MORNING

Will there really be morning?
  Is there such a thing as day?
Could I see it from the mountains
  If I were tall as they?

Has it feet like water-lilies?
  Has it feathers like a bird?
Is it brought from famous countries
  Of which I never heard?

Oh, some scholar! Oh, some sailor!
  Oh, some wise man from the skies!
Please to tell a little pilgrim
  Where the place called morning lies!

❧ *Emily Dickinson, in* St. Nicholas, *1891*

Over the River and Through the Wood

❦ AN ANTHOLOGY OF NINETEENTH-CENTURY
AMERICAN CHILDREN'S POETRY

Edited by Karen L. Kilcup and Angela Sorby

JOHNS HOPKINS UNIVERSITY PRESS | BALTIMORE

© 2014 Johns Hopkins University Press
All rights reserved. Published 2014
Printed in the United States of America on acid-free paper
9 8 7 6 5 4 3 2 1

Johns Hopkins University Press
2715 North Charles Street
Baltimore, Maryland 21218–4363
www.press.jhu.edu

Library of Congress Cataloging-in-Publication Data

Over the river and through the wood : an anthology of nineteenth-century American
children's poetry / edited by Karen L. Kilcup and Angela Sorby.
pages cm
Includes bibliographical references and index.
ISBN 978-1-4214-1139-2 (hardcover : alk. paper) — ISBN 978-1-4214-1140-8 (pbk. : alk.
paper) — ISBN 978-1-4214-1144-6 (electronic) — ISBN 1-4214-1139-3 (hardcover : alk.
paper) — ISBN 1-4214-1140-7 (pbk. : alk. paper) — ISBN 1-4214-1144-X (electronic)
1. Children's poetry, American. 2. American poetry—19th century.
I. Kilcup, Karen L. editor of compilation. II. Sorby, Angela editor of compilation.
PS586.3.O84 2013
811'.30809282—dc23   2013010973

A catalog record for this book is available from the British Library.

Frontispiece. Girl Reading, by Sarah S. Stilwell. From Mary Mapes Dodge,
Rhymes and Jingles, 1904.

*Special discounts are available for bulk purchases of this book. For more information,
please contact Special Sales at 410-516-6936 or specialsales@press.jhu.edu.*

Johns Hopkins University Press uses environmentally friendly book
materials, including recycled text paper that is composed of at least 30 percent
post-consumer waste, whenever possible.

CONTENTS

16. HISTORIES

This anthology offers twenty-first-century readers a generous and diverse selection of nineteenth-century American children's poetry. Our title, *Over the River and Through the Wood,* is taken from one of the most famous nineteenth-century children's poems, Lydia Maria Child's *A New England Boy's Song about Thanksgiving Day.* To travel "over the river and through the wood" is to traverse familiar territory that can nonetheless produce surprises and adventures. Accordingly, as editors, we have tried to balance old favorites with new discoveries—and indeed, there are many discoveries to be made, since most nineteenth-century children's poetry has long languished, inaccessible and unread, in old periodicals, gift books, and primers.

We have organized the poems in this collection by topic rather than by author or according to a timeline. Such an approach hearkens back to nineteenth-century editorial practices (Whittier and Larcom's *Child Life in Poetry,* for instance, was organized thematically), but it is also intended to spark connections and conversations among new generations of readers and scholars. Thematic clusters keep the focus on the poems, rather than on individual authors, which matters because some of the most delightful poems in the collection were written by little-known, or even anonymous, writers. Of course, given the Northeastern location of nineteenth-century publishing centers, the weight inevitably falls on white, middle-class authors, but we have ensured that writers from the South (for example, Caroline Howard Gilman), the Midwest (the Cary sisters), and West (Gelett Burgess and Joaquin Miller) also appear. In addition, the volume encompasses poetry by African American and Native American authors, as well as by children themselves. In addition to the verses by Thomas Hall Shastid, George R. Allen, and others from the New-York African Free-School and poems by the ex-slave Islay Walden, we have included a generous selection of work by the North Carolina writer Christina Moody, who composed much of her work between the ages of 13 and 16. We also feature work by Canadian poet E. Pauline Johnson (Mohawk), students from the Cherokee Female Seminary ("Corinne" and Lily Lee), Adella Washee, and Hellen Rebecca Anderson, the 8-year-old daughter of well-known Cherokee writer Mabel Washbourne Anderson.

In amassing this work, our first recourse was to survey prominent children's periodicals—*The Juvenile Miscellany, Merry's Museum, Our Young Folks, Harper's Young People, St. Nicholas, Wide Awake,* and *Youth's Companion*—which we supplemented with more regional journals, such as the (southern) *Rose-Bud.* In addition, we consulted volumes of children's poetry, adult volumes that explicitly or implicitly included children's verse, and readers and primers published between about 1800 and 1919. The only later poems are a handful of oral texts collected by Thomas Talley in the 1920s, but, as Talley notes, these works were circulating much earlier and thus fall within our nineteenth-century time frame. In most cases, we've used the first published version of a given poem. Occasionally it was more feasible to gather from later collections or to choose a later version that was clearly preferred by the poet or the public. The sources for individual poems are identified in the table of contents, as well as in the chronological appendix. For those poets who wrote as children, we have provided the age at which they wrote their poems. Pseudonyms of a first name, set of initials, or descriptor (like "A Lady of Boston") appear within quotation marks, with the author's real name, if known, appearing in brackets.

We have tried to provide coverage of every major trend in children's poetry while also giving some rein to our own contemporary tastes and biases. A perfectly representative anthology would contain more "funny" ethnic stereotypes, more plantation-tradition dialect verses, more evangelical Christianity, more deathbed sermons, and more botanical garden poems—but it would also be much less readable. We will admit outright that our editorial approach has generally favored charm over convention, even at the expense of some representativeness. In the end, we have selected poems that touched, amused, or at least intrigued us—and by doing so, we hope that we have constructed a living children's canon that has scholarly value but that also resonates with readers of all ages, in the academy and beyond.

ACKNOWLEDGMENTS

This anthology required the help of many hands. We would like to thank our Research Assistants: Jennifer Anderson, Kathleen Burt, and Adrianne Wojcik (Marquette University) and Christine Tobin and Logen Cure (University of North Carolina at Greensboro). Also from Marquette, Susan Hopwood afforded library research help. The Interlibrary Loan staff at UNCG helped us gather difficult-to-obtain materials, including images; special thanks to Gaylor Callahan.

Outside our home institutions, Ivan Roth provided important technical help. Anna Mae Duane and Kate Capshaw Smith shared research findings that have made the book more diverse. Richard Flynn, our outside reader, gave us generous praise and support when we needed it. At the Johns Hopkins University Press, we are grateful to our acquisitions editor, Matt McAdam; his assistant, Melissa Solarz; art director Martha Sewall; and managing editor Julie McCarthy. We also thank our copyeditor, Lynn Weber.

Stephen Crane's "I'd Rather Have—" appears courtesy of the Stephen Crane Collection, Special Collections Research Center, Syracuse University Library.

Karen thanks her husband, Chris, who daily reminds her of the value of play. Angela thanks her husband, Chris, as well, and also her three children, upon whom many of these poems were field-tested.

 OVER THE RIVER AND THROUGH THE WOOD

"Pretty New Moons"

Contact Zones in Nineteenth-Century American Children's Poetry

In 1877, when Thomas Edison made the first phonographic recording of a human voice, he chose a verse by Sarah Josepha Hale. As his assistant, Charles Batchelor, remembered:

> We fixed the instrument onto a table and I put in a strip of paper and adjusted the needle point down until it just pressed lightly on the paper. Mr. Edison sat down and putting his mouth to the mouthpiece delivered one of our favorite stereotyped sentences used in experimenting on the telephone, "Mary had a little lamb," whilst I pulled the paper through.[1]

Edison thus brought print culture into the age of mechanical voice reproduction via the medium of a children's poem. His use of "Mary's Lamb" dramatizes the ways that children's poetry was intertwined with the nineteenth century's seismic cultural and material transformations. Hale's poem was so deeply familiar to Edison and his team that it could serve as a "stereotyped" phrase. And indeed, the most famous nineteenth-century children's poems—"Mary's Lamb," "Account of a Visit from St. Nicholas," "A New England Boy's Song about Thanksgiving Day" (more often known as "Over the River and Through the Wood"), "The Three Little Kittens"—remain familiar even to Edison's heirs, the digital native children of the twenty-first century.[2]

Since the 1980s, American scholars have been revising the formerly narrow canon of nineteenth-century poetry, "profoundly reshaping," as Philip Schweighauser puts it, "how we read this verse and the parameters we set for the field as a whole."[3] A handful of famous children's poems (Hale's "Mary's Lamb," Riley's "Little Orphant Annie") thus appear in newer anthologies, such as John Hollander's landmark *American Poetry: The Nineteenth Century*.[4] In such contexts, the distinctive charm of such poems is evident: in an era when many poets labored under a set of stultifying literary conventions, children's poets were often able to break the rules. The subgenre demanded that poets compress their language and extend their sense of play in ways that produced some of the century's most amusing, readable, and durable verses. The social energy of a poem like "Mary's Lamb," however, is not confined to that poem; it stems from a vast discursive field of poetry about girls, boys, pets, natural rights, and education—a field that has not, up to now, been visible to most scholars or general readers. One aim of this anthology, then, is to recover children's poetry, not as a lower or lesser branch of American poetry, but as a field that is connected to, but also distinct from, the adult verse of the period.

As Beverly Lyon Clark has pointed out, children's literature is unique among literary subgenres because it defines itself, not in terms of authors or schools, but in terms of audience.[5] Children's poems, to state the obvious, are poems read by child readers. This definition, however, is fraught with complications. To be a children's poem, must a poem be written especially for children, like "Mary's Lamb," or can it be a poem that came to be read largely by children, like "Paul Revere's Ride"? How do poems written *by* children complicate the category? And what about Emily Dickinson? Some of her poems use a child's voice, and a few were published posthumously in *The Youth's Companion*, but are they therefore children's poems?[6] This latter question is especially vexing because *The Youth's Companion* was not a children's magazine per se, but rather a family publication aimed at a mixed readership of children and adults. In *Child Life: A Collection of Poems* (1871), John Greenleaf Whittier highlighted the imbrication of child and adult audiences: "While the compiler has endeavored to accommodate his book to the especial tastes of the young, he has not been without hope that maturer readers may find something of interest in it—something to bring back the freshness of the past,—hints and echoes from the lost world of childhood."[7] As editors we must thus ask: can children's poetry, as a genre, ever be defined?

Jacqueline Rose's 1984 book *The Case of Peter Pan*, famously declares children's literature impossible because the child is essentially a construct invented by adults to satisfy adult needs.[8] There can be no sharply delineated category of children's literature, she argues, because adults never just write for children; they write for themselves, projecting their desires onto the child. Rose's tone is scandalized—she goes so far as to use the word "sin"—but in editing this anthology, we have found the impurity of children's poetry to be the wellspring of its power. These poems are contact zones between adults and children: they register agendas, mixed motives, and competing desires. They circulated among child readers, but adults facilitated their circulation. They express, to some extent, children's experiences, but they also voice adult aspirations and fears.

Most of the poems from this collection connect with more familiar versions of literary history, as exemplified by Hollander's anthology or by Jay Parini's critical *Columbia Anthology of American Poetry*.[9] Virtually all nineteenth-century American poets—from canonical writers such as Nathaniel Hawthorne and Ralph Waldo Emerson to less familiar ones such as George W. Ranck and Clara Doty Bates—wrote poetry that was read by children. Readers will observe the influence of the Knickerbocker school (Clement Clark Moore's "Account of a Visit from St. Nicholas"), the New England tradition (John Greenleaf Whittier's "The Barefoot Boy"), the "sentimental poetry" tradition (Lydia Sigourney's "The Dove"), transcendentalism (Emerson's "Fable"), Civil War poetry (Margaret Sangster's "A Drummer"), progressive African American literature (Frances Harper's "The Little Builders"), dialect and regional verse (James Whitcomb Riley's "The Nine Little Goblins"), and naturalism (Charlotte Perkins Gilman's "Little Cell"). This continuity makes sense, because children's poets generally wrote in other—less marginal, more profitable—genres as well, involving themselves in the literary discourses of the day. The discourses that were most important to adult readers, however, were perhaps less important—or important in a different way—to children.

Our thematic approach intends to bring the poems into conversation with one another and into larger conversations as well. Scholars of nineteenth-century American and transatlantic culture will note that these poems add new dimensions to familiar areas of inquiry, from the history of the book to childhood studies to sentimentalism. They are also, frankly, delightful to read. Although the genre of children's poetry often sought to teach lessons, despite (or perhaps because of) this didacticism, poets were often tempted to bend rules and skirt conventions, crafting verses that brim with tension. Moreover, because they open space for playfulness, curiosity, and cultural resistance, many remain appealing and rewarding to modern sensibilities.[10]

❧ THE EMERGENCE OF CHILDREN'S PUBLISHING

The enterprise of children's publishing emerged in fits and starts over the course of the nineteenth century. In 1800, most children's books published in the United States were British reprints, illustrated (if at all) with woodcuts and sold directly by printers. By 1900, middle-class American children could enjoy an array of illustrated books and magazines that reflected the growth of mass market advertising, color illustration, national distribution networks, public schools, and libraries.

In the early nineteenth century, most commercially available children's poetry collections catered to small children who were learning to read. The educational meat poems ("Pork and Beef," "What Is Veal?") in our anthology are taken from one such volume, *Juvenile Poems*, printed by J. Metcalf of Northampton, Massachusetts. *Juvenile Poems* opens with the upper- and lower-case alphabet and uses a question-and-answer format reminiscent of Christian catechisms such as those in the *New England Primer*. The use-value of a poem like "What Is Veal?" seeps into its form, which structures the poem as a dialogue between a mother and child, while its secular, pragmatic content signals a move away from the *Primer*'s patriarchal doctrinal approach.

Once children could read well, they could engage with family-oriented volumes such as Lydia Sigourney's *Select Poems*, which mixes direct appeals to young readers, such as "A Mother's Counsel" or "Frost and the Flower Garden," with seemingly adult fare, such as "Recollections of an Aged Pastor." The third edition (1838) opens with an illustration of a prepubescent girl reading a book with her mother, as if inviting families to read *Select Poems* together. Since middle-class families were still unlikely to own many books, this image makes sense; Sigourney, always a canny self-marketer, suggests that all her work is appropriate for all ages: the more readers the merrier.

The Schoolroom poets—Longfellow, Whittier, and Bryant—also bound children's verses with their adult work in "Household" editions. Indeed, for these poets, the line between adult and juvenile poetry was highly mobile and often nonexistent.[11] A poem like Longfellow's "Paul Revere's Ride," published in the sophisticated *Atlantic Monthly* as a response to Civil War tensions, could also pass as a rollicking schoolroom recitation-piece. Indeed, as educational opportunities expanded, schoolrooms became key sites for the transmission of American poetry. School textbooks, including the famous McGuffey's Reader series, helped build a canon of poems that generations of students learned by heart. The repetition of poetry—Bryant's "Lines to a Waterfowl," Longfellow's "Paul Revere's Ride," Whittier's "The Barefoot Boy"—became a way for students to affirm their status as educated Americans. And later, when students were grown, these same poems acted as mnemonic devices through which adults recalled (and retroactively defined) "childhood."

As fiction ventured into lurid corners with authors such as George Lippard, most poetry remained solidly family oriented, exciting readers' emotions through biblical and historical stories, stirring hymns to nature, and touching deathbed scenes. Poetry, in antebellum America, was a genre that adults and children could share, and virtually every popular poem in America functioned, at least partly, as children's fare, including such curious choices as Bryant's "Thanatopsis," with its stern images of the world as a mass grave. While we have included some of the most famous schoolroom "chestnuts" in our anthology, to include all would be to burst its bindings and blur the definition of children's poetry beyond reason.

At the same time, even as children recited "Thanatopsis" in classrooms and parlors across the country, a nascent popular culture industry was beginning to generate a few texts exclusively for children. Samuel Griswold Goodrich entered this new niche market as "Peter Parley," producing *Parley's Magazine* for a select group of aspirational, middle-class young people, including Emily Dickinson and her siblings. Magazines like *Parley's* provided a small market for poets, although many of the poems they published were written by the editors themselves. It was impossible to forge a career as a children's poet, and many of the antebellum poets featured in this anthology were also involved in editing and publishing: Caroline Gilman edited the southern *Rose-Bud* (1832–1839), Sarah Josepha Hale succeeded Lydia Maria Child at the *Juvenile Miscellany* (1826–1836), and Hannah Flagg Gould ran the *Fireside Miscellany* (1850–1851).

In antebellum magazines, prose articles typically conveyed information while poetry sought to capture and cultivate feelings. When Goodrich launched *Merry's Museum,* he announced his aims in romantic terms:

> I will not claim a place for my numbers upon the marble table of the parlor, by the side of songs and souvenirs, gaudy with steel engravings and gilt edges. These bring to you the rich and rare fruitage of the hot-house, while my pages will serve out only the simple, but I trust wholesome productions of the meadow, field, and common of Nature and Truth. The fact is, I am more particular about my company than my accommodations. I like the society of the young—the girls and the boys; and whether in the parlor, the library, or the school-room, I care not, if so be they will favor me with their society.[12]

Goodrich defines his readership by its simplicity; children are not, or should not be, products of the hothouse. In keeping with romantic ideology, they are, like Rousseau's Émile, the most natural humans.

But if natural children were the most wholesome, then educators faced a problem, since education is by definition a civilizing process, as Mark Twain's Huck would later discover. Poetry helps ease the contradiction, in *Merry's Museum* and elsewhere, by tapping into what were assumed to be children's existing strengths: their affinity with plants and animals, their capacity to empathize with other weak creatures, and their responsiveness to rhythm and music. Not surprisingly, then, the first poem in the first issue of *Merry's Museum,* written by Goodrich himself, celebrates "My First Whistle":

> I blew that whistle, full of joy—
> It echoed o'er the ground;
> And never, since that simple toy,
> Such music have I found.

This whistle is carved from a willow tree, and the adult speaker prefers its pastoral pleasures to all his "manly toys" and fine wines.

Although antebellum children's poetry is often dismissed as didactic, it guides and celebrates children's emotions more frequently than it seeks to impart information. While antebellum poetry can certainly be preachy (see, for example, Nancy Sproat's "The Little Liar"), its romantic affinities with music and nature often counterbalance fixed messages with a degree of playfulness and pathos. In other words, poetry's unique contribution to children's education was affective: it taught them, by example, how to *feel*. In this respect, it paralleled the larger cultural trend embodied most famously by Harriet Beecher Stowe, who responded to readers' imagined question "what can any individual do?" when confronted by cultural problems with "they can see to it that *they feel right*."[13]

Visuals frequently supplemented children's affective education, although before the Civil War the children's picture book industry was in its infancy. The *New England Primer*, which continued to circulate in multiple incarnations, is often cited as the earliest children's picture book published in America. Its crude woodcuts link rhymes to images, embedding the alphabet in the specific world of New England Puritans. Later versions of the alphabet book offered different kinds of images to accompany their rhymes, illustrating, as Patricia Crain has argued, an "empire of things" rooted in domestic ideology. Alphabets—fanciful blends of letters, rhymes, and images—could inculcate cultural assumptions in the very youngest children and at the most elemental linguistic level. Our text includes some early woodcut illustrations of animals from the carefully titled volume *Juvenile Poems; or the Alphabet in Verse. Designed for the Entertainment of All Good Boys and Girls, and No Others* (1804). One wonders what the bad children read.

Children's verses and illustrations were still closely tied to folk culture, as evidenced by the "Cries" series, which recorded the calls of peddlers—in rhyme—for the amusement of children. The cover page of an 1828 edition, called *New-York Cries, in Rhyme*, depicts a peddler with a cart full of baskets and is enticingly captioned "Many sights in New-York there be, / Come buy this book, and you will see."[14] The volume proper includes appeals to cleanliness ("SAND O!" [used to clean floors]), scissor-sharpening ("Scissors to Grind!"), locksmithing ("Locks or Keys"), and, most notably, health and hunger ("NEW MILK," "Oranges!"). Each illustration advertises New York's wares, accompanied by a poem and an explanatory note, such as that accompanying "Potatoes, O!":

> Great quantities of Potatoes of different kinds, are carried about the streets of New-York, for sale. None make so much noise as those people who cry the Sweet Carolinas. These are held in high esteem by most persons, and one can buy them ready boiled and roasted at the cook-shops. They are of an oblong form, of many sizes, and when boiled, taste much like a roast chesnut [sic]. They sell from 75 cents to 1 dollar per bushel.

Educating children in consumption as well as promoting New York as a flourishing commercial center, *Cries* heralds the growth of the middle class and its purchasing might, while also hawking itself as an illustrated novelty.

Early periodicals such as the *Juvenile Miscellany* also included some illustrations, but they were scarce. Sometimes decorative—and floral or vegetable in character—they also included images of animals, such as the *Miscellany*'s images of a moose and a rabbit in the May 1829 issue.[15] One noteworthy image follows a little boy's poem to a dead brother and may or may not be related; untitled and murky, it depicts a mother outside a gate holding one child by the arm while her older sister reaches toward the gate. Such images possess little of the direct, earthy allure of the *Cries* series, which integrates text and image in ways that anticipate later children's picture books.

After the Civil War the children's market—like all markets—expanded dramatically. As the middle class established itself more firmly and consumerism became a signifier of social status, households bought more and displayed those possessions to others; leisure, including leisure to read, became another distinctive class marker. Better distribution networks, improved printing techniques (especially for illustrations), and urbanized populations all made children's books and magazines more accessible and appealing.[16] Moreover, the nascent social sciences emphasized pseudo-Darwinian ages and stages, influencing everything from graded school classrooms to standardized shoe sizing. To "have a childhood" suddenly entailed having age-appropriate possessions, many of which were acquired from Santa Claus, so it's not surprising that one of the most successful Gilded Age magazines was called *St. Nicholas*.

The social functions of poetry diversified along with the diversifying economy. Poetry's older use-value—as a tool for sentimental education—remained alive and well. At the same time, emerging social forces pushed children's poetry in new directions: if children still learned what to feel, they also learned how to behave socially, what to play, what to buy, and even how to be naughty within acceptable bounds. Magazines for children became more professionalized and widely distributed, although the trend of editors doubling as poets continued. Among the most influential titles were *St. Nicholas* (edited by Mary Mapes Dodge); *Our Young Folks* (edited by John Townsend Trowbridge, Lucy Larcom, and Gail Hamilton); *Harper's Young People* (edited by Horace Scudder); and of course, the longest-running of all, *Youth's Companion* (edited by Nathaniel Willis and later Daniel Sharp Ford).

Physical beauty also became a selling point for children's periodicals, as new printing techniques allowed for more lavish productions. *St. Nicholas*, in particular, offered extravagant black-and-white illustrations that engaged with, and expanded on, children's verses. Our anthology reprints several, including "The Punjaubs of Siam," whose pachyderm protagonists confront a train. "Mr. Bull-Frog's Party," from the August 1875 issue, depicts the eponymous host presiding over a harmonious, even comical gathering of amphibians, mammals, and insects, with Mr. Water-Rat tipping his hat to the assembled multitude. Conjuring a family reunion, the image collaborates with the poem's message critiquing bad boys who treat animals like enemies and celebrating the humane boy to whom the group concludes to send a valentine. Illustrated by L. Hopkins, Howell Fisher's "What Happened" is enclosed by the serious image of the hanging kangaroo in combination with mourning mammals that include a lion, a rhinoceros, and a chimpanzee, offering readers a counterpoint to a rollicking narrative distinctive not only for its content but also for its rhythm and rhyme ("An over-sensitive she-Gorilla / Declared that the shock would surely kill her").

Illustrations could reinforce or compete with the poem's ostensible message, but they could also spin readers outward into the greater unknown or offer innovative creative possibilities close to home. C. P. Cranch's "The Earth, the Moon and the Comet" is interspersed with stellar bodies whose humanized faces reflect the comet's relative proximity and the danger it poses, "robed in fire and mist," to its more domestic counterparts; the illustrator, perhaps the poet, remains unnamed. Among the most whimsical and imaginative illustrations accompany "Germs of Genius" by "I.R." Again interspersed with the poem, attracting readers and propelling them forward, the images mimic (or reproduce?) the mother-narrator's son's comically terrifying drawings, with a prickly, toothy beast with one eye on a stem and curlicue antennae, and then a Halloweenish pair of stick figures, one of which lassoes the other's head. As with "What Happened," the language—and, here, the form—reproduces the illustrations' playful delight:

> And Gustave Doré
> In his night-marish way
> Never pictured such terrible creatures as they;
> For ichthyosauri or pliocene snakes
> Would look gentle as doves by the drawings he makes.

In some sense, "I.R."'s poem visually represents the child's audaciousness, his playful ability to supersede discipline, while at the same time demonstrating a collaboration between mother and child.

Book publishers also took advantage of advances in illustration. Many of the volumes from which we gathered selections were lavishly and elegantly illustrated by professional artists, as we see with the modernist-inflected drawings of Sarah S. Stilwell for the 1904 reprint of Mary

Mapes Dodge's *Rhymes and Jingles*, first published in 1874. Dodge's pride emerges in the "Author's Note" to the new edition, where she admires the elegance and imagination of Stilwell's professional contributions.[17] Perhaps the most influential firm in the development of illustrated American children's books was the McLoughlin Brothers of New York. According to Gillian Avery, prior to the early 1860s, the pictures were "laboriously hand-coloured, using stencils," but John Jr., the successor to the firm's founder, developed a "process of printing from relief-etched zinc plates," which enabled his firm to overwhelm its competition. Avery claims that "at worst, the illustrations are strident," and most of the individual illustrators, with the noteworthy exception of Thomas Nast, were anonymous—but she acknowledges that "many books are delectably attractive."[18] To children accustomed to black-and-white engravings, or even to more muted and restrained colored images, the McLoughlin volumes fused rhymes with compelling visual images, paving the way for turn-of-the-century poets like Peter Newell, whose images and words are fully interdependent.

Interestingly, the period between the Civil War and First World War has often been seen as an "interregnum" in American poetry, an era that produced few stellar poems apart from Stephen Crane and (maybe) Sarah Piatt. But for children's poetry, this era was a golden age, in which writers such as Laura E. Richards, Paul Laurence Dunbar, Eugene Field, James Whitcomb Riley, Gertrude Heath, Gelett Burgess, and Palmer Cox composed pieces that have aged well, retaining their liveliness and social energy across the generations. A full consideration of why children's poetry was so abundant and of such high quality lies beyond the scope of this introduction, but partial answers lie in how these poems register the powerful discourses that shaped nineteenth-century life. These verses do not confine themselves to the schoolroom or the nursery; instead, they address the natural world in scientific and romantic terms; embrace social causes from abolition to animal rights to support for the armed forces; examine the sentimental terrain of death and suffering; break the boundaries between word and image; and redefine the lines separating play, work, and discipline. Even as "childhood" emerged as a separate social category, children's poetry continued to function as a contact zone, where adults and children could explore—together—the delights and complexities of their rapidly changing world.

❧ THE NATURE OF CHILDHOOD

Nineteenth-century children were often associated with nature, and this association possessed both positive and negative valences: positive, inasmuch as the romantic child represented nature's freedom; negative, in that these putatively wild creatures required civilizing. Beyond the ideological framing of childhood, however, practical historical circumstances figured in such representations. When we consider that in 1850 a huge percentage of Americans were farm people,[19] it is not surprising that a significant number of children's poems, like those intended for adults, focused on the natural world. Many, such as "The Wind," which represents a dialogue between mother and child, attempted to explain that world to young readers.

Hannah Flagg Gould's antebellum poem "The Mushroom's Soliloquy" offers two lessons. The first highlights the astonishing strangeness of the mushroom, which has "No fruit—no branch—nor leaf, nor bud," "No spicy odors," and, "in my sober suit," "scarce a root." Seemingly unnatural, the eponymous speaker questions her status as "Less like her [Nature's] work than like a piece of art, / Whirled out and trimmed exact in every part." Reflecting the Enlightenment emphasis on scientific observation and natural religion, this message conveys the interworkings of nature and divinity. The second lesson proposes the resignation expected of religious children: humility, for even the supposedly least beautiful, lowest being reflects an unknown divine purpose and artful creativity. Charlotte Perkins Gilman's "Tree Feelings" similarly attempts to enter the tree's perspective, but her turn-of-the-century moment permits a more sensual and ecstatic approach; the poem concludes with a series of exclamations, celebrating "the blossoms! And the wild seeds lost! / And jeweled martyrdom of fiery frost!" With its evocation of nature's wonder and its ending's emphasis on decline, Gilman's poem looks backward to mainstream romantic poetry and forward to modernism.

Depending on nature for their well-being, and organizing their lives around the seasons, every family member on the farm contributed to its economy: men with agricultural labor, especially raising crops for family and animals; women with indoor work that included sewing, preserving food, and cooking, but also outdoor tasks such as tending poultry, milking cows, and minding gardens; and children of both genders with age-appropriate tasks ranging from driving cows to pasture to picking berries.[20] Many of our selections reflect the writers' sense of respect and wonder: for the cycle of the seasons, plentiful water, and—though less directly—America's agricultural tradition, which John Greenleaf Whittier's "The Barefoot Boy" perhaps most famously represents. With his "cheek of tan" and "red lip, redder still / Kissed by strawberries on the hill," the boy is a native "prince" who possesses admirable health and insider knowledge "never learned of schools": "How the tortoise bears his shell, / How the woodchuck digs his cell"; "Where the whitest lilies blow, / Where the freshest berries grow." One reason Whittier's poem may have become so successful was that, in an environment in which hard work was expected of all, his boy has leisure to play, offering imaginative compensation to harried adults for their hardworking, postlapsarian realities. Although it reappeared in children's collections well into the twentieth century, the poem was collected in the writer's 1857 *Poetical Works*, suggesting its multiple audiences. Similar in impulse to Lucy Larcom's "Swinging on a Birch Tree," its greater optimism reflects its antebellum origins.

Beyond opportunities for play, nature provided sustenance, wonder, and spiritual insight. Springtime generated scores of appreciative, anticipatory verses, including Gertrude Heath's incantatory "Wake," while summer promises ripe cherries and honey for the young Cherokee writer Adella Washee. In her autobiography, *A New England Girlhood*, Lucy Larcom reflects the child's view of impending spring: "Very few of us lived upon carpeted floors, but soft green grass stretched away from our doorsteps, all golden with dandelions in spring. Those dandelion fields were like another heaven dropped down upon the earth, where our feet wandered at will among the stars."[21] The poets' repeated sense of exhilaration and wonder at everyday nature is echoed in contributions by Emily Dickinson, such as "The Sea of Sunset" and "As children bid the guest good-night." Although Dickinson intended some poems specifically for children, such as those she sent to her beloved nephew Ned, a number were gathered by later editors into children's collections, suggesting not only their versatility and wide appeal, but the continuity between poetry for children and that ostensibly for adults.

We see this continuity in another Dickinson poem, "The Mountain," which elevates the mountain to a divine status, "Grandfather of the days" and "Of dawn the ancestor." In the century's opening decades, many writers celebrated the country's wonders for readers of all ages; in 1834 William Cullen Bryant published "The Prairies," lauding these "gardens of the Desert," while Lydia Sigourney included one of many versions of "Niagara" in her 1844 travelogue *Scenes in My Native Land*. Romantic, myth-making, and reflecting an expanding vision of America, such work often reappeared in books and periodicals intended specifically for children. One noteworthy poem in this vein is the anonymous "Distant Worlds," which appeared in the pioneering children's periodical *Robert Merry's Museum* in July 1852. In awe at the immensity of the galaxy and what lies beyond, the poem attempts to concretize—for children and their parents—the vast distances covered by the light from distant stars, imagining a racehorse galloping without stopping from one star to Earth on "the morn of Moses' birth": "Not half its journey would be done, / Not half the distance now be run."

Like "The Seven Ages," "The Earth, the Moon and the Comet," and "Around the World on a Telegraph Wire," "Distant Worlds" reflects the nineteenth century's interest in—we might almost say obsession with—science, natural history, and technology. Celebrating scientific discovery, the poem points toward the Rosse Telescope, built in 1845 for the third Earl of Rosse (from Birr, County Offlay, Ireland), president of the British Royal Society from 1848 to 1854. With a 72-inch reflector, it represented a leap forward for astronomical observation and remained one of the world's largest telescopes until the mid-twentieth century.[22] Through it, viewers could easily perceive the mountains of the moon, including, as the poem suggests, Mount Tycho, named for the celebrated sixteenth-century Danish astronomer Tycho Brahe. The end of "Distant Worlds" reflects the ongoing tension between science and religion in the period, pondering the "mystery" of "bright and shooting stars" and suggesting that "Angels may all God's wonders tell, / When in eternity we dwell." This spiritual emphasis appears early and continues throughout the century, including in Lucy Larcom's poem, "Plant a Tree," which remains ubiquitous, appearing on various Internet sites, including the invitation to the 2010 Arbor Day celebration in Baton Rouge, Louisiana.[23]

Thomas Jefferson's Louisiana Purchase and the Lewis and Clark Expedition also fired the nation's imagination to look closely at nature—both its beauty and potential for profit. Beavers receive repeated attention from the explorers, but so do snakes and insects. On May 30, 1806, Lewis describes "a large speceis of frog which resorts [to] the water considerably larger than our bull frog, it's shape seems to be a medium between the delicate and lengthy form of our bull frog and that of our land frog or toad . . . like the latter their bodies are covered with little pustles or lumps . . . I never heard them make any sound or nois."[24] In the same entry, he catalogs various insects, including butterflies, various flies, the silkworm, beetles, hornets, and wasps. A review of the published volume that resulted from that expedition praises the explorers' courage and observes, "We almost imagine ourselves to be of the party; and the journal seems like a vehicle by which we are enabled to keep pace with the travellers."[25] The explorers' numerous scientific discoveries propelled naturalists such as John James Audubon to depict new species such as "Lewis's Woodpecker."[26]

Publications for both children and adults reflected their readers' fascination with natural history. Earlier in the century insects represented an opportunity to teach children about provisioning for the future and to warn them about vanity, as we see in Lydia Sigourney's "The Ladybug and the Ant." Benjamin Franklin King's "The Woodticks," written in a boy's comic dialect, makes readers squirm as the ticks "crawl up in yer hair" and "The devil's darnin' needle too, / 'Ill come and sew yer ear"; such work reflects the later period's more embodied and direct approach. On a different note, Eliza Lee Cabot Follen's "Butterflies Are Pretty

Things" teaches children to observe with interest—not to destroy—nature's loveliness, while Cooke's "Peter Parrot" explores the perspective of a bird removed from its native habitat and imprisoned in a northern household, inviting children and adults to understand nature from a more ecocentric perspective. Such works invoking animals' perspectives bespoke the Enlightenment connection between children and animals—both powerless and vulnerable to abuse—and sought to advance legal rights of both groups through sentimental education of their readers.[27]

William Cullen Bryant's 1854 "Robert of Lincoln" follows the bobolink—Emily Dickinson's "chorister" in "Some Keep the Sabbath Going to Church"—through its nesting cycle. While the poem romanticizes and anthropomorphizes the bird—for example, many take multiple mates rather than, as Bryant suggests, being monogamous, and both parents feed the young[28]—it promotes observing and listening to the bobolink carefully. Probably based in her childhood experience as a lighthouse keeper's daughter, Celia Thaxter's "Inhospitality" contrasts feminine and masculine approaches to a hawk seeking shelter in a winter storm; while "the little sister" urges the family to offer the bird refuge, her family laughs at her impulse to protect the "cruellest bird that flies" and that kills the beloved "song-sparrow." Her much older brother goes for his rifle, "But the wild wind seizes his yellow beard, / And blows it about like flame." Blinded by the gusting snow, he cannot see his prey, who disappears into the storm: "The fierce wind catches and bears him away / O'er the bleak crest of the hill." Merging information about natural enemies with an allegory of gender differences, the poem teaches lessons on several levels.

Emily Dickinson's "In the Garden," another poem that has often circulated as children's literature, similarly bridges the ostensible divide between younger and older audiences. Reflecting children's literature's emphasis on littleness, the poem also promotes careful observation of nature, presenting a robin in both domestic terms—his "rapid eyes" "looked like frightened beads"—and transcendental ones. When the narrator offers the bird "a crumb,"

> he unrolled his feathers
> And rowed him softer home
>
> Than oars divide the ocean,
> Too silver for a seam,
> Or butterflies, off banks of noon,
> Leap, plashless, as they swim.

In the poet's wonder-full world, nature's mysteries provide ample opportunity for contemplation and self-observation.

To observe the world was also, inevitably, to observe its evils. Nineteenth-century American children's poets engaged in debates ranging from slavery and immigration to class differences and environmental concerns, sometimes presenting these issues indirectly through the lens of natural history. Debates about race or nature, which evolved from earlier conceptual legacies, were always interdependent. The pre-Darwinist discourse of developmentalism, for example, sought to establish the relationship of human beings to animals, and it proposed a hierarchical vision of this relationship, with the former at the summit.[29] While critiquing dehumanizing portraits of enslaved persons such as the autistic musical prodigy Thomas Bethune, stories such as Rebecca Harding Davis's "Blind Tom" reinforced such attitudes. Regarded by his owners as nearly vegetable, a kind of "mushroom-growth," "Tom, through his very helplessness, came to be a sort of pet in the family."[30]

In emphasizing the spiritual and moral worth, and hence the humanity, of enslaved persons, Native Americans, immigrants, the disabled, women—and children, who were often associated with animals[31]—some children's poetry conveyed subtle or overt political messages. "Difference of Color" connects children, whether "A brow of sable dye," "a cheek of olive," or "a form / Of fairer, whiter clay," to their geographical origins, arguing for the equality of their souls. On a more comic note, Eliza Follen's "A Question of Color" uses the homely metaphor of "Mrs. Strawberry Jam" and "Mr. Blackberry Jam" to highlight the latter's virtues. Ex-slave Islay Walden's Reconstruction-era poem to a female friend sewing a shirt for the first time speaks quietly to domestic tranquility and agency. Early in the twentieth century, youthful African American poet Christina Moody could explicitly explore "The Depth from Whence We Came" and, in "The Negro's Flag and Country," proudly assert that America belonged to her, too. One of several poems by children in our anthology, Frank Printz Bixton, a fifteen-year-old student at the Ohio Institute for the Blind, suggests through natural metaphors the hidden brilliance of disabled people and thus forcefully humanizes them.

Alternatively, poems such as Alice Cary's "Three Bugs" deploys natural metaphors to convey a message about sharing scarce resources. Cary counterpoints the characteristic emphasis in children's literature on smallness and snugness—her subject is "Three little bugs in a basket"—with an undercurrent of scariness.[32] Enlisting white readers' sympathies in her description ("one was yellow, and one was black, / And one like me, or you"), the narrator focuses on the bugs' lack of food, for there were "hardly crumbs for two," and their selfishness. The "strong ones" consume all the bread, leaving one out in the cold, but the latter, "frozen and starved at the last," draws strength from his weakness "And killed and *ate*" his antagonists. Cary's moral message resonates in the concluding stanza:

Now, when bugs live in a basket,
Though more than it well can hold,
It seems to me they had better agree—
The white, and the black, and the gold—
And share what comes of the beds and the crumbs,
And leave no bug in the cold!

Avoiding selfishness, children must share, she argues, for their own well-being. Published in an era convulsed by racism, Reconstruction, and anti-Chinese unrest—the transcontinental railroad had recently been completed by Chinese laborers, and mounting anti-Asian sentiment, due in part to the weak economy in the 1870s, would culminate a few years later with the passage of the first Chinese Exclusion Act—the poem makes palpable a more immediate moral imperative to parents.

Engaging with a different kind of social problem that directly affected the natural world, Celia Thaxter published several children's poems that attacked the feather trade. Feathers, and even whole birds, were fashionable decorations for hats in the closing decades of the nineteenth century. In 1886, American Museum of Natural History ornithologist Frank Chapman recorded his observations during two walks through New York City's shopping districts. He counted 700 women's hats, nearly 80 percent of which bore some feathered decoration; many of the remainder belonged to elderly women or those in mourning, who otherwise might be sporting feathers as well. "On average, the millinery trade's demand for plumage and skins resulted in the destruction of as many as fifteen million American birds annually, from songbirds to waterfowl."[33] Thaxter, who became vice president of the Massachusetts Audubon Society, the first such group in the nation, included children in her audience as she sought to end the feather trade. Often reflecting a hybrid approach combining scientific and romantic-sentimental appeals, such poems about birds were particularly important to nineteenth-century readers, especially children, who were regarded "as a critical political constituency even though they could not vote."[34] A significant number of such poems, including Thaxter's "The Sandpiper," became part of political discourses urging bird protection.

"The Great Blue Heron" epitomizes this work, depicting the eponymous bird possessing consciousness and spectacular beauty. As he stands "lost in a reverie" beside the sea, he appears to the narrator "as if carved from the broken block / On which he was standing," simultaneously animate and, like a classical statue, inanimate. The narrator's apostrophe urges the heron to "'Fly! before over the sand / This lord of creation arrives / With his powder and shot, and his gun in his hand." Thaxter highlights the bird's right to "live and be happy," a message appealing to children; but adult readers would not have missed the ironic biblical reference to dominion over the birds of the air. It is worth noting that Thaxter uses sentimental rhetoric (highlighting the bird's "sweet life") with nationalist overtones, perhaps referencing the U.S. Declaration of Independence's phrase asserting the values of life, liberty, and the pursuit of happiness.

Given Thaxter's subtle reference to national ideologies, we should observe the imbrication of many poems in questions of identity, particularly national identity. The Histories section includes many that address these questions directly. Some, such as "Grandmother's Story of Bunker-Hill Battle" and "Revolutionary Tea," trace the nation's history from a humorous, domestic perspective, the latter highlighting the youthful country's resistance to taxation on tea. Others, such as "The Landlord's Tale" ("Paul Revere's Ride") represent dangers overcome, providing the foundation for an expansionist nationalism that gripped the nation as easterners began to comprehend the land's rich diversity. "Whitman's Ride for Oregon" makes this perspective clear with its opening line: "'An empire to be lost or won!'" Missionary doctor Marcus Whitman and his wife Narcissa forged what would become the Oregon Trail, opening this part of the West to white settlement on the historical homelands of the Cayuse and Nez Percé nations. The poem mythologizes Whitman's accomplishments, confirming conquest at the conclusion: near the "unmarked" graves of the first settlers,

> The flag waves o'er them in the sky
> Beneath whose stars are cities born,
> And round them mountain-castled lie
> The hundred states of Oregon.

Romanticizing the conquest of the West, invoking an almost mythical ("mountain-castled") present, the poem celebrates triumphant national growth by claiming to redeem "savage hordes." Commensurate with this "taming" of Native Americans through bringing "the Word"—and, not insignificantly, published just before the Wounded Knee massacre that ended the western Indian wars—Whitman must also negotiate nature's wildness: the "wandering eagle," "dizzy crag," "cloudy chasms," "pine-roofed gorges," and "wildering mazes."

Some selections in the Holidays grouping reiterate the nation-building theme. Larcom's "The Volunteer's Thanksgiving," which appeared in *Our Young Folks* near the end of the Civil War in January 1865, celebrates the perspective of a northern soldier. Recalling his geography and history lessons including "the boundaries of the States" and "the wars with England, the history and the dates," the narrator grounds himself in a romantic New England landscape overseen by "bald Monadnock" and the "pleasant northern river," the Merrimack. The speaker imagines his family at Thanksgiving dinner, enjoying "the crispy turkey" and the "golden squares of pumpkin, the flaky rounds of mince." Inviting readers to share in the celebration, Larcom conjures the idyllic, playful past, where boys and girls ramble outdoors among "fern-leaves and checkerberries red." What is at stake is this past, which emblematizes "home and love and honor and freedom." As the poem concludes, the speaker, Larcom's avatar, envisions a future domesticity that mirrors a desired national family at home and at peace.

❧ SENTIMENTAL NEGOTIATIONS

Children and animals—two essentials in the sentimental arsenal—could be turned to a number of purposes, from abolition to temperance to nationalism, but they most often appear in poems that explore the metaphysics of suffering and death. Although sentimentalism is often associated with earlier nineteenth-century figures like Stowe's Little Eva, it was a guiding force in much popular culture, including children's literature, up to the turn of the century and beyond—and its influence has not always been strictly conventional. With its associated tropes of family cares, vulnerable youth, early death, and affiliated religious fervor, sentimentalism appears even in the earliest works in *Over the River and Through the Wood*, including the sampler verses collected in the Homework and Handwork section. Samplers provided material examples of young girls' needlework skills; wrought by children as young as seven or eight years old, they demonstrated mastery of various stitches and, typically, the alphabet. Parents often proudly framed and displayed them. In addition to depicting such images as homes, farm animals, and flowers, many presented verses, often composed by a schoolmistress or mother, but sometimes by the girls themselves. It's unlikely, for example, that an adult composed the resentful couplet, "I cannot perceive This business design'd / For anything more Than to pleas[e] a raw mind."

Yet such individual responses were far less common than more conventional sentiments. Ten-year-old Rachel Anderson expressed a widespread attitude when she confronted future viewers: "When I am dead / And laid in Grave / And all my flesh decay[e]d / When this you see / Pray think on me / A poor young harmless maid."[35] Child death was a fact of life throughout the nineteenth century, and—whatever their venue—poets harnessed this anxiety, sometimes to push religious agendas, sometimes to ask hard questions. Susan Warner's novel *The Wide, Wide World* has become an ur-text for the study of nineteenth-century women's sentimentalism, but in 1860 she co-wrote, with her sister-in-law

Anna Bartlett Warner, a novel that launched the career of an even more influential text. In *Say and Seal*, a newly converted man, Mr. Linden, cradles a dying child and repeats: "Jesus loves me, this I know / For the Bible tells me so." In 1862 the lyrics were set to music by William Batchhelder Bradbury, becoming a staple of Protestant Sunday schools and missions.

While the verses referring directly to death are usually omitted from modern renderings, in the early to mid-nineteenth century, confronting death was precisely the point. In *Say and Seal* the lyric ushers little Johnny into the afterlife; in Mrs. G. S. Beaney's *The Sermon in Baby's Shoes* (1876) it accompanies one little Annie; and in Alfred Alsop's *Ten Years in the Slums* (1879) little Joey the newsboy dies with the words on his lips. The practice and politics of sentimentalism have been debated exhaustively elsewhere and need not be rehashed at length. It is notable, though, that when "Jesus Loves Me" is embedded in stories, its use-value is clear: it is not a sermon, per se, but a means of reassurance aimed at frightened parents and children of both sexes. Moreover, like most sentimental verse, it takes children seriously as the conduits of spiritual truth: the implied child speaker in "Jesus Loves Me" has a theologically weighty voice that is, from an evangelical Christian perspective, neither trivial nor cute.

In the decades following the Civil War, then, there was still plenty of deathbed sentimentalism to be had. However, parents and educators began to question texts that promoted, in the words of *Public Libraries* magazine, "a morbid sentiment among little folks which is neither natural nor healthy."[36] Many later nineteenth-century children's poems about death engage directly with sentimental rhetoric while also revising it, as two Gilded Age poems from our Death cluster can serve to illustrate. The first, "Little Boy Blue" by Eugene Field, was hugely popular around the turn of the century and seems at first to epitomize maudlin sentimentalism. But while it was included in many anthologies and school primers for child readers, the text is notable because the child at its center is absent. The poem is spoken in the voices of adults, who gaze sadly at the dead child's tin soldiers and toy dog. Instead of talking about Jesus (there is no religion in "Little Boy Blue"), the parents fixate on the uncanny afterlife of toys. Sentimental mourning remains, but its central narrative—the passage into heaven—is gone, replaced by the inadequate compensations of the material world.

By contrast, Annette Bishop's "Sissy's Ride to the Moon" is spoken in the voice of a child who is wrestling with her baby sister's death. Unlike Johnny in *Say and Seal*, Sissy can't accept death; and unlike "Little Boy Blue" she is not sweetly passive. Rather, she imagines that she can harness technology to fight death. She'll use the moon, she declares, as a spaceship to rescue her little sister from the angels:

"It was little Sissy," papa would say,
   "She went in the moon to-night,
And found little May, and coaxed her away
   From the angels all so white."

Then mamma would kiss me, and call me good,
   And we'd all go in at the door,
And have some supper; and May never would
   Go up in the sky any more.

Sissy values supper more than she values heaven, and this attitude gar-
ners her mother's kiss of approval. Child death was ubiquitous and pre-
dictably Christian in antebellum American poetry, and it virtually disap-
pears from twentieth-century children's verse. But in the interim, during
the Gilded Age, it was possible for children to "puzzle" out (as Frances
Harper put it in "Jamie's Puzzle") a range of responses to the mystery, in
collaboration with adult interlocutors who were just as uncertain as their
children.

One striking instance of this uncertainty appears in Sarah Piatt's vir-
tuoso "The Funeral of a Doll." Adult and child voices converge and over-
lap, as Piatt conjures Dickens's sentimental heroine "Little Nell" at the
opening, while deliberately eliding the poem's subject ("her"). The nar-
rator goes on to describe a "small and sad" doll's funeral that, we learn,
parallels and painfully evokes that of a dead sister. Stanza two begins to
conjoin the two, mourning that

   The very sunshine seem'd to wear
Some thought of death, caught in its gold,
That made it waver wan and cold.

But the next lines insert the gallows humor that suggests the poem's
ironic sentimentalism:

Then, with what broken voice he had,
   The Preacher slowly murmured on
(With many warnings to the bad)
   The virtues of the Doll now gone.

Piatt's narrator's voice emerges here and again more explicitly a few lines
later. The child's voice of the last stanza ventriloquizes the narrator's—
and perhaps the poet's—as she laments,

   Oh,
   Poor Little Nell is dead, is dead.
How dark!—and do you hear it blow?
   She is afraid."

By the poem's open-ended conclusion, neither child nor adult readers enjoy the comfort intended from either the funeral or the sentimental mourning poem itself. Anticipating grim modernist attitudes toward death and suggesting the absence of divine consolation, "The Funeral of a Doll" uses multiple voices and speaks to multiple audiences.

❧ PLAY ZONES

Children have always played when given a chance, but in the nineteenth century play became an object of fascination and study. Many nineteenth-century verses depict children at play while negotiating what it means to play and how play should be valued. In 1871, the famous and influential educator Jacob Abbott defended play in his child-rearing manual *Gentle Measures in the Management and Training of the Young*: "That rapid succession of bodily movements and of mental ideas, and the emotions mingling and alternating with them, which constitutes what children call play, must be regarded not simply as an indulgence, but as a necessity for them." But play, he insists, must be managed by parents, who need to realize that "this exuberance of energy is something to be pleased with and directed, not denounced and restrained."[37] Like most popular advice writers, Abbott was less a revolutionary than a consolidator of emergent social norms. His defense of play merges two basic nineteenth-century assumptions about play, both of which are reflected in our anthology. The first (more romantic) assumption is that children's play reflects their innocent state of nature. The second (more pragmatic) assumption is that children's play promotes their moral, physical, and social development.

Two antebellum poems included in this volume seem to reflect earlier Americans' emphasis on practicality over play.[38] In "The Skater's Song," the child narrator celebrates the freedom offered by skating: "Like a bird we glide, / Or a dart from an Indian's quiver." "Merry," "blithe and gay," the participants "outvie" the wind, "And our spirits keep time with the flight." Yet a counterbalancing responsibility attaches to this romantic freedom: "And though we play / With such glee to-day, / We'll study the better to-morrow." Eliza Lee Follen's "It Can't Be So" simultaneously lauds a boy's imagination of "a golden castle" and "a flying pony" while it brings his romantic flights of fancy down to earth, concluding—while perhaps silently commiserating—"O, no! O, no! O, no! / My little boy, it can't be so." Representing the mother's admonitory voice responding to the boy's, the poem offers an entry for readers of all ages, ambiguous in its attitudes toward play.

By the post–Civil War period, play had acquired greater status, at least as represented in the children's periodicals. For example, for northern poets, nature in winter offered multiple opportunities, including sleigh riding, snow fights, and ice skating. Louise Chandler Moulton's "Out in the Snow" (1867) conjures the "glittering ghost of the vanished night" that invites "Kate with her dancing scarlet feather," "Joe and Jack with their pealing laughter," and "half a score of roisterers after, / Out in the witching, wonderful snow." The poet acknowledges the distinction between adult and youthful perspectives in the last stanza:

> Shivering graybeards shuffle and stumble,
> Righting themselves with a frozen frown,
> Grumbling at every snowy tumble,—
> But the young folks know why the snow came down.

Despite the ostensibly divided perspective here, children and adults both participated in the pleasures of outdoor life. Such pleasures were amply represented in nineteenth-century popular culture, perhaps most visibly in the immensely popular hand-colored lithographs of Currier & Ives. *American Homestead Winter*, for example, centers on a sleigh ride in front of a well-kept home, although work is clearly being done by one man hauling wood and another overseeing chickens and a cow from a barn door opening.[39] Other images by the publisher suggest the decidedly middle-class, and racialized, inflection of such pleasures.[40]

Published in the same year as Moulton's poem, Lucy Larcom's "Swinging on a Birch Tree" spins out the possibilities inherent in the romantic view of childhood play. In this poem, children are remote from adults, "swinging on a birch-tree" to a tune that is "hummed by all the breezes." The tree releases the children's imaginations, so that they see themselves on a see-saw, then on a ship, and finally as masters of the globe: "And the world's our vessel: / Ho! she sails so fast!" The purpose of the poem is not to spur development per se, but to mark the specific value of childhood as a time before civilization ravages all innocence. Larcom's mid-century romantic assumptions also register in the form of the poem, which is a collective dramatic monologue spoken in the idealized voice, not of an individual child, but of Childhood. At the same time, we might read the poem, published in *Our Young Folks* only two years after the close of the Civil War, as reflecting a willed, postlapsarian impulse to celebrate and preserve childhood innocence, a precursor poem to Robert Frost's "Birches."[41] As we have suggested, such poems also reflect the realities of rural life in the mid-century United States, where farming was the norm and opportunities for play for most children were characteristically outdoors.

Agnes Lee's "Finding Things" also depicts outdoor play, but Lee—born a generation after Larcom—is not content to celebrate the child as a romantic *isolato*. Lee's speaker is an individuated "lucky boy," describing how he finds objects (a bun, a penny, a corkscrew) on his rambles.

In Lee's poem, the manufactured world literally litters the pastoral landscape, reflecting the incursion of industrialization—and, not coincidentally, of new ways to engineer childhood. The speaker's play has a purpose; he subtly teaches his readers to be close observers, so that they are developing a pragmatic life skill even as they have fun. To use Abbott's phrase, Lee frames ludic scavenging as something to be "pleased with and directed."

Toys are relatively scarce in nineteenth-century American children's poetry, and many of the toys depicted, such as Noah's arks or toboggans, were created at home or in small workshops run by European immigrants. Two mass-manufactured exceptions—roller skates and lifelike dolls—are worth considering for the ways that they navigate the tensions of modernity when they appear in poems. The New York–based inventor James Leonard Plimpton invented maneuverable quad roller skates in 1863, and by the 1880s roller skating was a craze and roller skates were being produced in factories all over the country. A.C.'s "The Song of the Roller Skates" speaks, like Larcom's "Birch Tree" children, in a collective voice. But instead of being captivated by the breezes of nature, the children are thrilled by visceral speed. Moreover, their bodies have been modified, and sped up, by the skates that unite them in a peer-based experience based on new consumer options. The poem not only weaves across the page but also invents a refrain to echo this essentially non-verbal (and modern) experience: Swoop-a-hoo! cheeks so red; / Full of laughter, the air! / Swoop-a-hoo! swoop-a-hoo! swoop-a-hoo!" *St. Nicholas* promoted a form of peer culture in which children identified more closely with age-mates than with their elders.[42] Not surprisingly, then, the poem promotes not only the fun of skating with age-mates but also a trendy tagline that child readers could presumably shout—"swoop-a-hoo"—when they roller skated themselves.

Manufactured dolls became staples of middle-class girlhood after the Civil War; as Miram Forman-Brunell puts it, a "conspicuous doll culture unfolded in widely available children's books and popular magazines."[43] If roller skates promoted egalitarian peer play, doll play replicated, in many cases, gendered hierarchies. The child speaker in Margaret Vandegrift's poem "The Dead Doll" fantasizes:

And papa will make me a tombstone, like the one he made for my bird;
And he'll put what I tell him on it—yes, every single word!
I shall say: "Here lies Hildegarde, a beautiful doll, who is dead;
She died of a broken heart, and a dreadful crack in her head."

Imported bisque dolls were susceptible to head cracks, so part of what ails Hildegarde is middle-class prosperity. Like a caged bird or a kept woman, she is as primarily decorative, and when her beauty fades (or cracks) she might as well be dead. The child speaker rebels against this fate by fantasizing that she can dictate words to her father—although the words she chooses are a passive-aggressive confirmation of Hildegarde's helplessness. If Hildegarde is helpless, her child owner is not, because she controls the language of the poem as well as the headstone.

Play poems, at their best, do not simply depict or direct play; rather, they explore its expressive possibilities. Even early in the century, poems such as "Arithmetical Epitaph"—which rhymes "biquadratics" with "mathematics"—embodied such practices. Ironically, the most linguistically playful poems in the anthology—which we've clustered as "nonsense"—were subject to the strictest controls by their nineteenth-century authors. Inspired by Edward Lear and Lewis Carroll, American nonsense writers (represented here by Laura Richards, Carolyn Wells, and Gelett Burgess) sought to purify the form of any didactic impulse. As Burgess complained in a 1902 essay:

> Today I heard of an otherwise estimable woman who has just read a carefully prepared paper on "Mother Goose" nonsense rhymes. It seems to have been written with the primary adoption of an artificial point of view, and a secondary attempt to manufacture evidence to fit. Her thesis was the ethical and educational value of this nursery classic, with pedantic essays in determination of its history. Was ever an alleged scientific theory so preposterous?[44]

Burgess thinks that nonsense cannot be educational; otherwise it generates extraliterary meaning that undermines its very raison d'être. Nonsense writers thus implicitly chart a theory of play that insists on its value, not as a developmental tool, but as an end in itself. In the context of nineteenth-century children's culture, this stance is difficult to maintain, since children's poetry circulated through such a heavily instructive network of magazines and books. Indeed, it's not surprising that the most famous American nonsense poem, Burgess's "Purple Cow," appeared, not in a children's magazine, but in an experimental San Francisco journal called *The Lark* that also featured a fanciful "map of Bohemia." To find space for nonsense, it was sometimes necessary to travel to society's margins.

Beginning in the 1880s, folklorists began to discover and record nonsense rhymes from the oral tradition. We have included examples from two important collectors: William Wells Newell and Thomas Talley. Newell's 1883 collection, *Games and Songs of American Children,* was an influential early work that attempted to link American folk rhymes with rhymes from England and Europe, emphasizing the peculiarly conservative nature of children's oral transmissions across generations and continents. Talley's 1922 collection technically falls outside the date purview of our anthology, but the rhymes themselves originated (insofar as folk materials can be said to "originate") during the eras of slavery and Reconstruction. Talley was the first African American folklorist to systematically gather this material, and while his use of dialect can be distracting to modern readers, his game and counting-out rhymes offer a rare, albeit mediated, window into the verse practices of African American children.

Nonsense purists would reject both Newell's and Talley's collections because the poems were used to play games or count out; in other words, they were not written to have no meaning, but rather to make gibberish meaningful: "eeny, meeny, miny, mo" is not nothing; it is a numbering system. And certainly, scholars of nonsense and folklore (two widely disparate fields) will need to return to the source materials to get a complete sense of how, say, Newell's "onery, uery, hickory, Ann" works differently than Richards's "Pillykin Willykin Winky Wee." When we consider this verse as a cluster, though, it is striking how effortlessly the oral tradition produced grotesque and playful language that even the most diligent students of nonsense (Richards, Wells) struggled to achieve.

Of course, the rise of supervised—and often commercialized—play included a disciplinary component, and children's poetry benefited from the tensions that arose between the capitalist economy (which supported more innovative, secular, peer relationships) and the domestic sphere (which supported more traditional, Christian, intergenerational relationships). And insofar as this struggle paired opposing worldviews, secular peer relationships almost always got the upper hand, especially as the century progressed. The very oldest lesson poems in our anthology, like "The Little Liar" by Nancy Sproat, are serious cautionary tales. But by the time Heinrich Hoffman's *Struwwelpeter* appeared in English (in 1848, three years after its original publication) readers were already willing to laugh at, and with, excessively bad children. Indeed, after the Civil War, "bad boys" inspired by Thomas Aldrich and Mark Twain (who had himself translated *Struwwelpeter*) were embraced by the reading public.

Not surprisingly then, the Lessons section of our anthology is—like pop culture more generally—full of ambivalence: bad behavior might be technically undesirable, but in small doses it's certainly more fun and marketable than lockstep obedience. For instance, a certain relish can be detected in poems like Gelett Burgess's "Table Manners":

The Goops they lick their fingers,
And the Goops they lick their knives;
They spill their broth on the table-cloth—
Oh, they lead disgusting lives!

And, indeed, Burgess tips his hand in another poem, confessing that he is qualified to write etiquette poems precisely because he, too, was once a Goop: "And almost every single rule / I broke, before I went to school!" In keeping with the assumptions of progressive child-rearing (not to mention pop Darwinism), to learn the rules of civilization everyone must pass through a primitive Goops stage. Moreover, Burgess's mock confession implies that the whole Goops cycle is an inside joke, shared by parents and children, rather than a hierarchical imposition of rules from above.

Nineteenth-century poets were similarly adept at this balancing act of conveying extravagant naughtiness and comforting safety expressed through form—rhythm and rhyme—and mechanics. Mrs. A. M. Diaz uses meter as a hammer in "Two Little Rogues" determined to "make a great hullaballoo!" With their mother safely departed, the older brother explains the word and extols the project's virtues to his little brother:

> "O, slammings and hangings,
>   And whingings and whangings;
>   And very bad mischief we'll do!
> We'll clatter and shout,
>   And knock things about,
>   And that's what's a hullabaloo!
>   Ri too! ri loo! loo! loo! loo!
>   And that's what's a hullabaloo!"

Diaz combines the pleasure of rhythm with that of repetition and sound, emphasizing that delight in the staccato "oo" sound repeated, not only within each stanza, but again and again down the ladder of the poem.[45] Diaz, no less than her successors Theodore Geisel and Shel Silverstein, understood her readers' pleasure in rhythm, rhyme, and sound.

In the end, the surprising number of flippant discipline poems in our anthology says more about the genre of poetry than about the practice of punishment. As contact zones, poems involve children and adults in collaborative reading practices that can suspend the authority of parents and institutions without seriously threatening them. Even in earnest educational contexts, the role of nineteenth-century children's poetry was seldom drably instructive or utilitarian, and its imagination was its signal strength: such poetry opened—to use Joseph Thomas's phrase— a "playground" where readers of all ages could explore their world in a fresh light.

Children's poetry, then—no less than adult literature of all kinds— reflects on playfulness and discipline, wildness and domesticity, and ultimately life and death. Nineteenth-century children's poets took their readers and themselves seriously as they explored almost every aspect of American culture. In "The End of the Rainbow," Sarah Piatt guides her readers past "pretty new moons" and into "wet dark leaves and the snow's white glare," where the narrator finds "Some little dead birds I had petted to sing, / Some little dead flowers I had gathered to wear, / Some withered thorns, and an empty ring." Ironically, Piatt's disenchanted fairy ring still has the power to enchant—precisely because she addresses, not just nineteenth-century children, but any reader, of any age, who wants to play with words.

NOTES

1 Charles Batchelor, "Invention of the Phonograph, as Recalled by Edison's Assistant," in *Thomas Edison and Modern America: A Brief History with Documents*, ed. Theresa Mary Collins, Lisa Gitelson, and Gregory Jankunis (New York: Palgrave, 2001), 66.

2 Like many poems that have passed at least partly into the oral tradition, or that circulated widely in newspapers without bylines, "A Visit from St. Nicholas" has been subject to author disputes. In this and other such cases we have adhered to the most widely accepted attribution.

3 Philipp Schweighauser, "Resources for the Study of Nineteenth-Century American Poetry: A Selective Guide," in *Teaching Nineteenth-Century American Poetry*, ed. Paula Bernat Bennett, Karen Kilcup, and Philipp Schweighauser (New York: MLA, 2007), 327.

4 John Hollander, ed., *American Poetry: The Nineteenth Century*, 2 vols. (New York: Library of America, 1996).

5 Beverly Lyon Clark, "Audience," in *Keywords for Children's Literature*, ed. Philip Nel and Lissa Paul (New York: New York UP, 2011), 14.

6 We have chosen to reproduce Dickinson's poems as they were first published, rather than as they were written by Dickinson in her fascicles. In doing so, we are attempting to place them in their cultural context as popular poems.

7 John Greenleaf Whittier, Preface, *Child-Life: A Collection of Poems* (Boston: James R. Osgood, 1872), viii. Doing most of the actual work, Lucy Larcom compiled several volumes with John Greenleaf Whittier (who was credited as sole editor), including *Child-Life*. See Karen L. Kilcup, "Lucy Larcom," *American Writers: A Collection of Literary Biographies*, Supplement XIII (New York: Scribner's, 2003), 137–157.

8 Jacqueline Rose, *The Case of Peter Pan, or the Impossibility of Children's Fiction* (London: Macmillan, 1984).

9 Jay Parini, ed. *The Columbia History of American Poetry* (New York: Columbia UP, 1995).

10 See Caroline F. Levander, *Cradle of Liberty: Race, the Child, and National Belonging from Thomas Jefferson to W. E. B. Du Bois* (Durham: Duke UP, 2006); Karen Sánchez-Eppler, *Dependent States: The Child's Part in Nineteenth-Century American Culture* (Chicago: U of Chicago P, 2005); Karen Sánchez-Eppler, "Playing at Class," in *The American Child: A Cultural Studies Reader*, ed. Caroline F. Levander and Carol J. Singley (New Brunswick: Rutgers UP, 2003), 40–62.

11 Angela Sorby, *Schoolroom Poets: Childhood, Performance, and the Place of American Poetry* (Lebanon, NH: UP of New England, 2005).

12 Samuel Goodrich, "Address to the Reader," *Robert Merry's Museum* 1 (1841): 1.

13 Harriet Beecher Stowe, *Uncle Tom's Cabin; or, Life among the Lowly*, vol. 2 (Boston: John P. Jewett, 1852), 317.

14 *The New-York Cries, in Rhyme* (New York: Mahlon Day, 1828), n.p.

15 *Juvenile Miscellany* 2.2 (1829): 136.

16 Gillian Avery highlights the innovative McLoughlin publishing house, which we discuss below. Avery, *Behold the Child: American Children and Their Books, 1621–1922* (London: Bodley Head, 1994), 125-26.

17 Mary Mapes Dodge, "Author's Note," *Rhymes and Jingles*, 2nd ed., illus. Sarah Stilwell (New York: Charles Scribner's Sons, 1904), xi–xii.

18 Avery, 125.

19 According to *The New York Times*, 4.9 million Americans, or about 64 percent of the nation's workers, were involved in farming. "Farm Population Lowest Since 1850's," *The New York Times*, July 20, 1988. PBS cites a figure of 90 percent in 1862, when President Lincoln established the U.S. Department of Agriculture. "Timeline of Farming in the U.S.," www.pbs.org/wgbh/amex/trouble/timeline/. See Herbert S. Klein, *A Population History of the United States* (New York: Cambridge UP, 2004), 61–94.

20 Chad Montrie, "'I Think Less of the Factory Than of My Native Dell': Labor, Nature, and the Lowell 'Mill Girls,'" *Environmental History* 9.2 (2004): 278.

21 Lucy Larcom, *A New England Girlhood* (Boston: Houghton Mifflin, 1889), 90.

22 John S. Rigden and Roger H. Stuewer, *The Physical Tourist: A Science Guide for the Traveler* (Basel: Birkhäuser, 2008), 16–19. .

23 Karen L. Kilcup, "Education by Poetry: Robert Frost, Women, and Children," in *Robert Frost in Context,* ed. Mark Richardson (Cambridge: Cambridge UP, forthcoming).

24 "The Journals of the Lewis and Clark Expedition," University of Nebraska, Lincoln, May 30, 1806. http://lewisandclarkjournals.unl.edu/read/?_xmlsrc=1806-05-30&_xslsrc=LCstyles.xsl.

25 "B," "Original Review—Lewis and Clarke's Travels," *Analectic Magazine* [Philadelphia], V February 1815, 127–149, and March 1815, 210–234.

26 John James Audubon, 1785–1851, "Plate CCLXXII: Lewis' Woodpecker," from Audubon, *The Birds of America from Drawings made in the United States.* 5 vols. (New York: J. J. Audubon; Philadelphia: J. B. Chevalier, 1842).

27 Angela Sorby, "Animal Poems and Children's Rights in America, 1820-1890," in *Poetry and Childhood*, ed. Morag Styles et al. (Stoke on Trent: Trentham Books, 2010), 179-86.

28 For scientifically correct information, see Cornell University's All About Birds website: www.birds.cornell.edu/BOW/boboli/ and www.allaboutbirds.org/guide/Bobolink/id.

29 See, for example, Ian Frederick Finseth, *Shades of Green: Visions of Nature in the Literature of American Slavery, 1770–1860* (Athens: U of Georgia P, 2009), 2, 137–148.

30 "The author of 'Margaret Howth' [Rebecca Harding Davis], Blind Tom," *Atlantic Monthly* 10.61 (November 1862): 580, 581. It is noteworthy that Davis compares Thomas Bethune's "instinct" to that of "a dog's or an infant's" (582).

31 See Karen L. Kilcup, *Fallen Forests: Redeeming American Women's Nature Writing* (Athens: U of Georgia P, 2013).

32 Jerry Griswold, *Feeling Like a Kid: Childhood and Children's Literature* (Johns Hopkins UP, 2006), 1–2.

33 Kathy S. Mason, "Out of Fashion: Harriet Hemenway and the Audubon Society, 1896–1905," *The Historian* 65.1 (December 2002): 3. See Kilcup, *Fallen Forests*, chapter 4.

34 Angela Sorby, "The Poetics of Bird Defense in America, 1860–1918," in *Poetry after Cultural Studies*, ed. Mike Chasar and Heidi Bean (Iowa City: U of Iowa P, 2011).

35 For more information on samplers and their verses, see Ethel Stanwood Bolton and Eva Johnston Coe, *American Samplers* (Boston: The Massachusetts Society of the Colonial Dames of America, 1921); Betty Ring, *Girlhood Embroidery: American Samplers and Pictorial Needlework, 1650–1850* (New York: Knopf, 1993); Betty Ring, *American Needlework Treasures: Samplers and Silk Embroideries from the Collection of Betty Ring* (New York: E.P. Dutton, 1987); Sue Studebaker, *Ohio Is My Dwelling Place: Schoolgirl Embroideries, 1803–1850* (Athens: Ohio UP, 2002); and various articles in *The Magazine Antiques*.

36 *Public Libraries* 6.2 (February 1901): 73.

37 Jacob Abbott, *Gentle Measures in the Management and Training of the Young* (New York: Harper & Brothers, 1871), 194, 195.

38 Gillian Avery asserts that American children's writing emphasizes work and profit far more than its English counterpart, which valued play and imagination (87ff., 123ff.).

39 Brooklyn Museum Collections: American Art: American Homestead Winter (1868–1869), //www.brooklynmuseum.org/opencollection/objects/147528/American_Homestead_Winter. However, even city folk could enjoy the winter; see Currier & Ives's *Central-Park Winter*, which depicts people of all ages happily ice skating (http://img2.etsystatic.com/008/0/7283944/il_fullxfull.404801358_md01.jpg and //www.antiquemapsandprints.com/p-0925.jpg).

40 *American Country Life: Pleasures of Winter* (1855) shows an affluent family—parents, son, and daughter—about to embark on a sleigh ride; the horses are held by a well-dressed African American servant. www.philaprintshop.com/images/cur123.jpg; www.aradergalleries.com/detail.php?id=3083; www.springfieldmuseums.org/the_museums/fine_arts/collection//view/611-american_country_life_pleasures_of_winter.

41 Karen L. Kilcup, "'Something of a Sentimental Sweet Singer': Robert Frost, Lucy Larcom, and 'Swinging Birches,'" in *Roads Not Taken: Rereading Robert Frost*, ed. Earl J. Wilcox and Jonathan Barron (Columbia: U of Missouri P, 2000), 11–31.

42 See Sorby, *Schoolroom Poets*, 68–97.

43 Miriam Forman-Brunell, "The Politics of Dollhood in Nineteenth-Century America," in *The Girls History and Culture Reader: The Nineteenth Century*, ed. Miriam Forman-Brunell and Leslie Paris (Urbana: U of Illinois P, 2011), 231.

44 Gelett Burgess, *The Romance of the Commonplace* (San Francisco: Elder & Shepard, 1902), 270.

45 This exciting rhythmic pattern continues to delight children today, as in Shel Silverstein's poem "Falling Up." Silverstein, *Falling Up* (New York: HarperCollins Children's Books, 1996), 7.

TREE FEELINGS

I wonder if they like it—being trees?
I suppose they do. . . .
It must feel good to have the ground so flat,
And feel yourself stand right straight up like that—
So stiff in the middle—and then branch at ease,
Big boughs that arch, small ones that bend and blow,
And all those fringy leaves that flutter so.
You'd think they'd break off at the lower end
When the wind fills them, and their great heads bend.
But then you think of all the roots they drop,
As much at bottom as there is on top,—
A double tree, widespread in earth and air
Like a reflection in the water there.

I guess they like to stand still in the sun
And just breathe out and in, and feel the cool sap run;
And like to feel the rain run through their hair
And slide down to the roots and settle there.
But I think they like wind best. From the light touch
That lets the leaves whisper and kiss so much,
To the great swinging, tossing, flying wide,
And all the time so stiff and strong inside!
And the big winds, that pull, and make them feel
How long their roots are, and the earth how leal!

And O the blossoms! And the wild seeds lost!
And jeweled martyrdom of fiery frost!
And fruit trees. I'd forgotten. No cold gem,
But to be apples—and bow down with them!

Lilian Taylor (age 9)

THE CRIMSON TREE

I saw a lovely crimson tree,
As fair and bright as it could be;
'T was robed in coral's richest hue,
And bathed in floods of evening dew.

'T was standing out in full relief
Against the sky, had I a sheaf
Of its bright leaves, a cluster rare,
Each perfumed by the scented air,

I'd twine it with the holly red
At Christmas time, and it would shed
Its lustrous radiance o'er our home
And from it may we never roam.

Wild vines were clustered 'round its stem,
Sweet perfumes floated forth from them;
'T was like a ruby on the green,
The fairest that was ever seen.

A softened brilliancy did glow
Around its boughs, as if to throw
A diamond brightness all around.
With it the head was softly crowned.

But now farewell, thou rosy tree,
For I must cease my strain to thee!
Farewell! I may not view thee more,
But thou wilt grace thy native shore.

Edna St. Vincent Millay (age 14)

FOREST TREES

Monarchs of long-forgotten realms, ye stand;
        Majestic, grand;
Unscarred by Time's destructive hand.
Enthroned on dais of velvet moss, inset
With the royal purple of the violet;
        And crowned with mistletoe.

How many ages o'er your heads have flown,
        To you is known—
To you, ye forest-founders of the past, alone.
No other eyes may scan the breadth of years,
        Each with its share of peace, and joy, and tears;
            Of happiness and woe.

Around you all is changed—where now is land
Swift vessels ploughed to foam the seething main;
Kingdoms have risen; and the fire-fiend's hand
Has crushed them to their Mother Earth again;
And through it all ye stand, and still will stand
Till ages yet to come have owned your reign.

Henry De Wolfe, Jr.

MAPLE LEAVES

When the grass is growing green,
And the ranging geese are seen
Flying forth
To their place of congregation in the rivers of the North,
Then within its heart of wood
Stirs and leaps the maple's blood,
Ever joyously ascending till the leaves begin to bud.
Over all the verdant meadows newly risen flowers are seen
In the bright unshadowed season when the maple leaves are green.

Like a dream the moments fly;
Now autumnal days are nigh;
All the summer's bloom is lost, and the fingers of the frost
Leave the maple leaves all radiant with a sanguinary dye.
All its lowly comrades scorning,
Careless of the season's warning,
Proudly towers the tinted maple, as it sought to reach the sky;
In its ire
Lifting higher;
From the withered earth arising like a pyramid of fire.
Now the maple leaves are dazzling in the clear September day,
While the splendor of their color hides the tokens of decay.

Still the cold is waxing stronger,
Days are shorter, nights are longer,
While the nipping breezes chill what the frost has failed to kill,
And the voices of the summer sound no more on plain or hill.
Now the maple leaves decayed
Fall and fade,
And the parent tree dismayed
Writhes and tosses, while the whirlwind, from its icy cave set free,
Shouts around the naked branches in demoniac jubilee.

꧁ Richard Le Gallienne

THE PINE LADY

O have you seen the Pine Lady—
Or heard her how she sings!
Have you heard her play
Your soul away
On a harp with moonbeam strings?
In a palace all of the night-black pine
She hides like a queen all day,
Till a moonbeam knocks
On her secret tree,
And she opens her door
With a silver key,
While the village clocks
Are striking bed
Nine times sleepily.

And, high in the
boughs
Of her haunted
house,
The moon and
she are sitting.

O come and hear the Pine Lady
Up in the haunted wood!
The stars are rising, the moths are flitting,
The owls are calling,
The dew is falling;
And, high in the boughs
Of her haunted house,
The moon and she are sitting.

Out on the moor the nightjar drones
Rough-throated love,
The beetle comes
With his silent drums,
And many a silent unseen thing
Frightens your cheek with its ghostly wing;
While there above,
In a palace builded of needles and cones,
The pine is telling the moon her love,
Telling her love on the moonbeam
    strings—
O have you seen the Pine Lady,
Or heard her how she sings!

PLANT A TREE

He who plants a tree,
    Plants a hope.
Rootlets up through fibers blindly grope;
Leaves unfold into horizons free.
    So man's life must climb
    From the clods of time
    Unto heavens sublime.
Canst thou prophesy, thou little tree,
What the glory of thy boughs shall be?

He who plants a tree,—
    Plants a joy;
Plants a comfort that will never cloy;
Every day a fresh reality,
    Beautiful and strong,
    To whose shelter throng
    Creatures blithe with song.
If thou couldst but know, thou happy tree,
Of the bliss that shall inhabit thee!

He who plants a tree,—
    He plants peace.
Under its green curtains jargons cease.
Leaf and zephyr murmur soothingly;
    Shadows soft with sleep
    Down tired eyelids creep,
    Balm of slumber deep.
Never hast thou dreamed, thou blessèd tree,
Of the benediction thou shalt be.

He who plants a tree,—
    He plants youth;
Vigor won for centuries in sooth;
Life of time, that hints eternity!
    Boughs their strength uprear;
    New shoots, every year
    On old growths appear,
Thou shalt teach the ages, sturdy tree,
Youth of soul is immortality.

He who plants a tree,—
    He plants love;
Tents of coolness spreading out above
Wayfarers, he may not live to see.
    Gifts that grow, are best;
    Hands that bless are blest;
    Plant! Life does the rest!
Heaven and earth help him who plants
    a tree,
And his work its own reward shall be.

Christina Moody (age 13–16)

THE LITTLE SEED

A little seed fell to the earth,
  'Twas the seed of an apple tree.
'Twas too small to grow as I could
    plainly see—
  Why it was'nt as large as a pea.

But the little seed planned of days to
    come,
  When his body would be great and tall,
But how could that be, when he was so
    wee,
  He could scarcely be seen at all?

By and by the seed broke in twain,
  'Twas the death of him I said,
But instead of death, a pretty stem
  Lifted up his little green head.

The stem grew up with perfect grace
  And looked with wondering eyes,
At the painting of Nature's wonderfull
    art,
  Until he became very wise.

Little leaflets too came forth,
  With beauty that can't be told.
So the seed that was wee, grew into a tree
  'Twas a wonderful sight to behold.

Paul Laurence Dunbar

THE SEEDLING

As a quiet little seedling
  Lay within its darksome bed,
To itself it fell a-talking,
  And this is what it said:

"I am not so very robust,
  But I'll do the best I can;"
And the seedling from that moment
  Its work of life began.

So it pushed a little leaflet
  Up into the light of day,
To examine the surroundings
  And show the rest the way.

The leaflet liked the prospect,
  So it called its brother, Stem;
Then two other leaflets heard it,
  And quickly followed them.

To be sure, the haste and hurry
  Made the seedling sweat and pant;
But almost before it knew it
  It found itself a plant.

The sunshine poured upon it,
  And the clouds they gave a shower;
And the little plant kept growing
  Till it found itself a flower.

Little folks, be like the seedling,
  Always do the best you can;
Every child must share life's labor
  Just as well as every man.

And the sun and showers will help you
  Through the lonesome, struggling
    hours,
Till you raise to light and beauty
  Virtue's fair, unfading flowers.

DAISIES

At evening when I go to bed
I see the stars shine overhead;
They are the little daisies white
That dot the meadow of the Night.

And often while I'm dreaming so,
Across the sky the Moon will go;
It is a lady, sweet and fair,
Who comes to gather daisies there.

For, when at morning I arise,
There's not a star left in the skies;
She's picked them all and dropped
  them down
Into the meadows of the town.

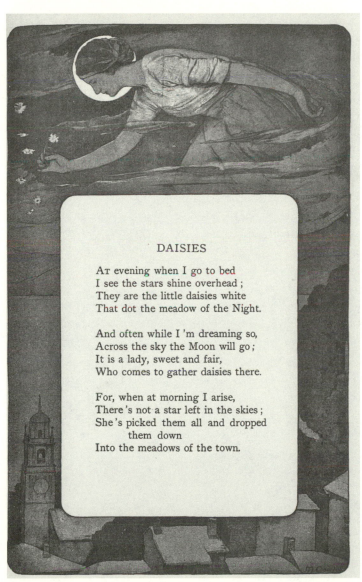

DAISIES

AT evening when I go to bed
I see the stars shine overhead ;
They are the little daisies white
That dot the meadow of the Night.

And often while I 'm dreaming so,
Across the sky the Moon will go ;
It is a lady, sweet and fair,
Who comes to gather daisies there.

For, when at morning I arise,
There 's not a star left in the skies ;
She 's picked them all and dropped
      them down
Into the meadows of the town.

THE PROFESSOR AND THE WHITE VIOLET

THE PROFESSOR.

Tell me little violet white,
If you will be so polite,
Tell me how it came that you
Lost your pretty purple hue?
Were you blanched with sudden fears?
Were you bleached with fairies' tears?
Or was Dame Nature out of blue,
Violet, when she came to you?

THE VIOLET.

Tell me, silly mortal, first,
Ere I satisfy your thirst
For the truth concerning me—
Why you are not like a tree?
Tell me why you move around,
Trying different kinds of ground,
With your funny legs and boots
In the place of proper roots?

Tell me, mortal, why your head,
Where green branches ought to spread,
Is as shiny smooth as glass,
With just a fringe of frosty grass?
Tell me—Why, he's gone away!
Wonder why he wouldn't stay?
Can he be—well, I declare!—
Sensitive about his hair?

Helen Hunt Jackson

MORNING-GLORY

Wondrous interlacement!
    Holding fast to threads by green and silky rings,
With the dawn it spreads its white and purple wings;
Generous in its bloom, and sheltering while it clings,
    Sturdy morning-glory.

    Creeping through the casement,
Slanting to the floor in dusty, shining beams,
Dancing on the door, in quick fantastic gleams
Comes the new day's light, and pours in tideless streams,
    Golden morning-glory.

    In the lowly basement,
Rocking in the sun, the baby's cradle stands.
Now the little one thrusts out his rosy hands;
Soon his eyes will open; then in all the lands
    No such morning-glory.

Mary McNeil Fenollosa

IRIS FLOWERS

My mother let me go with her,
  (I had been good all day),
To see the iris flowers that bloom
  In gardens far away.

We walked and walked through hedges
    green,
  Through rice-fields empty still,
To where we saw a garden gate
  Beneath the farthest hill.

She pointed out the rows of "flowers";—
  I saw no planted things,
But white and purple butterflies
  Tied down with silken strings.

They strained and fluttered in the breeze,
  So eager to be free;
I begged the man to let them go,
  But mother laughed at me.

She said that they could never rise,
  Like birds, to heaven so blue.
But even mothers do not know
  Some things that children do.

That night, the flowers untied themselves
  And softly stole away,
To fly in sunshine round my dreams
  Until the break of day.

OUR WREATH OF ROSE BUDS

I.

We offer you a wreath of flowers
Culled in recreation hours,
Which will not wither, droop, or die,
Even when days and months pass by.

II.

Ask you where these flowers are found?
Not on sunny slope, or mound;
Not on prairies bright and fair
Growing without thought or care.

III.

No, our simple wreath is twined
From the garden of the mind;
Where bright thoughts like rivers flow
And ideas like roses grow.

IV.

The tiny buds which here you see
Ask your kindly empathy;
View them with a lenient eye,
Pass each fault, each blemish by.

V.

Warmed by the sunshine of your eyes,
Perhaps you'll find to your surprise,
Their petals fair will soon unclose,
And every bud become—a Rose.

VI.

Then take our wreath, and let it stand
An emblem of our happy band;
The *Seminary*, our *garden* fair,
And *we*, the *flowers* planted there.

VII.

Like roses bright we hope to grow,
And o'er our home such beauty throw
In future years—that all may see
Loveliest of lands,—the Cherokee.

Mary E. Wilkins [Freeman]

A SONG

Sing a song of a little lass (*red blow the roses, O*),
About a lovely little lass, who was so like a rose, you know,
(*Red blow the roses, O*), so very like when placed together,
They only told her from a rose because she bloomed in winter weather.

Mary E. Wilkins [Freeman]

CARAWAY

Past the lavender-bed and the parsley,
    Close to the wall where the sweet-brier blows,
Green grows the caraway Grandma planted,
    Though scarce one lover to-day it knows.

When dear old Grandma her "meetin' bunnit"
    Had carefully tied, on the Sabbath Day,
She always put in her best-gown pocket
    A generous handful of caraway.

For the dear old soul would grow a-weary
    To sit so long in the cushionless pew;
And oft the parson's doctrinal sermon
    Would trouble her tender feelings too.

And when she had heard so much "election"
    That her heart for the others began to bleed,
She sensed the better God's love behind it
    By eating a bit of her "meetin' seed."

Solemn and mild upraised to the parson
    Was her dear old face on the Sabbath Day;
She drank the sweet there was in the sermon
    The bitter she flavored with caraway.

Though caraway is not fair to look at,
    Though you may not fancy its taste indeed,
Yet still it shall grow there down in the garden
    Because it was Grandma's "meetin' seed."

Mary E. Wilkins [Freeman]

TIGER LILIES

How keepeth my lady the weeds from her posies,
　　All in the gay summer-time!
Why is it the rose-chafer eats not her roses
From the song of the lark till the four-o'clock closes?

Five fierce lily-tigers in spotted cuirasses
She posteth at each of her green garden-passes,
And they frighten away the chafers and grasses,
　　All in the gay summer-time.

Marian Douglas

COW-LILIES

A great, green ring of water-reeds
　　Around the pool is growing,
And here and there the pickerel-weed
　　Its pale blue flower is showing;
Close by that tuft of cat-tails, look!
　　I see a minnow shine,
And there's a yellow cow-lily,
　　I wish that it were mine!
'T is more a memory than a wish,
　　For, when that flower I see,
My happy childhood, like a bird,
　　Comes flying back to me.

For then, though I, the summer long,
　　Had wood and field to play in,
A marshy meadow was the place
　　It pleased me most to stray in;
Around the pools we used to flit,
　　The dragon-flies and I,
Where, moored like golden boats, I saw
　　The yellow lilies lie.
The choicest treasures of the year
　　They seemed to me, but, O,
Just where I could not reach, those flowers
　　Were always sure to grow.

The purple clover, where all day
　　The bees were honey sucking,
The briar-roses offered me
　　Their blossoms for the plucking;
The roadside elder sought my hand,
　　Its silver mantle clad;
I left them all untouched; they were
　　Too easy to be had!
But, O, the lily's golden glow
　　Upon the pool's green breast!
The flowers that mocked my wishes were
　　The ones I liked the best!

Gay preacher in the yellow gown,
　　Thy silent lesson teach:
"A thing to charm Mortality
　　Must lie beyond its reach."

FLOWERS FOR THE BRAVE

Here bring your purple and gold,
  Glory of color and scent!
Scarlet of tulips bold,
  Buds blue as the firmament.

Hushed is the sound of the fife
  And the bugle piping clear:
The vivid and delicate life
  In the soul of the youthful year

We bring to the quiet dead,
  With a gentle and tempered grief:
O'er the mounds so mute we shed
  The beauty of blossom and leaf.

The flashing swords that were drawn,
  No rust shall their fame destroy!
Boughs rosy as rifts of dawn,
  Like the blush on the cheek of joy,

Rich fires of the gardens and meads,
  We kindle these hearts above!
What splendor shall match their deeds?
  What sweetness can match our love?

❧ Emily Dickinson

[TO MAKE A PRAIRIE]

To make a prairie it takes a clover and one bee,—
One clover, and a bee,
And reverie.
The reverie alone will do
If bees are few.

❧ Eudora May Stone* (about age 13)

PRAIRIE FIRES

The autumn frost begins to blight,
    But here and there late blossoms linger:
The maple leaves are glowing bright,
    Red-painted all by Autumn's finger.

The birds are gone; the chill wind grieves
    Among the dry and withered grasses,
And showers of gold or scarlet leaves
    It flings from every tree it passes.

But, see, a spark has fallen there
    Among the grasses of the prairie;
And high and higher in the air
    The flames are leaping light and airy.

Now, farmers, guard your hoarded grain;
    The flames are wider, fiercer growing,
And urging on the fiery train,
    The raging wind is wildly blowing.

The sun sinks low, the waning light
    Is fading fast from hills and meadows;
The night, so strangely, grandly bright,
    Mantles the earth in fitful shadows.

Now fiercer still the wild winds blow—
    The sky the fiery color catches;
And brighter yet the red flames glow,
    And wide the blackened prairie stretches.

* Nebraska.

🍀 *Author Unknown*

THE JOHNNY CAKE

This is the seed,
So yellow and round,
That little John Homer hid in the ground.

These are the leaves,
So graceful and tall,
That grew from the seed so yellow and small.

This is the stalk
That came up between
The leaves so pretty and graceful and green.

These are the tassels,
So flowery, that crowned
The stalk so smooth, so strong, and so round.

These are the husks
With satin inlaid,
That grew 'neath the tassels that drooped and swayed.

This is the silk
In shining threads spun:
A treasure it hides from the frost and the sun.

This is the treasure—
Corn, yellow as gold—
That satin and silk so softly unfold.

This is the cake,
For Johnny to eat,
Made from the corn so yellow and sweet.

🍀 *Fr. John Banister Tabb*

THE TRYST

Potato was deep in the dark under
    ground,
Tomato, above in the light.
The little Tomato was ruddy and round,
The little Potato was white.

And redder and redder she rounded
    above,
And paler and paler he grew,
And neither suspected a mutual love
Till they met in a Brunswick stew.

Hannah Flagg Gould

THE MUSHROOM'S SOLILOQUY

O what, and whence am I, 'mid damps and dust,
And darkness, into sudden being thrust?
What was I yesterday? and what will be,
Perchance, to-morrow, seen or heard of me?

Poor, lone, unfriended, ignorant, forlorn,
To bear the new, full glory of the morn,
Beneath the garden wall I stand aside,
With all before me beauty, show, and pride.

Ah! why did Nature shoot me thus to light,
A thing unfit for use—unfit for sight;
Less like her work than like a piece of art,
Whirled out and trimmed exact in every part?

Unlike the graceful shrub, and flexile vine,
No fruit—no branch—nor leaf, nor bud, is mine.
No humming bird, nor butterfly, nor bee
Will come to cheer, caress, or flatter me.

No beauteous flower adorns my humble head,
No spicy odors on the air I shed;
But here I'm stationed, in my sober suit,
With only top and stem—I've scarce a root.

Untaught of my beginning or my end,
I know not whence I sprung, or where I tend:
Yet I will wait, and trust; and ne'er presume
To question Justice—I, a frail Mushroom!

THE PEACH BLOSSOMS

Come here! come here! Cousin Mary, and see
What fair ripe peaches there are on the tree—
On the very same bough that was given to me
   By father, one day last spring.
When it look'd so beautiful, all in the blow,
And I wanted to pluck it, he told me, you know,
That I might—but that waiting a few months would show
   The fruit that patience might bring.

And, as I perceived by the sound of his voice,
And the look of his eye, it was clearly his choice
That it should not be touch'd, I have now to rejoice
   That I told him we'd let it remain.
For, had it been gather'd when full in the flower,
Its blossoms had wither'd, perhaps, in an hour,
And nothing on earth could have given the power
   That would make them flourish again!

But now, of a fruit so delicious and sweet
I've enough for myself, and my playmates a treat;
And they tell me, besides, that the kernels secrete
   What, if planted, will make other trees;
For the shell will come open to let down the root—
A sprout will spring up, whence the branches will shoot,
There'll be buds, leaves, and blossoms, and then comes the fruit—
   Such beautiful peaches as these!

And Nature, they say, like a mighty machine,
Has a wheel in a wheel, which, if ought comes between,
It ruins her work, as it might have been seen
   Had it not given patience this trial.
From this, I'll be careful to keep it in mind,
When the blossoms I love, that there lingers behind
A better reward, that the trusting shall find
   For a trifling self-denial!

THE PETRIFIED FERN

In a valley, centuries ago,
    Grew a little fern-leaf, green and slender,
    Veining delicate and fibres tender;
Waving when the wind crept down so low.
    Rushes tall, and moss, and grass grew round it,
    Playful sunbeams darted in and found it,
    Drops of dew stole in by night, and crowned it,
    But no foot of man e'er trod that way;
    Earth was young and keeping holiday.

Monster fishes swam the silent main,
    Stately forests waved their giant branches,
    Mountains hurled their snowy avalanches,
Mammoth creatures stalked across the plain;
    Nature revelled in grand mysteries;
    But the little fern was not of these,
    Did not number with the hills and trees;
    Only grew and waved its wild sweet way,
    No one came to note it day by day.

Earth, one time, put on a frolic mood,
    Heaved the rocks and changed the mighty motion
    Of the deep, strong currents of the ocean;
Moved the plain and shook the haughty wood,
    Crushed the little fern in soft moist clay,—
    Covered it, and hid it safe away.
    O, the long, long centuries since that day!
    O, the changes! O, life's bitter cost,
    Since that useless little fern was lost!

Useless? Lost? There came a thoughtful man
    Searching Nature's secrets, far and deep;
    From a fissure in a rocky steep
He withdrew a stone, o'er which there ran
    Fairy pencillings, a quaint design,
    Veinings, leafage, fibres clear and fine,
    And the fern's life lay in every line!
    So, I think, God hides some souls away,
    Sweetly to surprise us, the last day.

❧ T[acie] T[ownsend] Purvis

WHAT THE LICHENS SANG

I heard the lichens singing
One cold and frosty morn;
When all the leaves had vanished
From tree and bush and thorn.

When the hills were brown all over,
And the fields seemed desert sands;
When the summer flowers were sleeping
'Neath the dead leaves' folded hands.
I heard the lichens singing
And the mosses sweet and clear,
Joined in the fairy concert,
As I hushed my breath to hear.

"If it were always summer
And the land were filled with flowers,
What eye would mark the lichens
That bloom in wintry hours?
What hand would pluck the mosses,
That make the old wood gay,
And who would come to bear them
Like precious gems away?
We are the winter's jewels
He hides us in his breast;
And only those who love us,
May find us 'neath his vest."

IN BLOSSOM TIME

It's O my heart, my heart,
    To be out in the sun and sing—
To sing and shout in the fields about,
    In the balm and the blossoming!

Sing loud, O bird in the tree;
    O bird, sing aloud in the sky,
And honey-bees, blacken the clover beds—
    There is none of you glad as I.

The leaves laugh low in the wind,
    Laugh low, with the wind at play;
And the odorous call of the flowers all
    Entices my soul away!

For O but the world is fair, is fair—
    And O but the world is sweet!
I will out in the gold of the blossoming mould,
    And sit at the Master's feet.

And the love my heart would speak,
    I will fold in the lily's rim,
That th' lips of the blossom, more pure and meek,
    May offer it up to Him.

Then sing in the hedgerow green, O thrush,
    O skylark, sing in the blue;
Sing loud, sing clear, that the King may hear,
    And my soul shall sing with you!

&❧ *Eudora M[ay] Stone** (age 10)

SIGNS OF SPRING

Breezes soft are blowing, blowing
    O'er the lea;
And the little flowers are growing,
    Fair to see.
And the grass is springing, springing
    'Neath our feet;
And the early birds are singing,
    Clear and sweet.

Little lambs are racing, racing
    All the day;
And the warm bright sunbeams chasing
    Clouds away.
Busy bees are humming, humming
    'Mong the flowers.
Clouds are shifting—rain is coming—
    April showers.

* Emerson, Otoe County, Nebraska

&❧ *Pauline Jenks* (age 12)

APRIL FLOWERS

Where forest tangle is the wildest
    And all is wet with April showers,
And where the wind's fierce roar is
    mildest,
    'T is there you find the spring's first
    flowers.

Where thrush sings on the leafless tree,
    Where all is lonely, still, and wet,
You'll see a fair anemone,
    And possibly a violet.

&❧ *Jennie G. Clarke*

SECRETS

What is the secret the pine-trees know
That keeps them whispering, soft and low?
All day long in the breezes swaying,
What can it be they are always saying?
The nodding daisies deep in the grass
Seem to beckon to me as I pass.
What have they that is worth the showing,
Out in the meadow where they're
    growing?
If I listen close where the brook flows
    strong,

I can hear it singing a low, sweet song.
Is it just because of the watch it's
    keeping,
There where the baby ferns are sleeping?
The sweet, white clovers out in the sun
Have told the bumble bees, every one,
And high in the maple-tree swinging,
    swinging,
Loud and clear is a robin singing.
Is the flower's secret for bird and bee,
And not for a little girl like me?

& Mary E. Wilkins [Freeman]

THE PRIZE

"Hie to the meadow, my dearies three,
And hunt for some sweet, pretty thing for me!
    There's a cake in the oven with almonds and spice,
    And raisins and citron, and all that's nice,
To pay for the sweetest, my dearies three!"

When home from the field came the dearies three,
One brought to her mother a wild rose-tree;
    And another brought her a blue jay's feather
    And one of a gray goose, tied together,
And she was sure of the prize, was she.

But the last little girl of the dearies three
Had sucked a clover-bell like a bee,
    And tasted a columbine's honeyed tips
    To sweeten a kiss for her mother's lips;
And she got the beautiful cake for tea.

& Sarah Piatt

I WANT IT YESTERDAY

"Come, take the flower,—it is not dead;
    'Twas kept in dew the whole night through."
"I will not have it now," he said:
    "I want it yesterday, I do."

"It is as red, it is as sweet"—
    With angry tears he turned away,
Then flung it fiercely at his feet,
    And said, "I want it—yesterday!"

🍀 *Lizette Woodworth Reese*

A STREET SCENE

The east is a clear violet mass
Behind the houses high;
The laborers with their kettles pass;
The carts are creaking by.

Carved out against the tender sky,
The convent gables lift;
Half way below the old boughs lie
Heaped in a great white drift.

They tremble in the passionate air;
They part, and clean and sweet
The cherry flakes fall here, fall there;
A handful stirs the street.

The workmen look up as they go;
And one, remembering plain
How white the Irish orchards blow,
Turns back, and looks again.

🍀 *Charles Leland*

THE FLOWER GIRL
*From an Algonquin Indian Story.**

I'm going to the garden
Where summer roses blow;
I'll make me a little sister
Of all the flowers that grow;

I'll make her body of lilies,
Because they're soft and white;
I'll make her eyes of violets,
With dew-drops shining bright;

I'll make her lips of rose-buds,
Her cheeks of rose-leaves red,

Her hair of silky corn-tops
All braided 'round her head;

With apple-tree and pear leaves
I'll make her a lovely gown,
With rows of golden buttercups
For buttons, up and down.

I'll dance with my little sister
Away to the river strand,
Away across the water,
Away into Fairy-land.

* Several of the Algonquin tribes have a legend of a girl who was made entirely
   of flowers [Leland's note].

🍀 *Elaine Goodale* [*Eastman*] (age 15)

ASHES OF ROSES

Soft on the sunset sky
   Bright daylight closes,
Leaving, when light doth die,
Pale hues that mingling lie—
   Ashes of roses.

When Love's warm sun is set,
   Love's brightness closes;
Eyes with hot tears are wet,
In hearts there linger yet
   Ashes of roses.

BURS

Dear me!
    What shall it be?
Such sticky affairs
    Did ever you see?
Let's make a basket,
    Let's make a mat,
Let's make a tea-board,
    Let's make a hat;
Let's make a cottage,
    Windows and doors;
You do the roof,
    And I'll do the floors.
Let's make a pancake,—
    Stick 'em together;
See how they fasten
    Close to each other!
Tied to one's heel
    They would answer for spurs;
Ah, how we love 'em,
    These comical burs!

Emily Dickinson

[AS CHILDREN BID THE GUEST GOOD-NIGHT]

As children bid the guest good-night,
And then reluctant turn,
My flowers raise their pretty lips,
Then put their nightgowns on.

As children caper when they wake,
Merry that it is morn,
My flowers from a hundred cribs
Will peep, and prance again.

LANDSCAPES AND SEASONS

E. Pauline Johnson [Tekahionwake; Mohawk]

THE SONG MY PADDLE SINGS

West wind blow from your prairie
    nest[,]
Blow from the mountains, blow from
    the west.
The sail is idle, the sailor too;
O! wind of the west, we wait for you.
Blow, blow!
I have wooed you so,
But never a favour you bestow.
You rock your cradle the hills between,
But scorn to notice my white lateen.

I stow the sail, unship the mast:
I wooed you long but my wooing's past;
My paddle will lull you into rest.
O! drowsy wind of the drowsy west,
Sleep, sleep,
By your mountain steep,
Or down where the prairie grasses
    sweep!
Now fold in slumber your laggard
    wings,
For soft is the song my paddle sings.

August is laughing across the sky,
Laughing while paddle, canoe and I,
Drift, drift,
Where the hills uplift
On either side of the current swift.

The river rolls in its rocky bed;
My paddle is plying its way ahead;
Dip, dip,
While the waters flip
In foam as over their breast we slip.

And oh, the river runs swifter now;
The eddies circle about my bow.
Swirl, swirl!
How the ripples curl
In many a dangerous pool awhirl!

And forward far the rapids roar,
Fretting their margin for evermore.
Dash, dash,
With a mighty crash,
They seethe, and boil, and bound, and
    splash.

Be strong, O paddle! be brave, canoe!
The reckless waves you must plunge
    into.
Reel, reel.
On your trembling keel,
But never a fear my craft will feel.

We've raced the rapid, we're far ahead!
The river slips through its silent bed.
Sway, sway,
As the bubbles spray
And fall in tinkling tunes away.

And up on the hills against the sky,
A fir tree rocking its lullaby,
Swings, swings,
Its emerald wings,
Swelling the song that my paddle sings.

Margaret Sangster

THE FOUR WINDS

The wind o' the West
I love it best.
The wind o' the East
I love it least.

The wind o' the South
Has sweet in its mouth.
The wind o' the North
Sends great storms forth.

Taken together, all sorts of weather
   The four old fellows are sure to bring—
Hurry and flurry, rush and scurry,
Sighing and dying, and flitting and flying,
   Through summer and autumn and winter
      and spring.

Walt Whitman

GIVE ME THE SPLENDID SILENT SUN

Give me the splendid silent sun, with all his beams full-dazzling;
Give me juicy autumnal fruit, ripe and red from the orchard;
Give me a field where the unmow'd grass grows;
Give me an arbor, give me the trellis'd grape;
Give me fresh corn and wheat—give me serene-moving animals, teaching content;
Give me nights perfectly quiet, as on high plateaus west of the Mississippi, and
   I looking up at the stars;
Give me odorous at sunrise a garden of beautiful flowers, where I can walk
   undisturb'd;
Give me for marriage a sweet-breath'd woman, of whom I should never tire;
Give me a perfect child—give me, away, aside from the noise of the world, a rural
   domestic life;
Give me to warble spontaneous songs, reliev'd, recluse by myself, for my own
   ears only;
Give me solitude—give me Nature—give me again, O Nature, your primal sanities!

Author Unknown

ON THE SUN

See yon majestic orb of day,
That makes Creation look so gay,
Dispels the darkness of the night,
And in its stead, diffuses light.

Emily Dickinson

A DAY

I'll tell you how the sun rose,—
A ribbon at a time.
The steeples swam in amethyst,
The news like squirrels ran.

The hills untied their bonnets,
The bobolinks begun.
Then I said softly to myself,
"That must have been the sun!"

. . . .

But how he set, I know not.
There seemed a purple stile
Which little yellow boys and girls
Were climbing all the while

Till when they reached the other side,
A dominie in gray
Put gently up the evening bars,
And led the flock away.

✎ *James Smith* (age 14)

NIGHT

Night is a time of sweet repose,
   When wearied man may rest;
Forgetting all his cares and woes,
   He dreams that he is blest.
The feather'd tribes to roost are gone;
   Beasts of the forest roam,

And, until morning's early dawn,
   The night'ngale sings alone.
Then while his master soundly sleeps,
   Behold his watchful tray
Guards well the house, and safely keeps
   The robbers far away.

✎ *Mary McNeil Fenollosa*

THE JISHIN (THE EARTHQUAKE)

A jishin
Will begin
With a tiny start and shiver.
   The *shoji* gently chatter,
   The mice and children scatter,
   For they know well what's the matter
When the ground begins to quiver.
   O jishin,
   Good jishin,
Please don't be, this time, a big one, be a small one,
   Good jishin!

Bad jishin
Tumbles in
With the howl and growl of thunder!
   The plaster walls are crashing,
   The kitchen dishes smashing,
   The broken roof-tiles gnashing,
Till the house is half asunder!
   O jishin,
   Bad jishin,
You're the worst we've felt for ages. O you horrid
   Bad jishin!

❧ Christina Moody (age 13–16)

OL' MAN RAIN, P'EASE GO AWAY

Rain, Rain, go away.
Us little chilluns wants to play.
Got to stay in de house all day,
    If ol' Man Rain don't go away.

W'ats de use in powing down
Like you wants to see us drown?
Wish dat you would'en stay,
    Ol' Man Rain, p'ease go away.

Got de place all soaking wet,
Front do' swollen so 'twont shet:
Can't you see you'se in de way?
    Ol' Man Rain p'ease go away.

Mammy's cross as de ol' scratch,
Papy's techus as a match.
How long is you gwine to stay?
    Ol' Man Rain, p'ease go away.

Fido he's a fussing
And a biting at de cat,
And I recon if dey keep on
    Dey will end up in a scrap.

Wat's de use of keep on drapping
And a being in de way,
When you knows for yo' se'f,
    Dat us chilluns wants to play?

❧ Mary McNeil Fenollosa

A TYPHOON

We knew the storm was coming
    Long, long before it came;
For the whole air woke to humming
    And the wind smelled hot, like flame.

The clouds sank low and lower;
    The crows wheeled close, for fear,
And the flat earth seemed to cower
    With sense of danger near.

Then like a nest of dragons
    It fell upon the town;
It overturned the wagons
    And knocked the drivers down.

It kicked the dust to billows
    That climbed the frightened air;
And backward jerked the willows
    As by a woman's hair.

The pond, so placid lying
    Was tilted like a dish;
It sent the roof-tiles flying
    As though it scaled a fish.

Our pretty wooden bucket
    That hangs beside the door
Rose as the monster struck it
    And came to earth no more.

In midst of fiercest motion
    And shrieks, it left the sky
To rush upon the ocean.
    Old Typhoon San, Good-bye!

Emily Dickinson

THE STORM

There came a wind like a bugle;
It quivered through the grass,
And a green chill upon the heat
So ominous did pass
We barred the windows and the doors
As from an emerald ghost;
The doom's electric moccason
That very instant passed.
On a strange mob of panting trees,
And fences fled away,
And rivers where the houses ran
The living looked that day.
The bell within the steeple wild
The flying tidings whirled.
How much can come
And much can go,
And yet abide the world!

Emily Dickinson

THE MOUNTAIN

The mountain sat upon the plain
In his eternal chair,
His observation omnifold,
His inquest everywhere.
The seasons prayed around his knees,
Like children round a sire:
Grandfather of the days is he,
Of dawn the ancestor.

Emily Dickinson

AUTUMN

The morns are meeker than they were,
The nuts are getting brown;
The berry's cheek is plumper,
The rose is out of town.
The maple wears a gayer scarf,
The field a scarlet gown.
Lest I should be old-fashioned,
I'll put a trinket on.

Ina Coolbrith

DECEMBER

Send the ruddy fire-light higher;
Draw your easy-chair up nigher;
    Through the winter, bleak and chill,
    We may have our summer still.
Here are poems we may read,
Pleasant fancies to our need:
    Ah, eternal summer-time
    Dwells within the poet's rhyme!

E. Pauline Johnson [Tekahionwake; Mohawk]

LADY ICICLE

Little Lady Icicle is dreaming in the north-land
And gleaming in the north-land, her pillow all a-glow;
    For the frost has come and found her
    With an ermine robe around her
Where little Lady Icicle lies dreaming in the snow.

Little Lady Icicle is waking in the north-land,
And shaking in the north-land her pillow to and fro;
    And the hurricane a-skirling
    Sends the feathers all a-whirling
Where little Lady Icicle is waking in the snow.

Little Lady Icicle is laughing in the north-land,
And quaffing in the north-land her wines that overflow;
    All the lakes and rivers crusting
    That her finger-tips are dusting,
Where little Lady Icicle is laughing in the snow.

Little Lady Icicle is singing in the north-land,
And bringing from the north-land a music wild and low;
    And the fairies watch and listen
    Where her silver slippers glisten,
As little Lady Icicle goes singing through the snow.

Little Lady Icicle is coming from the north-land,
Benumbing all the north-land where'er her feet may go;
    With a fringe of frost before her
    And a crystal garment o'er her,
Little Lady Icicle is coming with the snow.

John James Piatt

SNOW FALLING

The wonderful snow is falling,
  Over river and woodland and wold;
The trees bear spectral blossom
  In the moonlight blurred and cold.

There's a beautiful garden in Heaven:
  And these are the banished flowers,
Fallen and driven and drifting
  To this dark world of ours!

SNOW-FLAKES

Whenever a snow-flake leaves the sky,
It turns and turns to say "Good-bye!
Good-bye, dear cloud, so cool and gray!"
Then lightly travels on its way.

And when a snow-flake finds a tree,
"Good-day!" it says—"Good-day to thee!
Thou art so bare and lonely, dear,
I'll rest and call my comrades here."

But when a snow-flake, brave and meek,
Lights on a rosy maiden's check,
It starts—"How warm and soft the day!
'Tis summer!"—and it melts away.

❧ *"Cora"* [*pseudonym*]

THE LITTLE BOY'S LAMENT

Oh dear! oh dear! do see the snow,
   How fast it melts away!
When only a few days ago,
   It seemed 'twould always stay.

For then the banks were broad and high,
   And white—*as white as snow*;
But now, do see them, there they lie
   All dirt, and soon they'll go.

I tried last night and drew my sled
   Quite up that long steep hill;
I could not slide. I went to bed
   And dreamed of "Jack and Gill."

And then the ice—I must not skate,
   For father says 'tis soft;
I can do nothing, but must wait
   Once more for old Jack Frost.

❧ *"Cora"* [*pseudonym*]

THE LITTLE GIRL'S REPLY

I'm glad, I'm glad 'tis warm to-day,
   For now the snow will melt;
But yesterday I thought 'twould stay,
   And then how sad I felt.

I'm glad, for spring will quickly come,
   With all its gentle showers,
Its singing birds, its beaming sun,
   And many fragrant flowers.

I'm tired of staying in the house,—
   I want to run and play;
I've been shut up just like a mouse,
   Each cold and snowy day.

But now they're gone, and I am sure
   Stern winter's power is lost;
I hope it is—I can't endure
   To think of old Jack Frost.

OUT IN THE SNOW

The snow and the silence came down together,
Through the night so white and so still,
And the young folks, housed from the bitter weather,—
Housed from the storm and the chill,—

Heard in their dreams the sleigh-bells jingle,
Coasted the hillsides under the moon,
Felt their cheeks with the keen air tingle,
Skimmed the ice with their steel-clad shoon.

They saw the snow, when they rose in the morning,
Glittering ghost of the vanished night,
Though the sun shone clear in the winter dawning,
And the day with a frosty pomp was bright.

Out in the clear cold winter weather,—
Out in the winter air like wine,—
Kate with her dancing scarlet feather,
Bess with her peacock plumage fine,

Joe and Jack with their pealing laughter,
Frank and Tom with their gay hallo,
And half a score of roisterers after,
Out in the witching, wonderful snow.

Shivering graybeards shuffle and stumble,
Righting themselves with a frozen frown,
Grumbling at every snowy tumble,—
But the young folks know why the snow came down.

Mary E. Wilkins [Freeman]

SLIDING DOWN HILL

There is ice on the hill, hurrah, hurrah!
We can slide quite down to the pasture-bar,
Where the cows at night, in the summer weather,
Would stand a-waiting and lowing together.
    "Tie your tippet closer, John,"
    That is what their mother said;
    "All of you put mittens on—
    The broom will answer for a sled!"

They had never a sled, but dragged in its room,
Just as gayly, behind them, the worn kitchen-broom;
John, Sammy, and Tom, and their sweet little sister,
With her cheeks cherry-red, where the wind had kissed her.
    "You can watch, sis, that's enough,"
    That was what her brothers said;
    "Keep your hands warm in your muff—
    Girls can't slide without a sled!"

"Oh! where in the world is there aught so nice
 As to slide down the pasture-hill on the ice?
 Quite down to the bar, sis, see, we are going,
 Where the cows each night in summer stood lowing."
    "If I were a boy, like you—"
    This was what their sister said,
    Watching as they downward flew—
    "I would make a girl a sled!"

HOW THE SNOW-MAN FELT

"The dear little hands are gone away,
  The small soft hands so busy and kind,
Which have toiled so faithfully all the day,
  And rounded and shaped me before, behind,
My head, my hat, and my wonderful clothes,
And the pipe in my mouth, and my queer long nose.

"As long as they stayed I was almost warm,
  I could feel a pulse that came and went,
A movement stirred in my frozen form;
  Or was it the children who shook and bent,
Who shook me and pounded until I felt
As if I were real, and going to melt?

"Now they are gone to their nursery tea;
  Pray! What is tea? I wish that I knew!
And the cold white lawn is left for me,
  And the cold round moon in the sky cold blue,
And the icicles hanging along the eaves,
And the crackling frost on the stiff, dead leaves.

"If I only could move these useless feet,
  Or open these heavy arms once more,
I would cross the brown grass, glazed with sleet,
  And pop through the crack of the nursery door.
How the little ones would laugh with glee,
When they saw their snow-man coming to tea!

"But no: I am fettered and prisoned well;
  I may not move for an inch, alas!
My pipe is as cold as an icicle,
  And my pockets are each a chill crevasse;
The long, long night must come and go,
And tomorrow will find me standing so."

When the children ran in the morning to seek
  The snowman who stood there stiff and drear,
The found a tear on his frozen cheek;
  But they never guessed that it was a tear!
"He's beginning to melt about his head;"
  That was all that the children said!

Author Unknown

WINTER

My pretty flowers are gone away,—
All covered o'er with snow—
And I must wait till next May-day,
To see my violets grow.

I'm very sure the leaves will peep
Again above the ground,
Although the root is buried deep,
And not a stem is found.

Mother says, when the grave shall close
O'er little Jane and I,
We, like our own sweet fading rose,
Shall only *seem* to die.

I know my mother tells me true—
I'm not afraid to go
To God, who showers my plants with dew,
And covers them with snow.

Gertrude Heath

WAKE

Wake up, grasses!
    Wake up, clover!
See! the cold is
    Almost over!

Here is April.
    See! she's weeping!
All her babes so
    Soundly sleeping!

Wake up, posies!
    April's going!
Comes the May-time,
    Time of blowing!

Wake up, grasses!
    Wake up, clover!
See! the cold is
    Almost over!

Lizette Woodworth Reese

SUNRISE

The east is yellow as a daffodil.
Three steeples—three stark swarthy arms—are thrust
Up from the town. The gnarlèd poplars thrill
Down the long street in some keen salty gust—
Straight from the sea and all the sailing ships—
Turn white, black, white again, with noises sweet
And swift. Back to the night the last star slips.
High up the air is motionless, a sheet
Of light. The east grows yellower apace,
And trembles: then, once more, and suddenly,
The salt wind blows, and in that moment's space
Flame roofs, and poplar-tops, and steeples three;
From out the mist that wraps the river-ways,
The little boats, like torches, start ablaze.

&❧ *Lucy Larcom*

MARCH

March! March! March! They are coming
  In troops to the tune of the wind:
Red-headed woodpeckers drumming,
  Gold-crested thrushes behind;
Sparrows in brown jackets hopping
  Past every gateway and door;
Finches with crimson caps stopping
  Just where they stopped years before.

March! March! March! They are slipping
  Into their places at last:
Little white lily-buds, dripping
  Under the showers that fall fast;

Buttercups, violets, roses;
  Snowdrop and bluebell and pink;
Throng upon throng of sweet posies,
  Bending the dewdrops to drink.

March! March! March! They will hurry
  Forth at the wild-bugle sound;
Blossoms and birds in a flurry,
  Fluttering all over the ground.
Hang out your flags, birch and willow!
  Shake out your red tassels, larch!
Up, blades of grass, from your pillow!
  Hear who is calling you—March!

SWINGING ON A BIRCH TREE

Swinging on a birch-tree
    To a sleepy tune,
Hummed by all the breezes
    In the month of June!
Little leaves a-flutter
    Sound like dancing drops
Of a brook on pebbles,—
    Song that never stops.

Up and down we seesaw:
    Up into the sky;
How it opens on us,
    Like a wide blue eye!
You and I are sailors
    Rocking on a mast;
And the world's our vessel:
    Ho! she sails so fast!

Blue, blue sea around us;
    Not a ship in sight;
They will hang out lanterns
    When they pass, to-night.
We with ours will follow
    Through the midnight deep;
Not a thought of danger,
    Though the crew's asleep.

O, how still the air is!
    There an oriole flew;
What a jolly whistle!
    He's a sailor, too.
Yonder is his hammock
    In the elm-top high:
One more ballad, messmate!
    Sing it as you fly!

Up and down we seesaw:
    Down into the grass,
Scented fern, and rose-buds,
    All a woven mass.

That's the sort of carpet
    Fitted for our feet;
Tapestry nor velvet
    Is so rich and neat.

Swinging on a birch-tree!
    This is summer joy,
Fun for all vacation,—
    Don't you think so, boy?
Up and down to seesaw,
    Merry and at ease,
Careless as a brook is,
    Idle as the breeze.

❧ "M.M." [pseudonym]

THE SLEEPING BEAUTY

Far down in the valley
    She lies asleep;
Around her the mountains
    A close watch keep.

The March winds whistle
    And roar and cry,
But never a whisper
    Comes in reply.

In the silent forest
    Alone she lies,
Unmindful of storm-wind
    Or cloudy skies.

But over the mountains
    Now crowned with snow,
A prince soon is coming,
    Whose kiss we know

Will waken the beauty;
    And hand-in-hand
They'll speed through the valley,
    And all the land

With blossoms will greet them,
    While south winds blow;
For the "sleeping beauty"
    Is "April," you know!

❧ I.D.D. ("A Little Girl")

PANSY'S LOVERS

SPRINGTIME.

Pansy, little pansy,
    Wrapped in velvet hues,
Pansy, little pansy,
    Bathed in morning dews;

Pansy, little pansy,
    I'm your lover true:
I am gentle Spring-time,
    Come to welcome you.

SUMMER.

Pansy, little pansy,
    Art thou here, my sweet,
Waiting for the lover
    Thou hast longed to meet?

I am he, my darling,
    I am Summer gay;
When I come, my sweetheart,
    Spring-time hastes away.

AUTUMN.

Pansy, little pansy,
    Dost thou not know me?
I am glorious Autumn,
    Tinting vine and tree.

Pansy, little pansy,
    Grant me this one boon—
Stay with me, my darling,
    Winter's coming soon.

WINTER.

Pansy, little pansy,
    Dost thou love us all?
Then, my darling pansy,
    Answer Winter's call.

Pansy, little pansy,
    I'm the flowers' night,—
I'll fold you in my arms, pet,
    Wrapped in mantles white.

❧ Mary Mapes Dodge

SUNLIGHT OR STARLIGHT

Sunlight or starlight
    Tilly, my nilly,
Find me a stem
    Of the tiger-lily;

I'll fill it full
    From the fountain there,
And flash the water
    Over your hair!

❧ John Greenleaf Whittier

THE BAREFOOT BOY

Blessings on thee, little man,
Barefoot boy, with cheek of tan!
With thy turned-up pantaloons,
And thy merry whistled tunes—
With thy red lip, redder still
Kissed by strawberries on the hill—
With the sunshine on thy face,
Through thy torn brim's jaunty grace:
From my heart I give thee joy,
I was once a barefoot boy!
Prince thou art,—the grown-up man
Only is republican,
Let the million-dollared ride—
Barefoot, trudging at his side,
Thou hast more than he can buy,
In the reach of ear and eye—
Outward sunshine, inward joy:
Blessings on thee, barefoot boy!

Oh! for boyhood's painless play,
Sleep that wakes in laughing day,
Health that mocks the doctor's rules,
Knowledge, never learned of schools,
Of the wild bee's morning chase,
Of the wild flower's time and place,
Flight of fowl, and habitude
Of the tenants of the wood
How the tortoise bears his shell,
How the woodchuck digs his cell,
And the ground-mole sinks his well;

How the robin feeds her young,
How the oriole's nest is hung;
Where the whitest lilies blow,
Where the freshest berries grow,
Where the ground-nut trails its vine,
Where the wood-grape's clusters shine;
Of the black wasp's cunning way,
Mason of his walls of clay,
And the architectural plans
Of gray hornet artizans!—
For, eschewing books and tasks,
Nature answers all he asks;
Hand in hand with her he walks,
Face to face with her he talks,
Part and parcel of her joy,—
Blessings on the barefoot boy!

Oh! for boyhood's time of June,
Crowding years in one brief moon,
When all things I heard or saw,
Me, their master, waited for.
I was rich in flowers and trees,
Humming birds and honey bees;
For my sport the squirrel played,
Plied the snouted mole his spade;
For my taste the blackberry cone
Purpled over hedge and stone;
Laughed the brook for my delight
Through the day and through the night,
Whispering at the garden wall,

Talked with me from fall to fall;
Mine the sand-rimmed pickerel pond,
Mine the walnut slopes beyond,
Mine on bending orchard trees,
Apples of Hesperides!
Still as my horizon grew,
Larger grew my riches too;
All the world I saw or knew
Seemed a complex Chinese toy,
Fashioned for a barefoot boy!

Oh for festal dainties spread,
Like my bowl of milk and bread,—
Pewter spoon and bowl of wood,
On the door-stone, gray and rude!
O'er me, like a regal tent,
Cloudy-ribbed, the sunset bent,
Purple-curtained, fringed with gold,
Looped in many a wind-swung fold;
While for music came the play
Of the pied frog's orchestra;
And, to light the noisy quire
Lit the fly his lamp of fire.
I was monarch: pomp and joy
Waited on the barefoot boy!

Cheerily, then, my little man,
Live and laugh, as boyhood can.
Though the flinty slopes be hard,
Stubble-speared the new-mown sward,
Every morn shall lead thee through
Fresh baptisms of the dew;
Every evening from thy feet
Shall the cool wind kiss the heat:
All too soon these feet must hide
In the prison cells of pride,
Lose the freedom of the sod,
Like a colt's for work be shod,
Made to tread the mills of toil,
Up and down in ceaseless moil—
Happy if their track be found
Never on forbidden ground—
Happy if they sink not in
Quick and treacherous sands of sin.
Ah! that thou couldst know thy joy
Ere it passes, barefoot boy!

Adella Washee

A SUMMER DAY

The cherries are ripe in the orchard,
  The wild birds are calling to me,
And out in the meadow the grasses
  Are rippling like waves on the sea;
The daisies are shaking so gayly
  Their white-ruffled caps in the sun,
And over the tall weeds beside me
  A long silken line has been spun.

I watch it sway upward and downward,
  And fancy a message so sweet
Has come to the bee, seeking honey
  In blossoms not far from my feet.
I sit in wonderful silence,
  And softly o're wires none can see
The many-toned voices of summer
  Are telling their story to me.

❧ Gertrude Heath

JULY

The air is still. A yellow haze
 Steals slowly o'er the sky;
The roadside grass is dry and brown;
 The cows go lagging by;
And scarce the grasses seem to stir;
No sound beside the cricket's whirr.

The air is still. The dusty steeds
 Go slowly homeward for the night;
And one by one in village homes
 Shines forth the cheery evening light.
But hark, that piping noise again!
The robin redbreast calls for rain.

❧ Sarah Piatt

IN PRIMROSE TIME
(Early Spring in Ireland.)

Here's the lodge-woman in her great cloak coming,
 And her white cap. What joy
Has touched the ash-man? On my word, he's humming
 A boy's song, like a boy!
He quite forgets his cart. His donkey grazes
 Just where it likes the grass.
The red-coat soldier, with his medal, raises
 His hat to all who pass;
And the blue-jacket sailor,—hear him whistle,
 Forgetting Ireland's ills!
Oh, pleasant land—(who thinks of thorn or thistle?)
 Upon your happy hills
The world is out! And, faith, if I mistake not,
 The world is in its prime
(Beating for once, I think, with hearts that ache not)
 In Primrose time.

Against the sea-wall leans the Irish beauty,
 With face and hands in bloom,
Thinking of anything but household duty
 In her thatched cabin's gloom;—
Watching the ships as leisurely as may be,
 Her blue eyes dream for hours.
Hush! There's her mother—coming with the baby
 In the fair quest of flowers.
And her grandmother!—hear her laugh and chatter,
 Under her hair frost-white!

Believe me, life can be a merry matter,
    And common folk polite,
And all the birds of heaven one of a feather,
    And all their voices rhyme,—
They sing their merry songs, like one, together,
    In Primrose time.

The magpies fly in pairs (an evil omen
    It were to see but one);
The snakes—but here, though, since St. Patrick, no man
    Has seen them in the sun;
The white lamb thinks the black lamb is his brother,
    And half as good as he;
The rival carmen all love one another,
    And jest, right cheerily;
The compliments among the milkmen savor
    Of pale gold blossoming;
And everybody wears the lovely favor
    Of our sweet Lady Spring.
And though the ribbons in a bright procession
    Go toward the chapel's chime,—
Good priest, there be but few sins for confession
    In Primrose time.

How all the children in this isle of faery
    Whisper and laugh and peep!
(Hush, pretty babblers! Little feet be wary,
    You'll scare them in their sleep,—
The wee, weird people of the dew, who wither
    Out of the sun, and lie
Curled in the wet leaves, till the moon comes hither.)—
    The new-made butterfly
Forgets he was a worm. The ghostly castle,
    On its lone rock and gray,
Cares not a whit for either lord or vassal
    Gone on their dusty way,
But listens to the bee, on errands sunny.—
    A thousand years of crime
May all be melted in a drop of honey
    In Primrose time!

CREEPY CRAWLIES

Lydia Sigourney

THE LADY-BUG AND THE ANT

The Lady-Bug sat in the rose's heart,
   And smil'd with pride and scorn,
As she saw a plainly dressed Ant go by,
   With a heavy grain of corn;
So, she drew the curtains of damask round,
   And adjusted her silken vest,
Making her glass of a drop of dew
   That lay in the Rose's breast.

Then she laugh'd so loud, that the Ant look'd up,
   And, seeing her haughty face,
Took no more notice, but travell'd on
   At the same industrious pace:—
But a sudden blast of Autumn came,
   And rudely swept the ground,
And down the rose with the Lady-Bug fell,
   And scatter'd its leaves around.

Then the houseless Lady was much amaz'd,
   For she knew not where to go;
And hoarse November's early blast
   Had brought both rain and snow,—
Her wings were chill, and her feet were cold,
   And she wished for the Ant's warm cell,—
And what she did when the winter came,
   I'm sure I cannot tell.

But the careful Ant was in her nest,
   With the little ones by her side;
She taught them all like herself to toil,
   Nor mind the sting of pride,—
And I thought, as I sat at the close of the day,
   Eating my bread and milk,
It was wiser to work and improve my time
   Than be idle and dress in silk.

ꙮ *Oliver Herford*

THE ANT

My child, ob-serve the use-ful Ant,
How hard she works each day.
She works as hard as ad-a-mant
(That's very hard, they say).
She has not time to gal-li-vant;
She has no time to play.
Let Fido chase his tail all day;
Let kitten play at tag:
She has no time to throw a-way,
She has no tail to wag.
She scurries round from morn till night;
She ne-ver, ne-ver sleeps;
She seiz-es ev-ery-thing in sight,
And drags it home with all her might,
And all she takes she keeps.

ꙮ *Oliver Herford*

THE ARTFUL ANT

Once on a time an artful Ant
   Resolved to give a ball,
For tho' in stature she was scant,
   She was not what you'd call
A shy or bashful little Ant.
   (She was not shy at all.)

She sent her invitations through
   The forest far and wide,
To all the Birds and Beasts she knew,
   And many more beside.
("You never know what you can do,"
   Said she, "until you've tried.")

Five score acceptances came in
   Faster than she could read.
Said she: "Dear me! I'd best begin
   To stir myself indeed!"
(A pretty pickle she was in,
   With five-score guests to feed!)

The artful Ant sat up all night,
   A-thinking o'er and o'er,
How she could make from nothing, quite
   Enough to feed five-score.
(Between ourselves I think she might
   Have thought of that before!)

She thought, and thought, and thought
    all night,
  And all the following day,
Till suddenly she struck a bright
  Idea, which was—(but stay!
Just what it was I am not quite
  At liberty to say.)

Enough, that when the festal day
  Came round, the Ant was seen
To smile in a peculiar way,
  As if—(but you may glean
From seeing tragic actors play
  The kind of smile I mean.)

From here and there and everywhere
  The happy creatures came,
The Fish alone could not be there.
  (And they were not to blame.
"They really could not stand the air,
  But thanked her just the same.")

The Lion, bowing very low,
  Said to the Ant: "I ne'er
Since Noah's Ark remember so
  Delightful an affair."
(A pretty compliment, although
  He really wasn't there.)

They danced, and danced, and danced,
    and danced;
  It was a jolly sight!
They pranced, and pranced, and
    pranced, and pranced,
  Till it was nearly light!
And then their thoughts to supper
    chanced
  To turn. (As well they might!)

Then said the Ant: 'It's only right
  That supper should begin,
And if you will be so polite,
  Pray *take each other in*."
(The emphasis was very slight,
  But rested on *"Take in."*)

They needed not a second call,
  They took the hint. Oh, yes,
The largest guest "took in" the small,
  The small "took in" the less,
The less "took in" the least of all.
  (It was a great success!)

As for the rest—but why spin out
  This narrative of woe?—
The Lion took them in about
  As fast as they could go.
(And went home looking very stout,
  And walking very slow.)

And when the Ant, not long ago,
  Lost to all sense of shame,
Tried it again, I chance to know
  That not one answer came.
(Save from the Fish, who "could not go,
  But thanked her all the same.")

Caroline Howard Gilman

INVITATION TO THE ANT

Come here, little ant,
For the pretty bird can't.
I want you to come,
And live at my home;

I know you will stay,
And help me to play.
Stop making that hill,
Little ant, and be still.

Come, creep to my feet,
Here is sugar to eat.
Say, are you not weary,
My poor little deary,

With bearing that load,
Across the wide road?
Leave your hill now, to me,
And then you shall see,

That by filling my hand,
I can pile up the sand,
And save you the pains,
Of bringing these grains.

THE ANT'S ANSWER

Stop, stop, little miss,
No such building as this
Will answer for me,
As you plainly can see.

I take very great pains,
And place all the grains
As if with a tool,
By a carpenter's rule.

You have thrown the coarse sand
All out of your hand,
And so fill'd up my door,
That I can't find it more.
My King and my Queen
Are choked up within;
My little ones too,
Oh, what shall I do?

You have smother'd them all,
With the sand you let fall.
I must borrow or beg,
Or look for an egg.*

To keep under my eye,
For help by and by,
A new house I must raise,
In a very few days,

Nor stand here and pine,
Because you've spoilt mine.
For when winter days come,
I shall mourn for my home;

So stand out of my way,
I have no time to play.

* *When an ant's nest is disturbed, there may be seen processions of ants bearing little white eggs, for more than a day. Ants are divided into workers, sentinels, etc., like bees, and they have their king and queen, also.* [Gilman's note]

❧ Mary Mapes Dodge

THE ANTS

Good Mistress Ant, I pray, what is the matter?
Why this commotion without any clatter?
"Alack! alack! we're ruined, you see;
I've lost my children, and they've lost me!
Our houses have fallen, our city is gone,
And thousands are murdered or running forlorn.
Ah me! who would think that such power to destroy
Could lurk in the heel of a bare-footed boy?"

❧ Mary Mapes Dodge

OLD BUM OF BUMBLEBY

Old Bum of Bumbleby bumped his nose,
Trying to light on a damask rose;
He bumped his nose, but he didn't care
As he pitched about in the dizzy air.
Whenever he tried to his love to fly,
He would shoot ahead and pass her by;
So he tumbled at last on a larkspur near,
And buzzed his business into her ear.

❧ Louisa May Alcott

MORNING SONG OF THE BEES

Awake! awake! for the earliest gleam
    Of golden sunlight shines
On the rippling waves, that brightly flow
    Beneath the flowering vines.
Awake! awake! for the low, sweet chant
    Of the wild-birds' morning hymn
Comes floating by on the fragrant air,
    Through the forest cool and dim;
        Then spread each wing,
        And work, and sing,
Through the long, bright sunny hours;
        O'er the pleasant earth
        We journey forth,
For a day among the flowers.

Awake! awake! for the summer wind
    Hath bid the blossoms unclose,
Hath opened the violet's soft blue eye,
    And wakened the sleeping rose.
And lightly they wave on their slender stems
    Fragrant, and fresh, and fair,
Waiting for us, as we singing come
    To gather our honey-dew there.
        Then spread each wing,
        And work, and sing,
Through the long, bright sunny hours;
      O'er the pleasant earth
      We journey forth,
For a day among the flowers.

❧ Hannah Flagg Gould

SONG OF THE BEES

We watch for the light of the morn to break
    And color the eastern sky
With its blended hues of saffron and lake,
Then say to each other, "Awake! awake!
"For our winter's honey is all to make,
    "And our bread for a long supply!"

Then, off we hie to the hill and the dell,
    To the field, the meadow and bower.
In the columbine's horn we love to dwell,
To dip in the lily snow-white bell,
To search the balm in its odorous cell,
    The mint and the rosemary-flower.

We seek the bloom of the eglantine,
    Of the painted thistle and brier;
And follow the steps of the wandering vine,
Whether it trail on the earth, supine,
Or round the aspiring tree-top twine,
    And reach for a state still higher.

As each on the good of her sisters bent,
    Is busy and cares for all,
We hope for an evening with hearts content,
For the winter of life without lament
That summer is gone with its hours misspent,
    And the harvest is past recall!

❦ *Gertrude Heath*

THE REASON WHY

To-day the first June rose bloomed out,
   Down by the daisies and clover;
All a-tremble, with leaves a-pout,
   Buttercups bending over.

"Sweet, so sweet!" the butterfly said,
   "Rose in your rustic splendor!"
And honey-bees lingered over her head,
   Murmuring love-words tender.

Sweet, little, blushing wayside Rose,
   Tell me what is the reason
All of your brothers and sisters sleep,
   You are first of the season?

All a-blushing the little Rose said:
   "I know they can not have missed me!
I waked this morning (she hung her head)
   Because a honey-bee kissed me!"

❦ *Hannah Flagg Gould*

THE FLY IN THE GLASS LAMP

Ah! thou lost, unwary thing,
Flutt'ring with a tortured wing—
Crying, with thy little feet
Scorch'd amid surrounding heat.
Poor, unhappy, suffering fly,
What a painful death to die!

Since, so rashly thou hast stray'd
'Twixt the funnel and the shade,
In the fiery prison lost,
Now, thy life must pay the cost
Of thy venturing near the glare,
Dazzling to allure thee there!

Oh! it fills my heart with pain,
Thus to see thee strive in vain
For escape; for I, alas!
Am too small to lift the glass.
Mother says I must not take
Things my little hands might break.

Here she comes! but 'tis too late!
Thou, poor thing, hast met thy fate.
Motion ceases—life has fled—
Dropping on the table, dead,
Now I see thee, thoughtless fly!
'Twas a foolish death to die.

"Yes, my child, in careless play,
Thus his life is thrown away—
For a thing that pleased the eye
He rush'd onward but to die!
Yet, remember, there was none
Warning him the blaze to shun.

"If thou think'st the untaught flies,
For their errors, so unwise,
Let this insect's fall be hence,
From temptation, thy defence!
On thy heart a picture stamp
Of *the fly about the lamp!* "

THE FLY

I.

Baby Bye,
Here's a Fly:
Let us watch him, you and I.
How he crawls
Up the walls—
Yet he never falls!
I believe, with those six legs,
You and I could walk on eggs!
There he goes,
On his toes,
Tickling Baby's nose!

II.

Spots of red
Dot his head:
Rainbows on his wings are spread!
That small speck
Is his neck;
See him nod and beck!
I can show you, if you choose,
Where to look to find his shoes:
Three small pairs
Made of hairs—
These he always wears.

III.

Black and brown
Is his gown;
He can wear it upside down!
It is laced
Round his waist;
I admire his taste.
Pretty as his clothes are made,
He will spoil them, I'm afraid,
If to-night
He gets sight
Of the candle-light!

IV.

In the sun
Webs are spun:
What if he gets into one!
When it rains
He complains
On the window-panes.
Tongues to talk have you and I:
God has given the little Fly
No such things;
So he sings
With his buzzing wings.

V.

He can eat
Bread and meat;
See his mouth between his feet!
On his back
Hangs a sack,
Like a peddler's pack.
Does the Baby understand?
Then the Fly shall kiss her hand!
Put a crumb
On her thumb:
Maybe he will come!

VI.

Round and round,
On the ground,
On the ceiling he is found.
Catch him? No:
Let him go:
Never hurt him so!
Now you see his wings of silk
Drabbled in the Baby's milk!
Fie, oh fie!
Foolish Fly!
How will he get dry?

VII.

All wet flies
Twist their thighs:
So they wipe their heads and eyes.
Cats, you know,
Wash just so:
Then their whiskers grow.
Flies have hair too short to comb!
Flies go barehead out from home!
But the Gnat
Wears a hat:
Do you laugh at that?

VIII.

Flies can see
More than we—
So how bright their eyes must be!
Little Fly,
Mind your eye—
Spiders are near by!
Now a secret let me tell:
Spiders will not treat you well!
So I say
Heed your way!
Little Fly, good day!

❧ *Gertrude Heath*

WHAT THE FLY THINKS

A fly went buzzing over my head;
      Buzz-z! Buzz-z!
And what do you think the little fly said?
      Buzz-z! Buzz-z!

I saw two babies as I flew by
Begin to quarrel and then to cry!
Pretty children, their Grandma thinks,
Calls them her "Rosy-posy pinks!"

What does it mean when the babies cry?
Isn't it better to be a fly?
Babies laugh though, coo and smile,
Shriek with laughter once in a while.

Wonder what creatures with two legs do!
I never could live with so very few!
How do they ever get about?
Wonder who pulled their other legs out!

There! They're going! How queer they
      crawl!
Funny world! said the fly on the wall!

A fly went buzzing over my head,
      Buzz-z! Buzz-z!
And these are the words the little fly said,
      Buzz-z! Buzz-z!

Alice Cary

SPIDER AND FLY

Once when morn was flowing in,
   Broader, redder, wider,
In her house with walls so thin
   That they could not hide her,
Just as she would never spin,
   Sat a little spider—
Sat she on her silver stairs,
Meek as if she said her prayers.

Came a fly, whose wings had been
   Making circles wider,
Having but the buzz and din
   Of herself to guide her.
Nearer to these walls so thin,
   Nearer to the spider,
Sitting on her silver stairs,
Meek as if she said her prayers.

Said the silly fly, "Too long
   Malice has belied her;
How should she do any wrong,
   With no walls to hide her?"
So she buzzed her pretty song
   To the wily spider,
Sitting on her silver stairs
Meek as though she said her prayers.

But in spite her modest mien,
   Had the fly but eyed her
Close enough, she would have seen
   Fame had not belied her—
That, as she had always been,
   She was still a spider;
And that she was not at prayers,
Sitting on her silver stairs.

Katharine Forrest Hamill

MRS. SPIDER

Brother Dick and I one day
Watched Mrs. Spider spin away:
My, how she spun, and spun, and spun,
Until she had her web all done!

Then, brother Dick, he said to me:
"Now, where can Mr. Spider be?"
We watched, but didn't see him come,
So I guess he didn't live at home.

Anne L. Huber

DADDY LONGLEGS

A big old daddy longlegs
   Creeping on the wall,
I wish that he would go away,
   I don't like him at all.

I know he will not hurt me,
   But I don't want him here;
So get you gone, old daddy,
   And don't come again so near.

✌ Anne L. Huber

WIDOW MCCREE

Old widow McCree
Caught a very big flea,
That had bit her in several places;
When he wasn't skipping,
He kept up a nipping,
That made her make very wry faces.

✌ Oliver Herford

THE FLY.

Ob-serve, my child, the House-hold Fly,
With his ex-traor-di-na-ry eye:
What-ev-er thing he may be-hold
Is mul-ti-plied a thou-sand-fold.
We do not need a com-plex eye
When we ob-serve the morn-ing Fly:
He is so vol-a-tile that he
In *ev-er-y* place at once can be;
He is the buzz-ing in-car-na-tion
Of an-i-mate mul-ti-pli-ca-tion.
Ah! chil-dren who can tell the Why
And Where-fore of the House-hold Fly?

Christina Moody (age 13–16)

THE PIE THAT SISTER MADE

Mama was eating a pie one day,
    And 'twas a fly in it.
She did'nt know it and took a bite,
    And down on the fly she bit.
My sister who made that pie was my mother's pet,
    But after mamma bit that pie, she was no more, you bet.
My mother grabbed a round out of the old armchair
    And on my poor sister's bones she took a liberal share.

Benjamin Franklin King

THE WOODTICKS

There's things out in the forest
    That's worser an' 'n owl,
'At gets on naughty boys 'n girls
    'At allers wears a scowl.
There's things out in the forest
    'At's worser'n a lion,
'At gets on wicked boys 'n girls
    'At's quarrelin' an' a-cryin'.
There 'a things out in the forest, mind,
    An' if you don't take care,
The woodticks—the woodticks—
    Will be crawlin' thro' yer hair.

An' they say as boys is naughty,
    An' their hearts is full o' sin,
They'll crawl out in the night time
    An' get underneath yer skin,
An' the doctor 'll have to take a knife
    An' cut 'em off jes' so,
An' if a bit of 'em is left
    Another one'll grow.
An' mebbe you won't feel 'em, too,
    Er ever know they're there,
But by and by they'll multiply
    And crawl up in yer hair.

The devil's darnin' needle too,
    'Ill come and sew yer ear.
An' make a nest inside like that,
    An' then you'll never hear;
An' the jigger bugs gets on you,
    An' the thousand-legged worm
'Ill make you writhe, an' twist, an' groan,
    An' cry, an' yell, an' squirm;
But the worst things 'at 'll git you
    If you lie, or steal, or swear,
Is the woodticks—the woodticks—
    A-crawlin' thro' yer hair.

&❧ *Author Unknown*

BEDBUG

De June-bug's got de golden wing,
De Lightning-bug de flame;
De Bedbug's got no wing at all,
But he gits dar jes de same.

De Punkin-bug's got a punkin smell,
De Squash-bug smells de wust;
But de puffume of dat ole Bedbug,
It's enough to make you bust.

Wen dat Bedbug come down to my house,
I wants my walkin' cane.
Go git a pot an' scald 'im hot!
Good-by, Miss Lize Jane!

🍀 *Clara Doty Bates*

THE CHEATED MOSQUITOES

Little Gold Locks has gone to bed,
Kisses are given and prayers are said.
Mamma says, as she turns out the light,
"Mosquitoes won't bite my child to-night.
They will try to come in, but won't know how,
For the nets are in the windows now."

First Mosquito. That is the window where we go in!
Second Mosquito. Is little girl Gold Locks fat or thin?
Third Mosquito. O, plump as the plumpest dairy mouse!
Fourth Mosquito. And the sweetest morsel in the house.
Fifth Mosquito. Hurry, I pray, and lead the way!
Sixth Mosquito. I haven't had a bite to-day!

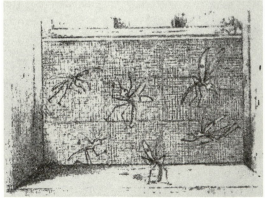

First Mosquito. What have I flown against now, I wonder?
Second Mosquito. There's something across here, let's crawl under.
Third Mosquito. These bars are as large as my body is!
Fourth Mosquito. I've broken the point of my bill on this!
Fifth Mosquito. I'm slim, perhaps I can crawl through!
Sixth Mosquito. Oh! what shall I do? Oh! what shall I do?

Chorus. Oh! what shall we do? Oh! what shall we do?

❧ *Marie Bruckman MacDonald*

THE 'SKEETER AND PETER
(A touching Limerick.)

There was a bright fellow named Peter,
Who struck at an active young 'skeeter,
But the 'skeeter struck first
And slackened his thirst,
For the 'skeeter was fleeter than Peter.

❧ *Mary Mapes Dodge*

[POOR LITTLE TODDLEKINS]

Poor little Toddlekins,
All full o' skeeter-bites—
Bodder him awful,
Baby can't sleep o' nights.
Buzzing all over him,
Singing and tickling,
In and out, round about,
Nipping and prickling.
Poor little Toddlekins,
All full o' skeeter-bites—
Bodder him awful,
Can't even sleep o' nights!

❧ *Mary E. Wilkins [Freeman]*

KATY-DID—KATY-DIDN'T

Who was Katy, who was she,
   That you prate of her so long?
Was she just a little lassie
   Full of smiles and wiles and song?

Did she spill the cups o' dew
   Filled for helpless, thirsty posies?
Did she tie a butterfly
   Just beyond the reach o' roses?

Slandered she some sweet dumb thing?
   Called a tulip dull and plain,
Said the clover had no fragrance,
   And the lily had a stain?

Did she mock the pansies' faces,
   Or a grandpa-longlegs flout?
Did she chase the frightened fireflies
   Till their pretty lamps went out?

Well, whatever 'twas, O Katy!
   We believe no harm of you;
And we'll join your stanch defenders,
   Singing "Katy-didn't," too.

❧ *Mary E. Wilkins [Freeman]*

THE ENLIGHTENMENT OF MAMMA

O mamma dear, just listen!
I ran away, you know;
I saw the grasses glisten,
A-bowing to me so,
The clovers shook their pink heads too—
You wouldn't care I ran away,
If how they did you only knew!
And I was dressed as much as they—
They didn't mind a bit—and Oh,
I saw there, fastened to the grass
With little shiny ropes of glass.

A spider's web! Mamma, you know
You've always said that spiders ate
For breakfast little frightened flies,
For which they long had laid in wait,
A-watching with their cruel eyes—
Well, mamma, in that spider's web—
Somebody told it wrong to you—
There wasn't any fly at all!
Mamma, you will believe it's true;
Everything for breakfast there
Was clover-tops and drops of dew!"

BUTTERFLIES ARE PRETTY THINGS

"Butterflies are pretty things,
    Prettier than you or I;
See the colours on his wings;
    Who would hurt a butterfly?

"Softly, softly, girls and boys;
    He'll come near us by and by;
Here he is, don't make a noise;—
    We'll not hurt you, butterfly."

Not to hurt a living thing,
    Let all little children try;
See, again he's on the wing;
    Good by! pretty butterfly!

Author Unknown

THE BUTTERFLY

Good-morning, pretty butterfly,
    Floating by on wings of light;
I hope you are as glad as I
    To have a day so fair and bright.

Come and rest here by my side,
    Here on this buttercup so fair;
Open thy rainbow wings so wide,
    And tell me, are you made of air?

You are a stranger, butterfly;
    Although I see you every day,
You're quickly, softly floating by
    Whenever I come out to play.

I want to count your tiny toes,
    I want to find your breathing place,
And see the downy horn that grows
    On either side your pretty face.

I'd like to see just how you're made,
    With stripes and spots and dust and
        rings;
I wish you'd show me how you played
    Just now upon your shining wings.

I could not trust you, little boy;
    You might not let me soon go free:
My life, is floating here in joy,
    My death would follow slavery.

BUTTERFLY AND BEE

Methought I heard a butterfly
  Say to a laboring bee,
'Thou hast no colors of the sky
  On painted wings like me.'

'Poor child of vanity, those dyes
  And colors bright and rare,
(With mild reproof the bee replies)
  Are all beneath my care.

'Content I toil from morn till eve,
  And scorning idleness,
To tribes of gaudy sloth I leave
  The vanities of dress.'

Author Unknown

KATYDID

When the evening star comes out,
  On pleasant summer eves,
You can hear the little Katydids,
  Crying out among the leaves,—
    Katy did, Katy did,
    She didn't, she didn't;
    Katy did, she did,
    No she didn't, Katy didn't.
How I wonder what they mean,
In the leaves, so thick and green,
What the mischief is that's hid,
Which little Katy did?

Was Katy once a little girl,
  Who didn't mind her mother;
Was it only known to Katydids,
  And not to any other?
    Katy did, Katy did,
    She didn't, she didn't;
    Katy did, she did,
    No she didn't, Katy didn't.
Was she such a naughty girl,
That, through time's unceasing whirl,
These insects are forbid
To tell what Katy did?

My darling on the porch,
  Each eve when they begin,
Tries, with eager little ears,
  To understand their din.
    Katy did, Katy did,
    She didn't, she didn't;
    Katy did, she did,
    No she didn't, Katy didn't.
But with all their constant cry,
My little one or I
Cannot make out the secret hid,
The dreadful thing that Katy did.

Author Unknown

TO THE KATYDID

Where are you little Katydid?
 I hear your funny song:
So safe among the bushes hid,
 Do you sing all night long?
I wonder if you're never tired
 Of chirping nothing new.
If I were you, I'd try for once
 To change a note or two.
But, Katy, it does seem to me
 You rather loudly sing;
You surely make too great a noise
 For such a little thing:

For don't you know big people say—
 And we must mind their word—
That young folks should, like you and me,
 Be seen, not often heard?
Now "Katy did," then "Katy didn't;"
 'Tis very sad to see
That children of one family
 Will sometimes disagree.
Don't quarrel, Katy; try to sing
 A little gentler song,
For mother tells me, Katy dear,
 To contradict is wrong.

Edna F. Wood (age 15)

THE FAIRY MESSENGER

O little, flashing firefly,
Flitter, flutter, guide me by,
Past the hornèd owl so grim,
Past the shadows, wavering dim.

Lead me, by your tiny light,
Down the hill and through the night,
O'er the wall, until we come
To the mystic, fairy home.

Elves and fairies hurry here,
Guided by the lights so clear.
From the shadows comes the queen,
Sparkling in her satin green.

All the fireflies form a row,
Swaying, swinging, to and fro;
With the frogs, the cricket choir
Lift their voices, soaring higher.

Loved and honored, just and fair,
Queen of fairies, follow there,
Torches light her mossy way.
Dance along, O sprites so gay.

Thus they dance the long night through,
Till the moon is pale in hue;
Till the fireflies' torches wane,
And the owls wing home again.

AFTER WINGS

This was your butterfly, you see.
    His fine wings made him vain?—
The caterpillars crawl, but he
    Pass'd them in rich disdain?—
My pretty boy says, "Let him be
    Only a worm again?"

Oh, child, when things have learn'd to wear
    Wings once, they must be fain
To keep them always high and fair.
    Think of the creeping pain
Which even a butterfly must bear
    To be a worm again!

Tacie Townsend

THE NIGHT-MOTH

When the sun goes down, and the air is filled
With the sound of rushing wings,
When the swallows fly, and the fire-flies flit,
The Night-Moth comes and sings:—

"O sweet is the flower, at the evening hour,
  When the wandering bee goes home;
  And dear to me are the sweets the bee
  Has left for my lips alone.
  I startle the child, in the garden wild,
  When my rustling wings are heard;
  But he laughs with glee my form to see,
  And calls me his humming-bird.

"The birds of day their roundelay
  May give to the sun and air,
  But the pale twilight and the fire-flies bright
  To the Night-Moth are more fair.
  O sweet is the flower, at the evening hour,
  When the wandering bee goes home;
  And dear to me are the sweets the bee
  Has left for my lips alone."

FEATHERED FRIENDS

ROBERT OF LINCOLN

Merrily swinging on brier and weed,
    Near to the nest of his little dame,
Over the mountain-side or mead,
    Robert of Lincoln is telling his name:
        Bob-o'-link, bob-o'-link,
        Spink, spank, spink;
Snug and safe is that nest of ours,
Hidden among the summer flowers.
            Chee, chee, chee.

Robert of Lincoln is gaily dressed,
    Wearing a bright black wedding-coat;
White are his shoulders and white his
                crest,
    Hear him call in his merry note:
        Bob-o'-link, bob-o'-link,
        Spink, spank, spink;
Look, what a nice new coat is mine,
Sure there was never a bird so fine.
            Chee, chee, chee.

Robert of Lincoln's Quaker wife,
    Pretty and quiet, with plain brown
                wings,
Passing at home a patient life,
    Broods in the grass while her husband
                sings:
        Bob-o'-link, bob-o'-link,
        Spink, spank, spink;
Brood, kind creature; you need not fear
Thieves and robbers while I am here.
            Chee, chee, chee.

Modest and shy as a nun is she;
    One weak chirp is her only note.
Braggart and prince of braggarts is he,
    Pouring boasts from his little throat:
        Bob-o'-link, bob-o'-link,
        Spink, spank, spink;
Never was I afraid of man;
Catch me, cowardly knaves, if you can!
            Chee, chee, chee.

Six white eggs on a bed of hay,
    Flecked with purple, a pretty sight!
There as the mother sits all day,
    Robert is singing with all his might:
        Bob-o'-link, bob-o'-link,
        Spink, spank, spink;
Nice good wife, that never goes out,
Keeping house while I frolic about.
            Chee, chee, chee.

Soon as the little ones chip the shell,
    Six wide mouths are open for food[;]
Robert of Lincoln bestirs him well,
    Gathering seeds for the hungry brood.
        Bob-o'-link, bob-o'-link,
        Spink, spank, spink;
This new life is likely to be
Hard for a gay young fellow like me.
            Chee, chee, chee.

Robert of Lincoln at length is made
    Sober with work, and silent with care;
Off is his holiday garment laid,
    Half forgotten that merry air:
        Bob-o'-link, bob-o'-link,
        Spink, spank, spink;
Nobody knows but my mate and I
Where our nest and our nestlings lie.
            Chee, chee, chee.

Summer wanes; the children are grown;
    Fun and frolic no more he knows;
Robert of Lincoln's a humdrum crone;
    Off he flies, and we sing as he goes:
        Bob-o'-link, bob-o'-link,
        Spink, spank, spink;
When you can pipe that merry old
                strain,
Robert of Lincoln, come back again.
            Chee, chee, chee.

Lydia Maria Child

LITTLE BIRD! LITTLE BIRD!

"Little bird! little bird! come to me!
I have a green cage ready for thee—
Beauty-bright flowers I'll bring to you,
And fresh, ripe cherries all wet with dew."

"Thanks, little maiden, for all thy care—
But I dearly love the clear, cool air;
And my snug little nest in the old oak tree
Is better than golden cage for me."

"Little bird! little bird! where wilt thou go,
When the fields are all buried in snow?
The ice will cover the old oak tree—
Little bird! little bird! stay with me."

"Nay, little damsel; away I'll fly
To greener fields and a warmer sky;
When Spring returns with pattering rain,
You will hear my merry song again."

"Little bird! little bird! who'll guide thee
Over the hills, and over the sea?
Foolish one, come in the house to stay;
For I am very sure you'll lose your way."

"Ah, no, little maiden! God guides me
Over the hills, and over the sea:
I will be free as the rushing air,
Chasing the sun-light every where!"

❧ Author Unknown [Samuel Goodrich?]

FOR MY YOUNGEST READERS

Little bird, roam
Quick to my home.
I'll give you to eat,
Every thing sweet;
Sugar and cake,
I'll save for your sake;
Melon and plum,
You shall have some;
A peach and a pear,
And every thing rare;
Some straw for your nest,

And what you like best;
A nice little house,
As snug as a mouse.
Come away from the tree,
And live here with me;
I will give you a brush,
To smooth down each feather,
And brother shall hush,
While we sing together.
Come away from the tree,
And live here with me.

❧ H. H. [Helen Hunt Jackson]

THE SHINING LITTLE HOUSE

It hung in the sun, the little house,
  It hung in the sun, and shone;
And through the walls I could hear his
   voice
  Who had it all for his own.

The walls were of wire, as bright as gold,
  Wrought in a pretty design;
The spaces between for windows served,
  And the floor was clean and fine.

There was plenty, too, to eat and drink,
  In this little house that shone;
A lucky thing, to be sure, you'd say,
  A house like this for one's own!

But the door was shut, and locked all
   tight,
  The key was on the outside;
The one who was in could not get out,
  No matter how much he tried.

'T was only a prison after all,
  This bright little house that shone;
Ah, we would not want a house like that,
  No matter if 't were our own!

And yet, through the walls I heard the
   voice,
  Of the one who lived inside:
To warble a sweeter song each day,
  It did seem as if he tried.

To open the door, he never sought,
  Nor fluttered in idle strife;
He ate, and he drank, and slept, and
   sang,
  And made the best of his life.

And I, to myself, said every day,
  As his cheery song I heard,
There's a lesson for us in every note
  Of that little prisoned bird.

We all of us live a life like his,
  We are walled on every side;
We all long to do a hundred things,
  Which we could not if we tried.

We can spend our strength all foolishly
  In a discontented strife;
Or we can be wise, and laugh and sing,
  And make the best of our life.

Esther B. Tiffany

FIRE! FIRE!

Oh, Birdie, fly! for the maple-tree,
Where your nest is hid so cunningly,
With scarlet flames is ablaze, I see.

For Autumn, that wanton, gold-haired boy,
Roams wild, with a flaming torch for a toy,—
And he fires the trees with a reckless joy.

On the maple's mantle the bright sparks fall,
On the creeping woodbine along the wall;
On the sturdy oak-trees, staunch and tall.

Oh, Birdie, fly! to the Southland hie,
For the woods are blazing beneath our sky,
And your home is on fire, Birdie,—fly!

Gertrude Heath

A FUNNY PARTY

Miss Robin Redbreast's Kettle-drum:
She hopes that all her friends will come.
From Four to Six P.M.——N. B.
Miss Golden Oriole pours the tea!

The little Sparrow in her nest
With careful touches plumed her breast.
The brown Thrush came, the shyest bird,
Who trembled at the lightest word!

The guests were gay; but all along
The party waited for a song.
The Robin came with eager wing
And begged the Bobolinks to sing.

The low tones trembled in their throats;
They could not sing without their notes!
The brown Thrush said, "Pray do not
      scold!
But O! I really have a cold!"

And so the party all took wing,
For not a single bird would sing!
A funny party all agree,
Where Golden Oriole poured the tea!

Edgar Allan Poe

THE RAVEN

Once upon a midnight dreary, while I pondered, weak and weary,
Over many a quaint and curious volume of forgotten lore,
While I nodded, nearly napping, suddenly there came a tapping,
As of some one gently rapping, rapping at my chamber door.
"'Tis some visiter," I muttered, "tapping at my chamber door—
                    Only this and nothing more."

Ah, distinctly I remember it was in the bleak December,
And each separate dying ember wrought its ghost upon the floor.
Eagerly I wished the morrow;—vainly I had sought to borrow
From my books surcease of sorrow—sorrow for the lost Lenore—
For the rare and radiant maiden whom the angels name Lenore—
                    Nameless here for evermore.

And the silken sad uncertain rustling of each purple curtain
Thrilled me—filled me with fantastic terrors never felt before;
So that now, to still the beating of my heart, I stood repeating
"'Tis some visiter entreating entrance at my chamber door—
Some late visiter entreating entrance at my chamber door;—
                    This it is, and nothing more."

Presently my soul grew stronger; hesitating then no longer,
"Sir," said I, "or Madam, truly your forgiveness I implore;
But the fact is I was napping, and so gently you came rapping,
And so faintly you came tapping, tapping at my chamber door,
That I scarce was sure I heard you"—here I opened wide the door;—
                    Darkness there and nothing more.

Deep into that darkness peering, long I stood there wondering, fearing,
Doubting, dreaming dreams no mortal ever dared to dream before;
But the silence was unbroken, and the stillness gave no token,
And the only word there spoken was the whispered word, "Lenore!"
This I whispered, and an echo murmured back the word, "Lenore!"
                    Merely this and nothing more.

Then into the chamber turning, all my soul within me burning,
Soon again I heard a tapping somewhat louder than before.
"Surely," said I, "surely that is something at my window lattice;
Let me see, then, what thereat is, and this mystery explore—
Let my heart be still a moment and this mystery explore;—
                    'Tis the wind and nothing more!"

Open here I flung the shutter, when, with many a flirt and flutter,
In there stepped a stately raven of the saintly days of yore;
Not the least obeisance made he; not a minute stopped or stayed he;
But, with mien of lord or lady, perched above my chamber door—
Perched upon a bust of Pallas just above my chamber door—
                              Perched, and sat, and nothing more.

Then this ebony bird beguiling my sad fancy into smiling,
By the grave and stern decorum of the countenance it wore,
"Though thy crest be shorn and shaven, thou," I said, "art sure no craven,
Ghastly grim and ancient raven wandering from the Nightly shore—
Tell me what thy lordly name is on the Night's Plutonian shore!"
                              Quoth the raven, "Nevermore."

Much I marvelled this ungainly fowl to hear discourse so plainly,
Though its answer little meaning—little relevancy bore;
For we cannot help agreeing that no living human being
Ever yet was blessed with seeing bird above his chamber door—
Bird or beast upon the sculptured bust above his chamber door,
                              With such name as "Nevermore."

But the raven, sitting lonely on the placid bust, spoke only
That one word, as if his soul in that one word he did outpour.
Nothing farther then he uttered—not a feather then he fluttered—
Till I scarcely more than muttered "Other friends have flown before—
On the morrow *he* will leave me, as my hopes have flown before."
                              Then the bird said "Nevermore."

Startled at the stillness broken by reply so aptly spoken,
"Doubtless" said I, "what it utters is its only stock and store
Caught from some unhappy master whom unmerciful Disaster
Followed fast and followed faster till his songs one burden bore—
Till the dirges of his Hope that melancholy burden bore
                              Of "Nevermore"—of "Nevermore."

But the raven still beguiling all my sad soul into smiling,
Straight I wheeled a cushioned seat in front of bird, and bust, and door;
Then upon the velvet sinking, I betook myself to linking
Fancy unto fancy, thinking what this ominous bird of yore—
What this grim, ungainly, ghastly, gaunt, and ominous bird of yore
                              Meant in croaking "Nevermore."

This I sat engaged in guessing, but no syllable expressing
To the fowl whose fiery eyes now burned into my bosom's core;
This and more I sat divining, with my head at ease reclining
On the cushion's velvet lining that the lamplight gloated o'er,
But whose velvet violet-lining with the lamplight gloating o'er,
                    She shall press, ah, nevermore!

Then, methought, the air grew denser, perfumed from an unseen censer
Swung by angels, whose faint foot-falls tinkled on the tufted floor.
"Wretch," I cried, "thy God hath lent thee—by these angels he hath sent thee
Respite—respite and Nepenthe from thy memories of Lenore!
Quaff, oh quaff this kind Nepenthe and forget this lost Lenore!"
                    Quoth the raven, "Nevermore."

"Prophet!" said I, "thing of evil!—prophet still, if bird or devil!—
Whether Tempter sent, or whether tempest tossed thee here ashore,
Desolate, yet all undaunted, on this desert land enchanted—
On this home by Horror haunted—tell me truly, I implore—
Is there—*is* there balm in Gilead?—tell me—tell me, I implore!"
                    Quoth the raven "Nevermore."

"Prophet!" said I, "thing of evil!—prophet still, if bird or devil!
By that Heaven that bends above us—by that God we both adore—
Tell this soul with sorrow laden if, within the distant Aidenn,
It shall clasp a sainted maiden whom the angels name Lenore—
Clasp a rare and radiant maiden whom the angels name Lenore."
                    Quoth the raven "Nevermore."

"Be that word our sign of parting, bird or fiend!" I shrieked, upstarting—
"Get thee back into the tempest and the Night's Plutonian shore!
Leave no black plume as a token of that lie thy soul hath spoken!
Leave my loneliness unbroken!—quit the bust above my door!
Take thy beak from out my heart, and take thy form from off my door!"
                    Quoth the raven "Nevermore."

And the raven, never flitting, still is sitting, still is sitting
On the pallid bust of Pallas just above my chamber door;
And his eyes have all the seeming of a demon that is dreaming,
And the lamp-light o'er him streaming throws his shadow on the floor;
And my soul from out that shadow that lies floating on the floor
                    Shall be lifted—nevermore!

Margaret Sangster

THE CALL OF THE CROW

Caw!   caw!   caw!
　　Over the standing corn
　　The cheery cry is borne—
Caw!   caw!   caw!

Caw!   caw!   caw!
　　Into the school-room door,
　　Over the clean-swept floor—
Caw!   caw!   caw!

Caw!   caw!   caw!
　　The crow he is free to fly,
　　But the boy must cipher and sight—
Caw!   caw!   caw!

Caw!   caw!   caw!
　　And I wish I could go with him
　　Where the woods are wild and dim—
Caw!   caw!   caw!

Lydia Sigourney

THE DOVE

There was a lonely ark,
That sail'd o'er waters dark;
　　And wide around,
Not one tall tree was seen,
No flower, nor leaf of green,
　　All—all were drown'd.

Then a soft wing was spread,
And o'er the billows dread,
　　A meek dove flew;
But on the shoreless tide
No living thing she spied,
　　To cheer her view.

There was no chirping sound
O'er that wide watery bound,
　　To soothe her wo;
But the cold surges spread
Their covering o'er the dead,
　　That slept below.

So to the ark she fled,
With weary, drooping head,
　　To seek for rest;
Christ is thy ark, my love,
Thou art the timid dove,—
　　Fly to his breast.

S. Conant Foster

THE CROW THAT THE CROW CROWED

"Ho! ho!"
Said the crow:
"So I'm not s'posed to know
Where the rye and the wheat
And the corn kernels grow—
Oh! no,
Ho! ho!

"He! he!
Farmer Lee,
When I fly from my tree,
Just you see where the tops
Of the corn-ears will be·
Watch me!
He! he!"

Switch-swirch,
With a lurch,
Flopped the bird from his perch
As he spread out his wings
And set forth on his search—
His search—
Switch-swirch.

Click!—bang!—
How it rang,
How the small bullet sang
As it sped through the air—
And the crow, with a pang,
Went spang—
Chi-bang.

THE TAILFEATHERS

Now know,
That to crow
Often brings one to woe;
Which the lines up above
Have been put there to show,
And so,
Don't crow.

THE SANDPIPER

Across the narrow beach we flit,
   One little sandpiper and I,
And fast I gather, bit by bit,
   The scattered driftwood bleached and dry.
The wild waves reach their hands for it,
   The wild wind raves, the tide runs high,
As up and down the beach we flit,—
   One little sandpiper and I.

Above our heads the sullen clouds
   Scud black and swift across the sky;
Like silent ghosts in misty shrouds
   Stand out the white light-houses high.
Almost as far as eye can reach
   I see the close-reefed vessels fly,
As fast we flit along the beach,
   One little sandpiper and I.

I watch him as he skims along
   Uttering his sweet and mournful cry;
He starts not at my fitful song,
   Or flash of fluttering drapery.
He has no thought of any wrong;
   He scans me with a fearless eye.
Staunch friends are we, well tried and strong,
   The little sandpiper and I.

Comrade, where wilt thou be to-night
   When the loosed storm breaks furiously?
My driftwood fire will burn so bright!
   To what warm shelter canst thou fly?
I do not fear for thee, though wroth
   The tempest rushes through the sky:
For are we not God's children both,
   Thou, little sandpiper, and I?

THE BUTCHER-BIRD

I'll tell you a story, children,
  The saddest you ever heard,
About Rupert, the pet canary,
  And a terrible butcher-bird.

There was such a blinding snow-storm
  One could not see at all,
And all day long the children
  Had watched the white flakes fall;

And when the eldest brothers
  Had kissed mamma good-night,
And up the stairs together
  Had gone with their bedroom light,

Of a sudden their two fresh voices
  Rang out in a quick surprise,
"Mamma! papa! come quickly
  And catch him before he flies!"

On a picture-frame perched lightly,
  With his head beneath his wing,
They had found a gray bird sitting;
  That was a curious thing!

Down stairs to the cosy parlor
  They brought him, glad to find
For the storm-tossed wanderer shelter;
  Not knowing his cruel mind!

And full of joy were the children
  To think he was safe and warm,
And had chosen their house for safety
  To hide from the raging storm!

"He shall stay with the pretty Rupert,
  And live among mother's flowers,
And he'll sing with our robin and
    sparrow;"
  And they talked about it for hours.

Alas, in the early morning
  There rose a wail and a cry,
And a fluttering wild in the cages
  And Rupert's voice rang high.

We rushed to the rescue swiftly;
  Too late! On the shining cage,
The home of the happy Rupert,
  All rough with fury and rage,

Stood the handsome, horrible stranger,
  With black and flashing eye,
And torn almost to pieces
  Did poor dead Rupert lie!

Oh, sad was all the household,
  And we mourned for Rupert long.
The fierce wild shrike was prisoned
  In a cage both dark and strong;

And would you like, O children,
  His final fate to know?
To Agassiz's Museum
  That pirate bird did go.

INHOSPITALITY

Down on the north wind sweeping
   Comes the storm with roaring din;
Sadly, with dreary tumult,
   The twilight gathers in.

The snow-covered little island
   Is white as a frosted cake;
And round and round it the billows
   Bellow and thunder, and break.

Within doors the blazing driftwood
   Is glowing, ruddy and warm,
And happiness sits at the fireside,
   Watching the raging storm.

What fluttered past the window,
   All weary and wet and weak,
With heavily drooping pinions,
   And the wicked, crooked beak?

Where the boats before the house door
   Are drawn up from the tide,
On the tallest prow he settles,
   And furls his wings so wide.

Uprises the elder brother,
   Uprises the sister too;
"Nay, brother, he comes for shelter!
   Spare him! What would you do?"

He laughs, and is gone for his rifle.
   And steadily takes his aim;
But the wild wind seizes his yellow
    beard,
   And blows it about like flame.

Into his eyes the snow sifts,
   Till he cannot see aright,—
Ah! the cruel gun is baffled!
   And the weary hawk takes flight;

And slowly up he circles,
   Higher and higher still;
The fierce wind catches and bears him
    away
   O'er the bleak crest of the hill.

Cries the little sister, watching,
   "Whither now can he flee?
Black through the whirling snow-flakes
   Glooms the awful face of the sea,

"And tossed and torn by the tempest,
   He must sink in the bitter brine!
Why couldn't we pity and save him
   Till the sun again should shine?"

They drew her back to the fireside,
   And laughed at her cloudy eyes,—
"What—mourn for that robber-fellow,
   The cruellest bird that flies!

"Your song-sparrow hardly would thank
    you,
   And which is the dearest, pray?"
But she heard at the doors and windows
   The lashing of the spray;

And as ever the shock of the breakers
   The heart of their quiet stirred,
She thought, "Oh would we had
    sheltered him,—
   The poor, unhappy bird!"

THE BIRDS' ORCHESTRA

Bobolink shall play the violin,
    Great applause to win;
Lonely, sweet, and sad, the meadow lark
    Plays the oboe. Hark!
That inspired bugle with a soul—
    'Tis the oriole;
Yellow-bird the clarionet shall play,
    Blithe, and clear, and gay.
Purple finch what instrument will suit?
    He can play the flute.
Fire-winged blackbirds sound the merry
    fife,
    Soldiers without strife;
And the robins wind the mellow horn
    Loudly eve and morn.
Who shall clash the cymbals? Jay and
    crow;
    That is all they know.
Hylas twang their harps so weird and
    high,
    Such a tuneful cry!
And to roll the deep, melodious drum,
    Lo! the bull-frogs come!
Then the splendid chorus, who shall sing
    Of so fine a thing?

Who the names of the performers call
    Truly, one and all?
Blue-bird, bunting, cat-bird, chickadee
    (Phoebe-bird is he),
Swallow, creeper, cross-bill, cuckoo,
    dove,
    Wee wren that I love;
Brisk fly-catcher, finches—what a crowd!
    King-bird whistling loud;
Sweet rose-breasted grosbeak, vireo,
    thrush—
    Hear these two, and hush;
Scarlet tanager, song-sparrow small
    (Dearer he than all;
At the first sound of his friendly voice
    Saddest hearts rejoice),
Redpoll, nuthatch, thrasher, plover
    gray—
    Curlew did I say?
What a jangling all the grackles make!
    Is it some mistake?
Anvil chorus yellow-hammers strike,
    And the wicked shrike
Harshly creaks like some half-open door;
    He can do no more.

Author Unknown

BIRD'S PICNIC

The birds gave a picnic, the morning was fine,
They all came in couples to chat and to dine;
Miss Robin, Miss Wren, and the two Misses Jay,
Were dressed in a manner decidedly gay.

And bluebird, who looks like a handful of sky,
Dropped in with her spouse as the morning wore by;
The yellowbirds, too, wee bundles of sun,
With the brave chickadees came along to the fun.

Miss Phoebe was there, in her prim suit of brown,
In fact, all the birds in the fair leafy town.
The neighbors, of course, were politely invited,
Not even the ants and the crickets were slighted.

The grasshoppers came, some in gray, some in green,
And covered with dust, hardly fit to be seen.
Miss Miller flew in with her gown white as milk,
And Lady Bug flourished a new crimson silk.

The bees turned out lively, the young and the old,
And proud as could be, in their spencers of gold,
But Miss Caterpillar, how funny of her,
She hurried along in her mantle of fur.

There were big bugs in plenty, and gnats great and small,
A very hard matter to mention them all.
And what did they do? Why they sported and sang,
Till all the green wood with their melody rang.

Who e'er gave a picnic so grand and so gay?
They hadn't a shower, I'm happy to say;
And when the sun fell, like a cherry, ripe red,
The fireflies lighted them all home to bed.

ℰ *Celia Thaxter*

THE GREAT WHITE OWL

He sat aloft on the rocky height,
  Snow-white above the snow,
In the winter morning calm and bright,
  And I gazed at him, below.

He faced the east where the sunshine
    streamed
  On the singing, sparkling sea,
And he blinked with his yellow eyes that
    seemed
  All sightless and blank to be.

The snow-birds swept in a whirling crowd
  About him gleefully,
And piped and whistled, sweet and loud,
  But never a plume stirred he.

Singing they passed and away they flew
  Through the brilliant atmosphere;
Cloud-like he sat with the living blue
  Of the sky behind him, clear.

"Give you good morrow, friend!" I cried.
  He wheeled his large round head
Solemn and stately from side to side,
  But never a word he said.

"O lonely creature, weird and white,
  Why are you sitting there,
Like a glimmering ghost from the still
    midnight
  In the beautiful morning air?"

He spurned the rock with his talons
    strong,
  No human speech brooked he;
Like a snow-flake huge he sped along,
  Swiftly and noiselessly.

His wide slow-waving wings so white
  Heavy and soft did seem,
Yet rapid as a dream his flight,
  And silent as a dream.

And when a distant crag he gained,
  Bright twinkling as a star,
He shook his shining plumes, and
    deigned
  To watch me from afar.

And once again, when the evening red
  Burned dimly in the west,
I saw him motionless, his head
  Bent forward on his breast.

Dark and still 'gainst the sunset sky
  Stood out his figure lone,
Crowning the bleak rock, far and high,
  By sad winds overblown.

Did he dream of the ice-fields, stark and
    drear,
  Of his haunts on the Arctic shore?
Or the downy brood in his nest last year
  On the coast of Labrador?

Had he fluttered the Esquimau huts
    among?
  How I wished he could speak to me!
Had he sailed on the icebergs, rainbow
    hung,
  In the open Polar Sea?

O, many a tale he might have told
  Of marvellous sounds and sights,
Where the world lies hopeless and
    dumb with cold
  Through desolate days and nights.

But with folded wings, while the darkness
    fell,
  He sat, nor spake nor stirred;
And charmed as if by a subtile spell
  I mused on the wondrous Bird.

A HOWL ABOUT AN OWL

It was an owl lived in an oak,
Sing heigh ho! the prowly owl!
He often smiled, but he seldom spoke,
And he wore a wig and a camlet cloak.
Sing heigh ho! the howly fowl!
Tu-whit! tu-whit! tu-whoo!

He fell in love with the chickadee,
Sing heigh ho! the prowly owl!
He asked her, would she marry he,
And they'd go and live in Crim Tartaree.
Sing heigh ho! the howly fowl!
Tu-whit! tu-whit! tu-whoo!

"'T is true," says he, "you are far from big."
Sing heigh ho! the prowly owl!
"But you'll look twice as well when I've bought you a wig,
And I'll teach you the Lancers and the Chorus Jig."
Sing heigh ho! the howly fowl!
Tu-whit! tu-whit! tu-whoo!

"I'll feed you with honey when the moon grows pale."
Sing heigh ho! the prowly owl!
"I'll hum you a hymn, and I'll sing you a scale,
Till you quiver with delight to the tip of your tail!"
Sing heigh ho! the howly fowl!
Tu-whit! tu-whit! tu-whoo!

So he went for to marry of the chickadee,
Sing heigh ho! the prowly owl!
But the sun was so bright that he could not see,
So he marrièd the hoppergrass instead of she.
And wasn't that a sad disappointment for he!
Sing heigh ho! the howly fowl!
Tu-whit! tu-whit! tu-whoo!

❧ Laura E. Richards

THE OWL AND THE EEL AND THE WARMING-PAN

The owl and the eel and the warming-pan,
They went to call on the soap-fat man.
The soap-fat man he was not within:
He'd gone for a ride on his rolling-pin.
So they came back by way of the town,
And turned the meeting-house upside down.

❧ Mary E. Wilkins Freeman

THE OSTRICH

The ostrich is a silly bird,
   With scarcely any mind.
He often runs so very fast,
   He leaves himself behind.—

And when he gets there, has to stand
   And hang about till night,
Without a blessed thing to do
   Until he comes in sight.

❧ Phoebe Cary

GRISELDA GOOSE

Near to a farm-house, and bordered round
   By a meadow, sweet with clover,
There lay as clear and smooth a pond
   As ever a goose swam over.

The farmer had failures in corn and hops,
   From drought and various reasons;
But his geese had never failed in their crops
   In the very worst of seasons.

And he had a flock, that any day
   Could defy all sneers and slanders;
They were certainly handsome,—that is
     to say,
   They were handsome for geese and
     ganders!

And, once upon a time, in spring,
   A goose hatched out another,—
The softest, cunningest, downiest thing,
   That ever gladdened a mother.

There was never such a gosling born,
   So the geese cried out by dozens;
She was praised and petted, night and
     morn,
   By aunts, and uncles, and cousins.

She must have a name with a lofty sound,
   Said all, when they beheld her;
So they proudly led her down to the pond,
   And christened her, Griselda!

Now you think, no doubt, such love and
        pride,
Must perfectly content her;
    That she grew to goosehood satisfied
To be what Nature meant her.

But folk with gifts will find it out,
    Though the world neglects that duty;
And a lovely female will seldom doubt,
    Though others may, her beauty!

And if she had thought herself a fright,
    And been content with her station,
She wouldn't have had a story to write,
    Nor I, my occupation.

But indeed the truth compels me to own,
    Whoever may be offended,
That my heroine's vanity was shown
    Ere her gosling days were ended.

When the mother tried to teach the art
    Of swimming to her daughter,
She said that she didn't like to start,
    Because it ruffled the water.

"My stars!" cried the parent, "do I dream,
    Or do I rightly hear her?
Can it be she would rather sit still on the
        stream,
    Than spoil her beautiful mirror?"

Yet, if any creature could be so fond
    Of herself, as to reach insanity,
A goose, who lives on a glassy pond,
    Has most excuse for such vanity!

And I do not agree with those who said
    They would glory in her disgraces;
Hers isn't the only goose's head
    That ever was turned by praises.

And Griselda swallowed all their praise:
    Though she said to her doting mother,
"Still, a goose is a goose, to the end of
        her days,
    From one side of the world to the other!

"And as to my name, it is well enough
    To say, or sing, or whistle;
But you just wait till I'm old and tough,
    And you'll see they will call me, Gristle!"

So she went, for the most of the time,
        alone,
    Because she was such a scoffer;
And, awful to tell! she was nearly grown
    Before she received an offer!

"Nobody will have her, that is clear,"
    Said those who spitefully eyed her;
Though they knew every gander, far and
        near,
    Was dying to waddle beside her.

And some of those that she used to slight,
    Now come to matronly honor,
Began to feel that they had a right
    To quite look down upon her.

And some she had jilted were heard to
        declare,
    "I do not understand her;
And I shouldn't wonder, and shouldn't
        care,
    If she never got a gander!"

But she said so all could overhear,—
    And she hoped their ears might tingle,—
If she couldn't marry above their sphere,
    She preferred remaining single!

She was praised and flattered to her face,
    And blamed when she was not present;
And between her friends and foes, her
        place
    Was anything but pleasant.

One day she learned what gave her a
        fright,
    And a fit of deep dejection;
And she said to herself, that come what
        might,
    She would cut the whole connection.

The farmer's wife to the geese proposed,
    Their spending the day in the stable;
And the younger ones, left out, supposed
    She would set an extra table.

So they watched and waited till day was
        done,
    With curiosity burning;
For it wasn't till after set of sun,
    That they saw them back returning.

Slowly they came, and each was bowed
    As if some disgrace was upon her;
They didn't look as those who are proud
    Of an unexpected honor!

Each told the naked truth: 'twas a shock,
    But who that saw, could doubt her?
They had plucked the pluckiest goose of
        the flock!
    Of all the down about her.

Said Miss Griselda, "That's my doom,
    If I stay another season;"
So she thought she'd leave her roosting
        room;
    And I think she had some reason.

Besides, there was something else she
        feared;
    For oft in a kind of flurry,
A goose mysteriously disappeared.
    And didn't come back in a hurry.

And scattered afterwards on the ground,—
    Such things there is no mistaking,—
Familiar looking bones were found,
    Which set her own a quaking.

She said, "There is danger if I stay,
    From which there are none exempted;
So, though I perish in getting away,
    The thing shall be attempted."

And, perfectly satisfied about
    Her claims to a foreign mission.
She slipped away, and started out
    On a secret expedition.

And oh! how her bosom swelled with
        pride;
    How eager hope upbore her;
As floating down the stream, she spied
    A broad lake spread before her.

And bearing towards her, fair and white,
    The pleasant breezes courting,
A flock of swans came full in sight,
    On the crystal waters sporting.

She saw the lake spread clear and wide,
    And the rich man's stately dwelling,
And felt the thrill of hope and pride
    Her very gizzard swelling.

"These swans," she said, "are quite un
        known.
    Even to their ranks and stations;
Yet I think I need not fear to own
    Such looking birds for relations.

"Besides, no birds that walk on lawns
    Are made for common uses;
Men do not take their pick of swans
    In the way they do of gooses.

"Blanche Swan! I think I'll take that name.
    Nor be ashamed to wear it;
Griselda Goose! that sounds so tame
    And low, I cannot bear it!"

Thought she, the brave deserve to win,
    And only they can do it:
So she made her plan, and sailed right in,
    Determined to go through it.

Straight up she went to the biggest swan,
    The one who talked the loudest;
For she knew the secret of getting on
    Was standing up with the proudest.

"Madam," she said, "I am glad you're
        home,
    And I hope to know you better;
You're an aunt of mine, I think, but I come
    With an introductory letter."

Then she fumbled, and said, "I've lost the
    thing!
    No matter! I can quote it;
And here's the pen," and she raised her
    wing,
    "With which Lord Swansdown wrote it.

"Of course you never heard of me,
    As I'm rather below your station;
But a lady famed like yourself, you see,
    Is known to all creation."

Then to herself the old swan said,
    "Such talk's not reprehensible;
Indeed, for a creature country-bred,
    She's very shrewd and sensible."

Griselda saw how her flattery took,
    And cried, on the silence breaking,
"You see I have the family look,
    My neck there is no mistaking.

"It doesn't compare with yours; you know
    I've a touch of the democracy;
While your style and manner plainly show
    Your perfect aristocracy."

Such happy flattery did the thing:
    Though the young swans doubtfully
        eyed her,
My Lady took her under her wing,
    And kept her close beside her.

And Griselda tried at ease to appear,
    And forget the home she had quitted;
For she told herself she had reached a
    sphere
    At last for which she was fitted.

Though she had some fits of common
    sense,
    And at times grew quite dejected;
For she wasn't deceived by her own pre
    tense,
    And she knew what others suspected.

If ever she went alone to stray,
    Some pert young swan to tease her
Would ask, in a patronizing way,
    If their poor home didn't please her?

Sometimes when a party went to sail
    On the lake, in pleasant weather,
As if she was not within the pale,
    She was left out altogether.

And then she would take a haughty tone,
    As if she scorned them, maybe;
But often she hid in the weeds alone,
    And cried like a homesick baby.

One day when she had gone to her room,
    With the plea that she was ailing,
They asked some rather gay birds to come
    For the day, and try the sailing.

But they said, "She will surely hear the stir,
    So we'll have to let her know it;
Of course we are all ashamed of her,
    But it will not do to show it."

So one of them went to her, and said,
    With a sort of stately rustle:
"I suppose you would rather spare your
        head
    Than join in our noise and bustle!

"If you wish to send the slightest excuse,
    I'll be very happy to take it;
And I hope you're not such a little goose
    As to hesitate to make it!"

Too well Griselda understood;
    And said, "Though my pain's distressing,
I think the change will do me good,
    And I do not mind the dressing."

'Twas the "little goose" that made her mad,
    So mad she wouldn't refuse her;
Though she saw from the first how very
        glad
    Her friend would be to excuse her.

She had overdone the thing, poor swan!
　As her ill success had shown her;
Shot quite beyond the mark, and her gun
　Recoiled and hit the owner.

"Don't you think," she cried, "I've done
　my best;
　But as sure as I'm a sinner,
That little dowdy, frightfully dressed,
　Is coming down to dinner!

"I tried in every way to show
　That I thought it an impropriety;
But I s'pose the creature doesn't know
　The manners of good society!"

Griselda thought, "If it comes to that,
　With the weapon she takes I'll meet her.
She's sharp, but I'll give her tit for tat,
　And I think that I can beat her."

So she came among them quite at ease,
　By her very look contriving
To say, "I'm certain there's nothing could
　please
　You so much as my arriving."

And her friend contrived to whisper low,
　As she made her genuflexion:
"A country cousin of ours, you know;
　A very distant connection!

"She hasn't much of an air, you see,
　And is rather new to the city;
Aunt took her up quite from charity,
　And keeps her just from pity."

But Griselda paid her, fair and square,
　For all her sneers and scorning;
And "the fête was quite a successful af
　fair,"
So the papers said next morning.

And yet she cried at the close of day,
　Till the lake almost ran over,
To think what a price she had to pay
　To get into a sphere above her.

"Alas!" she said, "that our common sense
　Should be lost when others flatter;
I was born a goose, and no pretense
　Will change or help the matter!"

At last she did nothing but mope and fret,
　And think of effecting a clearance!
She got as low as a lady can get,—
　She didn't regard her appearance!

She got her pretty pink slippers soiled
　By wearing them out in bad weather;
And as for her feathers, they were not
　oiled
　Sometimes for a week together.

Had she seen just how to bring it about,
　She would have left in a minute;
But she found it was harder getting out
　Of trouble than getting in it.

She looked down at the fish with envious
　eyes,
　Because each mother's daughter,
Content in her element, never tries
　To keep her head above water!

She wished she was by some good luck,
　Turned into a salmon finny;
Into a chicken, or into a duck:
　She wished herself in Guinea.

One day the Keeper came to the lake,
　And if he didn't dissemble,
She saw that to her he meant to take,
　In a way that made her tremble.

With a chill of fear her feathers shook,
　Although to her friend she boasted
He had such a warm, admiring look,
　That she feared she should be roasted;

And that for very modesty's sake,
　Since nothing else could shield her,
She would go to the other end of the lake,
　And stay till the night concealed her.

So, taking no leave, she stole away,
  And nobody cared or missed her;
But the geese on the pond were
    surprised, next day
  By the sight of their missing sister.

She told them she strayed too far and
    got lost;
  And though being from home had
  pained her,
Some wealthy friends that she came
    across,
  Against her will detained her.

But it leaked from the lake, or a bird of
    the air
  Had carried to them the matter;
For even before her, her story was there,
  And they all looked doubtfully at her.

Poor Griselda! unprotected, alone,
  By their slights and sneers was nettled;
For all the friends that her youth had
    known
  Were respectably married and settled;

Or all but one,—a poor old coot,
  That she used to scorn for a lover;

He was shabbier now, and had lost a foot,
  That a cart-wheel had run over.

But she said, "There is but one thing to
    be done
  For stopping sneers and slanders;
For a lame excuse is better than none,
  And so is the lamest of ganders!"

So she married him, but do you know,
  They did not cease to flout her;
For she somehow couldn't make it go
  With herself, nor those about her.

They spoke of it with scornful lip,
  Though they didn't exactly drop her;
As if 'twas a limited partnership,
  And not a marriage proper.

And yet in truth I'm bound to say
  Her state was a little better;
Though I heard her friend say yesterday
  To another one, who met her,—

"Oh, I saw old Gristle Goose to-night,—
  Of course I did not seek it;
I suppose she is really Mrs. White,
  Though it sticks in my crop to speak it!"

Frank Dempster Sherman

THE SNOW-BIRD

When all the ground with snow is white,
The merry snow-bird comes,
And hops about with great delight
To find the scattered crumbs.

How glad he seems to get to eat
A piece of cake or bread!
He wears no shoes upon his feet,
Nor hat upon his head.

But happiest is he, I know,
Because no cage with bars
Keeps him from walking on the snow
And printing it with stars.

❧ Frank Dempster Sherman

HUMMING-BIRD SONG

Humming-bird,
Not a word
  Do you say;
Has your throat
No sweet note
  To repay
Honey debts
It begets
  When you go
On the wing
Pilfering
  To and fro?

May be you
Whisper to
  Bloom and leaf
On the vine
Secrets fine
  In your brief
Calls on them,
Wingèd gem,
  Not a word
You reply!
Off you fly,
  Humming-bird!

❧ Eudora May Stone (age 12)

THE CHICKADEE

The birds have all flown to their homes in the south,
The flowers are withered and dead,
The feathery snow-flakes come hurrying down,
And the pleasant south breezes have fled:
But the brave little chickadee, cheery and bold,
Stays with us all winter, not minding the cold.

Though the meadow-lark's carol is sweeter by far,
And the bluebird is gaylier dressed,
Still of all the sweet songs of all the bright throngs,
Little chickadee's song is the best.
For this brave little chickadee, cheery and bold,
Stays with us all winter, not minding the cold.

When the birds have all flown to their homes in the south,
And the snow-flakes have earth gently pressed,
The chickadee comes in the winter to stay,
And that's why I like him the best.
Yes, the brave little chickadee, cheery and bold,
Stays with us all winter, not minding the cold.

PETER PARROT

Peter in the window sits,
   Turning round his cool, red eye,
   Looking strange, and cross and shy,
As from ring to perch he flits,
   Hanging there by claw or beak—
   Sometimes looking up to speak.

"Pretty Polly," oft he says—
   Half in question, half to see
   If his simply vanity
Finds an echo in my praise;
   Sometimes he will laugh and cry
   At the people passing by.

Then he stops to sneeze or cough;
   All his red, and green and gold
   Cannot fright away the cold,
Cannot keep the winter off;
   Ruffled feathers, rough and dim,
   Tell Jack Frost hath bitten him.

Much I wonder if he thinks,
   Sitting in the pallid sun,
   Of that life, so long since done,
Where the long liana's links,
   Swinging slow, from palm to palm,
   Cradled him in tropic calm.

Does he hear the bell-bird's cry,
   When we think him half asleep?
   Or, do forest odors creep
Through his troubled memory,
   Telling tales of happy hours,
   'Mid a thousand gorgeous flowers?

Does he ever seem to see
   Gayer brethren of his kind
   Flying on the torrid wind—
Perched on every stately tree,—
   Toucans, paroquets, macaws,
   Chattering on without a pause?

Does he see the monkeys swinging
   Here and yon along the vines;
   Or, when cool the moonlight shines,
Hear the Indian shrilly singing,
   On the river's gleaming breast,
   Floating homeward to his rest?

Pretty Polly! homesick bird!
   Or, is all my pity wasted?
   Are these joys, that once you tasted,
Vanished like a song half heard?
   Are you just as pleased to squall
   From the window, "Pretty Poll?"

Emily Dickinson

IN THE GARDEN

A bird came down the walk:
He did not know I saw;
He bit an angle-worm in halves
And ate the fellow, raw.

And then he drank a dew
From a convenient grass,
And then hopped sidewise to the wall
To let a beetle pass.

He glanced with rapid eyes
That hurried all abroad,—
They looked like frightened beads,
   I thought;
He stirred his velvet head

Like one in danger; cautious,
I offered him a crumb,
And he unrolled his feathers
And rowed him softer home

Than oars divide the ocean,
Too silver for a seam,
Or butterflies, off banks of noon,
Leap, plashless, as they swim.

Lily Lee

LITERARY DAY AMONG THE BIRDS

Dark night at last had taken its flight,
Morn had come with her earliest light;
Her herald, gray dawn, had extinguished each star,
And gay banners in the east were waving afar.

That lovely goddess, Beautiful Spring,
Had fanned all the earth with her radiant wing;
"Had calmed the wild winds with fragrant breath,"
And gladden'd nature with an emerald wreath.

Within the precincts of the Bird Nation,
All was bustle and animation;
For that day was to witness a literary feast,
Where only Birds were invited guests.

The place of meeting was a leafy nook,
Close by the side of a sparkling brook.
Soon were assembled a merry band,
Birds from every tree in the land.

Mrs. DOVE came first, in soft colors drest;
Then Mr. CANARY, looking his best.
The family of MARTINS, dressed in brown,
And Mr. WOODPECKER, with his ruby crown.

The exercises opened with a scientific song,
By the united voices of the feathered throng.
Then was delivered a brilliant oration,
By 'Squire RAVEN, the wisest bird of the nation.
Master WHIP-POOR-WILL next mounted the stage,
Trying to look very much like a sage.

Eight pretty green PARROTS then spoke with art;
Though small, with credit they carried their part.
Again an oration by Mr. QUAIL,
Spoken as fast as the gallop of snail.
And lastly, Sir BLACKBIRD whistl'd off an address,
Of twenty odd minutes, more or less.

Then came the applause, so loud and long,
That the air echoed the joyous song.
But the sun was low, so soon they sped
To their quiet nests and their grassy beds;
And rocked by the breeze, they quietly slept,
Ere the firstling star in the blue sky crept.

DOMESTIC ANIMALS

Eliza Lee Cabot Follen

TRUSTY LEARNING A B C

"Be quiet, good Trusty,
    See how still you can be,
For I've come to teach you
    Your A B C.

"I will show you the way
    Mother reads it to me;
She looks very sober,
    And says, A B C.

"Tom says you can't learn;
    But father says, he

Saw a little dog once
    That knew A B C.

"So, good Trusty, attend;
    Let us show them that we
Can learn if we please,
    Our A B C."

To what little Frank said
    Trusty seemed to agree.
Do you think he learned much
    Of his A B C?

Eliza Lee Cabot Follen

WALTER AND HIS DOG

There was a little boy,
    And he had a piece of bread,
And he put his little cap
    On his head, head, head.

Upon his hobby-horse
    Then he went to take a ride,
With his pretty Spaniel Flash
    By his side, side, side.

Little Walter was his name,
    And he said to little Flash,
"Let us gallop round the house,
    With a dash, dash, dash."

So he laid down his bread
    In a snug little place,
And away Walter went
    For a race, race, race.

But Flash had a plan
    In his little roguish head,
Of taking to himself
    Walter's bread, bread, bread.

So he watched for a moment
    When Walter did not look,

And his nice piece of bread
    Slyly took, took, took.

When Walter saw the rogue,
    He cried, "O, naughty Flash;"
And he showed his little whip
    With a lash, lash, lash.

But Flash looked so good-natured,
    With his tail curled up behind,
That his aunty said to Walter,
    "Never mind, mind, mind.

"Flash is nothing but a puppy,
    So, Walter, do not worry,
If he knew that he'd done wrong,
    He'd be sorry, sorry, sorry.

"And don't be angry, Walter,
    That Flash has had a treat;
Here's another piece of bread
    You may eat, eat, eat."

So Walter ate his bread,
    And then to Flash he cried,
"Come, you saucy little dog,
    Let us ride, ride, ride."

THE DINERS IN THE KITCHEN

Our dog Fred
Et the bread.

Our dog Dash
Et the hash.

Our dog Pete
Et the meat.

Our dog Davy
Et the gravy.

Our dog Toffy
Et the coffee.

Our dog Jake
Et the cake.

Our dog Trip
Et the dip.

And—the worst,
From the first,—

Our dog Fido
Et the pie-dough.

Author Unknown

LITTLE DOGS

I had a liddle dog; his name wus Ball;
Wen I give him a liddle, he want it all.

I had a liddle dog, his name wus Trot;
He helt up his tail, all tied in a knot.

I had a liddle dog, his name wus Blue;
I put him on de road, an' he almos' flew.

I had a liddle dog, his name wus Mack;
I rid his tail fer to save his back.

I had a liddle dog, his name wus Rover;
W'en he died, he died all over.

I had a liddle dog, his name wus Dan;
An' w'en he died, I buried 'im in de san'.

Christopher P. Cranch

AN OLD CAT'S CONFESSIONS

I am a very old pussy,
    My name is Tabitha Jane;
I have had about fifty kittens,
    So I think that I mustn't complain.

Yet I've had my full share of cat's troubles:
    I was run over once by a cart;
And they drowned seventeen of my babies,
    Which came near breaking my heart.

A gentleman once singed my whiskers,—
    I shall never forgive him for that!
And once I was bit by a mad dog,
    And once was deceived by a rat.

I was tied by some boys in a meal-bag,
    And pelted and pounded with stones;
They thought I was mashed to a jelly,
    But it didn't break one of my bones.

For cats that have good constitutions
    Have eight more lives than a man;
Which proves we are better than humans
    To my mind, if anything can.

One night, as I wandered with Thomas,—
    We were singing a lovely duet,—
I was shot in the back by a bullet;
    When you stroke me, I feel it there yet.

A terrier once threatened my kittens;
    O, it gave me a terrible fright!
But I scratched him, and sent him off howling,
    And I think that I served him just right.

But I've failed to fulfill all my duties:
    I have purred half my life in a dream;
And I never devoured the canary,
    And I never lapped half enough cream.

But I've been a pretty good mouser,
    (What squirrels and birds I have caught!)
And have brought up my frolicsome kittens
    As a dutiful mother-cat ought.

Now I think I've a right, being aged,
    To take an old tabby's repose;
To have a good breakfast and dinner,
    And sit by the fire and doze.

I don't care much for the people
    Who are living with me in this house,
But I own that I love a good fire,
    And occasional herring and mouse.

Eliza Lee Cabot Follen

THE THREE LITTLE KITTENS [adapted from English traditional verse]

(A CAT'S TALE, WITH ADDITIONS.)

Three little kittens lost their mittens;
 And they began to cry,
  Oh! mother dear,
  We very much fear
  That we have lost our mittens.
LOST YOUR MITTENS!
YOU NAUGHTY KITTENS!
THEN YOU SHALL HAVE NO PIE.
  Mee-ow, mee-ow, mee-ow.
NO, YOU SHALL HAVE NO PIE.
  Mee-ow, mee-ow, mee-ow.

The three little kittens found their
  mittens,
 And they began to cry,
  Oh mother dear,
  See here, see here;
  See, we have found our mittens.
PUT ON YOUR MITTENS,
YOU SILLY KITTENS,
AND YOU MAY HAVE SOME PIE.
  Purr-r, purr-r, purr-r,
 Oh! let us have the pie,
  Purr-r, purr-r, purr-r.

The three little kittens put on their
  mittens,
 And soon ate up the pie;
  Oh! mother dear,
  We greatly fear,
  That we have soil'd our mittens.
SOIL'D YOUR MITTENS!
YOU NAUGHTY KITTENS!
 Then they began to sigh,
  Mi-ow, mi-ow, mi-ow.

The three little kittens washed their
  mittens,
 And hung them out to dry;
  Oh! mother dear,
  Do not you hear,
  That we have washed our mittens?
WASHED YOUR MITTENS!
OH! YOU'RE GOOD KITTENS,
BUT I SMELL A RAT CLOSE BY:
  Hush! hush! mee-ow, mee-ow.
 We smell a rat close by,
  Mee-ow, mee-ow, mee-ow.

Clara Doty Bates

NAMING THE KITTEN

Is Rose a nice name for kitty? Do you like Rose?
You see she's a bit of pink at the end of her nose.

Gray isn't the prettiest color for flowers, of course.
Besides, to be streaked like a tiger does make it worse.

If she were only a white puss Rosy would do,
Or even yellow—for roses are yellow too.

She's scratched me, here, on my finger; pussy, for shame!
When I was thinking to give you the sweetest name.

Just see the mark—it is bleeding, and burns like fire;
You shall never be Rose—never! I'll call you Brier!

THE BROKEN PIPE

Come here, little Willy,—
    Why what is the trouble?
"I've broke my new pipe, Ma,
    And can't make a bubble!"

Well, don't weep for that, child!
    But brighten your face;
And tell how this grievous
    Disaster took place.

"Why, Puss came along,
    And said I, 'now she'll think
This white, frothy water
    Is milk she may drink!"

"So I set it before her,
    And dipped her mouth in—
When, up came both paws,
    And stuck fast on my chin!

"Then, I gave her a blow
    With my pipe, and it flew
Into three or four pieces—
    And what shall I do?

"I can't make a bubble—
    I wish naughty kit
Had been a mile off!
    See! there's blood on me yet!"

I'm sorry, my boy;
    Yet, your loss is but just,

For sporting with Puss
    By deception, at first.

When, failing in this,
    You compelled her; and thence
Came the wound on your face,
    By her just self-defence.

And, when you so cruelly
    Beat her, you know,
Your pipe and yourself
    Had the worst of the blow.

May this ever teach you,
    You never should stoop,
With man, or with brute,
    But to make him your dupe.

That when you have power,
    It should not be abused,
In oppressing the weaker;
    Nor strength be misused.

For often will torture
    Return whence it came;
And cruelty ever
    Be followed by shame.

Remember this, William,—
    And here end your troubles!
I've one more pipe left—
    You may go and make bubbles.

THE SAD STORY OF THE DANDY CAT

To Sir Green-eyes Grimalkin de Tabby de Sly
  His mistress remarked one day,
"I'm tormented, my cat, both by mouse and by rat,
  Come rid me of them, I pray.

"For though you're a cat of renowned descent,
  And your kittenhood days have flown,
Yet never a trace of the blood of your race
  In battle or siege you've shown."

Sir Green-eyes Grimalkin de Tabby de Sly
  Arose from his downy bed,
He washed himself o'er, from his knightly paw
  To the crown of his knightly head.

And he curled his whiskers and combed his hair,
  And put on his perfumed gloves;
And his sword he girt on, which he never had done
  Save to dazzle the eyes of his loves.

And when he had cast an admiring glance
  On the looking-glass tall and fair,
To the pantry he passed; but he stood aghast,
  For lo! the pantry was bare.

The pickles, the cookies, the pies, were gone;
  And naught remained on the shelf
Save the bone of a ham, which lay cold and calm,
  The ghost of its former self.

Sir Green-eyes Grimalkin stood sore amazed,
  And he looked for the mice and rats;
But they, every one, had been long since gone
  Far, far from the reach of cats.

For while he was donning his satin pelisse,
  And his ribbons and laces gay,
They had finished their feast, without hurry the least,
  And had tranquilly trotted away.

The mistress of Green-eyes Grimalkin de Sly,
    A woman full stern was she,
She came to the door, and she rated him sore,
    And punished him over her knee.

She grasped him, spite of his knightly blood,
    By the tip of his knightly tail.
His adornments she stripped, and his body she dipped
    Three times in the water-pail.

She plunged him thrice 'neath the icy flood,
    Then drove him outside to dry.
And terror and cold on his feelings so told,
    That he really was like to die.

And now in this world 't would be hard to find,
    Although you looked low and high,
A cat who cares less for the beauties of dress
    Than Sir Green-eyes Grimalkin de Sly.

&❧ *Margaret Vandegrift*

CATCHING THE CAT

The mice met in council;
    They all looked haggard and worn,
For the state of affairs was too terrible
    To be any longer borne.
Not a family was out of mourning—
    There was crape on every hat,
They were desperate—something must
        be done,
    And done at once, to the cat.

An elderly member rose and said:
    "It might prove a possible thing
To set the trap which they set for us—
    That one with the awful spring!"
The suggestion was applauded
    Loudly, by one and all,
Till somebody squeaked: "That trap
        would be
    About ninety-five times too small!"

Then a medical mouse suggested—
    A little under his breath—
They should confiscate the very first
        mouse
    That died a natural death,
And he'd undertake to poison the cat,
    If they'd let him prepare the mouse.
"There's not been a natural death," they
        shrieked,
    "Since the cat came into the house!"

The smallest mouse in the council
    Arose with a solemn air,
And, by way of increasing his stature,
    Rubbed up his whiskers and hair.
He waited until there was silence
    All along the pantry shelf,
And then he said with dignity,
    "I will catch the cat myself!"

"When next I hear her coming,
　　Instead of running away
I shall turn and face her boldly,
　　And pretend to be at play;
She will not see her danger,
　　Poor creature! I suppose;
But as she stoops to catch me,
　　I shall catch her, by the nose!"

The mice began to look hopeful,
　　Yes, even the old ones, when
A gray-haired sage said slowly,
　　"And what will you do with her
　　　then?"
The champion, disconcerted,
　　Replied with dignity, "Well,
I think if you'll excuse me,
　　T'would be wiser not to tell!

We all have our inspirations—"
　　This produced a general smirk—
"But we are not all at liberty
　　To explain just how they'll work.
I ask you then, to trust me;
　　You need have no farther fears—
Consider our enemy done for!"
　　The council gave three cheers.

"I do believe she's coming!"
　　Said a small mouse, nervously,
"Run, if you like" said the champion
　　"But I shall wait and see!"
And sure enough she was coming—
　　The mice all scampered away
Except the noble champion,
　　Who had made up his mind to stay.

The mice had faith, of course they had—
　　They were all of them noble souls,
But a sort of general feeling
　　Kept them safely in their holes,
Until some time in the evening;
　　Then the boldest ventured out,
And saw, in the distance,
　　The cat prance gayly about!

There was dreadful consternation,
　　Till some one at last said, "Oh,
He's not had time to do it,
　　Let us not prejudge him so!"
"I believe in him, of course I do,"
　　Said the nervous mouse with a sigh,
"But the cat looks uncommonly happy,
　　And I wish I did know why!"

The cat, I regret to mention,
　　Still prances about that house,
And no message, or letter or telegram
　　Has come from the champion mouse.
The mice are a little discouraged;
　　The demand for crape goes on;
They feel they'd be happier if they knew
　　Where the champion mouse had gone.

This story has a moral—
　　It is very short you see;
So no one, of course, will skip it,
　　For fear of offending me.
It is well to be courageous,
　　And valiant, and all that,
But—if you are mice—you'd better think
　　twice,
　　Before you catch the cat.

THE DOG AND THE CAT, THE DUCK AND THE RAT

Once on a time in rainy weather
   A dog and a cat,
   A duck and a rat,
All met in a barn together.
   The dog he barked,
   The duck she quarked,
The cat she humped up her back;
   The rat he squeaked,
   And off he sneaked
Straight into a nice little crack.

The little dog said, and he looked very wise,
   "I think, Mrs. Puss,
   You make a great fuss
With your back and your great green eyes;
   And you, Madam Duck,
   You waddle and cluck,
Till it gives one the fidgets to hear you.
   You had better run off
   To the old pig's trough,
Where none but the pigs, ma'am, are near you."

The duck was good-natured, and she ran away,
   But old pussy cat
   With her back up sat,
And said she intended to stay;
   And she showed him her paws.
   With her long sharp claws,
So the dog was afraid to come near;
   For puss if she pleases,
   When a little dog teases,
Can give him a box on the ear.

Eliza Lee Cabot Follen

THE FARM YARD

The cock is crowing,
The cows are lowing,
The ducks are quarking,
The dogs are barking,
The ass is braying,
The horse is neighing;
Was there ever such a noise!

The birds are singing,
The bell is ringing,
The pigs are squeaking,
The barn door creaking,
The brook is babbling,
The geese are gabbling
Mercy on us, what a noise!

The sheep are baaing,
The boys hahaing,
The swallows twittering,
The girls are tittering,
Father is calling,
The cook is bawling;
I'm nigh crazy with the noise.

Betty is churning,
The grindstone's turning,
John is sawing,
Charles hurrahing,
Old Dobson's preaching,
The peacock's screeching;
Who can live in such a noise!

Phoebe Cary

THE HAPPY LITTLE WIFE

"Now, Gudhand, have you sold the cow
    You took this morn to town?
And did you get the silver groats
    In your hand, paid safely down?

"And yet I hardly need to ask;
    You hardly need to tell;
For I see by the cheerful face you bring,
    That you have done right well."

"Well! I did not exactly sell her,
    Nor give her away, of course;
But I'll tell you what I did, good wife,
    I swapped her for a horse."

"A horse! Oh, Gudhand, you have done
    Just what will please me best,
For now we can have a carriage,
    And ride as well as the rest."

"Nay, not so fast, my good dame,
    We shall not want a gig:

I had not ridden half a mile
    Till I swapped my horse for a pig."

"That's just the thing," she answered,
    "I would have done myself:
We can have a flitch of bacon now
    To put upon the shelf.

"And when our neighbors come to dine
    With us, they'll have a treat;
There is no need that we should ride,
    But there is that we should eat."

"Alack! alack!" said Gudhand,
    "I fear you'll change your note,
When I tell you I haven't got the pig—
    I swapped him for a goat."

"Now, bless us!" cried the good wife,
    "You manage things so well;
What I should ever do with a pig
    I'm sure I cannot tell.

"If I put my bacon on the shelf,
    Or put it in the pot,
The folks would point at us and say
    'They eat up all they've got!'

"But a good milch goat, ah! that's the
        thing
    I've wanted all my life;
And now we'll have both milk and
        cheese,"
    Cried the happy little wife.

"Nay, not so fast," said Gudhand,
    "You make too long a leap;
When I found I couldn't drive my goat,
    I swapped him for a sheep."

"A sheep, my dear! you must have tried
    To suit me all the time;
'Twould plague me so to have a goat,
    Because the things will climb!

"But a sheep! the wool will make us
        clothes
    To keep us from the cold;
Run out, my dear, this very night,
    And build for him a fold."

"Nay, wife, it isn't me that cares
    If he be penned or loose:
I do not own the sheep at all,
    I swapped him for a goose."

"There, Gudhand, I am so relieved;
    It almost made me sick
To think that I should have the wool
    To clip, and wash, and pick!

"'Tis cheaper, too, to buy our clothes,
    Than make them up at home;
And I haven't got a spinning-wheel,
    Nor got a carding-comb.

"But a goose! I love the taste of goose,
    When roasted nice and brown;
And then we want a feather bed,
    And pillows stuffed with down."

"Now stop a bit," cried Gudhand,
    "Your tongue runs like a clock;
The goose is neither here nor there,
    I swapped him for a cock."

"Dear me, you manage everything,
    As I would have it done;
We'll know now when to stir our
        stumps,
    And rise before the sun.

"A goose would be quite troublesome
    For me to roast and stuff;
And then our pillows and our beds
    You know, are soft enough."

"Well, soft or hard," said Gudhand,
    "I guess they'll have to do;
And that we'll have to wake at morn,
    Without the crowing, too!

"For you know I couldn't travel
    All day with naught to eat;
So I took a shilling for my cock.
    And bought myself some meat."

"That was the wisest thing of all,"
    Said the good wife, fond and true;
"You do just after my own heart,
    Whatever thing you do.

"We do not want a cock to crow,
    Nor want a clock to strike;
Thank God that we may lie in bed
    As long now as we like!"

And then she took him by the beard
    That fell about his throat,
And said, "*While you are mine, I want
    Nor goose, nor swine, nor goat!*"

And so the wife kissed Gudhand,
    And Gudhand kissed his wife;
And they promised to each other
    To be all in all through life.

THE PIGS

"Do look at those pigs as they lie in the straw!"
    Little Richard once said to papa;
"They keep eating longer than ever I saw;
    What wonderful eaters they are!"

"I see they are feasting," his father replied;
    "They eat a great deal, I allow:
But let us remember, before we deride,
    'Tis the nature, my dear, of the sow.

"But when a great boy such as you, my dear Dick,
    Does nothing but eat all the day,
And keeps tasting good things till he makes himself sick,
    'What a piggy indeed!' we may say!"

ও *Hellen Rebecca Anderson* (age 8)

The following poem was written by a little Cherokee girl just eight years of age—Hellen Rebecca Anderson, daughter of Mrs. Mabel Washbourne Anderson, a contributor to Twin Territories. *The poem is entirely original with little Hellen, and we give it just as she submitted the manuscript to* Twin Territories.*—Editor [Ora Eddleman Reed]*

THE UNRULY PIGS

Billy Wiggs once caught some pigs.
    And he put them in a pen,
But the pen was not strong,
    And so all went wrong,
And the pigs were gone again.

He followed them fast,
    And found them at last
And put them in another;
    They ate and they fussed,
As if they would bust,
    And he sold them to his mother.

🍀 *Sarah Josepha Hale*

MARY'S LAMB

Mary had a little lamb,
   Its fleece was white as snow,
And every where that Mary went
   The lamb was sure to go;
He followed her to school one day—
   That was against the rule,
It made the children laugh and play
   To see a lamb at school.

And so the Teacher turned him out,
   But still he lingered near,
And waited patiently about,
   Till Mary did appear.

And then he ran to her and laid
   His head upon her arm,
As if he said—"I'm not afraid—
   You'll shield me from all harm."

"What makes the lamb love Mary so,"
   The little children cry;
"O, Mary loves the lamb you know,"
   The Teacher did reply,
"And you each gentle animal
   In confidence may bind,
And make them follow at your call,
   If you are always *kind*."

🍀 *Various, Authors Unknown*

"MARY'S LAMB" PARODIES

FROM *GODEY'S LADY'S BOOK*, 1872

Mary had a little lamb,
   Its eyes were heavenly blue;
And if you touch that little lamb,
   "I'll put a head on you."

And so the teacher turned him out,
   But still he lingered near,
And waited patiently about,
   Then walked off on his ear.

She put him in his little bed,
   And bade him go to rest,
"You bet," the little lambkin said,
   "I'll do my level best."

🍀 🍀 🍀

Marie had von little scheep,
   His vohl vas black as ink:
She dook him out to sckate von tay,
   Und tround him in der rink.

Unt ven she go mit bed dat night,
   She tream she hear him pleating;
But ven she vake, she vas misdake,
   He only vas a skeeding.

🍀 🍀 🍀

Mary had a little lamb,
   It drank cold water freely,
And looked so innocently wise,
   She called it Horace Greely.

FROM *THE VIRGINIA SPECTATOR*, 1872

Mary had a little lamb,
   Its tail was long and straight,
And every time it ope'd its mouth,
   It bleated, *"vaccinate!"*

Mary had a little lamb,
    Whose fleece was white as snow,
And every place that Mary went
    That lamb it would *not* go.

So Mary took that little lamb,
    And beat it for a spell;—
The family had it fried next day—
    And it went very well!

FROM *INDIANA SCHOOL JOURNAL*, 1877

Mary had a little lamb,
    We've heard it o'er and o'er,
Until that little lamb becomes
    A perfect little bore.

So I propose to make a grave,
    And dig it deep and wide,
That Mary's lamb and all its bards
    Be buried side by side.

❧ *Christina Moody (age 13–16)*

MARY'S LITTLE GOAT

Mary had a little goat
    With wool upon his back;
And every time the goat did wrong,
    He got a little slap.

He followed her to school one day,
    And butted all around,
After Mary got him home,
    She whipped him good and sound.

She carried him to the sea-shore
    And took him to the bay,
When the tide was coming in,
    He'd butt the tide away.

She carried him for a motor ride,
    To see the country fair,
He butt the chauffeur out the car
    Away up in the air.

She carried him to the country
    To get a little fat,
He chased the cows and butt the pigs,
    And fought duels with a cat.

She carried him to a circus;
    So he thought he'd butt the clown
But he didn't stop a butting,
    'Till the tent was up side down.

So Mary took her goat
    And whipped him 'till he cried,
And gave him bread and water
    Until he up his heels and died.

Then Mary had his funeral,
    And she wept for her dead;
But late that night he rose again
    And butt her out of bed.

Marian Douglass

THE MOTHERLESS TURKEYS

The White Turkey was dead! The White Turkey was dead!
How the news through the barn-yard went flying!
Of a mother bereft, four small turkeys were left,
And their case for assistance was crying.
E'en the Peacock respectfully folded his tail,
As a suitable symbol of sorrow,
And his plainer wife said, "Now the old bird is dead,
Who will tend her poor chicks on the morrow?
And when evening around them comes dreary and chill
Who above them will watchfully hover?"
"Two, each night, *I* will tuck 'neath my wings," said the Duck,
Though I've eight of my own I must cover!"
"I have so *much* to do! For the bugs and the worms,
In the garden, 't is tiresome pickin';
I have nothing to spare,—for my own I must care,"
Said the Hen with one chicken.

"How I wish," said the Goose, "I could be of some use,
For my heart is with love over-brimming;
The next morning that's fine, they shall go with my nine
Little, yellow-backed goslings, out swimming!"
"I will do what I can," the old Dorking put in,
"And for help they may call upon me too,
Though I've ten of my own that are only half grown,
And a great deal of trouble to see to.
But those poor little things, they are all heads and wings,
And their bones through their feathers are stickin'!"
"Very hard it may be, but, O, don't come to me!"
Said the Hen with one chicken.

"Half my care, I suppose, there is nobody knows,—
I'm the most overburdened of mothers!
They must learn, little elves! how to scratch for themselves,
And not seek to depend upon others."
She went by with a cluck, and the Goose to the Duck
Exclaimed, in surprise, "Well, I never!"
Said the Duck, "I declare, those who have the least care,
You will find, are complaining forever!
And when all things appear to look threatening and drear,
And when troubles your pathway are thick in,
For some aid in your woe, O, beware how you go
To a Hen with one chicken!"

CHICKENS

"I didn't!" says Chip. "You did!" says Peep—
"How do you know?—you were fast asleep."
"I was under Mammy's wing,
  Stretching my legs like anything,
  When all of a sudden I turned around,
  For close beside me I heard a sound—
  A little tip and a little tap."
"Fiddle-de-dee! You'd had a nap,
  And, when you were only half-awake
  Heard an icicle somewhere break."
"What's an icicle?" "I don't know;
  Rooster tells about ice and snow,
  Something that isn't as good as meal,
  That drops down on you and makes you squeal."
"Well! swallow Rooster's tales, I beg,
  And think you didn't come out of an egg!
  I tell you I heard the old shell break,
  And the first small noise you ever could make;
  And Mammy croodled, and puffed her breast,
  And pushed us further out of the nest,
  Just to make room enough for you;
  And there's your shell—I say it's true!"
  Chip looked over his shoulder then,
  And there it lay by the old gray hen—
  Half an eggshell, chipped and brown,
  And he was a ball of yellow down,
  Clean and chipper, and smart and spry,
  With the pertest bill and the blackest eye.
"H'm!" said he, with a little perk,
"That is a wonderful piece of work!
  Peep, you silly! don't you see
  That shell isn't nearly as big as me?
  Whatever you say, Miss, I declare
  I never, never could get in there!"
"You did!" says Peep. "I didn't!" says Chip;
  With that he gave her a horrid nip,
  And Peep began to dance and peck,
  And Chip stuck out his wings and neck.
  They pranced and struck and capered about,
  Their toes turned in and their wings spread out,

As angry as two small chicks could be,
Till Mother Dorking turned to see.
She cackled and clucked, and called in vain,—
At it they went with might and main—
Till at last the old hen used her beak,
And Peep and Chip, with many a squeak
Staggered off on either side
With a very funny skip and stride.
"What dreadful nonsense!" said Mother Hen,
When she heard the story told again;
"You're bad as the two-legs that don't have wings,
Nor feathers nor combs—the wretched things!
That's the way they fight and talk
For what isn't worth a mullein-stalk.
What does it matter, I'd like to know,
Where you came from, or where you go?
Keep your temper and earn your food;
I can't scratch worms for a fighting brood.
 I won't have quarrels—I will have peace;
I hatched out chickens, so don't be geese!"
Chip scratched his ear with his yellow claw,
The meekest chicken that ever you saw;
And Peep in her feathers curled one leg,
And said to herself: "But he *was* an egg!"

Ella Wheeler Wilcox

THE HEN'S COMPLAINT

Beside an incubator stood
The would-be mother of a brood.

With drooping wings and nodding head,
These are the clucked-out words she said:

"O, vile invention of the age,
You fill me with a burning rage!

Unfeeling monster, moved by steam,
You rob me of life's sweetest dream!

Deprived of offspring which I crave,
I must go childless to my grave.

My aching wings which long to cover
A chirping brood of nestlings over,

No more may know that comfort sweet,
Since chickens may be hatched by heat.

Three weeks of quiet expectation
(Full many a flighty hen's salvation)

I am denied, for now men say
A hen should be content to lay,

And furnish eggs to incubate,
And setting hens are out of date.

Alas, for such a cruel fashion—"
The angry fowl paused, choked with passion,

While from behind a strong hand caught her
And doused her in a tub of water.

❧ *Anna Maria Wells*

THE COW-BOY'S SONG

"Mooly cow, mooly cow, home from the wood
    They sent me to fetch you as fast as I could.
    The sun has gone down: it is time to go home.
    Mooly cow, mooly cow, why don't you come?
    Your udders are full, and the milkmaid is there,
    And the children all waiting their supper to share.
    I have let the long bars down,—why don't you pass through?"
        The mooly cow only said, "Moo-o-o!"

"Mooly cow, mooly cow, have you not been
    Regaling all day where the pastures are green?
    No doubt it was pleasant, dear mooly, to see
    The clear running brook and the wide-spreading tree,
    The clover to crop, and the streamlet to wade,
    To drink the cool water and lie in the shade;
    But now it is night: they are waiting for you."
        The mooly cow only said, "Moo-o-o!"

"Mooly cow, mooly cow, where do you go,
    When all the green pastures are covered with snow?
    You go to the barn, and we feed you with hay,
    And the maid goes to milk you there, every day;
    She pats you, she loves you, she strokes your sleek hide,
    She speaks to you kindly, and sits by your side;

Then come along home, pretty mooly cow, do."
    The mooly cow only said, "Moo-o-o!"

"Mooly cow, mooly cow, whisking your tail,
The milkmaid is waiting, I say, with her pail;
She tucks up her petticoats, tidy and neat,
And places the three-leggéd stool for her seat:—
What can you be staring at, mooly? You know
That we ought to have gone home an hour ago.
How dark it is growing! O, what shall I do?"
    The mooly cow only said, "Moo-o-o!"

Peter Newell

PLAID RABBITS

I have a pair of bunnies, and their eyes are large and sad;
The coats are white as buttermilk, and also somewhat plaid.

A VICIOUS GOAT

I do not love my billy-goat, I wish that he were dead,
Because he kicked me, so he did—he kicked me with his head.

A PROPER SELECTION

A bat was caught out in a storm, and very badly fared;
So an umbrella-man he sought, and had himself repaired.

THE LITTLE RABBIT'S MISTAKE

"Hello, some rabbit's lost its tail! Too bad, I
   do declare!"
(He saw a fluffy thistle-down afloat up in
   the air.)

E. Pauline Johnson [Tekahionwake; Mohawk]

THE TRAIN DOGS

Out of the night and the north;
  Savage of breed and bone,
Shaggy and swift comes the yelping band,
Freighters of fur from the voiceless land
  That sleeps in the Arctic zone.

Laden with skins from the north,
  Beaver and bear and raccoon,
Marten and mink from the polar belts,
Otter and ermine and sable pelts—
  The spoils of the hunter's moon.

Out of the night and the north,
  Sinewy, fearless and fleet,
Urging the pack through the pathless snow,
The Indian driver, calling low,
  Follows with moccasined feet.

Ships of the night and the north,
  Freighters on prairies and plains,
Carrying cargoes from field and flood
They scent the trail through their wild red blood,
  The wolfish blood in their veins.

WILD ANIMALS

THE REINDEER AND THE RABBIT

Mary.
I wish I was a reindeer,
To gallop o'er the snow;
Over frosty Lapland drear,
So merrily I'd go.

Ann.
A little rabbit I would be,
With fur so soft and sleek,
And timid ears raised prettily,
And looks so very meek.

Mary.
But then perhaps some cruel rat,
Would find your burrow out;
Or the furious old grey cat
Might scratch your peepers out.

Ann.
'Tis true they might—but don't you know
The reindeer's wretched lot?
His dinner and his bed is snow,
And supper he has not.

Mary.
But then he is so useful, Ann;
His masters love him so!
Dear creatures, they do all they can,
And are content with snow.

Ann.
And rabbits they do naught but play,
And feed on tender clover;
They frisk and eat the live-long day,
And sleep when that is over.

Both.
Then we would be the good rein-deer,
Because he is so kind—
If useful, we need never fear,
But friends and food we'll find.

❧ *J. Steeple Davis*

THE WILD RABBITS

Among the sand-hills,
   Near by the sea,
Wild young rabbits
   Were seen by me.

They live in burrows
   With winding ways,
And there they shelter
   On rainy days.

The mother rabbits
   Make cozy nests,
With hairy linings
   From their breasts.

The tender young ones
   Are nursed and fed,
And safely hidden
   In this warm bed.

And when they are older,
   They all come out
Upon the sand-hills,
   And frisk about.

They play, and nibble
   The long, dry grass,
But scamper away
   When-ever you pass.

❧ *Eliza Lee Cabot Follen*

Billy Rabbit was a little rabbit which a boy caught in the woods, and gave to a little girl of the name of Mary. She was very attentive to the little prisoner, gave him an abundance of good things to eat, and tried her best to make him happy; but all in vain. After many attempts, he at last succeeded in making his escape, and instantly disappeared in the woods. In the course of the day, the above letter, sealed with a sharp thorn, was received by his friend Mary.

BILLY RABBIT TO MARY

ARTICHOKE WOODS

You thought, my dear Mary, you had Billy fast,
But I tried very hard, and escaped you at last;
The chance was so tempting, I thought I would *nab* it—
It was not very naughty, I'm sure, in a rabbit.

O, let not your kind heart be angry with me;
But think what a joy it is to be free,
To see the green woods, to feel the fresh air,
To skip, and to play, and to run everywhere.
The food that you gave me was pleasant and sweet,
But I'd rather be free, though with nothing to eat.

O, how glad they all were to see me come back,
And every one wanted to give me a smack.
Dick knocked over Brownie, and jumped over Bun,
And the neighbours came in to witness the fun.
My father said something, but could not be heard;
My mother looked at me, but spoke not a word;
And while she was looking, her eyes became pink,
And she shed a few tears, I verily think.

To him who a hole or a palace inhabits,
To all sorts of beings, to men, and to rabbits,
Ah! dear to us all is sweet Liberty,
Especially, Mary, to you and to me.
So I hope you'll forgive me for sending this letter,
To tell you I'm safe, and feel so much better,
Cut all sorts of capers, and act very silly,
And am your devoted, affectionate

                              BILLY.

❦ Ralph Waldo Emerson

FABLE

The mountain and the squirrel
Had a quarrel;
And the former called the latter "Little Prig";
Bun replied,
"You are doubtless very big;
But all sorts of things and weather
Must be taken in together,
To make up a year
And a sphere.
And I think it no disgrace
To occupy my place.
If I'm not so large as you,
You are not so small as I,
And not half so spry.
I'll not deny you make
A very pretty squirrel track;
Talents differ; all is well and wisely put;
If I cannot carry forests on my back,
Neither can you crack a nut."

J. Warren Newcomb, Jr.

WORK AND PLAY

In the depths of a cool and breezy wood
　　Three little children romping all day,
Frolicsome, laughing, and bright, and good,
　　Happily passing the time away.
And the old woods ring, as the children sing:
　　"O Work is all evil, and Life is all Play!"

There came a red squirrel over the ground,
　　Pattering, clattering, frisking along;
And he paused in his run at the joyous sound,
　　And stopped to list to the children's song.
"O you are not wise," he cries with surprise;
　　"You dear little ones, you are wrong, you are wrong.

"My wife and I in an old oak-tree
　　Have laid up a store of nuts and corn;
And five little babies there have we,—
　　The prettiest squirrels that ever were born.
Can we play? Nay! nay! we must work all day,
　　Till late in the night, from the earliest morn.
We gather a store for the winter cold,
　　And rest in peace when the year grows old."

There came an old crow flying over the trees,
　　Dusky and hoarse and ragged of wing;
And he paused when he heard on the passing breeze
　　The happy sound as the children sing.
And the song he broke with a surly croak:
　　"You silly young creatures, 't is no such thing!

"In the top of a tall and ancient pine,
　　Rough and rugged and ugly to see,
Is a great, strong nest,—'t is my mate's and mine;
　　And we worked hard to build it, indeed did we.
And there hide inside, their mouths open wide,
　　Nine little crows, whom we feed, you see.
We pull them corn, and we pluck them meat,
　　And we must work hard that our young may eat."

There came a fox, with a stealthy tread,—
　　Sharp nose before and long tail behind,—

And he pricked up his ears, and he tossed his head,
  As the song of the children came down the wind.
And he laughed with glee: "Yes, I see," said he,
 "One needn't go far young geese to find!

"In a burrow deep, by a ledge of rocks,
  Cosey and warm and very secure,
Is dozing in comfort good Mrs. Fox,
  With the little foxes, three or four.
And chickens we kill, their stomachs to fill,—
  It's hard enough work to do that, I'm sure.
We creep and crawl when the nights are dark,
  And shake when we hear the watch-dog's bark."

A wood-thrush sat upon a hanging spray,
  And poured from its beautiful, swelling breast
The cheerfullest, happiest roundelay,—
  All of its speckled eggs and its nest.
"We work for our young," was the song it sung;
 "To work for our loved ones is best, is best!"

In the depths of a cool and breezy wood
  Three little children romping all day,
Frolicsome, laughing, and bright, and good,
  Happily passing the time away.
And the old woods ring, as the children sing:
 "Give Work to the old folks.—the young must have Play!"

&❧ *Charles de Kay*

BOOZY LITTLE BAT

    Bat, little bat,
Up the chimney there what are you at?
Now that the Christmas clouds in the sky
Rattle with snowflakes, warm and dry,
  Wrapped in your soft leather wings,
Are you hooked up there by the toes,
    Do you doze
  Like Tommy the cat who sings
By the fender a bass to the kettle?
See him hang his head over the settle
  All upside down,
    You would think him done brown—
Yet he's in the finest of fettle!

    Bat, little bat,
Wherever you are you've a brick in
    your hat,
  Don't deny it!
How else, winters through
Could you hang in a flue
  So quiet, so quiet
Head downward? Just answer me that,
    little bat!

Oh, the secret was told me:—
  A gnarl pated goblin (no matter
  What name! small bats mustn't
    chatter)

Has blabbed, little bat,
Of the brick in your hat
Every autumn—hush, hush now, don't
scold me!
For he said, On the green
Where Titania the queen
Of fairy-land held harvest revel
You were seen
After dawn
When the fairies were gone
Fie! drinking the dregs of the nectar
potheen!

Oh, oh, who'd have thought
You, batlet, a sot

Who dwell on so lofty a level!
Teehee, little bat,
So we find it is that
Makes you snooze without care
With your heels in the air
Through the draught be tremendous and
ever so hot!

But it's never too late,
Next year when you mate
And your children are fledge,
Come down to our fire
Small brown-coated friar
And sign, like a good Father Matthew,
The temperance pledge.

Mary E[lizabeth] Burt

THE FLYING SQUIRREL

Of all the woodland creatures,
    The quaintest little sprite
Is the dainty flying squirrel
    In vest of shining white;
In coat of silver gray,
    And vest of shining white.

His furry quaker jacket
    Is trimmed with stripe of black;
A furry plume to match it
    Is curling o'er his back;
New curved with every motion,
    His plume curls o'er his back.

No little new-born baby
    Has pinker feet than he;
Each tiny toe is cushioned
    With velvet cushions three;

Three wee, pink, velvet cushions,
    Almost too small to see.

Who said, "The foot of baby
    Might tempt an angel's kiss"?
I know a score of schoolboys
    Who put their lips to this—
This wee foot of the squirrel,
    And left a loving kiss.

Gnaw on, my elfish rodent!
    Lay all the sages low!
My pretty lace and ribbons,
    They're yours for weal or woe.
My pocket-book's in tatters
    Because you like it so.

Mary L. B. Branch

A LITTLE CAPTIVE

Some one has prisoned in a cage
    A little chipmunk with black eyes;
Sometimes he gnaws the wires in rage,
    Sometimes in weary dullness lies.
        It's clear to me, he longs to be
            Over the stone wall leaping,
        Up the tall tree, nimble and free,
            Or in its hollow sleeping.

He has a soft bright coat of brown
    With pretty stripes of darker hue,
In the woods scampering up and down,
    With merry mates he throve and grew.
        And oh! and oh! he longs to go
            Back to the forest flying—
        He has a nest, for aught I know,
            Where little ones are crying.

His captor looks at him each morn,
    But has no loving word to say,
Brings him some water and some corn,
    And then forgets him all the day.
        Poor little thing! who fain would bring
            Nuts from the great trees yonder,
        Drink water from some hill-side
            spring,
            And freely, wildly wander.

Pent in a narrow wire-walled box,
    He pines in vain, no joy he takes;
The moss, the leaves, the woods, the rocks,
    For these his little sad heart aches.
        My word I plight that I to-night
            Will wake, while some are sleeping,
        And to the woods by bright moonlight
            The chipmunk shall go leaping!

❦ Anna Maria Wells

DISAPPOINTMENT

"Tick tock! tick tock!"
 Twelve at night by the clock.
  The fire is dead
  And all are in bed.
"Tick tock! tick tock!"

"Tick tark! tick tark!"
 Pussy asleep in the dark?
  Cuddled up there
  In the soft arm-chair?
"Tick tark! tick tark!"

"Tick tock! tick tock!"
 Half past one by the clock.
  Out from his hole
  The little mouse stole.
"Tick tock! tick tock!"

"Tick tock! tick tock!"
 Nothing is heard but the clock.
  The mouse ran out,—
  Puss chased him about.
"Tick tock! tick tock!"

"Tick tack! tick tack!"
 The mouse to his hole ran back.
  "No, Pussy," said he,
  "You cannot have me."
"Tick tack! tick tack!"

"Tick tock! tick tock!"
 Pussy looked up at the clock.
  The clock struck two.
  The cat cried " Mew!"
"Tick tock! tick tock!"

❦ Laura E. Richards

AN OLD RAT'S TALE

He was a rat, and she was a rat,
And down in one hole they did dwell.
And each was as black as your Sunday hat,
And they loved one another well.

He had a tail, and she had a tail;
Both long and curling and fine.
And each said, "My love's is the finest tail
In the world, excepting mine!"

He smelt the cheese, and she smelt the cheese,
And they both pronounced it good;
And both remarked it would greatly add
To the charms of their daily food.

So he ventured out and she ventured out;
And I saw them go with pain.
But what them befell I never can tell,
For they never came back again.

❧ Author Unknown

BRIDLE UP ER RAT

Bridle up er rat,
Saddle up er cat,
An' han' me down my big straw hat.

In come de cat,
Out go de rat,
Down go de baby wid 'is big straw hat.

❧ George W. Ranck

THE WAR OF THE RATS AND MICE (ALMOST A FAIRY TALE)

Far back within an age remote,
Which common history fails to note,
When dogs could talk, and pigs could sing,
And frogs obeyed a wooden king,
There lived a tribe of rats so mean,
That such a set was never seen.
For during all the livelong day
They fought and quarreled in the hay,
And then at night they robbed the mice,
Who always were so kind and nice.
They stole their bread, they stole their meat,
And all the jam they had to eat;
They gobbled up their pies and cake,
And everything the mice could bake;
They stuffed themselves with good, fresh meal,
And ruined all they could not steal;
They slapped their long tails in the butter
Until they made a frightful splutter;
Then, sleek and fine in coats of silk,
They swam about in buttermilk.
They ate up everything they found,
And flung the plates upon the ground.
And catching three mice by their tails,
They drowned them in the water-pails;
Then seeing it was morning light,
They scampered home with all their might.

The mouse-tribe, living far and near,
At once this awful thing did hear,
And all declared, with cries of rage,
A war against the rats they'd wage.
The mouse-king blew a trumpet blast,
And soon the mice came thick and fast
From every place, in every manner,
And crowded round the royal banner.
Each had a sword, a bow and arrow;
Each felt as brave as any sparrow,
And promised, in the coming fight,
To die or put the rats to flight.
The king put on a coat of mail,
And tied a bow-knot to his tail;
He wore a pistol by his side,
And on a bull-frog he did ride.
"March on!" he cried. And, hot and thick,
His army rushed, in "double quick."
And hardly one short hour had waned,
Before the ranks the rat-camp gained,
With sounding drum and screaming fife,
Enough to raise the dead to life.
The rats, awakened by the clatter,
Rushed out to see what was the matter,

Then down the whole mouse-army flew,
And many thieving rats it slew.
The mice hurrahed, the rats they
    squealed,
And soon the dreadful battle-field
Was blue with smoke and red with fire,
And filled with blood and savage ire.
The rats had eaten so much jam,
So many pies and so much ham,
And were so fat and sick and swollen
With all the good things they had stolen
That they could neither fight nor run;
And so the mice the battle won.
They threw up rat-fur in the air;
They piled up rat-tails everywhere;
And slaughtered rats bestrewed the
    ground
For ten or twenty miles around.

The rat-king galloped from the field
When all the rest were forced to yield;
But though he still retained his skin,
He nearly fainted with chagrin,
To think that in that bloody tide
So many of his rats had died.

Fierce anger blazed within his breast;
He would not stop to eat or rest;
But spurring up his fiery steed,
He seized a sharp and trusty reed—
Then, wildly shouting, rushed like hail
To cut off little mouse-king's tail.
The mouse-king's face turned red with
    passion
To see a rat come in such fashion,
For he had just that minute said
That every thieving rat was dead.
The rat was scared, and tried to run,
And vowed that he was just in fun;
But nought could quell the mouse-king's
    fury,—

He cared not then for judge or jury;
And with his sharp and quivering spear,
He pierced the rat right through the ear.
The rat fell backward in the clover,
Kicked up his legs, and all was over.
The mice, with loud and joyful tones,
Now gathered all the bad rats' bones,
And with them built a pyramid,
Down which their little children slid.
And after that eventful day
The mice in peace and joy could play,
For now no wicked rats could steal
Their cakes and jam and pies and meal,
Nor catch them by their little tails,
And drown them in the water-pails.

❦ *Author Unknown*

STORY OF A LITTLE MOUSE

I'll tell you a tale of a little gray mouse,
That lived in the pantry of grandma's old house;
He nibbled the pastry, the cake, and the cheese,
Then gambolled about at his pleasure and ease.

The moment he heard grandma open the door,
He'd scamper away to his hole in the floor;
While grandma, amazed at the loss of her cake,
Would think it was Billy, or else little Jake.

At last she espied mouse's crumbs lying round.
And said, "Ah, the rogue! he must surely be found."
And so she went hunting all over the house.
But naught could she find of the little gray mouse.

For mousey was cunning, it must be confessed,
And kept very still in his snug little nest
Until all the hunting and searching was o'er,
Then into the pantry he went as before.

He climbed on the table, then ran up the shelf—
To cake rich and creamy went helping himself;
Then into the cheese-box he poked his gray nose,
And even the butter showed marks of his toes.

One day little mousey came out as before,
And scattered the cake crumbs all over the floor,
Until of its richness he'd eaten his fill,
Then up he went, climbing a shelf higher still.

A jar partly filled with some rich golden cream,
Was partly concealed by a large wooden beam.
"Now for a feast," said the mouse, with a sigh,
"If I can but reach it—at least, I can try!"

And so he leaped up to the edge of the jar,
And took a peep down, but the cream was too far.
With all his exertion, it just touched his chin,
And he then lost his balance, and tumbled right in.

The cream filled his nose, it filled up his eyes,
It filled up his mouth and it stifled his cries.
He struggled and struggled, but all was in vain;
The cream drew him under again and again.

At last all was silent; not even his head
Was seen in the cream-pot, for mousey was dead.
With rich satisfaction did pussy's eyes gleam,
When she feasted on mousey, all covered in cream!

Laura E. Richards

A LEGEND OF LAKE OKEEFINOKEE

There once was a frog,
And he lived in a bog,
On the banks of lake Okeefinokee.
And the words of the song
That he sang all day long
Were, "Croakety croakety croaky."

Said the frog, "I have found
That my life's daily round
In this place is exceedingly poky.
So no longer I'll stop,
But I swiftly will hop
Away from Lake Okeefinokee."

Now a bad mocking-bird
By mischance overheard
The words of the frog as he spokee.
And he said, "All my life
Frog and I've been at strife,
As we lived by Lake Okeefinokee.

"Now I see at a glance
Here's a capital chance
For to play him a practical jokee.
So I'll venture to say
That he shall not to-day
Leave the banks of Lake Okeefinokee."

So this bad mocking-bird,
Without saying a word,
He flew to a tree which was oaky.
And loudly he sang,
Till the whole forest rang,
"Oh! Croakety croakety croaky!"

As he warbled this song,
Master Frog came along,
A-filling his pipe for to smokee,
And he said, "'T is some frog
Has escaped from the bog
Of Okeefinokee-finokee.

"I am filled with amaze
To hear one of my race
A-warbling on top of an oaky;
But if frogs can climb trees,
I may still find some ease
On the banks of Lake Okeefinokee."

So he climbed up the tree;
But alas! down fell he!
And his lovely green neck it was brokee;
And the sad truth to say,
Never more did he stray
From the banks of Lake Okeefinokee.

And the bad mockingbird
Said, "How very absurd
And delightful a practical jokee!"
But I'm happy to say
He was drowned the next day
In the waters of Okeefinokee.

❧ *Gertrude Heath*

IN FROGLAND

Have you heard of the country of Bogland,
    In the famous Kingdom of Frogland?
Where each plump mother frog
    On a water-soaked log
Rocks Johnny and Peter and Polly Wog?

At night in this country of Bogland,
    In this famous Kingdom of Frogland,
Have you heard the poor mother
    Scold Peter and his brother,
And the froggies in turn each scolding each other?

In this curious country of Bogland,
    In the famous Kingdom of Frogland,
Frogs are naughty, I fear,
    Each night of the year;
Just listen some evening and you shall hear!

MR. BULL-FROG'S PARTY

Mr. Bull-frog gave a supper,
　And bade his friends to the feast,
From the lower world and the upper—
　Fish, insect, bird, and beast.

The table was spread by the river,
　On a gently sloping ground;
To the water guests ran if ever
　They heard an alarming sound.

The minnows came by the dozens;
　The turtles came one by one;
The frogs brought their aunts and
　　cousins,
　But the water-rat came alone.

Each guest had his seat allotted—
　Birds, butterflies, one, two, and three;
And a little field-mouse trotted
　To her place by the side of a bee.

They ate every cress and berry,
　And they drank their dew-drop tea
To the health of their host, with merry
　And rousing three times three.

Soon after this demonstration,
　The Bull-frog rose for a speech:
"We will hold a consultation;
　I should like to hear from each.

"By enemies we're surrounded
　(My friends, you feel this is true);
We are caught, crushed, lamed, and
　　pounded;
　To stop this, what can we do?

"Life would be perfect without them;
　These creatures are all called—boys;
There's but one good thing about
　　them—
　Their coming is known by the noise.

"My friends, we'll all sign a paper,
　With fin, antenna, or wing,
To get us out of the scrape, or
　These boys to sorrow we'll bring.

"We'll bite, scratch, worry and sting them
　When we've a chance so to do,
And thus to sorrow we'll bring them;
　Now, friends, I'll listen to you."

Mistress Mousie spoke; "Remember
　That *all* boys are not so bad.
One whom I knew last September,
　To hurt would make me quite sad.

"One of my distant relations
　He did, I confess, just seize,
While he made some observations;
　But he gave him lots of cheese.

"In twenty-four hours he hurried
　To open the cage door wide,
And Mousie home to his worried
　Mamma and family hied."

Miss Mousie ceased, and Bumble Bee
　Rose, with a hum and a buzz:
"I speak for self and friend," said he,
　"Friend Caterpillar—Miss Fuzz.

"With eagerness he has sought us,
　But never has hurt at all,
I've only said 'Hum' when he caught us,
　While Fuzz rolled up in a ball."

Then up rose a gay Grasshopper,
　So fine in his green dress-coat:
"For others I care not a copper;
　On *this* boy I really dote.

"Through all the bright Summer weather,
　Through all the sunny days long,
We played in the grass together,
　And he never stopped my song."

When Dorr-Bug knocked on the table,
  "Father Long-legs" left his seat;
To speak he was quite unable,
  But showed all his legs complete.

So Bull-frog told the story
  For his venerable guest,
Adding his mite to the glory
  Of this boy of boys the best.

A gray Moth rose; "My friends," said he,
  "Pray list to this plan of mine.
On the right day, next Februar-ee,
  We'll send him a valentine.

"And it shall say—if he takes care
  To injure no living thing,
All beasts and birds of earth and air
  Will join in the offering."

'Twas settled. The supper was ended;
  The creatures went homeward with
    glee.
The way I heard it was splendid—
  A little bird told it to me.

"Olive A. Wadsworth" [*Katharine Floyd Dana*]

OVER IN THE MEADOW

Over in the meadow,
  In the sand, in the sun,
Lived an old mother-toad
  And her little toadie one.
"Wink!" said the mother;
  "I wink," said the one:
So she winked and she blinked
  In the sand, in the sun.

Over in the meadow,
  Where the stream runs blue,
Lived an old mother-fish
  And her little fishes two.
"Swim!" said the mother;
  "We swim," said the two:
So they swam and they leaped
  Where the stream runs blue.

Over in the meadow,
  In a hole in a tree,
Lived a mother-bluebird
  And her little birdies three.
"Sing!" said the mother;
  "We sing," said the three:
So they sang, and were glad,
  In the hole in the tree.

Over in the meadow,
  In the reeds on the shore,
Lived a mother-muskrat
  And her little ratties four.
"Dive!" said the mother;
  "We dive," said the four:
So they dived and they burrowed
  In the reeds on the shore.

Over in the meadow,
  In a snug beehive,
Lived a mother-honeybee
  And her little honeys five.
"Buzz!" said the mother;
  "We buzz," said the five:
So they buzzed and they hummed
  In the snug beehive.

Over in the meadow,
  In a nest built of sticks,
Lived a black mother-crow
  And her little crows six.
"Caw!" said the mother;
  "We caw," said the six:
So they cawed and they called
  In their nest built of sticks.

Over in the meadow,
 Where the grass is so even,
Lived a gay mother-cricket
 And her little crickets seven.
"Chirp!" said the mother;
 "We chirp," said the seven:
So they chirped cheery notes
 In the grass soft and even.

Over in the meadow,
 By the old mossy gate,
Lived a brown mother-lizard
 And her little lizards eight.
"Bask!" said the mother;
 "We bask," said the eight:
So they basked in the sun
 On the old mossy gate.

Over in the meadow,
 Where the clear pools shine,
Lived a green mother-frog
 And her little froggies nine.
"Croak!" said the mother;
 "We croak," said the nine:
So they croaked, and they plashed,
 Where the clear pools shine.

Over in the meadow,
 In a sly little den,
Lived a gray mother-spider
 And her little spiders ten.
"Spin!" said the mother;
 "We spin," said the ten:
So they spun lace webs
 In their sly little den.

Over in the meadow,
 In the soft summer even,
Lived a mother-fire-fly
 And her little flies eleven.
"Shine!" said the mother;
 "We shine," said the eleven:
So they shone like stars
 In the soft summer even.

Over in the meadow,
 Where the men dig and delve,
Lived a wise mother-ant
 And her little anties twelve,
"Toil!" said the mother;
 "We toil," said the twelve:
So they toiled, and were wise,
 Where the men dig and delve.

Hannah Flagg Gould

THE ENVIOUS LOBSTER

A Lobster from the water came,
And saw another, just the same
In form and size; but gayly clad
In scarlet clothing; while she had
No other clothing on her back
Than her old suit of greenish black.

"So ho!" she cried, "'tis very fine!
 Your dress was yesterday like mine;
And in the mud below the sea,

You lived, a crawling thing, like me.
But now, because you've come ashore,
You've grown so proud, that what you
 wore—
Your strong old suit of bottle-green,
You think improper to be seen.
To tell the truth, I don't see why
You should be better dressed than I.
And I should like a suit of red
As bright as yours, from feet to head.

I think I'm quite as good as you,
And might be clothed in scarlet too."

"Will you be boiled," her owner said,
"To be arrayed in glowing red?
Come here, my discontented miss,
And hear the scalding kettle hiss!
Will you go in, and there be boiled,
To have your dress, so old and soiled,
Exchanged for one of scarlet hue?"
"Yes," cried the Lobster, "that I'll do,
And twice as much, if needs must be,
To be as gayly clad as she."
Then, in she made a fatal dive,
And never more was seen alive!

Now, if you ever chance to know,
Of one as fond of dress and show
As that vain Lobster, and withal
As envious, you'll perhaps recall
To mind her folly, and the plight
In which she reappeared to sight.

She had obtained a bright array,
But for it, thrown herself away!
Her life and death were best untold,
But for the moral they unfold!

❧ Author Unknown

FISHING SIMON

Simon tuck his hook an' pole,
An' fished on Sunday we's been told.
Fish dem water death bells ring,
Talk from out'n de water, sing—
"Bait yō' hook, Simon!
Drap yō' line, Simon!
Now ketch me, Simon!
Pull me out, Simon!
Take me home, Simon!
Now clean me, Simon!
Cut me up now, Simon!
Now salt me, Simon!
Now fry me, Simon!
Dish me up now, Simon!
Eat me all, Simon!"
Simon e't till he wus full.
Still dat fish keep his plate full.
Simon want no mō' at all,
Fish say dat he mus' eat all.
Simon's sick, so he throw up!
He give Sunday fishin' up.

Laura E. Richards

THE SHARK

Oh, blithe and merrily sang the shark,
   As he sat on the house-top high,
A-cleaning his boots, and smoking cheroots,
   With a single glass in his eye.

With Martin and Day he polished away,
   And a smile on his face did glow,
While merry and bold the chorus he trolled
   Of "Gobble-em-upsky ho!"

He sang so loud he astonished the crowd
   Which gathered from far and near,
For they said, "Such a sound in the country round
   We never, no never did hear."

He sang of the ships he'd eaten like chips,
   In the palmy days of his youth;
And he added, "If you don't believe it is true,
   Pray examine my wisdom tooth!"

He sang of the whales who'd have given their tails
   For a glance of his raven eye;
And the swordfish too, who their weapons drew,
   And vowed for his sake they'd die.

He sang about wrecks, and hurricane decks
   And the mariner's perils and pains,
Till every man's blood up on end it stood,
   And their hair ran cold in their veins.

But blithe as a lark the merry old shark
   Sat on the sloping roof;
Though he said, "It is queer that no one draws near
   To examine my wisdom tooth!"

He carolled away by night and by day,
   Until he made every one ill;
And I'll wager a crown that unless he's come down
   He is probably carolling still.

THE REVENGE OF THE LITTLE HIPPOPOTAMUS

A fat young hippopotamus
    Sat grimly by the Nile,
Contriving dire vengeance
    On a lady crocodile,
Who, that morning, for her breakfast
    Ate up his brothers twain;
So he pondered long and deeply
    How to pay her back again.

All at once an idea struck him,
    And he broke into a smile.
"I have it!" cried he, joyfully;
    "I'll fix that crocodile!"
Then he trotted through the rushes
    Until he reached dry land,
When he crept along quite silently
    To a mound in the hot sand,

Where the crocodile had buried
    Her eggs, because she knew
The torrid sun would hatch them
    Within a month or two.
Now, the savage mother-reptile
    Was nowhere to be seen,
For she was calmly slumbering
    Among the rushes green.

The little hippopotamus
    Moved cautiously and slow,
Until he saw the heap of eggs,—
    Then laughed he long and low.

Then boldly he marched forward,
    And stamped upon that nest,
And jumped and kicked and pranced about
    As if he were possessed,

Till all the eggs were scattered
    And broken every one,
While all the little crocodiles
    Forth from the shells did run.
The ancient mother-crocodile,
    Hearing her young ones' wail,
Came rushing from her muddy couch,
    Waving her frightful tail.

The little hippopotamus
    Was having then huge fun.
Stepping upon the babies,
    To smash them one by one;
So he failed to see the mother,
    Nor dreamed of his mishap,
Till—whack! against his side so fat
    There came an awful slap.

It lifted him from off his feet,
    And hurled him up on high,
And away he went careering
    Like a rocket in the sky.
How far he flew I know not,
    But 't is said that he was thrown
On the pyramid of Cheops,
    Straddling the topmost stone.

Being too fat to clamber down,
   He may be there this day,
Unless some one in a balloon
   Has carried him away.
But of this you may be certain,
   That if he is not found
In the air or in the water,
   He's somewhere on the ground.

✿ *Oliver Herford*

THE GIRAFFE

See the Gi-raffe; he is so tall
There is not room to get him all
Upon the page. His head is high-er—
The pic-ture proves it—than the Spire.
That's why the natives, when they race
To catch him, call it stee-ple-chase.
His chief de-light is to set
A good example: shine or wet
He rises ere the break of day,
And starts his break-fast right away.
His food has such a way to go,—
His throat's so very long,—and so
An early break-fast he must munch
To get it down ere time for lunch.

SONG OF THE TURTLE AND FLAMINGO

(Written for BOYLY BUMPS and WILLY BO LEE.)

A lively young turtle lived down by the
    banks
  Of a dark-rolling stream called the Jingo,
And one summer day, as he went out to
    play,
  Fell in love with a charming flamingo—
    An enormously genteel flamingo!
    An expansively crimson flamingo!
    A beautiful, bouncing flamingo!

Spake the turtle in tones like a delicate
    wheeze:
  "To the water I've oft seen you in go,
And your form has impressed itself deep
    on my shell,
    You perfectly modeled flamingo!
    You uncommonly brilliant flamingo!
    You tremendously 'A one' flamingo!
    You inex-pres-*si*-ble flamingo!

"To be sure I'm a turtle, and you are a
    belle,
  And *my* language is not your fine lingo;
But smile on me, tall one, and be my
    bright flame,
    You miraculous, wondrous flamingo!
    You blazingly beauteous flamingo!
    You turtle-absorbing flamingo!
    You inflammably gorgeous flamingo!"

Then the proud bird blushed redder than
    ever before,
  And that was quite un-nec-ces-*sa*-ry,
And she stood on one leg and looked out
    of one eye,
  The position of things for to vary,—
    This aquatical, musing flamingo!
    This dreamy, uncertain flamingo!
    This embarrassing, harassing
      flamingo!

Then she cried to the quadruped, greatly
    amazed:
  "Why your passion toward *me* do you
    hurtle?
I'm an ornithological wonder of grace,
  And you're an illogical turtle,—
    A waddling, impossible turtle!
    A low-minded, grass-eating turtle!
    A highly improbable turtle!"

Then the turtle sneaked off with his nose
    to the ground,
  And never more looked at the lasses;
And falling asleep, while indulging his
    grief,
  Was gobbled up whole by Agassiz,—
    The peripatetic Agassiz!
    The turtle-dissecting Agassiz!
    The illustrious, industrious Agassiz!

Go with me to Cambridge some cool,
    pleasant day,
  And the skeleton-lover I'll show you;
He's in a hard case, but he'll look in your
    face,
  Pretending (the rogue!) he don't know
    you!
    Oh, the deeply deceptive young turtle!
    The double-faced, glassy-cased turtle!
    The *green*, but a very *mock*-turtle!

Oliver Herford

A CHAMELEON

A use-ful lesson you may con,
My Child, from the Cha-me-le-on:
He has the gift, ex-treme-ly rare
In an-i-mals, of sav-oir-faire.
And if the se-cret you would guess
Of the Cha-me-le-on's suc-cess,
A-dapt your-self with great-est care
To your sur-round-ings ev-er-y-where;
And then, un-less your sex pre-vent,
Some day you may be Pres-i-dent.

Charles Edward Carryl

THE PLAINT OF THE CAMEL

Canary-birds feed on sugar and seed,
    Parrots have crackers to crunch;
And, as for the poodles, they tell me the
        noodles
    Have chickens and cream for their
        lunch.
        But there's never a question
        About MY digestion—
    ANYTHING does for me!

Cats, you're aware, can repose in a chair,
    Chickens can roost upon rails;
Puppies are able to sleep in a stable,
    And oysters can slumber in pails.
        But no one supposes
        A poor Camel dozes—
    ANY PLACE does for me!

Lambs are enclosed where it's never
        exposed,
    Coops are constructed for hens;
Kittens are treated to houses well heated,
    And pigs are protected by pens.
        But a Camel comes handy
        Wherever it's sandy—
    ANYWHERE does for me!

People would laugh if you rode a giraffe,
    Or mounted the back of an ox;
It's nobody's habit to ride on a rabbit,
    Or try to bestraddle a fox.
        But as for a Camel, he's
        Ridden by families—
    ANY LOAD does for me!

A snake is as round as a hole in the
        ground,
    And weasels are wavy and sleek;
And no alligator could ever be straighter
    Than lizards that live in a creek,
        But a Camel's all lumpy
        And bumpy and humpy—
    ANY SHAPE does for me!

TOYS AND PLAY

Agnes Lee

FINDING THINGS

I love to roam around,
And look on trees and skies.
Yet sometimes fixed upon the ground
I keep my watchful eyes.

For finding things is fun!
Now have you ever tried?
One day I found a little bun
With berries baked inside.

And once it was a cent,
And once it was a dime!
A corkscrew very oddly bent
I found, another time.

I found a little toy,
Down where the wild brook sings.
Oh! am I not a lucky boy,
To find so many things?

Josephine Preston Peabody

THE BUSY CHILD

I have so many things to do
I don't know when I shall be through.

To-day I had to watch the rain
Come sliding down the window-pane.

And I was humming all the time,
Around my head, a kind of rhyme;

And blowing softly on the glass
To see the dimness come and pass.

I made a picture, with my breath
Rubbed out to show the underneath.

I built a city on the floor;
And then I went and was a War.

And I escaped from square to square
That's greenest on the carpet there.

Until at last I came to Us;
But it was very dangerous.

Because if I had stepped outside,
I made believe I should have died!

And now I have the boat to mend,
And all our supper to pretend.

I am so busy, every day,
I haven't any time to play.

PLAYTHINGS

Not much to make us happy
   Do any of us need;
But just the right thing give us,
   And we are rich indeed.

Even as with men and women
   It is with girls and boys;
Why should you shower on Jeanie
   So many dear-bought toys?

Some bits of broken china,
   A handful of corn-floss,
A shred or two of ribbon,
   A strip of velvet moss;

With her family of rag-children,
   And the wide clean earth around,—
No happier little housewife
   Can anywhere be found.

But Nannie dear would rather
   Leave Jeanie to her play,
And wander by the streamlet,
   Or on the hill-top stray.

For a little white cloud passing,
   A ripple on the brook,
Much more her heart enriches
   Than playhouse, doll, or book.

Half Nannie's wealth lies hidden
   Under the rock's green shelf:
You cannot find it for her;
   She keeps the key herself.

Wild John likes forest-freedom,
   And room for boundless noise,
Better than spending-money,
   Or a cityful of toys.

And small Ned with a shingle
   Digs in his heap of sand;
Never swayed Inca sceptre
   Upon a throne so grand.

With large and little children
   The trouble is the same;
What pleases us, to others
   Is wearisome and tame.

Good friends, your entertainment
   A well-meant plan may be;
But he's our benefactor
   Who simply leaves us free.

*Andrew R. Smith

LINES ON THE SCHOOL FAIR

The work of children here you find,
The fruit of labor and of mind,
Three months are past, the day is come,
And he that gains shall have the sum.
   Although our minds are weak and
      feeble.
   Some can use a knife or needle:
   If fortune by my side will stand,
   I mean to join the happy band.

A girl can make a frock or coat,
A boy, a pretty little boat;
Another girl, a pretty quilt,
A handsome cap, or gown of silk.
   T' excel we all will work and strive,
   Till to perfection we arrive;
   Many will work and strive in vain,
   The fifty tickets to obtain.
Our little fair to us is great

As any other in the state;
It is a cheerful time to some,
Though idle scholars will not come.
   The child that comes to this good
      school
   Should never rest an idle fool;
   Though there are many, once were so,
   We find them daily wiser grow.

The beauties of our little fair
You will not know, if you're not there;
It will be taking too much time,
To enter all the things in rhyme.
   You'll find mistakes I do not doubt,
   And if you do, please leave them out.

❧ *Amos Russel Wells*

BY PROXY

Young Timothy Timid is cautious and wealthy;
He has heard that bicycle owners are healthy,
And being himself but a weak-chested youth,
He bought him a wheel,—and a beauty, in truth.
"A pity," he said, as he viewed it with pride,
"To scar it and batter it learning to ride;
And worse (what is likely) to batter myself.
I cannot do better than hire with my pelf
Some cycler to ride in my stead, and be rid
Of all danger and worry and work." So he did.

❧ *Anne L. Huber*

WON'T I, AND I WON'T

When I shall grow to be a man,
   Won't I have lots of fun?
Then I shall have a high-crowned hat,
   And a righty, dighty gun.

Then I won't have to wear a bib,
   Or have my hair in curls,
And I can dance in high-heeled boots,
   With all the pretty girls.

Then I won't play with pussy-cat
   Or with the big dog Dash,
And I shall have my second teeth,
   And a handsome, curled moustache.

Samuel Griswold Goodrich

MY FIRST WHISTLE

Of all the toys I e'er have know,
　　I loved that whistle best;
It was my first, it was my own,
　　And I was doubly blest.

'T was Saturday, and after noon,
　　That school-boys' jubilee,
When the young heart is all in tune,
　　From book and ferule free.

I then was in my seventh year;
　　The birds were all a singing;
Above a brook, that rippled clear,
　　A willow tree was swinging.

My brother Ben was very 'cute,
　　He climbed that willow tree,
He cut a branch, and I was mute,
　　The while, with ecstasy.

With penknife he did cut it round,
　　And gave the bark a wring;
He shaped the mouth and tried the sound,—
　　It was a glorious thing!

I blew that whistle, full of joy—
　　It echoed o'er the ground;
And never, since that simple toy,
　　Such music have I found.

I've seen blue eyes and tasted wines—
　　With manly toys been blest,
But backward memory still inclines
　　To love that whistle best.

Eugene Field

THE DUEL

The gingham dog and the calico cat
Side by side on the table sat;
'Twas half past twelve, and (what do you think!)
Nor one nor t'other had slept a wink!
   The old Dutch clock and the Chinese plate
   Appeared to know as sure as fate
There was going to be a terrible spat.
        (I wasn't there; I simply state
        What was told to me by the Chinese plate!)

The gingham dog went "bow-wow-wow!"
And the calico cat replied "mee-ow!"
The air was littered, an hour or so,
With bits of gingham and calico,
   While the old Dutch clock in the chimney place
   Up with its hands before its face,
For it always dreaded a family row!
        (Now mind: I'm only telling you
        What the old Dutch clock declares is true!)

The Chinese plate looked very blue,
And wailed, "Oh dear! what shall we do!"
But the gingham dog and the calico cat
Wallowed this way and tumbled that,
   Employing every tooth and claw
   In the awfullest way you ever saw—
And, oh! how the gingham and calico flew!
        (Don't fancy I exaggerate—
        I got my news from the Chinese plate!)

Next morning, where the two had sat
They found no trace of dog or cat;
And some folks think unto this day
That burglars stole that pair away!
   But the truth about the cat and pup
   Is this: they ate each other up!
Now what do you really think of that!
        (The old Dutch clock it told me so,
        And that is how I came to know.)

AMONG THE ANIMALS

One rainy morning,
    Just for a lark,
I jumped and stamped
    On my new Noah's Ark:
I crushed an elephant,
    Smashed a gnu,
And snapped a camel
    Clean in two;
I finished the wolf
    Without half tryin',
And wild hyena,
    And roaring lion;
I knocked down Ham,
    And Japhet, too,
And cracked the legs
    Of the kangaroo;

I finished, beside,
    Two pigs and a donkey,
A polar bear,
    Opossum, and monkey;
Also the lions,
    Tigers, and cats,
And dromedaries,
    And tiny rats—
There wasn't a thing
    That didn't feel,
Sooner or later,
    The weight o' my heel;
I felt as grand
    As grand could be—
But oh the whipping
    My mammy gave me!

A. C.

THE SONG OF THE ROLLER SKATES

(THE START.)

Swoop-a-hoo! swoop-a-hoo!
To the left, to the right;
Swoop-a-hoo! swoop-a-hoo!
On our rollers so bright!
Swoop-a-hoo! here we go;
All a-gliding along;
Swoop-a-hoo! here we go;
With a roller-skate song!

Whiz-a-whir! whiz-a-whir!
What a rush, what a stir!
All the children in the town
Whining down, whizzing down!

(THE TURN.)

Slower now. Have a care!
Here's the corner,—beware!
See the curb! It is near;
We must carefully steer.
Sweep around, one and all!
Make the curve,—do not fall!
    —That was gracefully done.
    Hurrah for the fun!

Whiz-a-whir! whiz-a-whir!
What a rush, what a stir!
Every child on the track
Whizzing back! whizzing back!

(*HOME AGAIN.*)

Swoop-a-hoo! swoop-a-hoo!
To the left,—to the right.
Swoop-a-hoo! swoop-a-hoo!
All aglow with delight!
Swoop-a-hoo! who's ahead?
Well, they're all nearly there.
Swoop-a-hoo! cheeks so red;
Full of laughter, the air!
Swoop-a-hoo! swoop-a-hoo! swoop-a-hoo!

✺ *Author Unknown*

THE SKATER'S SONG

To be said or sung, with a nimble tongue

Here we go,
　Steady and slow,
Plodding awhile behind;
　Faster we hie,
　Till away we fly,
Swift as the northern wind.

　Blithe and gay,
　We speed our way,
Over the ice-bound river;
　From side to side,
　Like a bird we glide,
Or a dart from an Indian's quiver.

　Look out! look out,
　Mind what you're about,
And skilfully guide your feet;
　Take care! take care!
　Or ere you're aware,
Your head will be cracking the sleet.

　There, down he goes—
　I pity his woes,
For he falls like a bar of lead;
　Now he can tell,
　I ween, pretty well,
Whether ice is as hard as his head.

　Ha! ha! you see
　He's as merry as we
And he's up and off again.
　Now for a race,
　With a quicker pace,
Over the glassy plain.

　Blithe and gay,
　We speed our way,
Over the ice-bound river;
　From side to side,
　Like a bird we glide,
Or a dart from an Indian's quiver.

　Away we fly
　And the wind outvie,
And our spirits keep time with the flight;
　Thus the day
　Glides away,
And sweetly blends with night.

　Thanks we'll give,
　While we live,
That our hearts are free from sorrow;
　And though we play
　With such glee to-day,
We'll study the better to-morrow.

From side to side,
  Like a bird we glide,
Till the twilight time is o'er;
  And when at last,
  Our sport is past,
We'll glide like a bird to the shore.

  And now we go
  Over the snow,
To our happy homes away,
  Tripping along,
  With mirth and song,
Till we come—to the end of our lay.

Benjamin Franklin King

TOBOGGAN

Down from the hills and over the snow
Swift as a meteor's flash we go,
  Toboggan! Toboggan! Toboggan!
Down from the hills with our senses lost,
Jealous of cheeks that are kissed by the
    frost,
  Toboggan! Toboggan! Toboggan!

With snow piled high on housetop and
    hill,
O'er frozen rivulet, river, and rill,
Clad in her jacket of sealskin and fur,
Down from the hills I'm sliding with her,
  Toboggan! Toboggan! Toboggan!

Down from the hills, what an awful
    speed!
As if on the back of a frightened steed,
  Toboggan! Toboggan! Toboggan!
Down from the hills at the rise of the
    moon,
Merrily singing the toboggan tune,
  "Toboggan! Toboggan! Toboggan!"

Down from the hills like an arrow we fly,
Or a comet that whizzes along through
    the sky;
Down from the hills! Oh, isn't it grand!
Clasping your best winter girl by the
    hand,
  Toboggan! Toboggan! Toboggan!

Down from the hills and both growing
    old,
Down from the hills we are nearing the
    fold:
  Toboggan! Toboggan! Toboggan!
Close to the homestead we hear the ring
Of children's voices that cheerily sing,
  "Toboggan! Toboggan! Toboggan!"

Down from the hills and we hear the
    chime
Of bells that are ringing out Old Father
    Time;
Down from the hills we are riding away,
Nearing the life with its endless day;
  Toboggan! Toboggan! Toboggan!

Henry Wadsworth Longfellow

THE CASTLE-BUILDER

A gentle boy, with soft and silken locks,
　A dreamy boy, with brown and tender eyes,
A castle-builder, with his wooden blocks,
　And towers that touch imaginary skies.

A fearless rider on his father's knee,
　An eager listener unto stories told
At the Round Table of the nursery,
　Of heroes and adventures manifold.

There will be other towers for thee to build;
　There will be other steeds for thee to ride;
There will be other legends, and all filled
　With greater marvels and more glorified.

Build on, and make thy castles high and fair,
　Rising and reaching upward to the skies;
Listen to voices in the upper air,
　Nor lose thy simple faith in mysteries.

Rudolph F. Bunner

THE GIPSIES

Where poplars run up in the air,
Where autumn fields lie wide and bare,
　Their tent the gipsies make;
And one white horse—'most lean as those
On which you dry the new-washed clothes—
　Now browses by a stake.

We know they never stole from us;
But since the neighbors make a fuss,
　We're told to stay away;
And flocks of geese no more can roam
O'er the wide fields afar from home,
　Where once we used to play.

But, standing by the mullen rocks,
Where little burs catch in our frocks,
    A flag of truce we wave
To Elta Geeze, the gipsy boy,
Who comes to trade, with toy for toy,
    And face so brown and grave.

He brings to trade the queerest toys
That ever were for girls or boys;
    And when we laugh he smiles.
We give him cookies, dolls, and cake;
He gives us things strange people make,
    Brought to us many miles.

And once he brought his violin,—
A queer green bag 't was carried in,—
    Then, like a magic spell,
He played us such a merry jig!
The village fiddler's twice as big
    But can't play half so well.

We see, from the last garden gate,
Their white-brown tent at twilight late,
    Where the red wood-fire gleams;
And when the doors are closed all round,
We know the gipsy boy sleeps sound,
    To dream his gipsy dreams.

Until, some morning—strange and bare
The fields look; for the gipsies fare
    On roads far, far away.
So we play we are gipsies now,
Where the tall poplar-trees bow,
    Near sumacs red and gay—
We play that we are gipsies, too,
In tents of quilts the light shines through,
    Where leafy shadows sway.

❧ Eliza Lee Cabot Follen

IT CAN'T BE SO

A boy once went the world around,
Till he a golden castle found;
    Then laughed the boy,
    Then thought the boy,
"O, were that golden castle mine,
  How brightly then my house would shine!"
        O, no! O, no! O, no!
  My little boy, it can't be so.

Again he went the world around,
Till he a flying pony found;
    Then laughed the boy,
    Then thought the boy,
"O, were that flying pony mine,
  Then I should be a horseman fine."
        O, no! O, no! O, no!
My little boy, it can't be so.

❧ Author Unknown

LOVE IN A NOAH'S ARK

  Only a wooden lady,
With but half an arm at most;
  Yet her look is so quaint,
  And so fresh is her paint,
My heart is forever lost!

  Only a wooden lady,
Is all that your eyes can see;
  But the straight up and down
  Of her plain wooden gown
Has a hundred charms for me.

  Only a wooden lady!
But that doesn't alter my plan,
  For, in spite of that clause,
  I can love her, because
I'm only a wooden man!

❧ Sarah Orne Jewett

ONLY A DOLL!

Polly, my dolly! why don't you grow?
    Are you a dwarf, my Polly?
I'm taller and taller every day;
    How high the grass is!—do you see that?
The flowers are growing like weeds, they say;
    The kitten is growing into a cat!
        Why don't you grow, my dolly?

Here is a mark upon the wall.
    Look for yourself, my Polly!
I made it a year ago, I think.
    I've measured you very often, dear,
But, though you've plenty to eat and drink,
    You haven't grown a bit for a year.
        Why don't you grow, my dolly?

Are you never going to try to talk?
    You're such a silent Polly!
Are you never going to say a word?
    It isn't hard; and oh! don't you see
The parrot is only a little bird,
    But he can chatter so easily.
        You're quite a dunce, my dolly!

Let's go and play by the baby-house;
    You are my dearest Polly!
There are other things that do not grow;
    Kittens can't talk, and why should you?
You are the prettiest doll I know;
    You are a darling—that is true!
        Just as you are, my dolly!

Lucy Larcom

A DOLL'S WEDDING

Says Ivanhoe to Mimi:
   "It is our wedding-day;
And will you promise, dearest,
   Your husband to obey?"

And this is Mimi's answer:
   "With all my heart, my dear;
If you will never cause me
   To drop a single tear;

"If you will ask me nothing
   But what I want to do,
I'll be a sweet, obedient,
   Delightful wife to you."

Says Mr. Fenwick, giving
   His brown mustache a twist:
"I shall command you, madam,
   To do whate'er I list!"

Miss Mimi answers, frowning,
   His very soul to freeze:
"Then, sir, I shall obey you
   Only just when I please!"

Says Ivanhoe to Mimi
   "Let us to this agree,—
I will not speak one word to you,
   If you'll not speak to me;

"Then we shall never quarrel,
   But through our dolly-life
I'll be a model husband,
   And you a model wife!"

And now all men and women
   Who make them wedding-calls,
Look on, and almost envy
   The bliss of these two dolls.

They seem so very smiling,—
   So graceful, kind, and bright!
And gaze upon each other
   Quite speechless with delight.

Never one cross word saying,
   They stand up side by side
Patterns of good behavior
   To every groom and bride.

Sweethearts, it is far better,—
   This truth they plainly teach,—
The solid gold of silence,
   Than the small change of speech!

Laura E. Richards

BELINDA BLONDE

Belinda Blonde was a beautiful doll,
With rosy-red cheeks and a flaxen poll;
Her lips were red, and her eyes were blue.
But to say she was happy would not be true;
For she pined for love of the great big Jack
Who lived in the box so grim and black.
She never had looked on the Jack his face,
But she fancied him shining with beauty and grace;

And all the day long she would murmur and pout,
Because Jack-in-the-box would never come out.
"Oh, beautiful, beautiful Jack-in-the-box!
Undo your bolts and undo your locks!
The cupboard is shut, and there's no one about;
Oh, Jack-in-the-box! jump out, jump out!"
But, alas, alas for Belinda Blonde!
And alas, alas for her dreamings fond!
There soon was an end to all her doubt,
For Jack-in-the-box really *did* jump out!—
Out with a crash, and out with a spring,
Half black and half scarlet, a horrible thing;
Out with a yell and out with a shout,
His great goggle-eyes glaring wildly about.
"Alas! Alas!" cried Belinda Blonde;
"Is this the end of my dreamings fond?
Is this my love, and is this my dear,
This hideous, glowering monster here?
Alas, alas!" cried Belinda fair.
She wrung her hands and she tore her hair,
Till at length, as the dolls who were witnesses say,
She fell on the ground and she fainted away.

MORAL

Now all you dolls, both little and big,
With china crown and with curling wig,
Before you give way to affection fond,
Remember the fate of Belinda Blonde;
And unless you wish to get terrible knocks,
Don't set your heart on a Jack-in-the-box.

Margaret Vandegrift

THE DEAD DOLL

You needn't be trying to comfort me—I tell you my dolly is dead!
There's no use in saying she isn't, with a crack like that in her head.
It's just like you said it wouldn't hurt much to have my tooth out, that day;
And then, when the man 'most pulled my head off, you hadn't a word to say.

And I guess you must think I'm a baby, when you say you can mend it with glue!
As if I didn't know better than that! Why, just suppose it was you?
You might make her *look* all mended—but what do I care for looks?
Why, glue's for chairs and tables, and toys, and the backs of books!

My dolly! my own little daughter! Oh, but it's the awfulest crack!
It just makes me sick to think of the sound when her poor head went whack
Against that horrible brass thing that holds up the little shelf.
Now, Nursey, what makes you remind me? I know that I did it myself!

I think you must be crazy—you'll get her another head!
What good would forty heads do her? I tell you my dolly is dead!
And to think I hadn't quite finished her elegant new Spring hat!
And I took a sweet ribbon of hers last night to tie on that horrid cat!

When my mamma gave me that ribbon—I was playing out in the yard—
She said to me, most expressly, "Here's a ribbon for Hildegarde."
And I went and put it on Tabby, and Hildegarde saw me do it;
But I said to myself, "Oh, never mind, I don't believe she knew it!"

But I know that she knew it now, and I just believe, I do,
That her poor little heart was broken, and so her head broke too.
Oh, my baby! my little baby! I wish *my* head had been hit!
For I've hit it over and over, and it hasn't cracked a bit.

But since the darling *is* dead, she'll want to be buried, of course;
We will take my little wagon, Nurse, and you shall be the horse;
And I'll walk behind and cry; and we'll put her in this, you see—
This dear little box—and we'll bury her then under the maple-tree.

And papa will make me a tombstone, like the one he made for my bird;
And he'll put what I tell him on it—yes, every single word!
I shall say: "Here lies Hildegarde, a beautiful doll, who is dead;
She died of a broken heart, and a dreadful crack in her head."

John Townsend Trowbridge

THE LITTLE THEATRE

I know a little theatre
  Scarce bigger than a nut.
Finer than pearl its portals are,
Quick as the twinkling of a star
  They open and they shut.

A fairy palace beams within:
  So wonderful it is,
No words can tell you of its worth,—
No architect in all the earth
  Could build a house like this.

A beautiful rose window lets
  A ray into the hall;
To shade the scene from too much light,
A tiny curtain hangs in sight,
  Within the crystal wall.

And O the wonders there beside!
  The curious furniture,
The stage, with all its small machinery,
Pulley and cord and shifting scenery,
  In marvelous miniature!

A little, busy, moving world,
    It mimics space and time,
The marriage-feast, the funeral,
Old men and little children, all
    In perfect pantomime.

There pours the foaming cataract,
    There speeds the train of cars;
Day comes with all its pageantry
Of cloud and mountain, sky and sea,
    The night, with all its stars.

Ships sail upon that mimic sea;
    And smallest things that fly,
The humming-bird, the sunlit mote
Upon its golden wings afloat,
    Are mirrored in that sky.

Quick as the twinkling of the doors,
    The scenery forms or fades;
And all the fairy folk that dwell

Within the arched and windowed shell
    Are momentary shades.

Who has this wonder holds it dear
    As his own life and limb;
Who lacks it, not the rarest gem
That ever flashed in diadem
    Can purchase it for him.

Ah, then, dear picture-loving child,
    How doubly blessed art thou!
Since thine the happy fortune is
To have two little worlds like this
    In thy possession now,—

Each furnished with soft folding-doors,
    A curtain, and a stage!
And now a laughing sprite transfers
Into those little theatres
    The letters of this page.

❧ *Carolyn Wells*

OUR CLUB

We're going to have the mostest fun!
    It's going to be a club;
And no one can belong to it
    But Dot and me and Bub.

We thought we'd have a Reading Club,
    But couldn't 'cause, you see,
Not one of us knows how to read—
    Not Dot nor Bub nor me.

And then we said a Sewing Club,
    But thought we'd better not;
'Cause none of us knows how to sew—
    Not me nor Bub nor Dot.

And so it's just a Playing Club,
    We play till time for tea;
And, oh, we have the bestest times!
    Just Dot and Bub and me.

Josephine Preston Peabody

SECRETS

I have a secret to myself
That no one else can see.
I hum it over to myself
And no one hears but me.
Something you don't know!
I knew it long ago.
And the more I never tell you it,
The more it gets to be.

It makes me feel as purry
As a kitten on your knee.
It makes me feel as round and warm
As a sparrow on that tree.
It makes me puff my feathers out
The way he puffs out his.
And if you think I haven't one,
I'll tell you what it is,
         —Maybe!

Clinton Scollard

THE POP-CORN MAN

There's a queer little man lives down the street
Where two of the broadest highways meet,
In a queer little house that's half of it glass,
With windows open to all who pass,
And a low little roof that's nearly flat,
And a chimney as black as Papa's best hat.
Oh, the house is built on this funny plan
Because it's the home of the pop-corn man!

How does he sleep, if he sleeps at all?
He must roll up like a rubber ball,
Or like a squirrel, and store himself
All huddly-cuddly under the shelf.
If he wanted to stretch he'd scarce have space
In his bare little, spare little, square little place.
He seems like a rat cooped up in a can,
This brisk little, frisk little pop-corn man!

I know he's wise by the way he looks,
For he's just like the men I've seen in books,
With his hair worn off, and his squinty eyes,
And his wrinkles, too,—oh, I know he's wise!
And then just think of the way he makes
The corn all jump into snowy flakes,
With a "pop! pop! pop!" in his covered pan,
This queer little, dear little pop-corn man!

BABEL

Three little maidens chanced, one day,
To meet together while at play;
"I'm very glad you came this way,"
The first, a social little maid,
Delighted, to the second said:
"Tell me your name, and I'll tell mine,—
It's Cora Dora Waterpine."

The second giggled, as she said
These words; she shook her curly head.
"Ach, ach! ich kann dich nicht versteh'n,"
Back laughingly the answer sped,
Whilst to the third she spoke again:
"Was sagt das Mädchen? Wenn du's
    weiszt,
Zu hören würde ich gereizt."

The third—she was a merry wight—
Stood giggling, too, with all her might:
But, suddenly, her cheeks grew bright,
"En vérité! En vérité!"
Softly, the others heard her say,
"Je sais que ce n'est pas poli—
Peut-on me blâmer si je ris?"

Three little maidens standing there,
Each with a puzzled, solemn air.
A moment silent, paused to stare
But, "If I ever!" Speedily
The first one cried: "It can not be
That my words are as yours to me;
Come, tell your names, and I'll tell
    mine,—
It's Cora Dora Waterpine."

'But still the second shook her head,
Backward the merry answer sped,
E'en merrier than before she said:
"Ach, ach, ich kann dich nicht versteh'n!"
So to the other spoke again.
"Was sagt das Mädchen? Wenn du's
    weiszt,
Zu hören würde ich gereizt."

And still the third—this jolly wight—
Stood giggling, too, with all her might:
Till once again her cheeks grew bright,
And once again they heard her say,
With accent soft and motion gay:
"En vérite! En vérité!
Je sais que ce n'est pas poli—
Peut-on me blâmer si je ris?"

Three little maidens, side by side,
Sat down and laughed until they cried,
And cried until they laughed again;
"Ach, ach, ich kann dich nicht versteh'n!"
Uproarius burst the old refrain,
"Tell me your name, and I'll tell mine,"
Cried Cora Dora Waterpine,
"En vérité! En vérité!"
It might have lasted all the day,
But such confusion breeding there,
There came a sudden deep despair—

With fingers in their ears, they say,
Three little maidens ran away.

℘❦ *Author Unknown*

INTERNATIONAL

She came from a round black dot on the map,—
This dear little girl, and she's called a Jap.
Maybe my sister will show it to you:—
The very place where this little girl grew.

I wish she knew some American words,
Such as "How do you do?" and "trees," and "birds."
I'd like to talk with her ever so much
But she can't tell a thing that I say from Dutch.

Well, our dollies will get us acquainted today
If she'll only come out in the Park to play!
If it were not for nodding, and taking their hands,
We could never know people from foreign lands.

℘❦ *D. C. W.*

DAISIES

"'*Wich man, poor man, beggar man, sief*'–
    Wait till I tell 'ou what 'ou 'll be;—
'*Doctor, lawyer, Inzun shief*'—
    'Ou couldn't be *zat* one, don't you see?
'*Wich man, poor man, beggar man, sief*'–
    Aren't 'ou glad it isn't zat one?
'*Doctor, lawyer, Inzun shief*'—
    Wait a minute, I'se almost done.
'*Wich* man'—zat's the lastest one,
    So zat it what 'ou 's doing to be.

'*Wich man, poor man, beggar man, sief*'–
    I dess I must see who'll marry me.—
'*Doctor, lawyer, Inzun shief*'—
    Who do 'ou s'pose it's going to be?

"'*Wich man*'—why, it tums ze same!
    I doesn't see how zat can be!—
O ess, I does—it's dest as plain,—
    O' course it means '*ou'll* marry me!"

[SWEET! SWEET!]

"Sweet! Sweet!
Come, come and eat
Dear little girls
With yellow curls;
For here you'll find
Sweets to your mind.
On every tree
Sugar-plums you'll see;
In every dell
Grows the caramel;
Over every wall
Gum-drops fall;
Molasses flows
Where our river goes;
Under your feet
Lies sugar sweet;
Over your head
Grow almonds red.
Our lily and rose
Are not for the nose;
Our flowers we pluck
To eat or suck;
And, oh! what bliss
When two friends kiss,
For they honey sip
From lip to lip!
And all you meet,
In house or street,
At work or at play,
Sweethearts are they.

So, little dear,
Pray feel no fear;
Go where you will;
Eat, eat your fill;
Here is a feast
From west to east;
And you can say,
Ere you go away:
'At last I stand
In dear Candy-land.'
Sweet! Sweet!
Tweet! Tweet!
Tweedle-dee!
Tweedle-dee!"

Anna M. Pratt

FIVE LITTLE PIGS

Five little pigs all rosy pink
Are shut in a pen as black as ink;
All day long in a close, dark pen
They wriggle and twist about, and then—

This little pig went to market
To buy him some crackers and cheese,
But instead of a lunch
He bought a big bunch
Of fresh mignonette and sweet peas.

This little pig stayed at home,
And said with a heart-rending wail,
"The air is so damp.
It will give me the cramp.
And take all the curl from my tail."

This little pig had a piece of bread and butter
"I'm tidy," quoth she, "tho' I'm fat."
Then it dropped on her gown
The buttered side down,
And oh, how she hiccoughed at that!

This little pig had none,
Not a crumb nor a morsel of bread;
So he swung on the gate
Until it was late,
And then he went hungry to bed.

This little pig said, "Wee, wee, wee,
  I can't find my way home!"
But no wonder the rogue went astray,
For he ran down the street,
When he heard the drums beat,
And he followed the circus all day.

Five little pigs as pink as a rose!
They're only the baby's tiny toes;
And before they are tucked in the blanket tight
I'll seize them and squeeze them, and kiss them good-night.

COUNTING APPLE-SEEDS

One, I love,
Two, I love,
Three, I love, I say,
Four, I love with all my heart,
And five, I cast away;
Six, he loves,
Seven, she loves,
Eight, they both love;
Nine, he comes,
Ten, he tarries,
Eleven, he courts,
Twelve, he marries;
Thirteen wishes,
Fourteen kisses,
All the rest little witches.

INTERY MINTERY

Intery mintery cutery corn,
Apple-seed and apple-thorn,
Wire, briar, limber lock,
Twelve geese in a flock;
Sit and sing by a spring,
O-u-t spells out, and in again.
Over yonder steep hills,
Where my father he dwells,
He has jewels, he has rings,
And very many pretty things.
Strike Jack, lick Tom,
Blow the bellows,
Black finger—out-of-the-game.

RHYMES FOR TICKLING

1. Tickle'e, tickle'e on the knee;
   If you laugh, you don't love me.

2. If you're a little lady, as I take you for to be,
   You will neither laugh nor smile when I tickle your knee.

3. Old maid, old maid, you'll surely be,
   If you laugh or you smile while I tickle your knee.

☙

RHYMES FOR COUNTING OUT

1. Onery, uery, hickory, Ann,
   Fillison, follasson, Nicholas John,
   Queevy, quavy, Virgin Mary,
   Singalum, sangalum, buck.

2. Onery, uery, ickory, Ann,
   Filisy, folasy, Nicholas John,
   Queevy, quavy, Irish Mary,
   Stingalum, stangalum, buck.

3. Onery, uery, ickory, Ann,
   Fillison, follason, Nicholas John,
   Queevy, quavy, English navy,
   Stinkalum, stankalum, John Buck.
   B-u-c-k spells buck.

4. Onery, uery, ickory, a,
   Hallibone, crackabone, ninery-lay,
   Whisko, bango, poker my stick,
   Mejoliky one leg!

5. Onery, uery, hickory, able,
   Hallowbone, crackabone, Timothy, ladle.

   . . . .

7. One-amy, uery, hickory, seven,
   Hallibone, crackabone, ten and eleven,
   Peep—O, it must be done,
   Twiggle, twaggle, twenty-one.

8. Onery, uery, ickery, see,
   Huckabone, crackabone, tillibonee;
   Ram pang, muski dun,
   Striddledum, straddledum, twenty-one.

9. Eny, meny, mony, my,
   Tusca, leina, bona, atry,
   Kay bell, broken well,
   We, wo, wack.

10. Eny, meny, mony, mine,
    Hasdy, pasky, daily, ine,
    Agy, dagy, walk.

11. Eny, meny, mony, mite,
    Butter, lather, bony strike,
    Hair cut, froth neck,
    Halico balico,
    We, wo, wack.

12. Ena, mena, mona, my,
    Padalona, bona, stry,
    Ee wee, fowl's neck,
    Hallibone, crackabone, ten and eleven,
    O-u-t spells out.

13. Intery, mintery, cutery corn,
    Apple-seed and apple-thorn,
    Wire, briar, limber lock,
    Five mice in a flock;
    Catch him Jack,
    Hold him Tom,
    Blow the bellows,
    Old man out.

14. Ikkamy, dukkamy, alligator, mole,
    Dick slew alligator slum,
    Hukka pukka, Peter's gum,
    Francis.

NONSENSE

Laura E. Richards

MY UNCLE JEHOSHAPHAT

My Uncle Jehoshaphat had a pig,
  A pig of high degree;
And it always wore a brown scratch wig,
  Most beautiful for to see.

My Uncle Jehoshaphat loved that pig,
  And the piggy-wig he loved him;
And they both jumped into the lake one day,
  To see which best could swim.

My Uncle Jehoshaphat he swam up,
  And the piggy-wig he swam down;
And so they both did win the prize,
  Which the same was a velvet gown.

My Uncle Jehoshaphat wore one-half,
  And the piggy-wig wore the other;
And they both rode to town on the brindled calf,
  To carry it home to its mother.

Laura E. Richards

BOBBILY-BOO AND WOLLYPOTUMP

Bobbily-Boo, the king so free,
He used to drink the Mango tea:
Mango tea and coffee, too,—
He drank them both till his nose turned blue.

Wollypotump, the queen so high,
She used to eat the Gumbo pie:
Gumbo pie and Gumbo cake,—
She ate them both till her teeth did break.

Bobbily-Boo and Wollypotump,
Each called the other a greedy frump;
And, when these terrible words were said,
They sat and cried till they both were dead.

Laura E. Richards

PUNKYDOODLE AND JOLLAPIN

Oh, Pillykin Willykin Winky Wee!
How does the Emperor take his tea?
He takes it with melons, he takes it with milk,
He takes it with syrup and sassafras silk.
He takes it without, he takes it within.
Oh, Punkydoodle and Jollapin!

Oh, Pillykin Willykin Winky Wee!
How does the Cardinal take his tea?
He takes it in Latin, he takes it in Greek,
He takes it just seventy times in the week.
He takes it so strong that it makes him grin.
Oh, Punkydoodle and Jollapin!

Oh, Pillykin Willykin Winky Wee!
How does the Admiral take his tea?
He takes it with splices, he takes it with spars,
He takes it with jokers and jolly jack-tars.
And he stirs it round with a dolphin's fin.
Oh, Punkydoodle and Jollapin!

Oh, Pillykin Willykin Winky Wee!
How does the President take his tea?
He takes it in bed, he takes it in school,
He takes it in Congress against the rule.
He takes it with brandy, and thinks it no sin.
Oh, Punkydoodle and Jollapin!

Mary Wiley Staver

[TWINKUM, TWUNKUM, TWANKUM, TWERRY]

Twinkum, twunkum, twankum, twerry;
Here's a peach, and there's a cherry;
Here's an apple, and there's a pear;
Here's a monkey, and there's a bear.
Twinkum, twunkum, twankum, twerry,
This is funny, ain't it? Very.

🍀 *Agnes Lee*

THE LITTLE MAN OF MICHIGAN

A little girl of Michigan
Declares she saw a tiny man,

No larger than the least of mice,
Skating far out upon the ice.

She thought, "How charming it will be
To take that small man home with me.

"I'll dress him in a coat of blue,
And he shall sleep inside my shoe.

"I'll put him in my pocket—O,
And take him everywhere I go.

"And proud I'll be, and show with joy
So dear a little living toy!"

Far o'er the ice she slid, she ran,
To catch her cunning little man.

But as she near and nearer drew,
That little man, he grew, and grew

Till she, quite close, beheld with awe
The biggest man she ever saw!

And fast her feet they slid, they ran,
Back to the shores of Michigan.

🍀 *James Whitcomb Riley*

A NONSENSE RHYME

RINGLETY JING!
And what will we sing?
Some little crinkety-crankety thing
That rhymes and chimes,
And skips, sometimes,
As though wound up with a kink in the spring.

Grunkety-krung!
And chunkety-plung!
Sing the song that the bullfrog sung,—
A song of the soul
Of a mad tadpole
That met his fate in a leaky bowl:
And it's O for the first false wiggle he made
In a sea of pale pink lemonade!
And it's O for the thirst
Within him pent,
And the hopes that burst
As his reason went—
When his strong arm failed and his strength was spent!

Sing, O sing
Of the things that cling,
And the claws that clutch and the fangs that sting—
Till the tadpole's tongue
And his tail upflung
Quavered and failed with a song unsung!
—Oh! the dank despair in the rank morass,
Where the crawfish crouch in the cringing grass,
And the long limp rune of the loon wails on
For the mad, sad soul
Of a bad tadpole
Forever lost and gone!

Jinglety-jee!
And now we'll see
What the last of the lay shall be,
As the dismal tip of the tune, O friends,
Swoons away and the long tale ends.
And it's O and alack!
For the tangled legs
And the spangled back
Of the green grigg's eggs,
And the unstrung strain
Of the strange refrain
That the winds wind up like a strand of rain!
And it's O,
Also,
For the ears wreathed low,
Like a laurel-wreath on the lifted brow
Of the frog that chants of the why and how,
And the wherefore too, and the thus and so
Of the wail he weaves in a woof of woe.
Twangle, then, with your wrangling strings,
The tinkling links of a thousand things!
And clang the pang of a maddening moan
Till the echo, hid in a land unknown,
Shall leap as he hears, and hoot and hoo,
Like the wretched wraith of a Whoopty Doo.

❧ *Gertrude Heath*

A JINGLE

As I was going to Kalamazoo,
   Kalamazoo Mazindy!
Oh, I met a Cat and a Kitten or two,
   Kalamazoo Mazindy!
"Oh! Madam Felicia," I said, said I,
   Kalamazoo Mazindy,
"I saw three mice in a lane hard by,"
   Kalamazoo Mazindy!

Now what came next, oh! never I knew,
   Kalamazoo Mazindy!
Away went a Cat and a Kitten or two,
   Kalamazoo Mazindy.
But I think that they dined on a mouse-
   ragout,
   Kalamazoo Mazindy!

❧ *Mary Mapes Dodge*

[LEMONS FOR MOLLY]

Lemons for Molly;
   Molly is sour.
Roses for Polly;
   Polly's a flower.

Ginger for Willie;
   Willie is quick.
Powders for Tillie;
   Tillie is sick.

❧ *Frederick Palmer*

LIMERICKS FROM *ST. NICHOLAS*

There was an old man of the Nile,
Who had a benevolent smile,
   When they said, "Smile again,"
   He replied, "I'm not vain,
But I think I do know how to smile."

❧

Said a sorrowing maiden named Han;
"That they stuff all the dollies with bran
   There is scarcely a doubt;
   I have just found it out.
What a horrid deceiver is man!"

❧

There once was a ve-ry rich pig,
Who wore spec-ta-cles, al-so a wig;
   And at last grew so stout
   That, to travel a-bout,
He had to in-dulge in a gig.

❦ Isabel Frances Bellows

LIMERICKS FROM *ST. NICHOLAS*

There once was an Ichthyosaurus,
Who lived when the earth was all porous,
    But he fainted with shame
    When he first heard his name,
And departed a long time before us.

❦

There once was a Mystic Macaw,
Who impressionist pictures could draw.
    He'd take lampblack and soot
    On the sole of his foot,
And then dash it about with his claw.

❦ Carolyn Wells

LIMERICKS FROM *ST. NICHOLAS*

There once was a happy Hyena
Who played on an old concertina.
    He dressed very well,
    And in his lapel
He carelessly stuck a verbena.

❦ Authors Unknown

SANITARY FAIR LIMERICKS

There was an old man of Woonsocket,
Who carried bomb-shells in his pocket;
    Endeavoring to cough
    One day—they went off,
And of course, up he went   like a rocket.

❦

There was a young man of Calcutta,
Who ate at his meals too much butter;
    Till a very kind niece
    Oiled him down into grease,
Which dissolved this young man of Calcutta.

There was a fine lady of Metz,
Continually surrounded by pets:
   Two cats very small,
   And two dogs rather tall,
With which she would walk about Metz.

There was a young lass of Kentucky,
Who tho' little was loyal and plucky;
   When her spark turned secesh,
   Though dear as her flesh,
She drummed him herself from Kentucky.

Newton Mackintosh

LIMERICKS

I.

There was a young lady named Hannah,
Who trod on a piece of banana.
   A slip and a slide,
   And more stars she espied
Than there are on the Star-spangled Banner.

II.

A gentleman sprang to assist her,
And picked up her muff and her wrister.
   "Are you hurt, ma'am?" he cried.
   "Did you think," she replied,
"I sat down for the fun of it, mister?"

There was a young fellow named Gustave,
Who said that a monkey he must have.
   His mother said not,
   For she thought she had got
Sufficient young monkey in Gustave.

Carolyn Wells

A BICYCLE BUILT FOR TWO

There was an ambitious young eel
Who determined to ride on a wheel;
    But try as he might,
    He couldn't ride right,
In spite of his ardor and zeal.

If he sat on the saddle to ride
His tail only pedalled one side;
    And I'm sure you'll admit
    That an eel *couldn't* sit
On a bicycle saddle astride.

Or if he hung over the top,
He could go, but he never could stop;
    For of course it is clear
    He had no way to steer,
And under the wheel he would flop.

His neighbor, observing the fun,
Said, "I think that the thing can be done,
    If you'll listen to me,
    You'll quickly agree
That two heads are better than one.

"And this is my project, old chap,
Around our two waists I will wrap
    This beautiful belt
    Of bottle-green felt
And fasten it firm with a strap."

This done, with a dignified mien
The two squirmed up on the machine,
    And rode gayly away,
    Or at least, so they say,
Who witnessed the wonderful scene.

Carolyn Wells

AN ALPHABET ZOO

A was an apt Alligator,
Who wanted to be a head-waiter;
    He said, "I opine
    In that field I could shine,
Because I am such a good skater."

B was a beggarly Bear,
Who carefully curled his front hair;
    He said, "I would buy
    A red-spotted tie,—
But I haven't a penny to spare."

C was a cool Chimpanzee,
Who went to an afternoon tea.
    When they said, "Will you take
    A caraway cake?"
He greedily took twenty-three!

D was a diligent Doe,
In summer she shovelled the snow;
    In the spring and the fall
    She did nothing at all,
And in winter the grass she would mow.

E was an erudite Ermine,
Who tried very hard to determine
    If he *should* earn a cent,
    How it ought to be spent,
And decided to purchase a sermon.

F was a fussy Flamingo,
Who remarked to his family, "By jingo!
    I think I would go
    To that animal show,
But they all talk such barbarous lingo."

G was a giddy Gazelle,
Who never could learn how to spell;
But she managed to pass
To the head of her class,
Because she did fractions so well.

H was a haughty young Hawk,
Who affected society talk;
But when introduced
At a large chicken roost
He excitedly screamed out, "Oh, Lawk!"

I was an idle Iguana,
Who lived upon curried banana;
With tears he'd protest
That he never could rest
Till he learned to sing "Eileen Alanna."

J was a jimp Jaguar,
Who purchased a Spanish guitar;
He played popular airs
At *fêtes* and at fairs,
And down at the Fancy Bazaar.

K was a kind Kangaroo,
Whose bonnet was always askew;
So they asked her to wait
While they put it on straight
And fastened it firmly with glue.

L was a lachrymose Leopard,
Who ate up twelve sheep and a shepherd,
But the real reason why
He continued to cry
Was his food was so lavishly peppered.

M was a mischievous Marten,
Who went to the Free Kindergarten;
When they asked him to plat
A gay-colored mat,
He tackled the job like a Spartan.

N was a naughty Nylghau,
Who wandered too near a buzz saw.
It cut off his toes,
And the shrieks that arose
Filled all of the neighbors with awe.

O was an ossified Oyster,
Who decided to enter a cloister.
He could not return,
So continued to yearn
For his home in the sea, which was
moister.

P was a poor old Poll Parrot,
Who had nothing to eat but a carrot,
And nothing to wear
But a wig of red hair,
And nowhere to live but a garret.

Q was a querulous Quab
Who at every trifle would sob;
He said, "I detest
To wear a plaid vest,
And I hate to eat corn from the cob!"

R was a rollicking Ram,
Attired in an old pillow sham.
When asked if he'd call
At the masquerade ball,
He said, "I'll go just as I am."

S was a shy Salamander,
Who slept on a sunny veranda.
She calmly reposed,
But, alas! while she dozed
They caught her and killed her and
canned her.

T was a tidy young Tapir,
Who went out to bring in the paper;
And when he came back
He made no muddy track,
For he wiped his feet clean on the scraper.

U was a young Unicorn,
The bravest that ever was born.
They bought him a boat
And they set him afloat,
And straightway he sailed for Cape Horn.

V was a vigorous Vulture,
Who taught animals physical culture;
    When a pupil dropped dead,
    The kind teacher said,
"You needn't consider sepulture."

W was a wild Worm,
All day he did nothing but squirm.
    They sent him to school,
    But he broke every rule,
And left at the end of the term.

X was a Xiphias brave,
Who lived on the crest of the wave.
    To each fish he would say,
    "Good day, sir, good day!"
And then a polite bow he gave.

Y was a young Yellowhammer,
Who raised a ridiculous clamor;
    And he chattered until
    An owl said, "Keep still!
I'm trying to study my grammar."

Z was a zealous old Zibet,
Toboggans he tried to prohibit.
    If any one tried
    To take a sly slide,
He ordered him hanged on a gibbet.

❧ *Carolyn Wells*

AN ALICE ALPHABET

A is for Alice, who wrote to her feet.
B is the Bandersnatch, frumious and
    fleet.
C is the Cheshire Cat, who slowly
    appears.
D is the Duchess, who boxed the
    Queen's ears.
E is the Eaglet who barred out long
    words.
F, the Flamingo, the queerest of birds.
G is the Gryphon, loquacious and gay.
H, Humpty-Dumpty in gorgeous array.
I for the Insects with curious names.
J is the Jabberwock, breathing forth
    flames.
K is the King who was whizzed through
    the air.

L is the Lobster who sugared his hair.
M, the Mock Turtle, whose tears freely
    flowed.
N is for Nobody, seen on the road.
O is for Oysters, with shoes on their
    legs.
P is for Pigeon who guarded its eggs.
Q is for Queen who breathlessly ran.
R is the Rabbit who hunted his fan.
S is the Sheep, on her knitting intent.
T, Tweedledum, with his noisy lament.
U is the Unicorn, valiant in feud.
V is the Violet, saucy and rude.
W's the Walrus with appetite keen.
X the Executioner employed by the
    Queen.
Y is the Youth Father William surveyed.
Z is the Zigzag the Mouse's tale made.

🍀 *Charles E. Carryl*

MEMORANDRUMS

Have Angleworms attractive homes?
   Do Bumble-bees have brains?
Do Caterpillars carry combs?
   Do Ducks dismantle drains?
Can Eels elude elastic earls?
   Do Flatfish fish for flats?
Are Grigs agreeable to girls?
   Do Hares have hunting-hats?
Do Ices make an Ibex ill?
   Do Jackdaws jug their jam?
Do Kites kiss all the kids they kill?
   Do Llamas live on lamb?
Will Moles molest a mounted mink?
   Do Newts deny the news?

Are Oysters boisterous when they drink?
   Do Parrots prowl in pews?
Do Quakers get their quills from quails?
   Do Rabbits rob on roads?
Are Snakes supposed to sneer at snails?
   Do Tortoises tease toads?
Can Unicorns perform on horns?
   Do Vipers value veal?
Do Weasels weep when fast asleep?
   Can Xylophagans squeal?
Do Yaks in packs invite attacks?
   Are Zebras full of zeal?

🍀 *Amos Russel Wells*

A PLANE STATEMENT

A very vicious Angle, a master of abuse,
Reviled a neighbor Angle, and shouted, "You're obtuse!"
(He himself was quite acute, as all angles like to be,
And the neighbor *was* obtuse, as any one could see.)
It wasn't many minutes, I much regret to say,
Before they came to blows in a very savage way.
And to make the matter worse, the Ellipse was strolling by,
And joining in the fray, almost lost a focus eye!
A Parabola, alas! stopped and mingled in the fight,
But was flattened to an oval, a very shocking sight!
A most aggressive Triangle, tall and rather thin,
Was carried from the combat with both his sides knocked in.
A smooth and perfect Circle came rolling on the ground,
And kindly counselled peace, but he couldn't bring them 'round.
They got to throwing points. There were many looking on,
And one of these was hit,—'twas a portly Polygon.
"Police! police!" he cried, and he shouted long and loud,
And soon a squad of Rectangles captured all the crowd!

A battered, sorry rabble, they stood before the Square,
Who frowned upon the culprits with a most judicial air,
And imposed a heavy sentence that none of them could shirk,—
A life, in Conic Sections, of unremitting work!
And that is why, my hearers, as wise professors say,
They're still in Conic Sections, and cannot get away.

&ℛ *Margaret Johnson*

A MODERN ARTIST

There was a small maid in our town
Who was sure she could win
    much renown
   By painting in oil
  So with infinite toil
She finished a "Study in Brown."
  She gazed at her picture and sighed
In a rapture of pleasure and pride.
    "It's exceedingly flat,
   But of course you like that."
To her wondering neighbors she cried.

"It is crooked perhaps in your sight
   Though to say so you're
    much too polite.
   But observe if you please
  It is so Japanese!"
And her friends all declared
   her quite right.

Palmer Cox

THE FUNNY MANDARIN

There was a funny mandarin
    Who had a funny way,
Of sliding down the balustrade
    A dozen times a day.

With arms in air and streaming hair,
    At risk of bone and brain,
Around and round the winding stair
    He slid the rail amain.

The "surest" aim may miss the game,
    The "safest" ship go down,
And one mistake will bring to blame
    The wisest man in town.

And thus it ran, that daring man,
    Who never thought to fail,
At last, in spite of every plan,
    Went gliding off the rail.

The servants then, unlucky men,
    Began to laugh and grin,
Which, like a lion in its den,
    Aroused that mandarin.

"Ho, ho!" said he, "you laugh at me?
    Now, slaves, you each shall slide!"
And when they all had met a fall,
    He laughed until he cried.

William H. Abbott

A "MOTHER-GOOSE"-Y JINGLE

    The cold moon is dead,
    The stars have turned red,
The sun's gone to bed with a cold in his head,
    The world's up side down,
    The mayor's out of town,
And the children are crying for bread, bread, bread!

❧ Anne L. Huber

THE MAN IN THE MOON

The man in the moon
 Was married last June,
And a beautiful star was his bride.
 Away up on high,
 In the bright blue sky,
She glitters and shines by his side.

On that wedding night,
 The stars came out bright,
And they sparkled and twinkled with glee;
 A meteor flew by,
 Across the blue sky,
And took the news over the sea.

❧ Anne L. Huber

THE LITTLE BOY'S POCKET

Starry, fiery, long-tailed rocket,
What does the little boy keep in his
 pocket?
A pair of mittens, with ragged thumbs,
A half-eaten cracker, and many crumbs;
A handkerchief that once had been white,
Some paper to make new tails for his kite;

A broken knife, with part of a blade,
A whistle some other boy has made;
A marble, a top, two dirty strings,
A button, a ball, and some other things.
And is that all he keeps in his pocket,
Starry, fiery, long-tailed rocket?

❧ Anne L. Huber

THE MONKEY AND THE PUSSY CAT

A monkey and a pussy cat
 Were married one fine night;
But before a week was over,
 The bride and groom did fight.

The monkey bit the pussy's tail,
 And slapped her with his paws;
And pussy spit with all her might,
 And scratched him with her claws.

So pussy ran away from him,
 And led a single life;
But monkey did not care at all,
 And got another wife.

&✿ *Anne L. Huber*

THE OLD MAID AND THE BACHELOR

A little old maid,
  Crabbed and crusty,
Married a bachelor,
  Old, rusty, and fusty.

They lived in an old house,
  High up in the garret;
She had a pet cat,
  And he had a parrot.

&✿ *Anne L. Huber*

MY WIFE PEGGY

My little wife Peggy
  Loves apples and pears;
Her left leg fell down
  And broke all our stairs.

Oh, no, that is not it.
  It was my wife Peg,
Who fell down our stairs
  And broke her left leg.

&✿ *Anne L. Huber*

THE KILKENNY CATS

The cats of Kilkenny,
Though not a great many,
Were famous for fighting,
And scratching, and biting.

From morning till night,
'Twas their greatest delight,
To spit, and to paw,
To scratch, and to claw.

Two Kilkenny cats
Once were hunting for rats,
When they got in a fight
That lasted all night.

And this they do say,
That when it was day,
That nothing was found,
But two tails on the ground.

THE SOMETHINGS

A Something met a Something
    In the mists of Shadowland.
They ran against each other,
    And came quickly to a stand.

"And who are you?" said Something One.
 And Something Two, said he,
"That's just the very question that
 At once occurred to me."

❧ *Ruth McEnery Stuart and Albert Bigelow Paine*

A WHAT-IS-IT

There was an old man of high feather,
Who said, "I can't really tell whether
I'm a man or a mouse,
Or the roof of a house,
So much may depend on the weather."

Benjamin Franklin King

THE PESSIMIST

Nothing to do but work,
    Nothing to eat but food,
Nothing to wear but clothes
    To keep one from going nude.

Nothing to breathe but air,
    Quick as a flash 'tis gone;
Nowhere to fall but off,
    Nowhere to stand but on.

Nothing to comb but hair,
    Nowhere to sleep but in bed,
Nothing to weep but tears,
    Nothing to bury but dead.

Nothing to sing but songs,
    Ah, well, alas! alack!
Nowhere to go but out,
    Nowhere to come but back.

Nothing to see but sights,
    Nothing to quench but thirst,
Nothing to have but what we've got;
    Thus thro' life we are cursed.

Nothing to strike but a gait;
    Everything moves that goes.
Nothing at all but common sense
    Can ever withstand these woes.

Mary Mapes Dodge

THE MAYOR OF SCUTTLETON

The Mayor of Scuttleton burned his nose
Trying to warm his copper toes;
He lost his money and spoiled his will
By signing his name with an icicle-quill;
He went bare-headed, and held his breath,
And frightened his grandame almost to death;
He loaded a shovel, and tried to shoot,
And killed the calf in the leg of his boot;
He melted a snow-bird, and formed the habit
Of dancing jigs with a sad Welsh rabbit;
He lived on taffy, and taxed the town;
And read his newspapers upside down;
Then he sighed, and hung his hat on a feather,
And bade the townspeople come together;
But the worst of it all was, nobody knew
What the Mayor of Scuttleton next would do.

THE TERRIBLE BALL

Give me your ear, good children all,
I'm going to set up a terrible ball—
A terrible ball that began to grow
From only the least little speckle of snow.
And, to make the lesson pointed and plain,
I'll just remark that life, in the main,
Is, etcet'ra—you know; and I hope you'll be good
In future to show that you've understood.

Three lovely, little artless boys,
All of them being mothers' joys,
One day decided, in innocent mirth,
To make a snow-ball as big as the earth.
What makes the story more touching still,
The big-eyed school-house on the hill
Was in session, under the cross Miss Stookey,
And these little boys were "playing hookey."

Hookey from Stookey, they worked with a will,
And, from making a ball like a tiny pill,
They rolled and rolled, till, no longer small,
'Twas big as Miss Stookey's waterfall.
Then, like a pumpkin fair and round,
They kept it rolling on the ground—
Bigger, bigger, bigger, bigger,
Bigger, bigger, bigger, bigger!
The boys could hardly push it along,
It steadily grew so mighty stout and strong.

Now, this mammoth ball that began as a pill,
Was made, you must know, on top of a hill;
This hill was so terribly steep and high,
That even the coasters would pass it by;
And, saving a road by the cattle made,
It sloped right down, at a fearful grade,
To the meadow, where stood a cottage red
Where these little children were born and bred.

"Halloo!" they cried, "let's have some fun,
There's Stookey's pig as sure as a gun!"
"Hooray! hooray!" cried the children three,
Thus giving vent to their youthful glee.

When—what do you think?—this ungrateful pill,
That they'd made so big on top of the hill,
With an air that said, "Now, I think I've got 'em!"
Resolved to roll all the way to the bottom.

The ball was swift, the ball was big,
Alas for Stookey's innocent pig!
Alas for lovers who walked that way,
They ne'er in their lives forgot the day!
Alas for the learned Professor Gath
Who happened to stroll in the snow-ball's path!
And alas, alas, for those children three,
Who shouted and cheered in their pretty glee!

Rolling, growing, demolishing all,
On and on went the terrible ball;
It left the cattle down on their knees,
It crushed the fences and bent the trees;
Even the hay-stacks went ker-flop.
It wouldn't turn, nor it wouldn't stop,
But still rolled on in steady motion,
Making a bee-line for the ocean!

With laugh and shout and merry hoot,
Those children followed in glad pursuit.
"Hooray! hooray!" they cried again,
And then gave chase with might and main;
They gave the chase with main and might,
But the terrible ball rolled out of sight.

And now comes the saddest part of all.
(Oh! That cruel, wicked, terrible ball!)
When at last the three little artless boys,
Tired of running and making a noise,
All resolved to go home to bed,
Where, oh! where was that cottage red?
Where, oh! where? Ask the terrible ball—
Never a home had those children small.
Gone, clean gone! with picket and paling—
And all their joy was turned to wailing!

MORAL

    Hence it is, and so we see
    Thus and so, it seems to me,
    As I'm sure you'll all agree.

Mary Mapes Dodge

TROTTY MALONE

Boys and girls, come riddle and ravel,—
Tell us how you would like to travel.

Crispy, crackly, snow and tingle,
"Give me sleighs!" said Jenny Jingle.

Stony, bumpty, bang and bolter,
"Give me carts!" said Johnny Jolter.

Slidy, glidy, jerky whiffter,
"Give me cars!" cried Sally Swifter.

Flippety, cricketty, elegant go,
"Give me a buggy!" cried Benjamin Beau.

"A fig for them all!" cried Trotty Malone,
"Give me a stout pair of legs of my own!"

Mary E. Wilkins [Freeman]

A SILLY BOY

O, A little boy sailed in a sugar-bowl, with silver spoons for oars,
  And his hold was full of sugar, the Frenchman's tea to sweeten;
But when he safely moored his craft beside those foreign shores—
  Alas, that silly little boy, his cargo he had eaten!

Mary E. Wilkins [Freeman]

A PRETTY AMBITION

The mackerel-man drives down the street,
  With mackerel to sell,
A-calling out with lusty shout:
  "Ha-il, Mack-e-rel!"

When I'm a man I mean to drive
  A wagon full of posies,
And sing so sweet to all I meet:
  "Hail, Hyacinths and Roses!"

Mary E. Wilkins [Freeman]

PUSSY-WILLOW

"Pussy, pussy, pussy!" There she stood a-calling,
"Pussy, pussy, pussy!" Her voice rang sweet, and shrill-o.
  Yet still her pussy lingered; but, on a bush beside her,
  Crept softly out in answer, a little pussy-willow.

& Mary E. Wilkins [Freeman]

THE THREE MARGERY DAWS

See-saw, see-saw, up and down we gayly go!
See-saw, see-saw, such a lovely teeter, O!
See-saw, see-saw, grass across a daisy-stalk—
Up and down the robins teetered with their silvery talk.

See-saw, see-saw! robins, they know how to play
See-saw, see-saw, as well as children any day;
See-saw, see-saw! lads and lassies, don't you know,
Grass across a daisy-stalk makes a lovely teeter, O!

& Gelett Burgess

THE PURPLE COW

I never saw a Purple Cow,
    I never hope to see one;
But I can tell you, anyhow,
    I'd rather see than be one.

ENVOI

Ah yes, I wrote the Purple Cow,
    I'm sorry now I wrote it.
But I can tell you anyhow,
    I'll kill you if you quote it.

& Gelett Burgess

THE LAZY ROOF

 The Roof it has a Lazy Time
    A-lying in the Sun;
The Walls they have to Hold Him Up;
    They do Not Have Much Fun!

& Gelett Burgess

MY FEET

My feet, they haul me Round the House,
    They Hoist me up the Stairs;
I only have to Steer them and
    They Ride me Everywheres.

WHAT HAPPENED

A very respectable Kangaroo
Died week before last in Timbuctoo;
A remarkable accident happened to him:
He was hung head down from a banyan-
  limb.
The Royal Lion made proclamation
For a day of fasting and lamentation,
Which led to a curious demonstration:
The Elephant acted as if he were drunk—
He stood on his head, he trod on his
  trunk;
An over-sensitive she-Gorilla
Declared that the shock would surely
  kill her;
A frisky, gay and frolicsome Ape
Tied up his tail with a yard of crape;
The Donkey wiped his eyes with his ears;
The Crocodile shed a bucket of tears;
The Rhinoceros gored a young Giraffe
Who had the very bad taste to laugh;
The Hippopotamus puffed and blew,
To show his respect for the Kangaroo;
And a sad but indignant Chimpanzee
Gnawed all the bark from the banyan-
  tree.

CAUTIONARY TALES

"A Lady of Boston" [Nancy Sproat]

THE LITTLE LIAR

The coach is tackled, sister, run,
And put your gloves and bonnet on;
It is about a week ago,
Our parents promised us, you know,
If we were good, that we today,
Should have the coach, and ride away.
Our cousins too, are all at home,
How glad they'll be to see us come!
And they're such lovely girls and boys,
And have so many pretty toys,
And we shall have the sweetest ride,
Through trees along the river side!—
Come, sister, come, make no delay,
'Tis time for us to start away.
What ails you, Mary? an't you well?
What makes you cry so? pri'thee tell—
"Harry, I can't—don't ask me why—
And yet I must—*I've told a lie!*
And here shut up I'm doom'd to stay,
And weep, and mourn, the live-long day,
I shall not dare to shew my face,
Nor join the children in their plays—
They'll see my tears and then enquire
What I have done—and call me *Liar.*
And, Harry, I'm afraid that you
And Harriet will hate me too—
But what is worst of all, Mamma
Don't speak to me nor does Papa—
Not once upon me have they smiled,
Since I was such a wicked child—
Oh! it will break my heart, I'm sure,
I never told a lie before,
And never, never, will again,
If I their pardon can obtain.
Go—it is time that you were gone,
And leave me here to cry alone."

THE LITTLE THIEF

"Edward, come here—how pale you are!
    What makes you look so wild?
And you've been crying sadly too;
    What's happened to my child?"

"You know Mamma, you sent me down
    To Mr. Brightman's shop,
With ninepence in my hand, to buy
    A little humming-top.

Well neighbor Brightman handed down;
    A dozen tops, or more,
For me to make a choice of one,
    Then stepped towards the door.

So then I caught one slily up,
    And in my pocket slid it,
That no one would suspect the thing,
    So cunningly I hid it.

And so I bought another top,
    And laid my ninepence down;
Then laughed to think I owned them both,
    But paid for only one.

But when I turned and left the shop
    I felt most dreadfully,—
For all the time I was in fear
    That he would follow me.

For sure, thought I, he'll find it out,
    The angry man will come,—
And I shall never see Mamma,
    And never more go home.

He'll tie a rope around my neck,
    And hang me up on high;
And leave the little wicked thief
    To hang there till he die.

And then I screamed, and ran so fast
    Adown the nearest lane;
And then I turned and looked behind,—
    Then screamed and ran again.

Trembling, at last, I reached my home,
    And straight I went to bed—
But, Oh! in such a shocking fright,
    That I was almost dead.

No rest or comfort could I get,—
    And not a wink of sleep,—
All I could do was toss and turn
    From side to side, and weep.

And what was worst of all Mama,
    I could not say my prayers;
And then I thought my heart would
        burst
    And I was drowned in tears.

No, no, I cried, God will not hear
    A child so wicked, pray,
I dare not hope he'll let me live
    To see another day.

Thus did I mourn till morning's dawn,
    And yet found no relief—
For oh! what comfort can there be,
    Or pleasure, for a *thief?*"

"Go, my poor wretched guilty child,
    Go, take the top you stole,
And give it to the man you've wronged;
    And own to him the whole.

Then, on your knees before your God,
    Confess how vile you've been—
Beg him to save you, and forgive
    This great and dreadful sin.

And never, while you live, again,
    To such a deed consent,
Lest he should take away you[r] life,
    Before you can repent."

LITTLE LYDIA AND THE RAZOR

"This box little Lydia may put in its place,"
    Said her uncle, "for I am quite lame;
My razor is nicely shut up in its case,
    Be careful, my dear, of the same."

But Lydia had seen this razor so bright
    In the hands of her uncle display'd,
And when she was fairly out of his sight,
She open'd the box, and saw with delight
    The beautiful handle and blade.

She met her young sister; "Dear Abby," she said,
    "This beautiful thing only see;
Sit down here directly, and hold up your head,
    I'll shave you as nice as can be."

Her sister consented, and now they begin
    Their dangerous play with delight;
But, lo! the first stroke brings blood from her chin,
    And both scream aloud with affright.

At the sound of these voices their mother appear'd
    And well might such figures amaze her;
For one little girl was with blood all besmeared,
    The other was holding a razor.

Now Abby was washed, and a plaster they bring
    For the cut on her face most befitting;
And Lydia was told what a terrible thing,
    She'd been on the point of committing.

They were warned for the future such play-things to shun,
    And I trust they remember their warning;
For I've heard of no mischief these children have done,
    Since that most unfortunate morning.

THE CAT O' NINE TAILS

The old cat o' nine tails is comin' 'round agin,
And the way he worries children sometimes is a sin;
He grabs 'em by the collar, an' he yanks 'em by the clothes
And reaches for a tender place. Why, what do you suppose
Will happen if you're impident an' set aroun' an' grin?
Well, I'll have to call the cat o' nine tails in—
Have to call him in; yes, have to call him in;

<pre>
                                              in
                              tails
              cat o' nine
        old
</pre>
I'll have to call the old cat o' nine tails in.
<pre>
        old
              cat o' nine
                              tails
                                    in.
</pre>

Are you sassy to yer father, are you fibbin' to yer mother?
Are you quarrellin' with yer sister an' a-pinchin' of yer brother,
Do you "ring around the rosey" till you have a dizzy feelin',
And you think yer goin' roun' an' walkin' on the ceilin'?
Well, you better stop yer screechin' an' a-makin' such a din,
Er I'll have to call the cat o' nine tails in—
Have to call him in; yes, have to call him in;

<pre>
                                              in
                              tails
              cat o' nine
        old
</pre>
I'll have to call the old cat o' nine tails in.
<pre>
        old
              cat o' nine
                              tails
                                    in.
</pre>

Do you allers mind your manners when company is come?
Er do you git 'nd yell, 'nd stomp around 'nd drum?
Do you show off at the table, too, 'nd try to act up smart,
'Nd p'int yer fingers at the things 'nd say: "Gimme a tart?"
If some one doesn't dress you down I think it is a sin;
So I'll have to call the old cat o' nine tails in—
Have to call him in; yes, have to call him in;

<pre>
                                    in
                    tails
            cat o' nine
        old
I'll have to call the old cat o' nine tails in.
            old
                    cat o' nine
                            tails
                                    in.
</pre>

❧ *C. C. S.*

HURRY AND WORRY

Hurry and Worry were two busy men;
They worked at the desk till the clock struck ten.
They gained high station, power, and wealth,
And lost youth, happiness, and health.

❧ *Sarah Orne Jewett*

DISCONTENT

Down in a field, one day in June,
  The flowers all bloomed together,
Save one, who tried to hide herself,
  And dropped, that pleasant weather.

A robin who had soared too high,
  And felt a little lazy,
Was resting near a buttercup
  Who wished she were a daisy.

For daisies grow so trig and tall;
  She always had a passion
For wearing frills about her neck
  In just the daisies' fashion.

And buttercups must always be
  The same old tiresome color,
While daisies dress in gold and white,
  Although their gold is duller.

"Dear robin," said this sad young flower,
  "Perhaps you'd not mind trying

To find a nice white frill for me,
  Some day, when you are flying?"

"You silly thing!" the robin said;
  I think you must be crazy!
I'd rather be my honest self
  Than any made-up daisy.

"You're nicer in your own bright gown,
  The little children love you;
Be the best buttercup you can,
  And think no flower above you.

"Though swallows leave me out of sight,
  We'd better keep our places;
Perhaps the world would all go wrong
  With one too many daisies.

"Look bravely up into the sky,
  And be content with knowing
That God wished for a buttercup,
  Just here where you are growing."

FAST LITTLE MISS CROCUS

Time folks was gettin' up—
　They're so slow.
I've been awake here
　Hours ago!

Reckon I'll peep out:—
　Who's afraid?
That dark ain't nothin',
　Only shade.

Been here long enough
　In my bed;
Guess I'll push blanket
　Off my head.

My stars! what a world!
　Ain't it white!
I b'lieve the clouds fell
　Down in the night.

I smell somethin':
　My, that's good!
Must be Arbutus
　Up in the wood.

If there ain't Snow-drop!
　Seems to me
She'd better stay where
　She oughter be.

Wonder what brought her
　Out so soon.
S'pose she thought 'twas
　Afternoon.

She'll get her nose nipped:
　Serve her right!
Small children like her
　Must keep out o' sight.

Wind needn't blow so!
　Makes such a din.
Good gracious!—guess I'd
　Better go in.

Where's my blanket gone?
　Cold hurts so.
Poor little Crocus is
　Freezin' up—oh!

B'lieve I'm an orphan, now;
　—Goin' to—die!
And be—an angel—
　Up in the sky!

OLD GREGORY

Old Gregory stood on a rising ground,
And, viewing the country spread around,
Said, "I'm worth a hundred thousand pound!"

His ample wealth had increased of late,
The cash at his banker's was growing great,
And he had just purchased a vast estate.

"We must look to those cots to-morrow morn;
They obstruct the view from my elegant lawn;
I'll sow the spot where they stand with corn!"

Then the kind old steward he shook his head,—
"And all those poor who toil for their bread,
Where will they hide their heads?" he said.

"They may hide their heads where they please, for me;
It's none of *my* business!" said Gregory.

"And yonder rickety, clackety mill,
That grinds and groans at the foot of the hill,
I'll stop its noise, and I'll keep it still!"

Then the kind old steward he looked forlorn:—
"But the mill was built before you were born,
And where will the villagers grind their corn?"

"They may go grind where they will, for me;
All that is *their* business!" said Gregory.

Jolly old Gregory supped very late,
He drank of the best, of the choicest he ate,
His soul was contented, his heart was elate.

Then he took his usual nap in his chair,
And, in his slumber, was never aware
Of an unexpected visitant there.

Unaware indeed! He is slumbering still
When the dusty miller reopens his mill,
And the cottagers never shall dread his will!

And I fear that the villagers laughed with glee,
That Death had had "business" with Gregory.

THE GOOPS

Let me introduce a Race
Void of Beauty and of Grace,
Extraordinary Creatures
With a Paucity of Features.
Though their Forms are fashioned ill,
They have Manners stranger still;
For in Rudeness they're Precocious,
They're Atrocious, they're Ferocious!
Yet you'll learn, if you are Bright,
Politeness from the Impolite.
When you've finished with the Book,
At your Conduct take a Look;
Ask yourself, upon the Spot,
Are you Goop, or are you Not?
For, although it's Fun to See them
It is TERRIBLE to Be them!

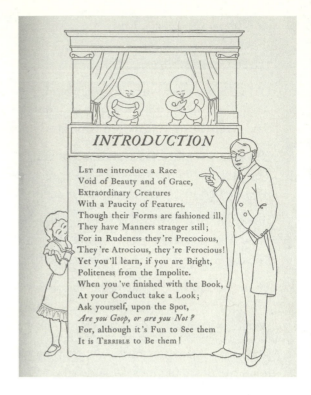

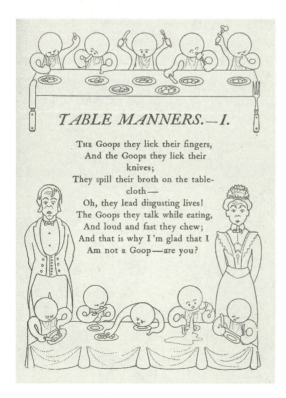

❦ *Gelett Burgess*

TABLE MANNERS I

The Goops they lick their fingers,
    And the Goops they lick their knives;
They spill their broth on the table-cloth—
    Oh, they lead disgusting lives!
The Goops they talk while eating,
    And loud and fast they chew;
And that is why I'm glad that I
    Am not a Goop—are you?

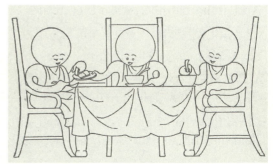

Gelett Burgess

DISFIGURATION

Have you ever seen the scrawls
On the fences and the walls,
All the horrid little pictures and the horrid
little names?
Don't you think it is a shame?
Are the Goops the ones to blame?
Did you ever catch them playing at their
horrid little games?

Gelett Burgess

A LOW TRICK

THE meanest trick I ever knew
Was one I know *you* never do.
I saw a Goop once try to do it,
And there was nothing funny to it.
He pulled a chair from under me
As I was sitting down; but he
Was sent to bed, and rightly, too.
It was a *horrid* thing to do!

Lilian Dynevor Rice

A FOURTH OF JULY RECORD

1   was a wide-awake little boy
Who rose at the break of day;

2   were the minutes he took to dress,
Then he was off and away.

3   were his leaps when he cleared the stairs,
Although they were steep and high;

4   was the number which caused his haste,
Because it was Fourth of July!

5   were his pennies which went to buy
A package of crackers red;

6   were the matches which touched them off,
    And then—he was back in bed.

7   big plasters he had to wear
    To cure his fractures sore;

8   were the visits the doctor made
    Before he was whole once more.

9   were the dolorous days he spent
    In sorrow and pain; but then

0   are the seconds he'll stop to think
    Before he does it again.

❧ *Amos Russel Wells*

TOM'S TOOTH

The word went forth from Fairyland,
    (From ugly fays, in sooth!)
"Young Tom's had too much candy;
    He needs an aching tooth!"

So Fever hurried from the south,
    And from the west came Grumps,
And from the east came Puffy Face,
    And from the north came Thumps.

They quickly spied a hollow tooth
    (Where Tom had failed to brush);
They clapped their little, impish hands,
    And made a silent rush.

They thumped the tooth, they banged the tooth,
    The mocking, cruel crew;
They rasped the nerve, they ground the nerve,
    They pierced it through and through.

From nine o'clock till twelve o'clock
    They racked the groaning child,
Till Tom was "almost crazy,"
    His mother, "fairly wild."

At length between his moans and cries
    Young Tom was heard to say,
"I'll give my teeth less candy,
    And brush them twice a day."

Bang, bang! The impish fairy four
    Each dealt a parting thwack,
Then off they flew, east, west, north, south
    And nevermore came back.

&❧ *Paul Laurence Dunbar*

WHEN A FELLER'S ITCHIN' TO BE SPANKED

W'en us fellers stomp around, makin' lots o' noise,
Gramma says, "There's certain times come to little boys
W'en they need a shingle or the soft side of a plank;"
She says "we're a-itchin' for a right good spank."
    An' she says, "Now thes you wait,
    It's a-comin'—soon or late,
W'en a feller's itchin' fer a spank."

W'en a feller's out o' school, you know how he feels,
Gramma says we wriggle 'roun' like a lot o' eels.
W'y it's like a man that's thes home from out o' jail.
What's the use o' scoldin' if we pull Tray's tail?
    Gramma says, tho', "Thes you wait,
    It's a-comin'—soon or late,
You'se the boys that's itchin' to be spanked."

Cats is funny creatures an' I like to make 'em yowl.
Gramma alwus looks at me with a awful scowl
An' she says, "Young gentlemen, mamma should be thanked
Ef you'd get your knickerbockers right well spanked."
    An' she says, "Now thes you wait,
    It's a-comin'—soon or late,
W'en a feller's itchin' to be spanked."

Ef you fin' the days is gettin' awful hot in school
An' you know a swinmin' place where it's nice and cool,
Er you know a cat-fish hole brimmin' full o' fish,
Whose a-goin' to set around school and wish?
    Tain't no use to hide your bait,
    It's a-comin'—soon or late,
W'en a feller's itchin' fer to be spanked.

Ol' folks know most ever'thing 'bout the world, I guess,
Gramma does, we wish she knowed thes a little less.
But I alwus kind o' think it 'ud be as well
Ef they wouldn't alwus haft to up an' tell;
        We kids wish 'at they'd thes wait,
        It's a-comin'—soon or late,
W'en a feller's itchin' to be spanked.

☙ Dora Read Goodale (age 10)

THE GRUMBLER

HIS YOUTH

His coat was too thick and his cap was too thin,
He couldn't be quiet, he hated a din;
He hated to write, and he hated to read,
He was certainly very much injured indeed;
He must study and work over books he detested,
His parents were strict, and he never was rested;
He knew he was wretched as wretched could be,
There was no one so wretchedly wretched as he.

HIS MATURITY

His farm was too small and his taxes too big,
He was selfish and lazy, and cross as a pig;
His wife was too silly, his children too rude;
And just because he was uncommonly good,
He never had money enough or to spare,
He had nothing at all fit to eat or to wear;
He knew he was wretched as wretched could be,
There was no one so wretchedly wretched as he.

HIS OLD AGE

He finds he has sorrows more deep than his fears,
He grumbles to think he has grumbled for years;
He grumbles to think he has grumbled away
His home and his fortune, his life's little day.
But, alas! 'tis too late,—it is no use to say
That his eyes are too dim, and his hair is too gray.
He knew he is wretched as wretched can be,
There *is* no one more wretchedly wretched than he.

cb Mary Mapes Dodge

LOOKING BACK
BY "DEACON GREEN"

If I were little again,—ah, me!—
How very, very good I'd be!
I would not sulk, I would not cry,
I'd scorn to coax for cake or pie.
I would not cause Mamma distress,
I'd never hate to wash and dress.
I'd rather learn a task than play,
And ne'er from school I'd run away.
I'd any time my jack-knife lend,
And share my toys with every friend.
I'd gladly go to bed at six,
And never be "as cross as sticks."
I'd run with joy to take a pill,
And mustard wear whenever ill.
I'd never wish to skate or swim,
But wisely think of dangers grim.
And, oh, I'd never, just for fun,
Beg to go hunting with a gun!
At every naughty thing I did—
For mischief might somewhere be hid—
I'd drop at once upon my knees,
And say, "Dear Teacher, flog me, please."

It's easy to be good, you see,
When looking back from sixty-three.

cb Mary Mapes Dodge

FARM LESSONS

"Ho! Plowman Kelly! How does it feel
  To get in a wagon by climbing the wheel?"
"Nay, nay, little master, don't try it, I beg,
  For that is the way that I broke my leg."

"Kelly, Kelly! Come, show me the way
  They turn this machine when they cut the hay!"
"No, no, little master, just let it be—
  That hay-cutter cut off my thumb for me."

"Ho, Kelly! The well-curb is rimmed with moss.
  Now look at me while I jump across!"
"Hold, hold, young master! 'Twould be a sin!
  I tried it once, and I tumbled in."

"Kelly, Kelly! Send me to jail,
  But I'll pluck a hair from your pony's tail."
"Oh, master, master! Come back! Don't try—
  That's the very way I lost my eye."

"Why, Kelly, man, how under the sun
  Can you be so frisky and full of fun?—
  With all your mishaps, you are never a spoon—
  You're as brave as a lion and wise as a coon."

"Well, well, young master, maybe it's so,
  And maybe it isn't. But this I know:
  It just brings trouble and mischief and slaughter,
  To be fussin' around where one hadn't ought ter."

&❧ *Christina Moody (age 13–16)*

ADVICE FROM UNCLE ENOUX

Mother, train yo' chillun jest de way yo'd hab 'em go,
'Cause jest like you bends de sapling, da't the way its gwine to grow.
Father, teach yo' sons jest de ting yo'd hab 'em know,
'Cause de way you aims yo' arrow dat's de way it's gwine to go.

Now don't you tink yo' chillun is too good to learn to work,
'Cause a little bit a hardship, now an den aint gwine to hurt,
For dey's got one ting to learn, and dat it—neber shirk
If dey's workin' in a office or a'diging in de dirt.

You may hab plenty money, and a plenty something eat
And may leave it to yo' chilluns when you lays you down to sleep;
And evyting at first will run right smooth and sweet
T'well de money dat you left 'em gine to sneak, and sneak, and sneak.

Den if you aint taught 'em nothing, but to set and hold dey hands
Dey can't earn demselves a libing, and a'how you spose dey can?
Den dey'll end up in de po' house 'cause 'tis jest is true and show
Dat de way you aim yo' arrow, dats de way its gwine to go.

ॐ Christina Moody (age 13–16)

SAM FOUND SOMETHING NEW
AND MAMMY DID TOO

I wants somet'ing new to do,
I'se tired of workin' an' playin' too,
   So I guess I'll git upon de she'f
   An' pitch into t'ings an' he'p myse'f.

Corse I knows dat hit aint right
But my jaws feels likes dey want to bite.
   But how's I gwine to git up dar?
   Oh, I knows, I'll git a cha'r.

Jist look—Lor's dar's chicken pie;
I eat my fill, unless I die.
   Dar's apple pie and ginger cake,
   'Tis 'nuff to make your jaw bones
     shake.

Well, I guess I'll 'gin to eat,
I'll first start on de chicken meat;
   And de pie nex' I t'ink I'll take,
   And den I'll hab de ginger cake.

Dis am my lucky day, whoopee!
Oh! here comes mammy Lawdy me!
   Wat' you doin' up dar, Sam?
   War's my strap—lam! de! lam!

Stealin' eh! you rascul you,
You jist wait 'twell I git thro'.
   Bip! Bam! "Oh! Mammy! wow!"
   Bam! Bam! "Oh, Lawdy! Ow!"

"I aint neber goin' steal no mo'"
 Bip! Bang! "You'll kill me sho'
   Oh! Lawdy, hear my humble cry.
 'Cause I b'leve I's gwine to die."

ॐ A[bby] M[orton] Diaz

TWO LITTLE ROGUES

Says Sammy to Dick,
"Come hurry! Come quick!
And we'll *do* and we'll *do* and we'll *do!*
Our mammy 's away,
She's gone for to stay,
And we'll make a great hullabaloo!
Ri too! ri loo! loo! loo! loo!
We'll make a great hullabaloo!"

Says Dicky to Sam,
"All weddy I am
To do, and to do, and to do.
But how doesth it go?
I so ittle to know.
Thay, what be a hullabawoo?
Ri too! ri loo! woo! woo! woo!
Thay, what be a hullabawoo?"

"O, slammings and hangings,
And whingings and whangings;
And very bad mischief we'll do!
We'll clatter and shout,
And knock things about,
And that's what's a hullabaloo!
Ri too! ri loo! loo! loo! loo!
And that's what's a hullabaloo!

Slide down the front stairs!
Tip over the chairs!
Now into the pantry break through!
Pull down all the tinware,
And pretty things in there!
All aboard for a hullabaloo!
Ri too! ri loo! loo! loo! loo!
All aboard for a hullabaloo!

Now roll up the table,
Far up as you're able,
Chairs, sofa, big easy-chair too!
Put the lamps and the vases
In funny old places.
How's this for a hullabaloo?
Ri too! ri loo! loo! loo! loo!
How's this for a hullabaloo?

Let the dishes and pans
Be the womans and mans;
Everybody keep still in their pew!
Mammy's gown I'll get next,
And preach you a text.
Dicky! hush with your hullabaloo!
Ri too! ri loo! loo! loo! loo!
Dicky! hush with your hullabaloo!"

As the preacher in gown
Climbed up and looked down
His queer congregation to view,
Said Dicky to Sammy,
"O, *dere* comes our mammy!
Se'll *pank* for dis hullabawoo!
Ri too! ri loo! woo! woo! woo!
Se'll *pank* for dis hullabawoo!"

"O mammy! O mammy!"
Cried Dicky and Sammy,
"We'll never again, certain true!"
But with firm step she trod
To take down the rod,—
O, then came a hullabaloo!
"Boohoo! boohoo! woo! woo! woo!"
O, then came a hullabaloo!

Arthur James Burdick

THE RUNAWAY BOY

Oh, the naughtiest, sauciest, wickedest boy
   That ever I chanced to see
Was the ragged and tattered and runaway boy
   Who happened to live near me.

Oh his parents and teachers he never would mind,
   And from school he'd run away,
With some other audacious and runaway boys,
   To indulge in idle play.

And the wob-ble-te-gob-ble-te-ketch-a-boy man
   Was one day passing that way,
And he captured that boy in the wink of an eye,
   And carried him far away.

He carried him deep in the wire-brier wood
   And left him all alone,
Where the bob-by-us-jump-py-us howled and roared,
   And the big boo-boo made moan.

And the hip-pi-o-hop-pi-o-not-si-ri-nos,
   He growled and prowled all day;
But which one of the hobgoblins made off with the boy
   I'm not quite ready to say.

Ella Wheeler Wilcox

THE DISCONTENTED MANICURE SCISSORS

Said the manicure scissors one day,
"The shears always have their own way,
    And I think it absurd
    That I am deterred
From entering into life's fray.

My task might be jolly for snails,
But I must confess that it fails
    To give pleasure to me;
    I am sick as can be
Of snipping the ends of pink nails.

I want to do work like the shears!"
So the scissors set out it appears,
    And very much wroth
    They tried to cut cloth,
And so split themselves open, my dears.

And the cloth, well you should have seen that;
It looked as if gnawed by a rat.
    Now little folks, you
    Must not think you can do
Whatever your elders are at.

Joel Stacy

THE NAUGHTY LITTLE EGYPTIAN

Long, long ago in Egypt land
    Where the lazy lotus grew,
And the pyramids, though vast and grand,
    Were rather fresh and new,
There dwelt an honored family,
    Called Scarabéus Phlat,
Whose duty 't was all faithfully
    To tend The Sacred Cat.

They brought the water of the Nile
    To bathe its precious feet;
They gave it oil and chamomile
    Whene'er it deigned to eat.

With gold and precious emeralds
    Its temple sparkled o'er,
And golden mats lay thick upon
    The consecrated floor.

And Scarabéus Phlat himself—
    A man of cheerful mood—
Held, not his trust from love of pelf,
    For he was very good.
He thought The Cat a catamount
    In strength and majesty;
And ever on his bronzéd face
    He wore a look of glee.

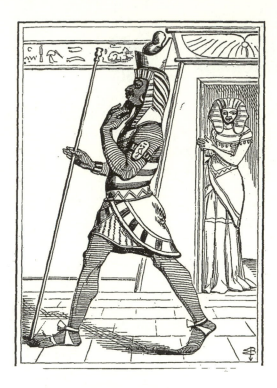

And Mrs. Scarabéus Phlat
   Was smiling, bright, and good;
For she, too, loved The Sacred Cat,
   As it was meet she should.
Never a grumpy syllable
   Came from this joyous pair;
And all the neighbors envied them
   Their very jolly air.

When Scarabéus went to find
   The Sacred Cat its store,
The pretty wife he left behind
   Stood smiling at the door.
He knew that sweetly, smilingly
   She'd welcome his return,
And brightly on the altar stone
   The tended flame would burn.

The Sacred Cat was different quite;
   No jollity he knew;
But, spoiled and petted day and night,
   Only the crosser grew.

Yet still they served him faithfully,
   And thought his snarling sweet;
And still they fed him lusciously,
   And bathed his sacred feet.

So far, so good. But hear the rest:
   This couple had a child,
A little boy, not of the best,—
   Ramesis, he was styled.
This little boy was beautiful,
   But soon he grew to be
So like The Cat in manners,—oh!
   'T was wonderful to see!

He might have copied Papa Phlat,
   Or Mamma Phlat, as well;
And why he didn't this or that
   No mortal soul could tell.
It wasn't want of discipline,
   Nor lack of good advice,
But just because he didn't care
   To be the least bit nice.

Besides, he noticed day by day
  How ill The Cat behaved,
And how (whatever they might say)
  His parents were enslaved;
And how they worshiped silently
  The naughty Sacred Cat.
Said he, "They'll do the same by me,
  If I but act like that."

At first the parents said: "How blest
  Are we, to find The Cat
Glow, humanized, within the breast
  Of a Scarabéus Phlat!"
But soon the neighbors, pitying,
  Whispered: "'T is very sad!
There's no mistake,—that little one
  Of Phlat's is very bad!"

He snarled, he squalled from night till
    morn,
  And scratched his mother's eyes.
The Sacred Cat, himself, looked on
  In undisguised surprise.
And here the record suddenly
  Breaks off. No more we know,

Excepting this: That happy pair
  Soon wore a look of woe.

Yes, then, and ever afterward,
  A look of pain they wore.
No more the wife stood smilingly
  A-waiting at the door.
No more did Scarabéus Phlat
  Display a jolly face;
But on his brow such sadness sat
  It gloomied all the place.

So, children, take the lesson in,
  And due attention give:
No matter when, or where, or how,
  Mothers and fathers live;
No matter be they Brown or Jones,
  Or Scarabéus Phlat,
It grieves their hearts to see their child
  Act like a naughty cat.
And Sacred Cats are well enough
  To those who hold them so;
But—oh, take warning of the boy
  In Egypt long ago!

&⁊ *Laura E. Richards*

WIGGLE AND WAGGLE AND BUBBLE AND SQUEAK

Wiggle and Waggle and Bubble and Squeak,
They went their fortunes for to seek;
They went to sea in a chicken-coop,
And they lived on mulligatawney soup.

Wiggle and Waggle and Bubble and Squeak,
They cooked their soup every day in the week;
They cooked their soup in a chimney-pot,
For there the water was always hot.

Wiggle and Waggle and Bubble and Squeak,
Each gave the other one's nose a tweak;
They tweaked so hard that it took their breath,
And so they met an untimely death.

☘ *Louisa May Alcott*

THE DOWNWARD ROAD

Two Yankee maids of simple mien,
   And earnest, high endeavor,
Come sailing to the land of France,
   To escape the winter weather.
When first they reached that vicious
    shore
   They scorned the native ways,
Refused to eat the native grub,
   Or ride in native shays.
"Oh, for the puddings of our home!
   Oh, for some simple food!
These horrid, greasy, unknown things,
   How can you think them good?"
Thus to Amanda did they say,
   An uncomplaining maid,
Who ate in peace and answered not
   Until one day they said,—
"How *can* you eat this garbage vile
   Against all Nature's laws?
How *can* you cut your nails in points,
   Until they look like claws?"
Then patiently Amanda said,
   "My loves, just wait a while,
The time will come you will not think
   The nails or victuals vile."
A month has passed, and now we see
   That prophecy fulfilled;
The ardor of those carping maids
   Is most completely chilled.

Matilda was the first to fall,
   Lured by the dark gossoon,
In awful dishes one by one,
   She dipped her timid spoon.
She promised for one little week
   To let her nails grow long,
But added in a saving clause
   She thought it very wrong.
Thus did she take the fatal plunge,
   Did compromise with sin:
Then all was lost, from that day forth
   French ways were sure to win.
Lavinia followed in her train,
   And ran the self-same road,
Ate sweet-bread first, then chopped-up
    brains,
   Eels, mushrooms, pickled toad.
She cries, "How flat the home *cuisine*,
   After this luscious food!
Puddings and brutal joints of meat,
   That once we fancied good!"
And now in all their leisure hours,
   One resource never fails,
Morning and noon and night they sit
   And polish up their nails.
Then if in one short fatal month,
   A change like this appears,
Oh, what will be the net result
   When they have stayed for years?

☘ *Phoebe Cary*

FEATHERS

You restless, curious little Jo,
I have told you all the stories I know,
   Written in poem or fable;
I have turned them over, and let you look
At everything like a picture-book
   Upon my desk or table.

I think it's enough to drive one wild
To be shut up with a single child,
   And try for a day to please her.
Oh, dear me! what does a mother do,
Especially one who lives in a shoe,
   And has a dozen to tease her?

"Aha! I've found the very thing,"
I cried, as I saw the beautiful wing
  Of a bird, and I said demurely:
"Now, if you'll be good the rest of the
    day,
I'll give you a bird with which to play;
  You know what a bird is, surely?

"Oh, yes!" and she opened wide her eyes,
"A bird is alive, and sings and flies;"
  Then, folding her hands together,
She archly shook her wise little head,
And, looking very innocent, said,
  "I know a bird from a feather!"

Well! of all the smart things uttered yet
By a baby three years old, my pet!
  It's enough to frighten your mother.
Why, I've seen women—yes, and men,
Who had lived for threescore years and
    ten,
  Who didn't know one from the other!

Now there is Kitty, past sixteen—
The one with the soldier beau, I mean—
  When he makes his bayonet rattle,
And acts so bravely on parade,
She thinks he wouldn't be afraid
  In the very front of battle.

But yet, if I were allowed to guess,
I should say her soldier was all in the
    dress,
  And you'll find my guess is the right
    one.
If ever he has to meet the foe,
The first, and only feather he'll show
  That day will be a white one.

There's Mrs. Pie, in her gorgeous plumes:
Why, half the folks who visit her rooms,
  Because she is dressed so finely
And holds herself at the highest price,
Pronounce her a bird of paradise,
  And say she sings divinely;

While many a one, with a sweeter lay,
Because her feathers are plain and gray,
  The world's approval misses,
And only gets its scorn and abuse;
She is called a failure, and called a goose,
  And her song is met with hisses.

Men will stick as many plumes on their
    head
As an Indian chief who has bravely shed
  The blood of a hostile nation,
When all the killing they've done or seen
Was killing themselves—that is, I mean
  In the public estimation.

When Tom to his pretty wife was wed,
"She's fuss and feathers," people said,
  That any woman could borrow;
And sure enough, her feathers fell,
Though the fuss was the genuine article,
  As Tom has found to his sorrow.

When Mrs. Butterfly, who was a grub,
First got her wings, she was such a snob,
  She scorned the folks around her,
And made, as she said, the feathers fly;
But when she fell, she had gone so high,
  She was smashed as flat as a flounder.

Alas, alas! my little Jo,
I'm sorry to tell it, and sorry it's so;
  But as to deceiving, I scorn to.
And I only hope that when you are grown
You will keep the wonderful wisdom
    you've shown,
  Nor lose the wit you were born to.

But whether folks, so wise when they're
    small,
Can ever live to grow up at all,
  Is one of the doubtful whethers.
I'm sure it happens but seldom, though,
Or there wouldn't be so many, you know.
  Who can't tell birds from feathers.

TELLING FORTUNES

"Be not among wine-bibbers; among riotous eaters of flesh; for the drunkard and the glutton shall come to poverty; and drowsiness shall clothe a man with rags."

—PROV. xxiii: 20, 21.

I'll tell you two fortunes, my fine little lad,
For you to accept or refuse.
The one of them good, and the other one bad;
Now hear them, and say which you choose!

I see by my gift, within reach of your hand,
A fortune right fair to behold;
A house and hundred good acres of land,
With harvest fields yellow as gold.

I see a great orchard, the boughs hanging down
With apples of russet and red;
I see droves of cattle, some white and brown,
But all of them sleek and well-fed.

I see doves and swallows about the barn-doors,
See the fanning-mill whirling so fast,
See men that are threshing the wheat on the floors;
And now the bright picture is past!

And I see, rising dismally up in the place,
Of the beautiful house and the land,
A man with a fire-red nose on his face,
And a little brown jug in his hand!

Oh! if you beheld him, my lad, you would wish
That he were less wretched to see;
For his boot-toes, they gape like the mouth of a fish,
And his trousers are out at the knee!

In walking he staggers now this way, now that,
And his eyes they stand out like a bug's,
And he wears an old coat and a battered-in hat,
And I think that the fault is the jug's!

For our text says the drunkard shall come to be poor
And drowsiness clothes men with rags;
And he doesn't look much like a man, I am sure,
Who has honest hard cash in his bags.

Now which will you choose? to be thrifty and snug,
And to be right side up with your dish;
Or to go with your eyes like the eyes of a bug,
And your shoes like the mouth of a fish!

❧ *Alice Cary*

BARBARA BLUE

There was an old woman
    Named Barbara Blue,
But not the old woman
    Who lived in a shoe,
And didn't know what
    With her children to do.

For she that I tell of
    Lived all alone,
A miserly creature
    As ever was known,
And had never a chick
    Or child of her own.

She kept very still,
    Some said she was meek;
Others said she was only
    Too stingy to speak;
That her little dog fed
    On one bone for a week!

She made apple-pies,
    And she made them so tart
That the mouths of the children
    Who ate them would smart;
And these she went peddling
    About in a cart.

One day, on her travels,
    She happened to meet
A farmer, who said
    He had apples so sweet
That all the town's-people
    Would have them to eat.

"And how do you sell them?"
    Says Barbara Blue.
"Why, if you want only
    A bushel or two,"
Says the farmer, "I don't mind
    To give them to you."

"What! Give me a bushel?"
    Cries Barbara Blue,
"A bushel of apples,
    And sweet apples, too!"
"Be sure," says the farmer,
    "Be sure, ma'am, I do."

And then he said if she
    Would give him a tart
(She had a great basket full
    There in her cart),
He would show her the orchard,
    And then they would part.

So she picked out a little one,
    Burnt at the top,
And held it a moment,
    And then let it drop,
And then said she hadn't
    A moment to stop,
And drove her old horse
    Away, hippity hop!

One night when the air was
    All blind with the snow,
Dame Barbara, driving
    So soft and so slow
That the farmer her whereabouts
    Never would know,

Went after the apples;
    And avarice grew
When she saw their red coats,
    Till, before she was through,
She took twenty bushels,
    Instead of the two!

She filled the cart full,
    And she heaped it a-top,
And if just an apple
    Fell off, she would stop,
And then drive ahead again,
    Hippity hop!

Her horse now would stumble,
    And now he would fall,
And where the high river-bank
    Sloped like a wall,
Sheer down, they went over it,
    Apples and all!

LEARNING LESSONS

❧ Ralph Waldo Emerson

FORBEARANCE

Hast thou named all the birds without a gun?
Loved the wood-rose, and left it on its stalk?
At rich men's tables eaten bread and pulse?
Unarmed, faced danger with a heart of trust?
And loved so well a high behavior,
In man or maid, that thou from speech refrained,
Nobility more nobly to repay?
O, be my friend, and teach me to be thine!

❧ Ralph Waldo Emerson

SO NIGH IS GRANDEUR

In an age of fops and toys,
   Wanting wisdom, void of right,
Who shall nerve heroic boys
   To hazard all in Freedom's fight,—
Break sharply off their jolly games,
   Forsake their comrades gay
And quit proud homes and youthful dames
   For famine, toil and fray?
Yet on the nimble air benign
   Speed nimbler messages,
That waft the breath of grace divine
   To hearts in sloth and ease.
So nigh is grandeur to our dust,
   So near is God to man,
When Duty whispers low, *Thou must,*
   The youth replies, *I can.*

❧ Henry David Thoreau

PRAYER

Great God, I ask thee for no meaner pelf
Than that I may not disappoint myself,
That in my action I may soar as high,
As I can now discern with this clear eye.

And next in value, which thy kindness lends,
That I may greatly disappoint my friends,
Howe'er they think or hope that it may be,
They may not dream how thou'st distinguished me.

That my weak hand may equal my firm faith,
And my life practise more than my tongue saith;
That my low conduct may not show,
    Nor my relenting lines,
That I thy purpose did not know,
    Or overrated thy designs.

❦ *Anna Bartlett Warner*

JESUS BIDS US SHINE

Jesus bids us shine
    With a pure, clear light,
Like a little candle,
    Burning in the night.
In the world is darkness
    So we must shine,
You in your small corner,
    And I in mine.

Jesus bids us shine,
    First of all, for Him:
Well He sees and knows it
    If one light is dim!

He looks down from heaven
    To see us shine;
You in your small corner,
    And I in mine.

Jesus bids us shine,
    Then for all around;
For many kinds of darkness,
    In the world are found.
There's sin, there's want, and sorrow,
    So we must shine,
You in your small corner,
    And I in mine.

❦ *Ella Wheeler Wilcox*

THE BARBAROUS CHIEF

There was a kingdom known as the Mind,
    A kingdom vast as fair,
And the brave king, Brain, had the right to reign,
    In royal splendor there.
Oh! that was a beautiful, beautiful land,
    Which unto this king was given;
Filled with everything good and grand,
    And it reached from earth to heaven.

But a savage monster came one day
    From over a distant border;
He warred with the king and disputed his sway,
    And set the whole land in disorder.
He mounted the throne, which he made his own,
    He sunk the kingdom in grief.
There was trouble and shame from the hour he came—
    Illtemper, the barbarous chief.

He threw down the castles of love and peace,
    He burned up the altars of prayers.
He trod down the grain that was planted by Brain,
    And scattered thistles and tares.
He wasted the store-house of knowledge and drove
    Queen Wisdom away in fright;
And a terrible gloom, like the cloud of doom,
    Shrouded that land in night.

Bent on more havoc away he rushed
    To the neighboring kingdom, Heart;
And the blossoms of kindness and hope he crushed—
    And patience he pierced with his dart,
And he even went on to the Isthmus Soul,
    That unites the mind with God,
And its beautiful bowers of fragrant flowers
    With a ruthless heel he trod.

To you is given this wonderful land
    Where the lordly Brain has sway;
But the border ruffian is near at hand,
    Be on your guard, I pray.
Beware of Illtemper, the barbarous chief,
    He is cruel as vice or sin,
And your beautiful kingdom will come to grief
    If once you let him in.

THE VILLAGE BLACKSMITH

Under a spreading chestnut-tree
  The village smithy stands;
The smith, a mighty man is he,
  With large and sinewy hands;
And the muscles of his brawny arms
  Are strong as iron bands.

His hair is crisp, and black, and long,
  His face is like the tan;
His brow is wet with honest sweat,
  He earns whate'er he can,
And looks the whole world in the face,
  For he owes not any man.

Week in, week out, from morn till night,
  You can hear his bellows blow;
You can hear him swing his heavy sledge
  With measured beat and slow,
Like a sexton ringing the village bell,
  When the evening sun is low.

And children coming home from school
  Look in at the open door;
They love to see the flaming forge,
  And hear the bellows roar,
And catch the burning sparks that fly
  Like chaff from a threshing-floor.

He goes on Sunday to the church,
  And sits among his boys;
He hears the parson pray and preach,
  He hears his daughter's voice,
Singing in the village choir,
  And it makes his heart rejoice.

It sounds to him like her mother's voice,
  Singing in Paradise!
He needs must think of her once more,
  How in the grave she lies;
And with his hard, rough hand he wipes
  A tear out of his eyes.

Toiling,—rejoicing,—sorrowing,
  Onward through life he goes;
Each morning sees some task begin,
  Each evening sees it close;
Something attempted, something done,
  Has earned a night's repose.

Thanks, thanks to thee, my worthy
    friend,
  For the lesson thou hast taught!
Thus at the flaming forge of life
  Our fortunes must be wrought;
Thus on its sounding anvil shaped
  Each burning deed and thought!

Joaquin Miller

FOR THOSE WHO FAIL

"All honor to him who shall win the prize,"
    The world has cried for a thousand years;
But to him who tries, and who fails and dies,
    I give great honor and glory and tears:

Give glory and honor and pitiful tears
    To all who fail in their deeds sublime;
Their ghosts are many in the van of years,
    They were born with Time in advance of Time.

Oh, great is the hero who wins a name,
    But greater many and many a time
Some pale-faced fellow who dies in shame,
    And lets God finish the thought sublime.

And great is the man with a sword undrawn,
    And good is the man who refrains from wine;
But the man who fails and yet still fights on,
    Lo, he is the twin-born brother of mine.

Julia A. F. Carney

LITTLE THINGS

Little drops of water
    Little grains of sand,
Make the mighty ocean,
    And the pleasant land.

Thus the little moments,
    Humble though they be,
Make the mighty ages
    Of eternity.

Thus our little errors
    Lead the soul away
From the path of virtue,
    Off in sin to stray.

Little deeds of kindness,
    Little words of love,
Make our earth an Eden,
    Like the heaven above.

ea *Anna M. Pratt*

A USEFUL POSSESSION

If a string is in a knot
   Patience will untie it.
Patience can do many things;
   Did you ever try it?
If it was sold at any shop
   I should like to buy it,
But you and I must find our own;
   No other can supply it.

ea *Walt Whitman*

THE COMMONPLACE

The commonplace I sing;
How cheap is health! how cheap nobility!
Abstinence, no falsehood, no gluttony, lust;
The open air I sing, freedom, toleration,
(Take here the mainest lesson—less from books—less from the schools),
The common day and night—the common earth and waters,
Your farm—your work, trade, occupation,
The democratic wisdom underneath, like solid ground for all.

ea *Edward Rowland Sill*

A BAKER'S DUZZEN UV WIZE SAWZ

Them ez wants, must choose.
Them ez hez, must lose.
Them ez knows, won't blab.
Them ez guesses, will gab.
Them ez borrows, sorrows.
Them ez lends, spends.
Them ez gives, lives.
Them ez keeps dark, is deep.
Them ez kin earn, kin keep.
Them ez aims, hits.
Them ez hez, gits.
Them ez waits, win.
Them ez *will, kin.*

Author Unknown

[ALPHABET]

ANT.

How wisely and frugal
　　The little ANT plies!
Come hither, ye sluggards,
　　And learn to be wise.

BIBLE.

Within this sacred book,
　　The words of life are given,
Wherein should all men look,
　　And learn the way to Heaven.

CAT.

The CAT with care
　　From rat and mouse,
Your trust to share,
　　Defends the house.

DOG.

With faithful diligence,
　　The DOG your house will keep;
And from the raging wolf,
　　Protect your tender sheep.

EGG.

Imprison'd in the shell,
　　The chick securely lies;
But when deliver'd from its cell,
　　Abroad for food it cries.

FOX.

Sly Reynard the fox,
　　Will certainly slay,
Your hens and your cocks,
　　If they come in his way.

GRAPES.

See, here are the grapes,
　　Which Reynard did want;
Tho' nimbly he leaps,
　　Yet catch them he can't.

HOUR-GLASS.

Mortals behold the hour-glass,
　　And leave your worldly care;
It shews how swift our minutes pass,
　　And bids us all for death prepare.

IDOL.

The ancient heathens, we are told,
　　Worship'd an idol made of gold;
Our misers still, as heretofore,
　　The precious idol do adore.

KEY.

To keep the golden glitt'ring store,
　　A smyth the key invented:
Many there are who thirst for more;
　　Scarce one that is contented.

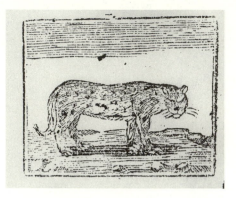

LEOPARD.

With native beauty see how fine
    This fierce but noble beast doth shine!
Nature here has far outdone
    All that art has ever known.

MONKEY.

See the monkey frisk and play,
    See him all his tricks display:
Ev'ry thing but speak he can,
    In all but speech a little man.

NIGHTINGALE.

Night and morn, on a thorn,
    The nightingale doth sing;
Sweet the note, soft the throat,
    Whence these sonnets spring.

OAK.

Of all the noble trees,
    That grace the forest wide,
The royal oak for bulk and strength,
    Has never been outvi'd.

PURSE.

Here you behold a purse of gold,
    All rich and dazzling to the sight;
Yet let not vice your mind entice,
    To take in gold too much delight.

QUILL.

What matchless skill is in the quill,
    Pluck'd from a goose's wing!
By this the wise their maxims teach,
    By this the poets sing.

ROSE.

Of ev'ry flow'r, the beauteous rose
    Sweetest smells and fairest blows;
Yet e'en rose[s] soon decay,
    Wither, fade, and die away.

SERPENT.

Bred in cunning, form'd in guile,
    See the shining serpent rise!
Skill'd in each deceitful wile,
    Hapless victims to surprize.

TEMPLE.

Holy temples were design'd,
    For each pure and humble mind,
To pray, and praise the Lord most high,
    Who all their wants can satisfy.

VIZARD.

Vizards but conceal the fate,
    Hypocrisy the heart;
Many put on a shew of grace,
    To act a navish part.

WIND-MILL.

Agitated by the wind,
    The flying fans go round,
And set the mill to work, we find,
    By which the corn is ground.

XERXES.

Xerxes in all his pomp and state,
　　Did like an infant cry,
To think his host, so vast, so great,
　　In one poor age must die.

YOUTH.

Youth to pastime is inclin'd,
　　Ever fix'd on play:
Sport unbends the studious mind,
　　And makes the heart more gay.

ZANY.

You here the antic zany view.
　　Quite void of sense or wit;
Yet what the wise in vain pursue,
　　The fool will sometimes hit.

❧ *"A Lady of Savannah"* [pseudonym]

WILLIE'S POLITICAL ALPHABET

Come, Willie, come study your State Alphabet:
First A's for the Army—now don't you forget—
And B's for the Banner, the "flag of the free,"
For Beauregard, Bartow, Bethel and Bee!
And C's for the "Southern Confederacy" brave,
Our bold little ship, all afloat on the wave!
And D's for Davis, oh, wide as the sea
Shall the fame of our glorious President be!
Next, E's for the Eighth, they were first in the fight,
And F is for Freedom, the freedom of right,
And G stands for Georgia,—the flower, the queen,
And H is for Hampton, his legion I mean!
Now I is the Infantry, sturdy and strong,
And the J's to the Johnsons and Jacksons belong,
And K's for "King Cotton" he sits on his throne,
The monarch of nations, alone, all alone!
And L stands for Lincoln, oh, woe to his crown!
"King Cotton," "King Cotton" is trampling him down!
And M's for Manassas, our glory, our pride,
And N for the Navy, the waters to guide,
And O's for the Oglethorpes, glorious name!
O write it in gold on the pages of fame!
And stamp Carolina the rebel the worst,
With a P for Palmetto, secession the first!
And Q is so twisted, so twisted and twirled,

That Q's for the traitors, all over the world,
And R for the Rebels, the rebels shall stand—
And S for Savannah, our own native land.
And U's for the Union, a wreck on the sea!
And V's for our Victory, bright as the sun,
And W for Washington, soon to be won!
And X still a place in your letters must keep,
O X is a cross for the heroes you weep!
Y for the Yankees, the Yankees is set,
Then Z for the Zouaves—now don't you forget—
For Z is the end of your State Alphabet.

&❧ *Authors Unknown*

LEFT OVERS FROM GOOD ENGLISH WEEK:
SLOGANS AND RHYMES BY VOCATIONAL IV, GIRLS

1. Hang,
    Slang!
2. While slang is in the atmosphere,
    We must treat it with a sneer.
3. Here's to the class of 1920!
    Good English we must have aplenty.
4. Be a good walker
    And a good talker.
5. Do not slave for master "Slanguage."
    Be your own master, uphold good language.
6. s—stands for spelling important for all,
    p—perseverance, for patience and pull.
    e—stands for effort put forth on our words.
    l—stands for leaders of which you have heard.
    l—stands for loyal, applied to this class,
    If we can spell, perhaps we shall pass.
7. Be clean in your speech
    Our slogan this week.
8. Hail to the class of '20!
    We're studious far than some.
    And when we speak, we'll use no slang,
    And chew no chewing gum.

Author Unknown

CURIOUS RHYMES

What is earth, sexton?
  A place to dig graves.
What is earth, rich man?
  A place to work slaves.

What is earth, gray beard?
  A place to grow old.
What is earth, miser?
  A place to dig for gold.

What is earth, school-boy?
  A place for my play.
What is earth, maiden?
  A place to be gay.

What is earth, seamstress?
  A place where I weep.
What is earth, sluggard?
  A good place to sleep.

What is earth, soldier?
  A place for battle.

What is earth, herdsman?
  A place to raise cattle.

What is earth, widow?
  A place of true sorrow.
What is earth, tradesman?
  I'll tell you to-morrow.

What is earth, sick man?
  'Tis nothing to me.
What is earth, sailor?
  My home is the sea.

What is earth, statesman?
  A place to win fame.
What is earth, author?
  I'll write there my name.

What is earth, monarch?
  For my realm, 'tis given.
What is earth, Christian?
  The gateway of heaven.

Kate Lawrence

QUESTIONS

Can you put the spider's web back in its place, that once has been swept away?
Can you put the apple again on the bough, which fell at our feet to-day?
Can you put the lily-cup back on the stem, and cause it to live and grow?
Can you mend the butterfly's broken wing, that you crushed with a hasty blow?
Can you put the bloom again on the grape, or the grape again on the vine?
Can you put the dewdrops back on the flowers, and make them sparkle and shine?
Can you put the petals back on the rose? If you could, would it smell as sweet?
Can you put the flour again in the husk, and show me the ripened wheat?
Can you put the kernel back in the nut, or the broken egg in its shell?
Can you put the honey back in the comb, and cover with wax each cell?
Can you put the perfume back in the vase, when once it has sped away?
Can you put the corn-silk back on the corn, or the down on the catkins—say?
You think that my questions are trifling, dear? Let me ask you another one:
Can a hasty word ever be unsaid, or a deed unkind, undone?

&8 *Peter Newell*

A YOUNG PHILOSOPHER

"My eyes are very much alike, as you can
    plainly see,
And act in perfect harmony, and never
    disagree.
When to the right I turn one eye, the
    other turns also,
And when I turn one to the left, so must
    the other go.
And when I wink with one eye, then the
    other wants to wink.
Oh, they are very much alike, my two eyes,
    Don't you think?"

&8 *Anne L. Huber*

HOW MUCH, AND HOW MANY

How many stars are in the sky?
You don't know, neither do I.

How many fishes are in the sea?
I'll tell you, if you'll tell me.

How much water is in the well?
Dip it out, then you can tell.

How many leaves are on the tree?
Pick them off, then you will see.

How many ding-dongs in a bell?
The clapper knows, but it won't tell.

How much love has my mother for me?
No tongue can tell, no eye can see.

A MERCANTILE TRANSACTION

"A pound of jumps!" and I looked in surprise
At little black Rose with her shining eyes.

"A pound of jumps!"—my mother said
"A pound of jumps," and she nodded her head.

"But, my dear, we've flour, and sugar in lumps,
And peanuts but never a pound of jumps,

With walnuts and chestnuts and corn that pops—"
"O, O! I forgot! it's a pound of hops!"

Authors Unknown

NEW MILK.

"Meeleck! Come Meeleck, Come!"

Here's New Milk from the Cow,
   Which is so nice and so fine,
That the doctors do say,
   It is much better than wine.

This wholesome beverage, is carried all round the city by men in carts, wagons, and very large tin kettles, as we see in the cut. The cows are pastured on the Island of New-York, some along the New-Jersey shore, and large droves on Long-Island. Milk sells from 4 to 6 cents per quart, delivered at our doors every morning in the winter season, and twice a day in summer.

SAND O!

"S-A-N-D! Here's your nice white S-A-N-D!"

Sand, O! white Sand O!
   Buy sand for your floor;
For so cleanly it looks
   When strewed at your door.

This Sand is brought from the sea shore in vessels, principally from Rockaway Beach, Long-Island. It is loaded into carts, and carried about the streets of New-York, and sold for about 12½ cents per bushel. Almost every little girl or boy, knows that it is put on newly scrubbed floors, to preserve them clean and pleasant.

BEANS, PEAS &C. &C.

"Here's Beans, Peas, Cucumbers, Cabbage, Onions, Potatoes, Here they go!"

Here's nice Beans or Peas,
   Only ten pence a peck!
Come buy if you please,
   I've an excellent stock.

In the summer time, you may see persons in carts, and others with hand-barrows, having a load of the above articles, that they cry along our streets, and sell to those families who live a distance from the markets.

What a vast garden it would take to raise vegetables enough for all the inhabitants of New-York! Long Island may be considered the garden of New-York: the produce brought to this city daily is very great.

HOT CORN!

"Here's your nice Hot Corn!
   "Smoking hot! piping hot!
"O what beauties I have got!"

Here's smoking hot Corn,
   With salt that is nigh,
Only two pence an ear,—
   O pass me not by!

From midsummer, till late in the autumn, our ears during the evenings, are saluted with this cry. The corn is plucked while green, and brought to our markets from the surrounding country, in great quantities. It is boiled in the husk, and carried about the streets in pails and large bowls, with a little salt, and sold from a penny to two pence an ear.

MATCHES!

"Will you have any matches to-day?
   Twenty bunches for 6d."

Fine Matches! good Matches!
   Will you please to have any,
In pity do take some,
   Three bunches a penny.

To sell matches, is the employment of women and children, who make a few pence honestly, by slitting pine or cedar sticks, or procuring a long thin shaving, the ends of which they dip in brimstone, which, when touched by a spark, will blaze directly.— Though a small matter, it is a great convenience to house-keepers.

This is a very humble business, but it is not to be despised on that account.

Author Unknown

PORK AND BEEF

Little Jane thinks she can tell
  What pork is when alive;
She knows their squeaking noise quite
    well,
  When pigs to market drive.

Well, Jane is right, for pork is pig,
  But does she know beside,
That when they older grow, and big,
  Bacon they make, if dried.

And what is beef? sure James must
    know,
  For often have we seen
The creature running to and fro
  When in the fields we've been.

She cannot guess, I must explain,
  The ox is then its name;
And other countries try in vain
  To equal ours in fame.

Author Unknown

WHAT IS VEAL

William ask'd how veal was made,
  His little sister smil'd
It grew in foreign climes, she said,
  And call'd him silly child.

Eliza, laughing at them both,
  Told to their great surprise,
The meat cook boil'd to make the broth,
  Once liv'd, had nose, and eyes;

Nay, more, had legs, and walk'd about;
  William in wonder stood,
He could not make the riddle out,
  But begg'd his sister would.

Well, brother, I have had my laugh,
  And you shall have yours now,
Veal, when alive, was called a calf—
  Its mother was a cow.

Author Unknown

WHAT IS MUTTON

If veal is calf, what's mutton, pray;
  That cannot be calf too?
No, William, no, but step this way,
  And mutton is in view.

Eliza, I see nothing there,
  But flocks of wooly sheep;
Yet stay, I think some lambs there are
  Grazing down yonder steep.

True brother, and when sheep we kill,
  Mutton becomes its name;
When young we call it lamb, but still
  The taste is much the same.

The wool which from its back we shear,
  Makes nice warm coats for you,
Flannel for Jane and I to wear.
  And other uses, too.

❦ M. A., Sisters of Mercy

THE GEOGRAPHY OF IRELAND

Written for Irish Children in Exile

My native home is Erin, my own, my Father's land,
I love its flowery valleys, I love its memories grand:
The wild Atlantic ocean between us pours its tide,
Yet will I try to know it from North to Shannon side.

The North, green, fertile Ulster—I love it well, for there
The green, soft grassy hills are set, its ramparts strong and fair;
There Monaghan and Armagh stand, Cavan and green Tyrone,
And Donegal and Derry, where James was overthrown.

Fermanagh there its lakes of blue spread to the sun's bright rays,
And Antrim where the Causeway stands, where shines the broad Lough Neagh;
The Bann and the Blackwater, and the Foyle's broad sweeping flood,
And a thousand springs are pouring free thro' valley, plain and wood.

Leinster has twelve broad counties where Dublin city stands,
Liffey and Boyne, and Barrow flow through its fertile lands;
Wicklow, Kilkenny, Wexford, Dublin, Louth and Meath,
Kildare and Carlow, may they all the sword of discord sheath.

Longford—the ancient Annaly's, a hospitable soil,
Though woefully her son's are pressed by tyranny and toil;
The ruins of her abbeys by the Crumlin's banks are seen,
And the name of Temple-Michael tells where a church hath been.

Alas, for Leix and Offaly! they bear an English name;
King's County and the Queen's they're called,—words redolent of shame;
And now I pass from Leinster and the ancient English pale,
Where Strongbow ravaged and where lived famous Granu Aile.

Old Connaught! O my country, how all the bygone days
Saw heroes fill its homestead, and harpers hymn its praise;
Leitrim, Roscommon, Sligo, and Galway's famous town,
And Mayo with its Abbeys and Aughrim's sad renown.

Five counties, many a battle field, and many a holy shrine,
And many a tale of stormy strife, old Connaught, all are thine—
Southward is fertile Munster with its old Milesian fame,
And its learning, wild and racy, and its soul of restless flame.

The Shannon sweeps through Limerick and Tipperary bounds,
And Kerry where O'Connell's voice still in our thought resounds;

Cork! the green island's borders contain no land more fair,
And in it Waterford is found, and westward ancient Clare.

Through Munster flows the pleasant Lee, and the sunny Avonmore,
And thy famous Lakes, Killarney, with all their fairy lore;
There Mangerton uplifts his brow, and Turk with all his woods
Of flowery arbutus, keeps guard around thy floods.

Thus thro' old Erin in sad and wistful thought,
My native land, my mother, may I love thee as I ought;
Thus early, early exiled, may still my heart be true,
O Martyr of the Nations! through good and ill to you!

To you I owe my faith, to you my hope in God on high—
Oh may His love still lead me on, till in that faith I die;
And may your long, dark sorrows cease, oh may we one day see
The Emerald Isle, the Ocean's gem, a happy land and free.

Laura E. Richards

TOMMY'S DREAM, OR THE GEOGRAPHY DEMON

I hate my geography lesson!
    It's nothing but nonsense and names.
To bother me so every Thursday,
    I think it's the greatest of shames.

The brooklets flow into the rivers,
    The rivers flow into the sea;
For my part, I hope they enjoy it!
    But what does it matter to me?

Of late, even more I've disliked it,
    And more disagreeable it seems,
Ever since that sad night of last winter,
    When I had that most frightful of
        dreams.

I dreamed that a horrible monster
    Came suddenly into my room—
A frightful Geography Demon,
    Enveloped in darkness and gloom;

His body and head like a mountain,
    A volcano on top for hat;
His arms and his legs were like rivers,
    With a brook round his neck for cravat.

He laid on my trembling shoulder
    His fingers, cold, clammy, and long;
And rolling his red eyes upon me,
    He roared forth this horrible song:

"Come! come! rise and come
    Away to the banks of the Muskingum!
It rolls o'er the plains of Timbuctoo,
With the Peak of Teneriffe just in view;
And the cataracts leap in the pale moon
        shine,
As they dance o'er the cliffs of Brandy
        wine.

"Flee! Flee! rise and flee
    Away to the banks of the Tombigbee!
We'll pass by Alaska's flowery strand,
Where the emerald towers of Pekin
        stand;
We'll pass it by, and we'll rest awhile
On Michillimackinack's tropic isle;
While the apes of Barbary frisk around,
And the parrots crow with a lovely
        sound.

"Hie! hie! rise and hie
  Away to the banks of the Yang-tse-kai!
  There the giant mountains of Oshkosh
    stand,
  And the icebergs gleam through the
    shifting sand;
  While the elephant sits in the palm tree
    high,
  And the cannibals feast upon bad-boy
    pie.

"Go! go! rise and go
  Away to the banks of the Hoang-ho
  There the Chickasaw sachem makes his
    tea,
  And the kettle boils and waits for thee.
  We'll smite thee, ho! and we'll lay thee
    low,
  On the beautiful banks of the Hoang-
    ho!"

These terrible words were still sounding
  Like trumpets and drums through my
    head,
When the monster clutched tighter my
    shoulder,
  And dragged me half out of the bed.

In terror, I clung to the bed-post;
  But the faithless bed-post, it broke;
I screamed out aloud in my anguish,
  And suddenly—well, I awoke!!—

He was gone. But I cannot forget him,
  The fearful Geography Sprite.
He has my first thought in the morning,
  He has my last shudder at night.

Do you blame me for hating my lesson?
  Is it strange that it frightful should
    seem?
Or that I more and more should abhor it
  Since I had that most horrible dream?

☙ C. Perry

A BOY'S REMONSTRANCE

I am feeling very badly; everything is going to smash:
All the things I have believed in are going with a crash!
The folks are growing learned, and all their wretched lore is
Used to shake a fellow's faith in his best-beloved stories.
The fairies have been scattered, and the genii they have gone,
There are no enchanted castles; they have vanished, every one.
Aladdin never lived, and the dear Scheherazade,
Though very entertaining, was a much mistaken lady.
Of course I see through Santa Claus, I had to, long ago;
And Christmas will be going, the next thing that I know,
For I heard, I wasn't listening—I heard the parson say,
He had really—yes had really—grave doubts about the day.
And as for Master Washington, they say the goose should catch it,
Who believed a single minute in that story of the hatchet.
They've given a rap at Crusoe, and dear old Friday. Why!
We'll all believe in Friday, we boys will, till we die!
They may say it's not "authentic," and such like if they dare!
When they strike a blow at Friday, they hit us boys. So there!

And I've been reading in a book, writ by some college swell,
That there never was a genuine, a real live William Tell!
That lie was just a myth, or what we boys would call a sell:
That he didn't shoot the apple, nor Gesler, not a bit—
That all the other nations have a legend just like it.
I think it's little business for a college man to fight
Against these dear old stories and send them out of sight.
And all the boys are just as mad! and so the girls are, too;
And so we called a meeting to decide what we should do.
And we passed some resolutions, because that is the one
And only way for meetings, when it's all that can be done.
I send you here a list: Resolved, that there was a William Tell;
That by his bow and arrow the tyrant Gesler fell.
Resolved, that he was not a myth, whatever that may be—
But that he shot the apple and Switzerland was free.
Resolved, that Crusoe lived, and Friday, and the goat.
Resolved, that little Georgy his father's fruit-tree smote,
And owned up like a hero. Resolved, that all the science
Of all the learned professors shall not shake our firm reliance
In the parties we have mentioned; and we do hereby make known
The fact that we boys feel that we have some rights of our own—
And request that in the future these rights be let alone.

Janet Miller

THE CRITIC

We were "practising scales" in the parlor,
    And the air was wild with our din,
When, happening to glance at the window,
    A robin was looking in,

His wee head turned sideways with wonder,
    As he listened in mute surprise;
For how those children could blunder
    In scales, he couldn't surmise.

Ah! robin, don't judge in a hurry,
    Though *your* scales are quite without flaws;
Don't you think you would be in a flurry,
    If you were obliged to use claws?

🍀 *Christina Moody (age 13–16)*

TO MY DEAR READER

Don't criticize my writing
    Cause I ain't well trained you know
I hab al-ways been so sickly
    Dat I haben had much show.

Don't laff and ridicule me
    Cause 'twill make me feel ashamed,
For I knows dat I ain't great
    Nor neither have I fame.

Some of dese poems you'er reading
    Was written long ago,
When I was just a little kid
    Of thirteen years or so.

Don't criticize my poems,
    'Cause I wrote 'em all for you;
I ain't had much training
    'Tis de best dat I can do.

And if you find's my book
    Ain't good as t'ought to be,
Jist leave it to my ignorance
    And don't you laff at me.

🍀 *Mary Mapes Dodge*

THE WAY TO DO IT

I'll tell you how I speak a piece:
    First, I make my bow;
Then I bring my words out clear
    And plain as I know how.

Next, I throw my hands up *so!*
    Then I lift my eyes—
That's to let my hearers know
    Something doth surprise.

Next, I grin and show my teeth,
    Nearly every one;
Shake my shoulders, hold my sides:
    That's the sign of fun.

Next I start and knit my brow,
    Hold my head erect:
Something's wrong, you see, and I
    Decidedly object.

Then I wabble at my knees,
    Clutch at shadows near,
Tremble well from top to toe:
    That's the sign of fear.

Now I start, and with a leap
    Seize an airy dagger.
"WRETCH!" I cry. That's tragedy,
    Every soul to stagger.

Then I let my voice grow faint,
    Gasp and hold my breath;
Tumble down and plunge about:
    That's a villain's death.

Quickly then I come to life,
    (Pardon me the fraud)
With a bow my speech is done—
    Now, you'll please applaud.

THE BOY IS COLD

I think I might get near the grate,
  My toes they grow colder and colder;
I am sure I wish, early and late,
  That I could be bigger and older.

There's grandma' stowed close by the fire,
  And she's managed to squeeze in my
    brother;
Aunt Polly has got her desire,
  And sits like a toast next to mother.

My teeth they all shake in my head,
  And my hands are like skimm'd milk so
    blue;
And my feet feel as if they were dead,
  And I'm sure I can't tell what to do.

I have tried once or twice to go near,
  And they cry out, "Oh, don't be a baby,
Run about and you'll warm yourself, dear;"
  They think I've no feeling then, may be.

I just wish that from now till to-morrow
  They and I could change fingers and
    toes,
And then they'd find out to their
    sorrow,
  How a fellow must feel when he's *froze.*

NOT READY FOR SCHOOL

Pray, where is my hat? It is taken away,
  And my shoe-strings are all in a knot!
I can't find a thing where it should be
    to-day,
  Though I've hunted in every spot.

My slate and my pencil nowhere can be
    found,
  Though I placed them as safe as can be;
While my books and my maps are all
    scattered around,
  And hop about just like a flea.

Do, Rachel, just look for my atlas up stairs,
  My Aesop is somewhere there, too;
And, sister, just brush down these
    troublesome hairs,
  And, mother, just fasten my shoe.

And, sister, beg father to write an excuse;
  But stop, he will only say "No";
And go on with a smile, and keep reading
    the news,
  While everything bothers me so.

My satchel is heavy, and ready to fall,
  This old pop-gun is breaking my map;
I'll have nothing to do with the pop-gun or
    ball,
  There's no playing for such a poor chap.

The town clock will strike in a minute,
    I fear,
  Then away to the foot I must sink;
There, look at my Eaton has tumbled down
    here,
  And my Worcester's covered with ink.

I wish I'd not lingered at breakfast the
last,
  Though the toast and the butter were
  fine;
I think that our Edward must eat pretty
fast,
  To be off when I haven't done mine.

Now Edward and Harry protest they
won't wait,
  And beat on the door with their
  sticks;
I suppose they will say *I was dressing too
late;*
  To-morrow, *I'll be up at six.*

☙ *Caroline Howard Gilman and Caroline Howard Gilman Jervey*

CANNOT WRITE POETRY

My paper is ruled very neat,
  Father's made me an *elegant* pen;
I sit quite upright on my seat,
  And have everything ready; what then?

I have scratched my head several times,
  And nothing comes out of it yet;
For my life I can't make out the rhymes;
  Not a word can I think of but—*fret.*

Dear mother, do help me a bit,
  I'm puzzled,—no matter,—here goes,—
But how the right measure to hit,—
  I have a good subject,—I know-s.

There once was a widow in trouble,
  She was aged and old, and advanced;
Not a word I can think of but *bubble,*
  And it won't do to say that she danced.

A widow she was of great feeling,
  Of great feeling this widow was she;
'Twill be shocking to speak of her squealing,
  And how can I lug in a flea!

This widow to woe was a votary,
  Oh, mother! you laugh at her woes,
And say I had better quit poetry,
  Until I know how to write prose.

SLAVERY AND FREEDOM

THE LITTLE SLAVE'S WISH

I wish I was that little bird
   Up in the bright blue sky,
That sings and flies just where he will,
   And no one asks him why.

I wish I was that little brook
   That runs so swift along,
Through pretty flowers, and shining
     stones,
   Singing a merry song.

I wish I was a butterfly,
   Without a fear or care,
Spreading my many-colour'd wings,
   Like a flower in the air.

I wish I was that wild, wild deer,
   That I saw the other day,
Who through the dark-green forest flew,
   Like an arrow far away.

I wish I was that little cloud
   By the gentle south wind driven,

Floating along so calm and bright
   Up to the gates of heaven.

I'd rather be a savage beast,
   And dwell in a gloomy cave,
And shake the forest when I roared,
   Than what I am,—a slave.

My mother calls me her good boy,
   My father calls me brave;
What wicked action have I done
   That I should be a slave?

They tell me God is very good,
   That his right arm can save;
Oh, is it, can it be his will
   That I should be a slave?

O, how much better 'tis to die,
   And lie down in the grave,
Than 'tis to be what I am now,—
   A little negro slave!

E.T.C.

LETTER FROM AN INFANT SLAVE TO THE CHILD OF ITS MISTRESS—BOTH BORN ON THE SAME DAY

Baby! be not surprised to see
A few short lines coming from me,
   Addressed to you;
For babies black of three months old
May write as well, as I've been told,
   Some white ones do.

There are some things I hear and see,
Which very much do puzzle me,
   Pray don't they you?
For the same day our lives began,
And all things here beneath the sun,
   To both are new.

Baby, sometimes I hear you cry,
And many run to find out why,
   And cure the pain;
But when I cry from pains severe,
There's no one round who seems to hear,
   I cry in vain.

Except it be when she is nigh,
Whose gentle love, I know not why,
   Is all for me;
Her tender care soothes all my pain,
Brings to my face those smiles again,
   She smiles to see.

With hunger faint, with grief distressed,
I once my wretchedness expressed,
  With urgent power;
Some by my eloquence annoyed,
To still my grief rough blows employed;
  Oh, dreadful hour!

When first *thy* father saw his child,
With hope, and love, and joy, he
      smiled—
  Bright schemes he planned;
Mine groaned, and said with sullen brow,
Another *slave* is added now
  To this free land.

Why am I thought so little worth,
You prized so highly from your birth?
  Tell, if you know;
Why are my woes and joys as nought,
With careful love yours shunned or
      sought?
  Why is it so?

My own dear mother, it is true,
Loves me as well as yours does you;
  But when she's gone,
None else to me a care extends;
Oh, why have you so many friends,
  I only one?

Why must that one be sent away,
Compelled for long, long hours to stay
  Apart from me?
I think as much as I she mourns,
And is as glad when she returns,
  Her child to see.

One day I saw my mother weep,
A tear fell on me when asleep,
  And made me wake;
Not for herself that tear was shed,
Her own woes she could bear, she said,
  But for my sake.

She could not bear, she said, to think,
That I the cup of woe must drink,
  Which she had drunk;
That from my cradle to my grave,
I too must live a wretched slave,
  Degraded, sunk.

Her words I scarcely understood,
They seemed to speak of little good,
  For coming years;
But joy with all my musings blends,
And infant thought not far extends
  Its hopes or fears.

I ponder much to comprehend
What sort of beings, gentle friend,
  We've got among;
Some things in my experience,
Do much confound my budding sense
  Of right and wrong.

Baby, I love you; 'tis not right
To love you less because you're white;
  Then surely you
Will never learn to scorn or hate,
Whom the same Maker did create
  Of darker hue.

Beneath thy pale uncolored skin,
As warm a heart may beat within,
  As beats in me.
Unjustly I will not forget,
Souls are not colored white or jet,
  In thee or me.

Your coming of the tyrant race,
I will not think in you disgrace,
  Since not your choice;
If you're as just and kind to me,
Through all our lives, why may not we,
  In love rejoice?

ॐ *Nellie L. Tinkham*

A QUESTION OF COLOR

"Dear me!" said Mrs. Strawberry Jam,
    A-growing very red,
"What a most unfortunate creature I am;
    I can scarce hold up my head.
To think that I should live to see
An insult offered, like this, to me!
That I should be placed on the very same shelf
(Oh dear! I hardly know myself)
By the side of that odious Blackberry Jam—
That vulgar, common, Blackberry Jam!"

So she fumed and fretted, hour by hour,
    Growing less and less contented,
Till her temper became so thoroughly sour
    That she at last fermented.
While Mr. Blackberry Jam kept still,
    And let her have her say,—
Kept a quiet heart, as blackberries will,
    And grew sweeter every day.

One morn there stopped at Dame Smither's fence
    The parson,—to say that he might,
By the kind permission of Providence,
    Take tea with her that night.
And the good old lady, blessing her lot,
Hastened to open her strawberry pot.
"Oh, what a horrible mess! Dear—dear!
    Not a berry fit to eat is here.
After all," putting it down with a slam,
"Nothing will keep like good Blackberry Jam,
    Honest, reliable, Blackberry Jam."

Mrs. Strawberry J. went into the pail;
    Oh my—what a dire disgrace!
And the pig ate her up, with a twitch of his tail
    And a troubled expression of face.
While Blackberry J., in a lovely glass dish,
    Sat along with the bread and honey,
And thought, while happy as heart could wish,
    "Well, things turn out very funny!"

AN INFANT ABOLITIONIST

How often by a sinless child
May we of error be beguiled;
How oft a single, simple word
The sealed springs of thought have
    stirr'd,
And waken'd feelings deep, to be
A lesson for futurity!

The gayest, most aerial thing,
That moves on earth without a wing,
Today such lesson taught to me.
How sweetly, yet unconsciously,
The infant maiden, artless, mild,
Reproved her elder playmate's pride!
And yet the babe has only smiled
Three years by her fond mother's side.

They stood before a picture—one
Where dark 'neath Afric's burning sun,
A wild and lonely native lay:
The child's companion turn'd to say,
"There's an *old nigger*, Anne, see!"
And pointed to the African;
The little one said quietly,
"I see he is a *colored man*."

Ah, well may sages bow to thee,
Loving and guileless infancy!
And sigh, amid their learned lore,
For one untaught delight of thine—
And feel they'd give their wisdom's store
To know again thy truth divine!

The boasted power of eloquence
Can sway the soul with magic art—
But simple words from innocence
May sink more deeply in the heart.

Sarah Josepha Hale

BIRDS

If ever I see,
On bush or tree,
Young birds in a pretty nest,
I must not, in my play,
Steal the birds away,
To grieve their mother's breast.

My mother I know,
Would sorrow so,
Should I be stolen away—
So I'll speak to the birds,
In my softest words,
Nor hurt them in my play.

❧ Sarah Josepha Hale

MY COUNTRY

America! my own dear land,—
O, 'tis a lovely land to me;
I thank my God that I was born
      Where man is *free*!

Our land—it is a glorious land—
And wide it spreads from sea to sea—
And sister States in Union join
      And all are *free*.

And equal laws we all obey,—
To kings we never bend the knee—
We may not own no Lord but God
      Where all are *free*.

We've lofty hills and sunny vales
And streams that roll to either sea—
And through this large and varied land
      Alike we're *free*.

You hear the sounds of healthful toil,
And youth's gay shout and childhood's glee,
And every one in safety dwells,
      And all are *free*.

We're brothers all from South to North,
One bond will draw us to agree—
We love this country of our birth—
      We love the *free*—

We love the name of Washington,
I lisped it on my father's knee—
And we shall ne'er forget the *name*
      While we are *free*.

My Land, my own dear native Land,
Thou art a lovely land to me;
I bless my God that I was born
      Where man is *free*!

❧ Louisa May Alcott

[THE WILD BIRDS SING IN THE ORANGE GROVES]

The wild birds sing in the orange groves,
   And brightly bloom the flowers;
The fair earth smiles 'neath a summer sky
   Through the joyous fleeting hours.
But oh! in the slave girl's lonely heart,
   Sad thoughts and memories dwell,
And tears fall fast as she mournfully sings,
   Home, dear home, farewell!

Though the chains they bind be all of flowers,
   Where no hidden thorn may be,
Still the free heart sighs 'neath its fragrant bonds,
   And pines for its liberty.
And sweet, sad thoughts of the joy now gone,
   In the slave girl's heart shall dwell,
As she mournfully sings to her sighing harp,
   Native land, native land, farewell!

Lydia Sigourney

DIFFERENCE OF COLOR

God gave to Afric's sons
   A brow of sable dye,
And spread the country of their birth
   Beneath a burning sky,
And with a cheek of olive, made
   The little Hindoo child,
And darkly stained the forest-tribes
   That roam our western wild.

To me he gave a form
   Of fairer, whiter clay;
But am I, therefore, in his sight
   Respected more than they?

No,—'tis the hue of deeds and thoughts
   He traces in his Book,
'Tis the complexion of the heart,
   On which he deigns to look.

Not by the tinted cheek,
   That fades away so fast,
But by the *color of the soul,*
   We shall be judged at last.
And God, the Judge, will look at me
   With anger in His eyes,
If I my brother's darker brow
   Should ever dare despise.

T[acie] T[ownsend] Purvis

RUTH, A BALLAD OF '36*

"Thee must turn the cows out, Benny, for I heard father say,
They were to go into the meadow, before he went away,
And let old Doll go with them, she'll have a day of rest;
For I cannot go to meeting, I know't would not be best.

O Benny, I'm so troubled, I could not sleep last night,
For thinking of that woman; I'm afraid it isn't right
To keep her here much longer, since father's so well known
As being an Abolitionist, Oh, I wish he were at home!

I think I would feel better, if thee'd take the time to go
To Avondale, to see friend Brown; for he would surely know,
If there is any danger; and do not forget to say
That father went with mother to Quarterly yesterday."

She stood within the door-way; and watched her brother ride,
Where the little road wound through the valley, with the little stream beside,
Among the new leafed maples, the robins gaily flew,
And the air was sweet with violets, that round the door-step grew.

She looked upon the valley, and the sloping hills of green;
And thought a place more lovely, was rarely to be seen.
It was a goodly heritage, but alas! that there should be
The blighting stain upon it, of human slavery!

While yet she gazed, a horseman rode swiftly down the hill,
And up the lane he hurried; her heart stood very still.
He waved his hand in greeting, and as he nearer drew;
She saw 'twas neighbor Jackson, a friend right brave and true.

"Ho, Ruth!" he cried, as quickly she hastened to the gate,
"The woman's master's coming, and I have no time to wait.
Our house they now are searching, and I away must ride;
To call the neighbors round me, and rouse the country side."

"What shall I do?" she murmured, in a low and frightened tone,
"If they should come and find her, for I'm here all alone?"
"Do what thee can, fear nothing, they'll harm thee not, I know;
And we will save the woman, so onward I must go."

There came an inspiration, as she saw him ride away,
For she heard a low voice saying: Thy people meet to-day!
Then up the garret stairway, with lightning speed she flew,
And from her place of hiding the frightened woman drew.

Right quickly she arrayed her, in her mother's shawl and gown;
And in the plain drab bonnet, she hid the face so brown,
Her thick green veil was doubled, to shield her from the sun,
"Now thee will pass for mother," she said, when all was done.

Then out in the meadow, with eager steps she sped,
And patient quiet Dolly, by her hand was homeward led;
And deftly moved her fingers to buckle trace and band,
While anxious eyes were gazing, far over all the land.

O, the maiden's heart was beating, as through the valley wide,
She drove out in the wagon, with the woman at her side;
She knew that she was bearding the lion in his den,
For sweeping down the valley, came the master and his men!

She felt the woman tremble, and her pale cheeks paler grew,
And quickened were her heart throbs, as the horsemen nearer drew;
Then close, beside the wagon, they stayed the bridle rein;
And looked within right boldly, and found their quest in vain!

One cried, as on they hurried, "O the Quakers meet to pray,
But this maid and her mother, will be there late to-day."
Ah, little dreamed the master, as he spurred his weary steed,
How near he had been to grasping—the object of his greed.

Right onward pressed the maiden, to neighbor Jackson's door,
And gave the poor slave trembling, to their friendly care once more.
And great was her rejoicing; as she took her homeward way,
That she had foiled the hunters, and snatched from them their prey.

*An incident related in the life of Dr. Ann Preston (author's note).

THE TREE OF SLAVERY

The

sin of

slavery

hardens the

heart, distempers

the mind, brutalizes

the holder, corrupts the

moral sense, inflames the

evil passions, turns men into

cruel monsters; it is "a witch

to the senses, a devil to the soul,

a thief to the pocket," a mildew to

the soil, and a curse to the nation; it

produces woe to man, woman, and child,

and draws from them sighs, tears, and

groans, that reach to the ear of the great God;

it reduces man to a beast—a thing—de-

faces the image of God on the mind,

takes away the key of knowledge,

robs man of the bible and his

soul!

The

root of this evil is

SLAVERY!!!!!!

MR. PREJUDICE

Pray who is Mr. Prejudice,
  We hear so much about,
Who wants to spoil our pleasant songs,
  And keep the white folks out?

They say he runs along the streets,
  And makes a shocking noise,
Scolding at little colored girls,
  And whipping colored boys.

This wizard we have never met—
  Although our mothers say
That colored folks, both old and young,
  He torments every day.

The colonizers tell us all
  They hate this wicked man—
Yet ask him every day to dine,
  And flatter all they can.

He must be very tall and stout—
  Quite dreadful in a rage—
For strongest colored men, they say,
  He'll toss out of a stage.

We wish that we could catch him *here!*
  We think he'd hold his tongue,
If he should see our smiling looks,
  And know how well we've sung.

However strong this rogue may be,
  Kind friends, if you'll unite,
Should he peep in, oh, never fear,
  We'll banish him to-night.

THE ANTI-SLAVERY ALPHABET

"In the morning sow thy seed."

TO OUR LITTLE READERS.

Listen, little children, all,
Listen to our earnest call:
You are very young, 'tis true,
But there's much that you can do.
Even you can plead with men
That they not buy slaves again,
And that those they have may be
Quickly set at liberty.
They may hearken what *you* say,
Though from *us* they turn away.
Sometimes, when from school you walk,
You can with your playmates talk,
Tell them of the slave child's fate,
Motherless and desolate.
And you can refuse to take
Candy, sweetmeat, pie or cake,
Saying "no"—unless 'tis free—
"The slave shall not work for me."
Thus, dear little children, each
May some useful lesson teach;
Thus each one may help to free
This fair land from slavery.

A is an Abolitionist—
    A man who wants to free
The wretched slave—and give to all
    An equal liberty.

B is a Brother with a skin
    Of somewhat darker hue,
But in our Heavenly Father's sight,
    He is as dear as you.

C is the Cotton-field, to which
    This injured brother's driven,
When, as the white man's *slave*, he toils,
    From early morn till even.

D is the Driver, cold and stern,
    Who follows, whip in hand,
To punish those who dare to rest,
    Or disobey command.

E is the Eagle, soaring high;
    An emblem of the free;
But while we chain our brother man,
    Our type he cannot be.

F is the heart-sick Fugitive,
    The slave who runs away,
And travels through the dreary night,
    But hides himself by day.

G is the Gong, whose rolling sound,
    Before the morning light,
Calls up the little sleeping slave,
    To labor until night.

H is the Hound his master trained,
    And called to scent the track
Of the unhappy Fugitive,
    And bring him trembling back.

I is the Infant, from the arms
    Of its fond mother torn,
And, at a public auction, sold
    With horses, cows, and corn.

J is the Jail, upon whose floor
    That wretched mother lay,
Until her cruel master came,
    And carried her away.

K is the Kidnapper, who stole
    That little child and mother—
Shrieking, it clung around her, but
    He tore them from each other.

L is the Lash, that brutally
    He swung around its head,
Threatening that "if it cried again,
    He'd whip it till 'twas dead."

M is the Merchant of the north,
    Who buys what slaves produce—
So they are stolen, whipped and worked,
    For his, and for our use.

N is the Negro, rambling free
    In his far distant home,
Delighting 'neath the palm trees' shade
    And cocoa-nut to roam.

O is the Orange tree, that bloomed
    Beside his cabin door,
When white men stole him from his
        home
    To see it never more.

P is the Parent, sorrowing,
    And weeping all alone—
The child he loved to lean upon,
    His only son, is gone!

Q is the Quarter, where the slave
    On coarsest food is fed,
And where, with toil and sorrow worn,
    He seeks his wretched bed.

R is the "Rice-swamp, dank and lone,"
    Where, weary, day by day,
He labors till the fever wastes
    His strength and life away.

S is the Sugar, that the slave
    Is toiling hard to make,
To put into your pie and tea,
    Your candy, and your cake.

T is the rank Tobacco plant,
    Raised by slave labor too:
A poisonous and nasty thing,
    For gentlemen to chew.

U is for Upper Canada,
    Where the poor slave has found
Rest after all his wandering,
    For it is British ground!

V is the Vessel, in whose dark,
    Noisome, and stifling hold,
Hundreds of Africans are packed,
    Brought o'er the seas, and sold.

W is the Whipping post,
    To which the slave is bound,
While on his naked back, the lash
    Makes many a bleeding wound.

X is for Xerxes, famed of yore;
    A warrior stern was he.
He fought with swords; let truth and love
    Our only weapons be.

Y is for Youth—the time for all
    Bravely to war with sin;
And think not it can ever be
    Too early to begin.

Z is a Zealous man, sincere,
    Faithful, and just, and true;
An earnest pleader for the slave—
    Will you not be so too?

Elizabeth Margaret Chandler

THE SUGAR-PLUMS

No, no, pretty sugar-plums! stay where you are!
Though my grandmother sent you to me from so far;
You look very nice, you would taste very sweet,
And I love you right well, yet not one will I eat.

For the poor slaves have labour'd, far down in the south,
To make you so sweet and so nice for my mouth;
But I want no slaves toiling for me in the sun,
Driven on with the whip, till the long day is done.

Perhaps some poor slave child, that hoed up the ground,
Round the cane in whose rich juice your sweetness was found,
Was flogg'd, till his mother cried sadly to see,
And I'm sure I want nobody beaten for me.

So grandma, I thank you for being so kind,
But your present, to-day, is not much to my mind;
Though I love you so dearly, I choose not to eat
Even what you have sent me by slavery made sweet.

Thus said little Fanny, and skipp'd off to play,
Leaving all her nice sugar-plums just where they lay,
As merry as if they had gone in her mouth,
And she had not cared for the slaves of the south.

Hannah Flagg Gould

THE BLACK AT CHURCH

God, is thy throne accessible to me—
    Me of the Ethiop skin? May I draw near
Thy sacred shrine, and humbly bend the knee,
    While thy white worshippers are kneeling here?

May I approach celestial purity,
    And not offend thee with my sable face?
This company of saints, so fair to see,
    Behold! already shrink from the disgrace!

Yet, in thine earthly courts, I'll gladly bow
    Behind my fellow-worms, and be denied
Communion with them, will my Lord allow
    That I may come and touch his bleeding side!

In that blest forest have I an equal claim
    To bathe, with all who wear the stain of sin?
Or, is salvation by another name
    Than thine?—or, must the Ethiop change his skin?

Thou art our Maker, and I fain would know
    If thou hast different seats prepared above,
To which the master and the servant go
    To sing the praise of thine eternal love!

There will my buyer urge the price of gold,
    Which here, for this uncomely clay he gave,
That he my portion may appoint, and hold
    In bondage still, the helpless, trembling slave?

Or, will the dearer ransom, paid for all,
    A Saviour's blood, impress me with the seal
Of everlasting freedom from my thrall,
    And wash me white, and this crushed spirit heal?

Then, will I meekly bear these lingering pains,
    And suffer scorn, and be by man opprest,
If at the grave, I may put off my chains,
    And thou wilt take me where the weary rest!

Ann Preston

HOWARD AND HIS SQUIRREL

Our Howard had a little squirrel,
    Its tale was long and gray,
He put it in a wiry cage,
    And there it had to stay.

Its hickory nuts and corn it ate
    From out its little paw,
And such a funny, active thing,
    I think, I never saw.

But Howard thought he should not like
    A little slave to be;
And God had made the nimble squirrel,
    To run, and climb the tree.

And so he opened Bunny's door,
    And laughed to see it run,
And spring right up the leafy tree,
    As if 'twas only fun.

A bird or squirrel in a cage
    It makes me sad to see;
It seems so cruel to confine
    The creatures made so free.

TOM AND LUCY: A TALE FOR LITTLE LIZZIE

Come Lizzie, and I'll tell the tale
   Of Tom and Lucy Lee,
Two little slaves, no bigger, dear,
   Than cousin Charles and thee.

They lived in Carolina state,
   Beside the great, deep sea;
Their mother was a weary slave
   And wanted to be free.

She only came to them at dark,
   For she must work all day,
And with her, on the cabin floor,
   They slept the night away.

Long sunny days they played alone,
   As little children play,
But never hurt the butterflies,
   Nor pelted frogs away.

Sometimes they rambled in the wood,
   Where moss and flowers grew,
And little birds sang them to sleep,
   As birds will often do.

But one dark night their mother dear
   Stayed all the night away,
And long they cried, and waited there;
   Until the break of day;

And then their master came, and bade
   Them to his house repair,
For they were old enough, he said,
   To earn their victuals there:

They met their mother in a drove
   Of slaves, upon their way;
Her heart was broke, for she was sold
   To go to Florida.

She gazed on them and cried, "my God"!
   She stopped, and begged to stay:
The driver fiercely called "move on,"
   And drove her fast away.

Through dreary days and dreary years
   Toiled Tom and Lucy there,
And when they stopped, the great whip cracked
   Upon their shoulders bare.

But though they'd none to pity them,
   They loved each other well,
And love will always bring some joy,
   Wherever it may dwell.

They said when they grew big and strong
   They both would run away,
And, up in Pennsylvania, learn
   To read and write, each day.

But once, I think it was May morn,
   A stranger came along,
While Lucy milked, and sadly sung
   Her mother's little song.

He called her master to the road,
   And told him he would pay
Six hundred dollars for that girl,
   And take her right away.

Her master took the trader's gold;—
   Such wicked things they do;
Just like a calf was Lucy sold,
   Though she was good as you.

Tom heard her scream, and ran to her;—
   To part they could not bear;
He held her fast, and cursed the men,
   Who stood in wonder there.

They knocked him down, and roughly took
    Poor Lucy far away;
And toiling in some cotton field
    She weeps, perhaps, today.

Tom ran away, but dogs and men
    Were set upon his track,
And broken-hearted from the swamp
    They brought him quickly back.

And then, 'twas said, they sold him off,
    All chained to Georgia men;
He may be dead, I never heard
    From that poor boy again.

Thomas Hall Shastid (est. age 14)

CLEOPATRA'S NEEDLES

It was in Africa's torrid clime,
    Two sisters stood alone,
And what they witnessed was a sight
    To melt a heart of stone.

The English came and carried off
    One sister, far away;
And now in London's haunts she stands
    And sorrows all the day.

They took her from her native spot,
    Where she was wont to stand,
And placed her in a foreign Clime,
    Within a foreign land.

Ah! how she feels, with other eyes
    Than on bright Egypt's shore;—
She stands where she had never been—
    To stand for evermore.

The others came with iron bonds,
    Her sister, too, they brought,
To grace America's bright parks
    Where pity ne'er was thought.

Ah! yes, in New York city's haunts
    That sister is to be;
Between the two the waters lie—
    A dark and stormy sea.

Ah! now when I to Egypt's plains
    Do wend my careful way,
I'll seek the spot where once they stood,
    And there respect I'll pay.

But, oh, the beauties will be gone—
    The sisters are not there,
Insulted by a grosser race,
    They stand where naught is fair.

George R. Allen (age 12)

ON SLAVERY

Slavery! oh, though cruel stain,
Thou dost fill my heart with pain:
See my brother, there he stands
Chain'd by slavery's cruel bands.

Could we not feel a brother's woes,
Relieve the wants he undergoes;
Snatch him from slavery's cruel smart,
And to him freedom's joy impart?

❧ Thomas S. Sidney (age 12)

ON FREEDOM

Freedom will break the tyrant's chain,
And shatter all his whole domain;
From slavery she will always free,
And all her aim is liberty.

❧ Author Unknown

[FOR THERE IS YET A LIBERTY UNSUNG]

[adapted from William Cowper, "The Task"]

For there is yet a liberty unsung
By poets and by Senators unprais'd,
Which Monarchs cannot grant, nor all the power
Of earth and hell confed'rate take away!
A liberty which persecution, fraud,
Oppression, prisons have no power to bind:
Which, whoso tastes, can be enslav'd no more.
He is the freeman whom the truth makes free,
And all are slaves beside. The oppressor holds his
Body bound, but knows not what a range
His spirit takes unconscious of a chain:
And that to bind him is a vain attempt,
Whom God delights in, and in whom he dwells.

❧ Henry Wadsworth Longfellow

THE SLAVE'S DREAM

Beside the ungathered rice he lay
  His sickle in his hand;
His breast was bare, his matted hair
  Was buried in the sand.
Again, in the mist and shadow of sleep,
  He saw his Native Land.

Wide through the landscape of his dreams
  The lordly Niger flowed;
Beneath the palm-trees on the plain
  Once more a king he strode;

And heard the tinkling caravans
   Descend the mountain-road.

He saw once more his dark-eyed queen
   Among her children stand;
They clasped his neck, they kissed his cheeks,
   They held him by the hand!
A tear burst from the sleeper's lids
   And fell into the sand.

And then at furious speed he rode
   Along the Niger's bank;
His bridle-reins were golden chains,
   And, with a martial clank,
At each leap he could feel his scabbard of steel
   Smiting his stallion's flank.

Before him, like a blood-red flag,
   The bright flamingoes flew;
From morn till night he followed their flight,
   O'er plains where the tamarind grew,
Till he saw the roofs of Caffire huts,
   And the ocean rose to view.

At night he heard the lion roar,
   And the hyaena scream,
And the river-horse, as he crushed the reeds
   Beside some hidden stream;
And it passed, like a glorious roll of drums,
   Through the triumph of his dream.

The forests, with their myriad tongues,
   Shouted of liberty;
And the Blast of the Desert cried aloud,
   With a voice so wild and free,
That he started in his sleep and smiled
   At their tempestuous glee.

He did not feel the driver's whip,
   Nor the burning heat of day
For Death had illumined the Land of Sleep,
   And his lifeless body lay
A worn-out fetter, that the soul
   Had broken and thrown away!

Frances E. W. Harper

THE LITTLE BUILDERS

Ye are builders little builders,
   Not with mortar, brick and stone,
But your work is far more glorious—
   Ye are building freedom's throne.

Where the ocean never slumbers
   Works the coral 'neath the spray,
By and by a reef or island
   Rears its head to greet the day.

When the balmy rains and sunshine
   Scatter treasures o'er the soil,
'Till a place for human footprints,
   Crown the little builder's toil.

When the stately ships sweep o'er them,
   Cresting all the sea with foam,
Little think these patient toilers,
   They are building man a home.

Do you ask me, precious children,
   How your little hands can build,
That you love the name of freedom,
   But your fingers are unskilled?

Not on thrones or in proud temples,
   Does fair freedom seek her rest;
No, her chosen habitations,
   Are the hearts that love her best.

Would you gain the highest freedom?
   Live for God and man alone,
Then each heart in freedom's temple,
   Will be like a living stone.

Fill your minds with useful knowledge,
   Learn to love the true and right;
Thus you'll build the throne of freedom,
   On a pedestal of light.

Christina Moody (age 13–16)

A TALE TOLD BY GRANDMA

I was seting in de cabin do',
   One moon shin' summers night,
When I heard a mighty nois,
   An' I seen a mazzing sight.

Some soldiers was a coming,
   Jest a tearing down de road
And dey busted Mis'us do' in
   An' thro' de house dey poured.

Mis'us had hur bacon,
   All packed up in de wall,
But de soldiers broke de wall in
   And I clar' dey took it all.

Dey called out po' ol' Hanner,
   An' dey made her cook some meat
An' I can't begin to tell you,
   How dem Yankee men did eat.

Dey catched every chichen,
   An' dey killed every pig
An' Mis'us had histericks
   'Twell she far'ly danced a jig.

Den dey went in de garden
   An' dey striped de place right bare
Left de place a lookin'
   Like a syclone passed thro dar.
Den dey went in de barn,
   An' took de co'n and wheat
An' dey clared de hol' plantation
   Of eberyting dats fit to eat.

Dey took all of Mis'us wine,
   An' dey camp out on de place
An' de way dem soldiers carried on
   I tinks it am disgrace.
Some of 'em got toxicated,
   An' dey cracked de wo'ses jokes
An' dey laffed an' squarled an' hollered
   'Twell I frought dey sho' would choke.

'Twernt nobody on de place,
   Got a drap of sleep dat night
Ebery eye was so red nex' mornin'
   Woulden a thought dey had a white.
Ol' Mar'ser he had gone to war,
   So po' Mis'us she was lef'
Dout a soal fer to pertect hur
   But her own po' measely sef'.

Well I neber was so sorry
   Fur a body in my life
As I was fur po' ol' Mis'us
   She was scared as little mice.
Why de way she ran across de yard,
   An' fell in Hanner's do'
Would of made you clar 'fore heben
   Dat she'd los' hur reason sho'.

Scared po' Hanner twell she hollered,
   Lowd enough to make you def'
Lawsy Mis'us w'ats de matter?
   Why you don't look lik' yo' sef'.
You am afraid about dem soldiers
   'Twell you'se white as any sheet.

But don't you worry honey
   You jest lay you down an' sleep.

But as I foremost told you
   'Twernt no sleep for us dat night,
We jest huddled up toget'er
   Watching fur de morning light.
Well at las' when mornin' came
   An' de soldiers went away
Dey diden leave us vittles nough
   To las us thro' one day.

But de Holy Father knowed,
   An' he woulden let us starb,
So he sent us to a neighbor
   Dat de soldiers didn't rob.
An' so my story's ended
   An' I aint gwine tell no mo,
So taint no use for to axe me
   Cause my answer will be no.

≈ *Christina Moody* (age 13–16)

THE DEPTH FROM WHENCE WE CAME

My fore-parents were slaves,
   I'm not ashamed to say;
Though many a one disdains the fact,
   And fain would drive it away.

Why should we be ashamed to know
   Of the depth from whence we came?
When we see the progress of our race—
   They have risen from slavery to fame.

We once were crushed to the earth
   And bound with a heavy chain,
And a seal was put upon us
   "Thou shalt lose and never gain."

How tight the chain did hold us,
   And the seal, how well it did last,
While the Negro toiled on and grew weary,
   The chain and the seal held fast.

For many long years did he toil thus,
    With no sign of deliverance near;
To God he prayed with patience,
    But it seemed that He did not hear.

The old men died and left the yoke
    For the younger ones to bear.
The young men grew old and others were born
    With the chain of slavery to wear.

But before the earth was created,
    God saw the slave bound man;
He wrote in His holy scripture
    "Ethiopia shall stretch forth her hand."

After many years of slavery
    God's lightning was seen in the sky,
His voice was heard in thunder saying,
    "Let the Negro rise."

Lo! the chain was broken,
    And the seal was torn away;
The Negro saw in the heavens
    The dawn of his coming day.

He shook the dust from his shoulders,
    And stood face to face with the world.
He has proved his grit and courage
    Though rocks at him were hurled.

He grasped every opportunity
    And rose in spite of all,
Whenever duty demanded him
    He did not need to be called.

You have risen, oh Mother Race,
    So be thou not ashamed,
Let the once cursed name of Negro
    Stand for the word of Fame.

Christina Moody (age 13–16)

THE NEGRO'S FLAG AND COUNTRY

"Why do you write of the American's Flag,
  Of its stripes of red and white?
And why do you call a flag your own
  To which you have no right?

Why do you praise the white man's flag,
  When you have not one of your own?
And why do you love this country
  When this country is not your home?"

These words were said to me by a member of my race.
The fire was kindled within me as I looked him in the face.
  I call this Flag *my own*, because long years ago
  A war broke out for freedom and the land was full of woe.

The white man old and young fought with all their strength and might.
But they found the field was pretty hot, then the Negro joined the fight.
  The Negro shed his blood without a murmur or complaint,
  And though they faced many a hardship, their brave hearts did not faint.

My claim upon this country is sealed with Negro blood.
That swept many a battle field in royal crimson flood.
  I claim it, yes! I claim it! because for many years,
  We have mourned the loss of our heroes with bitter hearts and briny tears.

Give me back my death bound warriors, and I'll bow my head and cease;
But no! they are gone, yes gone forever, so let their bones rest on in peace.
  Then sing it in the school house, then cheer the Negro's Flag.
  Ring it in the school bell, don't let its banners drag.

Sing of the Negro heroes who fought in the days of yore;
Sing it until it echoes on the banks of eternity's shore.
  The Negro's Flag and country, long may thy glory shine,
  And know ye that I, a Negro, claim the Royal Flag as mine.

POLITICS AND SOCIAL REFORM

THREE BUGS

Three little bugs in a basket,
And hardly room for *two!*
And one was yellow, and one was black,
And one like me, or you.
The space was small, no doubt, for all;
But what should *three* bugs do?

Three little bugs in a basket,
And hardly crumbs for two;
And all were selfish in their hearts,
The same as I or you;
So the strong ones said, "We will eat the bread,
And that is what we'll do."

Three little bugs in a basket,
And the beds but two would hold;
So they all three fell to quarreling—
And two of the bugs got under the rugs,
And *one* was out in the cold!

So he that was left in the basket,
Ah, pity, 'tis true, 'tis true!
But he that was frozen and starved at the last,
A strength from his weakness drew,
And pulled the rugs from *both* of the bugs,
And killed and *ate* them, too!

Now, when bugs live in a basket,
Though more than it well can hold,
It seems to me they had better agree—
The white, and the black, and the gold—
And share what comes of the beds and the crumbs,
And leave no bug in the cold!

Lydia Sigourney

WAR

War is a wicked thing,
    It strikes the strong man dead,
And leaves the trampled battle-field
    With blood and carnage red,
While thousand mangled forms
    In hopeless suffering bleed,
And vultures and hyenas throng
    Upon their flesh to feed.

See with what bitter grief
    Those widowed ones deplore;
And children for their fathers mourn,
    Who must return no more.
And aged parents sink
    In penury and despair,
And sorrow dwells in many a home,—
    War makes the weeping there.

It comes with sins and woes,
    A dark and endless train,
It fills the breast with murderous hate,
    Where Christian love should reign;
It desolates the land
    With famine, death, and flame,
And those are in a sad mistake
    Who seek the warrior's fame.

Oh, may I guard my heart
    From every evil thing,
From thoughts of anger and revenge,
    Whence wars and fighting spring.
And may the plants of peace
    Grow up serene and fair,
And mark me for a child of heaven,
    That I may enter there.

Mary Norton Bradford

HER PAPA

My papa's all dressed up to-day;
He never looked so fine;
I thought when I first looked at him,
My papa wasn't mine.

He's got a beautiful new suit—
The old one was so old—
It's blue, with buttons, Oh! so bright,
I guess they must be gold.

And papa's sort o' glad and sort
O' sad—I wonder why?
And every time she looks at him
It makes my mamma cry.

Who's Uncle Sam? My papa says
That he belongs to him;
But papa's joking, 'cause he knows
My uncle's name is Jim.

My papa just belongs to me
And mamma. And I guess
The folks are blind who cannot see
His buttons, marked U. S.

U. S. spells us. He's ours—and yet
My mamma can't help cry,
And papa tries to smile at me
And can't—I wonder why?

THE THREE COPECKS

Crouched low in a sordid chamber,
   With a cupboard of empty shelves,—
Half starved, and alas! unable
   To comfort or help themselves,—

Two children were left forsaken,
   All orphaned of mortal care;
But with spirits too close to Heaven
   To be tainted by Earth's despair,—

Alone in that crowded city,
   Which shines like an Arctic star,
By the banks of the frozen Neva,
   In the realm of the mighty Czar.

Now, Max was an urchin of seven;
   But his delicate sister, Leeze,
With the crown of her rippling ringlets,
   Could scarcely have reached your
     knees!

As he looked on his sister weeping,
   And tortured by hunger's smart,
A Thought like an Angel entered
   At the door of his opened heart.

He wrote on a fragment of paper,—
   With quivering hand and soul,—
"Please send to me, Christ! three copecks,
   To purchase for Leeze a roll!"

Then, rushed to a church, his missive
   To drop,—ere the vesper psalms,—
As the surest mail bound Christward,—
   In the unlocked Box for Alms!

While he stood upon tiptoe to reach it,
   One passed from the priestly band,
And with a smile like a benediction
   Took the note from his eager hand.

Having read it, the good man's bosom
   Grew warm with a holy joy:

"Ah! Christ may have heard you
     already,—
   Will you come to my house, my boy?"

"But not without Leeze?" "No, surely,
   We'll have a rare party of three;
Go, tell her that somebody's waiting
   To welcome her home to tea." . . .

That night, in the coziest cottage,
   The orphans were safe at rest,
Each snug as a callow birdling
   In the depths of its downy nest.

And the next Lord's Day, in his pulpit,
   The preacher so spake of these
Stray lambs from the fold, which Jesus
   Had blessed by the sacred seas;—

So recounted their guileless story,
   As he held each child by the hand,
That the hardest there could feel it,
   And the dullest could understand.

O'er the eyes of the listening fathers
   There floated a gracious mist;
And oh, how the tender mothers
   Those desolate darlings kissed!

"You have given your tears," said the
     preacher,—
   "Heart-alms we should none despise;—
But the open palm, my children,
   Is more than weeping eyes!"

Then followed a swift collection,
   From the altar steps to the door,
Till the sum of two thousand rubles
   The vergers had counted o'er.

So you see that unmailed letter
   Had somehow gone to its goal,
And more than three copecks gathered
   To purchase for Leeze a roll!

"A Lady of Boston" [Nancy Sproat]

THE BEGGAR

Look, sister, see how rich I be!
Six cents Mamma has given me,
Because it is a holyday,
And now I'm going off to play.
But let me think—what shall I buy?
A cake—or else some pretty toy?
I've wanted long a *Jumping Jack*—
Well, *that* I'll buy and not a cake.
But stop, dear sister, who is this?
A poor old man! how lame he is!

How lean he looks and ragged too—
Give him some dinner, sister,—do.
Now he will have to go away,
And beg his dinner every day.
I wish I had a dollar now—
Six cents will buy some biscuit though—
And as he travels on the road,
A biscuit would taste very good—
And he shall have them—so I'll play
Without a Jumping Jack to-day.

"A Lady of Boston" [Nancy Sproat]

LAZY JANE

Who was that, dear Mamma, who ate
  Her breakfast here this morn?
With tangled hair and ragged shoes,
  And gown and apron torn?

They call her *Lazy Jane*, my dear,
  She begs her bread all day;
And gets a lodging in a barn,
  At night among the hay.

For when she was a little girl,
  She loved her play too well;
At school she would not mind her book,
  To learn to read and spell.

"Dear Jane," her mother oft would say,
  "Pray learn to work and read;
Then you'll be able when you're grown,
  To earn your clothes and bread."

But lazy Jenny did not care,
  She'd neither knit nor sew;
To romp with naughty girls and boys,
  Was all that she would do.

So she grew up a very dunce,—
  And when her parents died,
She knew not how to teach a school,
  Nor work, if she had tried.

And now an idle vagabond,
  She strolls about streets;
And not a friend can Jenn find,
  In any one she meets.

And now, my child, should you neglect
  Your book or work again,
Or play, when you should be at school,
  Remember *Lazy Jane*.

THE WORTHY POOR

A dog of morals, firm and sure,
Went out to seek the "worthy poor."
"Dear things!" she said, "I'll find them
    out,
And end their woes, without a doubt."

She wandered east, she wandered west,
And many dogs her vision blest,—
Some well-to-do, some rich indeed,
And some—ah! very much in need.

So poor they were!—without a bone,
Battered and footsore, sad and lone;
No friends, no help. "What lives they've
    led,
To come to this!" our doggie said.

"I ought not give to them; I'm sure
They cannot be the worthy poor.
They must have fought or been dis-
    graced;
My charity must be well placed."

Some dogs she found, quite to her mind;
So thrifty they—so sleek and kind!
"Ah me!" she said, "were they in need,
To help them would be joy indeed."

'T was the same, day in, day out,—
The poorest dogs were poor, no doubt;
But they were neither clean nor wise,
As she could see with half her eyes.

'T is strange what faults come out to
    view
When folks are poor. She said: "'T is
    true
They need some help; but as for me,
I must not waste my charity."

So home she went and dropped a tear.
"I've done my duty, that is clear.
I've searched and searched the village
    round,
And not one 'worthy poor' I've found."

And all this while, the sick and lame
And hungry suffered all the same.
They were not pleasant, were not neat—
But she had more than she could eat!

And don't you think it was a sin?
Was hers the right way to begin?
No, no!—it was not right, I'm sure,
For she was rich and they were poor.

O ye who have enough to spare!
To suffering give your ready care;
Waste not your charitable mood
Only in sifting out the good.

For, on the whole, though it is right
To keep the "worthy poor" in sight,
This world would run with scarce a hitch
If all could find the *worthy rich.*

Bessie Hill

[SOME CHILDREN ROAM THE FIELDS AND HILLS]

Some children roam the fields and hills,
And others work in noisy mills;
Some dress in silks and dance and play,
While others drudge their life away;
Some glow with health and bound with song,
And some must suffer all day long.

Which is your lot, my girl and boy?
Is it a life of ease and joy?
Ah, if it is, its glowing sun
The poorer life should shine upon.—
Make glad one little heart to-day,
And help one burdened child to play.

Fenton Johnson

THE PLAINT OF THE FACTORY CHILD

I.
Mother, must I work all day?
All the day? Ay, all the day?
Must my little hands be torn?
And my heart bleed, all forlorn?
I am but a child of five,
And the street is all alive
With the tops and balls and toys,—
Pretty tops and balls and toys.

II.
Day in, day out, I toil—toil!
And all that I know is toil;
Never laugh as others do,
Never cry as others do,
Never see the stars at night,
Nor the golden glow of sunlight,—
And all for but a silver coin,—
Just a worthless silver coin.

III.
Would that death might come to me!
That blessed death might come to me,
And lead me to waters cool,
Lying in a tranquil pool,
Up there where the angels sing,
And the ivy tendrils cling
To the land of play and song,—
Fairy land of play and song.

H.H. [Helen Hunt Jackson]

THE HAND-ORGAN MAN'S LITTLE GIRL

From nine in the morning till six at night—
    A weary march for the strongest feet—
She trudges along, a pitiful sight,
    To be seen every day in the city street.

She is tired, and hungry, and cold and wet;
    She trembles with wretchedness where she stands;
But she knows if she falters a moment, she'll get
    A cruel, hard blow from the cruel hands.

Her tambourine feels as heavy as lead;
    She wearily shifts it from side to side;
Her poor little knuckles are bruised and red;
    Her pale, sunken eyes show how much she has cried.

But she must keep step to the gayest tunes,
    With merry, quick flings of her tambourine;
And watch for the crowds, in the late afternoons.
    —How soon they forget the sad face they have seen!

Oh, how do you think she feels when she sees,
    In the pleasant parks on a sunny day,
The rows of nurses, all taking their ease,
    With children who've nothing to do but play?

"Who have nothing to do but play!"—The thought!
    She cannot imagine it, if she tries;
Nor how such wonderful playthings are bought,—
    The dolls that can walk and open their eyes!

"Who have nothing to do but play!" It seems
    To her that such children in Heaven live.
Not all her wildest, most beautiful dreams
    A happiness greater than that could give.

O children, who've nothing to do but play,
    And are happy, do not forget
The poor little children who work all day,
    And are tired and hungry and cold and wet!

THE IDIOT BOY

The following melancholy story is said to be founded on fact.

A stranger's eye this poor child ever caught;
But there was something which they always sought,
Beyond his blue eye and his pensive smile,
His snowy cheek, and lip that knew no guile.
A father's pride he *was*,—a mother's joy,—
Now he is naught but a poor idiot boy!
It was not always so—for once they say,
He was unrivalled at his books and play;
And few could see the smiling happy one,
'Ere four bright summers of his life were run,
Without deep love toward the curly head,
That shone in sport, and every pastime led.
He was a tiny fellow—and some older one,
In careless gaiety, or heedless fun,
When they were playing "hide-and-then-go-seek,"
Placed him within a clock,—and not to speak
They charged him—The clock door then was closed,
And the scared child in silence there reposed.
Between the tickings he could plainly hear
Voices, that seemed to him, oh very, very near—
And yet he would not call—that clock struck four!
They took the poor boy out—he knew no more.
From that hour after, he did naught but mock
The solemn music of that ticking clock;
And as the sad hours struck in slow review,
He with a little wand would strike them too.
With artful fondness they would try to wean,
His childish mem'ry from that fatal scene;
But all their care and kindness were in vain—
He had forgotten all things,—e'n his name!
All save the clock—to that his mind would cling
As if it were the only precious thing;
He's like a young vine torn from parent stem,
'Scorched by the sun, and ne'er to bloom again;
And his fond parents find no other joy,
Than love and pity for their idiot boy.

GLEN CRERAN.

TO THE CHILDREN OF THE RICH
FOR THE CHILDREN OF THE POOR

Dear little friends, whose eyes bespeak the gladness.
That in your hearts like God's bright sunshine dwells;
Whose lives are filled with rays of home-affection.
Twining o'er all such blissful, fairy spells.

List ye, and know, that hearts like yours are flowing
With bitter sorrow,—and that bare, cold feet
Travel the city's walks, while ye are sleeping,—
Seeking for warmth and shelter, in the street.

That little childish heads are bowed in anguish,
That tiny fingers toil and know not play;
That crouching figures fear their home's reception,
And shrink e'en from that sweet word, "home," away.

To them it echoes not in love,—they know not
The cherished tenderness with which yon hail
Each eve's unbroken circle,—joys and pleasures,—
No! they but see life's weary, darksome veil.

No gentle mother's smile to crown their labor—
Perchance her soul hath winged its flight above;
Or if remaining,—'tis the earth's cold bosom
That speaks to her of future peace and love.

Sadly she folds her dear and suffering children
Unto her heart, that would their comfort be;
But it is broken, and its songs are silent:
Sorrow is very sad in infancy.

So, for the love of Jesus in His childhood,
If to His Infant-Heart you would be dear,—
Cherish and keep the legacy He leaves you:
His own afflicted little ones to cheer.

Think of your happy homes,—deal out a portion
Of kindly comfort to your sadder friends;
Believe their prayers will reach the Heart of Jesus,
Deepening the love, which on you now He spends.

🎕 *H.H. [Helen Hunt Jackson]*

GRAB-BAG

A fine game is Grab-bag, a fine game to see!
For Christmas, and New Year, and birthdays, and all.
Happy children, all laughing and screaming with glee!
If they draw nothing more than a pop-corn ball,
'T is a prize they welcome with eyes of delight,
And hold it aloft with a loud, ringing cheer;
Their arms waving high, all so graceful and white;
Their heads almost bumping, so close and so near.
The laughter grows louder; the eyes grow more bright.
Oh, sweet is the laughter, and gay is the sight—
A fine game is Grab-bag! a fine game to see!

A strange game of Grab-bag I saw yesterday;
I'll never forget it as long as I live.
Some street-beggars played it,—poor things, not in play!
A man with a sack on his back, and a sieve,—
A poker to stir in the barrels of dirt,—
A basket to hold bits of food he might find,—
'T was a pitiful sight, and a sight that hurt,
But a sight it is well to keep in one's mind.

His children were with him, two girls and three boys;
Their heads held down close, and their eyes all intent;
No sound from their lips of glad laughter's gay noise:
No choice of bright playthings to them the game meant!
A chance of a bit of waste cinder to burn;
A chance of a crust of stale bread they could eat;
A chance—in a thousand, as chances return—
Of ragged odd shoes they could wear on their feet!

The baby that yet could not totter alone
Was held up to see, and, as grave as the rest,
Watched wistful each crust, each cinder, each bone,
And snatched at the morsels he thought looked the best.
The sister that held him, oppressed by his weight—
Herself but an over-yeared baby, poor child!—
Had the face of a woman, mature, sedate,
And looked but the older whenever she smiled.

Oh, a sad game is Grab-bag—a sad game to see!
As beggars must play it, and their chances fall;
When Hunger finds crusts an occasion for glee,
And Cold finds no rags too worthless or small.
O children, whose faces have shone with delight,
As you played at your Grab-bag with shouting and cheer,
And stretched out your arms, all so graceful and white,
And gayly bumped heads, crowding near and more near,
With laughter and laughter, and eyes growing bright,—
Remember this picture, this pitiful sight,
Of a sad game of Grab-bag—a sad game to see!

❧ *Mary E. Wilkins [Freeman]*

THE BEGGAR KING

"Hark! hark! hark! the dogs do bark!
The Beggars have come to town,
Some in rags, and some in tags,
And some in velvet gowns."
                    Old Nursery Rhyme.

Half frantic, down the city streets
    The barking dogs they tore;
The dust it flew, and no man knew
    The like of it before.
The St. Bernard's deep booming bass,
    The hound's sepulchral howl,
The terrier-whelp's staccato yelp,
    And the bull-dog's massive growl,
In chorus sounded thro' the town:
    The windows up they went,
Thro' every space a gaping face
    Inquiringly was bent.
The burgher's daughter clean forgot
    Her snood of silk and pearls,
And, full of dread, popped out her head,
    With its tumbled yellow curls.
A rosebud smote her on the lips:
    Down went the rattling blind;
But still the maid, all curious, staid,
    And slyly peeped behind.

A handsome lord, with smiling lips,
    Leaned from the opposite tower;
Two withered hags, in dirt and rags,
    Did from their garret glower.
The tailor left his goose to see,
    And got his coat ablaze;
Three peasant maids, with shining braids,
    Looked on in wild amaze.
The emperor's palace windows high,
    All open they were set—
From the gray stone red jewels shone,
    All gold and violet.
The ladies of the emperor's court
    Leaned out with stately grace;
And each began her peacock fan
    To wave before her face.
"Hark! hark! hark! the dogs do bark!"
    The emperor left his throne
At the uproar, and on the floor
    He dropped his emerald crown.

The dogs press round the city-gates,
    The guards they wave them back;
But all in vain, with might and main
    Dance round the yelping pack.
"Hark! hark! hark! the dogs do bark!"
    There sounds a trumpet-call!
Now, rat-tat-tat; pray, what is that
    Outside the city-wall?
Airs from the Beggar's Opera
    On broken fiddles played;
On pans they drum and wildly strum,
    Filched from a dairy-maid.
With tenor-whine, and basso-groan,
    The chorus is complete;
And, far and wide, there sounds beside
    The tramp of many feet!
"Hark! hark! hark! the dogs do bark!"
    Ah, what a horrid din!
The Beggars wait outside the gate,
    And clamor to get in.
A herald to the emperor rode:
    "Save! save the emerald crown!
For, hark! hark! hark! the dogs do bark!
    The Beggars storm the town!"
The emperor donned his clinking mail,
    Called out his royal guard,
The city-gate, with furious rate,
    Went galloping toward.
A captain with a flag of truce
    Thus parleyed on the wall:
"Why do ye wait outside the gate,
    And why so loudly call?"
He spoke, then eyed them with dismay;
    For o'er the valley spread
The clamoring crowd, and stern and proud
    A king rode at their head.
In mothy ermine he was drest;
    As sad a horse he rode,
With jaunty air, quite *débonnaire*,
    As ever man bestrode.
The Beggars stumped and limped behind,
    With wails and whines and moans—
"Some in rags, and some in tags,
    And some in velvet gowns."

A great court-beauty's splendid dress
    Was there, all soiled and frayed;
The scarf, once bright, a belted knight
    Wore at his accolade;
A queen's silk hose; a bishop's robe;
    A monarch's funeral-pall;
The shoes, all mud, a prince-o'-the-blood
    Had danced in at a ball.
The Beggars stumped and limped along,
    Aping their old-time grace:
Upon the wind, flew out behind,
    Ribbons of silk and lace.
A wretched company it was
    Around the city gate—
The sour and sad, the sick and bad,
    And all disconsolate.
But in the wretched company
    There was one dainty thing:
A maiden, white as still moonlight,
    Who rode beside the king.
Her hands were full of apple-flowers
    Plucked in the country lanes;
Her little feet, like lilies sweet,
    O'erlaced with violet veins,
Hung down beneath her tattered dress;
    A bank of lilies, showed
Her shoulders fair; her dusky hair
    Down to her girdle flowed.
Up spoke the haughty Beggar King:
    "I want no parleying word!
Bid come to me, right speedily,
    The emperor, your Lord!"
Wide open flew the city-gate!
    Out rode the emperor bold;
His war-horse pranced and lightly danced
    Upon his hoofs of gold.
"What wouldest thou, O Beggar King?
    What wouldest thou with me?
For all the gold the town doth hold
    Would not suffice for thee."
"Beholdest thou my daughter dear,
    O emperor! by my side?
Though wild the rose, it sweetly grows,
    And she shall be thy bride,

"And thou shalt seat her on thy throne.
  When thou thy troth hast pledged,
Her beauty grace with gems and lace,
  And robes with ermine edged;
"Or else, on thee, O emperor!
  Like locusts we'll come down,
And naught that's fair or rich or rare
  We'll leave within the town!
"The children all shall lack for food,
  And the lords and ladies pine;
For we will eat your dainties sweet,
  And drink your red old wine!
"Now, what say'st thou, O emperor?—
  Wed thou my daughter dear,
To-morrow day, by dawning gray,
  Thy borders shall be clear."
The emperor looked upon the maid:
  She shyly dropped her head;
Her apple-flowers fell down in showers,
  Her soft white cheeks grew red.
The emperor loved her at the sight:
  "I take your terms!" cried he;
"Nor wilt thou fear, O maiden dear!
  To wed to-night with me?"
Her long, dark lashes swept her cheek;
  A word she could not find,
For to and fro her thoughts did blow,
  Like lilies in a wind.
She toward him reached her little hand,
  Then—drew it back again;
She smiled and sighed—all satisfied,
  He grasped her bridle-rein.
Then clattered courtiers thro' the street,
  Fast ran the folk, I ween,

And under feet strewed roses sweet,
  And boughs of apple-green.
The emperor, on his gold-shod horse,
  Came pacing thro' the town,
And by his side his timid bride
  Rode in her tattered gown.
A crocus-broidered petticoat,
  Robes stiff with threads of gold,
The maids found soon, and satin shoon,
  And lace in spices rolled.
They led the trembling beggar-maid
  All gently up the stair,
Thro' golden doors with sills of flowers,
  Into a chamber fair.
They loosed from her her faded gear;
  They kissed her gentle face;
From head to feet clad her so sweet
  In linen fine and lace;
They clasped her golden-threaded robe—
  "Darling, thou art so fair!"
With strings of pearls, amid the curls,
  They dressed her flowing hair.
"Now, pardy!" cried the emperor,
  "The rose-tree is in flower!
In the world green was never seen
  Queen half so sweet before!"
The people, dressed as for a feast,
  Thronged round the palace doors;
The minstrels sung, the joy-bells rung,
  The roses fell in showers.
The Beggar King looked toward the town:
  "Farewell, my daughter dear!"
The east was gray—he rode away,
  And swallowed down a tear.

NIKOLINA

O tell me, little children, have you seen her—
The tiny maid from Norway, Nikolina?
O, her eyes are blue as cornflowers 'mid the corn,
And her cheeks are rosy red as skies of morn!

O buy the baby's blossoms if you meet her,
And stay with gentle words and looks to greet her;
She'll gaze at you and smile and clasp your hand,
But no word of your speech can understand.

Nikolina! Swift she turns if any call her,
As she stands among the poppies hardly taller,
Breaking off their scarlet cups for you,
With spikes of slender larkspur, burning blue.

In her little garden many a flower is growing—
Red, gold, and purple in the soft wind blowing;
But the child that stands amid the blossoms gay
Is sweeter, quainter, brighter even than they.

O tell me, little children, have you seen her—
This baby girl from Norway, Nikolina?
Slowly she's learning English words, to try
And thank you if her flowers you come to buy.

IN THE DORY

Now, if there's anything I hate,—
    And there is some, perhaps,—
It's the way you have with you,
    You city chaps!

But, then, I didn't ask you out
    (You pull the dory round!)
For a chance to blow you up;
    (She'll run aground!)

Because I think that wouldn't be—
    It's an idea I have—
Just the way a gentleman
    Would like behave.

Fact is, I'd like to show you how,
    Before we're squared off quits,
All the gentlemen ain't grown
    In Boston streets.

But here! You called me that, just now,
    I've heard you say before
This summer (Look out there!
    You hug the shore!)

It's really more than I can stand—
    A pretty word! "Dock-rat!"
Just because a fellow don't
    Wear such a hat.

And doesn't wear a fancy shirt,
    With anchors to the sleeve;
And don't wear his stockings weeks.
    You'd best believe

That all this living round the wharves,
    And picking drift-wood up,
And such like vacation chores
    (Just see that pup

Those there ladies took to bathe,
    With patent corks tied on!)
I tell *you* this sort o' life
    Aint such a one

As needs be sarsed at specially
    To be uncomf'table,
Though I like it, on the whole,
    Tolerable.

Perhaps the boarding-folks round here
    May have a sprucer look;
May be, now, you Boston chaps
    Can read a book

That's bigger by an inch or so
    Than I can easy steer;
You may clean up more than me—
    But now look here!

In all my life I never did—
    And I'm just square gone ten—
Put the name of "Paddy" on
    To Irishmen.

Nor called a boy a "nigger," just
    Because his face was black;
Nor I don't hail sailors round:
    "Oh, here you, Jack!"

If so a chap is not exact
    So nice or smart as I,
I don't make an imperence
    To know him by.

Now, don't you see, this dory here
    Don't need to hold two men?
Just duck *you* under! Who'd be
    The "dock-rat" then?

But, sir! I *asked* you out to row;
    Now tell me, if you can,
Which of *us* two is most like
    A gentleman?

🍀 *Phoebe Cary*

THE CROW'S CHILDREN

A huntsman, bearing his gun a-field,
  Went whistling merrily;
When he heard the blackest of black
    crows
  Call out from a withered tree:—

"You are going to kill the thievish birds,
  And I would if I were you;
But you musn't touch my family,
  Whatever else you do!"

"I'm only going to kill the birds
  That are eating up my crop;
And if your young ones do such things,
  Be sure they'll have to stop."

"Oh," said the crow, "my children
  Are the best ones ever born;
There isn't one among them all
  Would steal a grain of corn."

"But how shall I know which ones they
    are?
  Do they resemble you?"
"Oh no," said the crow, "they're the
    prettiest birds,
  And the whitest that ever flew!"

So off went the sportsman, whistling,
  And off, too, went his gun;
And its startling echoes never ceased
  Again till the day was done.

And the old crow sat untroubled,
  Cawing away in her nook;
For she said, "He'll never kill my birds,
  Since I told him how they look.

"Now there's the hawk, my neighbor,
  She'll see what she will see, soon;
And that saucy, whistling blackbird
  May have to change his tune!"

When, lo! she saw the hunter
  Taking his homeward track.
With a string of crows as long as his gun
  Hanging down his back.

"Alack, alack!" said the mother,
  "What in the world have you done?
You promised to spare my pretty birds,
  And you've killed them every one."

"Your birds!" said the puzzled hunter;
  "Why, I found them in my corn;
And besides, they are black and ugly
  As any that ever were born!"

"Get out of my sight, you stupid!"
  Said the angriest of crows;
"How good and fair her children are,
  There's none but a parent knows!"

"Ah! I see, I see," said the hunter,
  "But not as you do, quite;
It takes a mother to be so blind
  She can't tell black from white!"

Christina Moody (age 13–16)

CHILLUN AND MEN

W'ats dat fretting mammy's chile?
You'se enough to set me wile.
  Stop my work and play wid you?
  Hum, dat's a pretty ting to do.

Here's I got dis fish to fry—
Hush, honey don't you cry—
  Dar now, dar now, shut right up.
  Lause dat youngon's broke my cup.

Le' go dat po cat's tail—
Why I just soon be in jail—
  Don't you know dat cat will scratch
  Land of goodness give me dat match.

Set yo' se'f down in dat chair;
And you jest move, sur, if you dare;
  Take yo' hands off dat air fish—
  Holy smokes dar goes de dish.

Good ting my hands is in dis doe,
If dey weren't I'd whip you sho.
  Getting sleppy? well I guess,
  Lay down dar and take yo' res'.

Don't you lemme see you move,
Turn over dar take off dem shoes.
  Look what a mess dis room is in,
  Tings and stroned from end to end.

Above all tings I do declare,
Just look'er yonder at dat chair.
  I never seed sich in all my life,
  Dat youngon's hacking it wid a knife.

Here comes Ben, well I be bless,
What'll he say about dis mess?
  Chillun and men, chillum and men;
  When a 'oman gits married
    Then hur trobles begin.

Hannah Flagg Gould

THE DISSATISFIED ANGLER BOY

I'm sorry they let me go down to the brook;
I'm sorry they gave the line and the hook;
And I wish I had staid at home with my book!
  I'm sure 'twas no pleasure to see
That poor, little, harmless, suffering thing
Silently writhe at the end of the string:
And to hold the pole, while I felt him swing
  In torture, and all for me!

'Twas a beautiful, speckled and glossy trout—
And when from the water I brought him out,
In the grass on the bank, as he floundered about,
  It made me shiver cold,
To think I had caused so much needless pain
And I tried to relieve him, but all in vain—
Oh! never as long as I live, again,
  May I such a sight behold!

O what would I give once more to see
The brisk little swimmer alive and free,
And darting about, as he ought to be,
    Unhurt, in his own native brook!
'Tis strange how people can love to play,
By taking innocent lives away!—
I wish I had staid at home to day
    With sister and read my book!

⁊ *Anna Maria Wells*

COMPASSION

Among the hills, one summer's day,
    I met a cottage lad;
Lonely and mute he took his way,
    As though his heart were sad.

'Why Reuben!—see the bright blue sky—
    Hath it no charm my boy?
The birds are singing merrily,—
    All wears the face of joy.

'Look up,—the sheep are on the hills,
    The bees are round the flowers;
The spicy east no breath distils
    Sweeter than this of ours.

'The fields of waving grain look glad;
    There's mirth among the trees;
What is it Reuben makes thee sad,
    Mid sights and sounds like these?'

'I know the earth is full of joy,
    The sheep are on the hills;
And even this,' replies the boy,
    'My heart with sorrow fills.

'I saw them lead a young ewe-lamb
    Away from all the rest;—
I heard the bleating of the dam:—
    What grief that cry expressed!

But, when I saw the gentle ewe
    Lay down its head to die—
I wondered they had hearts to do,
    Such act of cruelty.

'I think I could not crush a flower,
    That bowed its head so low;
It may be pleasant to have power,
    But not to use it so.'

Hannah Flagg Gould

THE LAME HORSE

O! I cannot bring to mind
When I've had a look so kind,
Gentle lady, as thine eye
Gives me, while I'm limping by;
Then, thy little boy appears
To regard me but with tears.
Dost thou think he'd like to know
What has brought my state so low?

When not half so old as he,
I was bounding, light and free,
By my happy mother's side
Ere my mouth the bit had tried;
Or my head had felt the rein
Drawn, my spirits to restrain.
But I'm now so worn and old,
Half my sorrows can't be told.

When my services began,
How I loved my master, man!
I was pampered and caressed,
Housed, and fed upon the best.
Many looked with hearts elate
At my graceful form and gait,
At my smooth and glossy hair,
Combed and brushed with daily care.

Studded trappings then I wore,
And with pride my master bore—
Glad his kindness to repay
In my free, but silent way.
Then was found no nimble steed
That could equal me in speed;
So untiring and so fleet
Were these now old, aching feet.

But my troubles soon drew nigh:
Less of kindness marked his eye,
When my strength began to fail,
And he put me off at sale.
Constant changes were my fate,
Far too grievous to relate.
Yet I've been, to say the least,
Mid them all, a patient beast.

Older, weaker, still I grew:
Kind attentions all withdrew.
Little food and less repose;
Greater burdens, heavier blows—
These became my hapless lot,
Till I sunk upon the spot!
This maimed limb beneath me bent
With the pain it underwent.

Now I'm useless, old and poor,
They have made my sentence sure;
And to-morrow is the day
Set for me to limp away
To some far, sequestered place,
There at once to end my race.
I stood by and heard their plot—
Soon my woes will be forgot.

Gentle lady, when I'm dead
By the blow upon my head,
Proving thus my truest friend
Him, who brings me to my end,
Wilt thou bid them dig a grave
For their faithful, patient slave;
Then, my mournful story trace,
Asking mercy for my race?

THE INDIAN BOY WITH HIS FATHER'S BOW

"I look on the bow that my father bent,
And I know the ways where the warrior went.
I remember the flash of the chieftain's eye;
When he heard the whoop of the foeman nigh!
I can see the fall of that stately head
On the dauntless breast, when its blood was shed;
And I bear in my heart the charge that hung,
To avenge his death, on the faltering tongue!

"My hand is as firm to bend the bow;
My foot through the forest as fleet to go;
I can aim my dart with as sure an eye;
And I am as ready as he to die!
My spirit is burning with thirst to meet
Our ancient foe—for revenge is sweet.
Lo! onward I go, and my father's shade
Shall be at my side, till the debt is paid!"

He leaps, and is gone, like the bounding deer;
But not like her, from the hound and spear.
He flies to his death—he has met the dart;
And 'tis drinking the blood of that fearless heart!
But it came too late, for his dying ear
The curse of his falling foe can hear—
The arrow was sped, which brings him low,
By the hand of the son, from the father's bow!

Robert Frost (age 16)

TENOCHTITLAN, FROM "LA NOCHE TRISTE"

Changed is the scene: the peace
And regal splendor which
Once that city knew are gone,
And war now reigns upon
That throng, who but
A week ago were all
Intent on joy supreme.
Cries of the wounded break
The stillness of the night,
Or challenge of the guard.
The Spaniard many days
Besieged within the place,
Where kings did rule of old,
Now pressed by hunger by

The all-relentless foe,
Looks for some channel of
Escape. The night is dark;
Black clouds obscure the sky—
A dead calm lies o'er all.
The heart of one is firm,
His mind is constant still,
To all, his word is law.
Cortes his plan hath made,
The time hath come. Each one
His chosen place now takes,
There waits the signal, that
Will start the long retreat.

Robert Frost (age 17)

THE SACHEM OF THE CLOUDS

(A Thanksgiving Legend)

When the sedge upon the meadows crosses, falls and interweaves,
Spent, the brook lies wrapt in silence on its bed of autumn leaves;
When the barren fields are moaning, where the Autumn winds rush by,
And the leaves start up in eddies and are whirled athwart the sky;

On the lonely hillside, darkened by the over-hurrying clouds,
Ghostly, stand the withered corn-rows, in their waving midnight shrouds,
Like the band of those departed, murmuring with discontent,
Come again to tell their sadness, hid in vengeance as they went.

Then the traveler, wending downward from the mountain's fading height,
Deep among the woody marshes, stretching back within the night,
Sees a hermit, grey and feeble, dwarfed beside a giant oak,
Sees the sachem of the storm-cloud, clad about with wreaths of smoke,

Piling high his pyre of hemlocks, weaving spell and crossing limb,
Till a hazy phosphorescence plays around the circle's rim;
All night long, 'mid incantations, hears the wizard's voice arise,
On the bleak wind wildly mingled with the forest's eerie cries.

And when far the flames up-reaching, lurid, gleam upon the vale,
Then the wizard's muttered croaking rises to a piercing wail:
"Come, O come, with storm, come darkness! Speed my clouds on Winter's breath.
All my race is gone before me, all my race is low in death!
Ever, as I ruled a people, shall this smoke arise in cloud;
Ever shall it freight the tempest for the ocean of the proud.
'Thanks!' I hear their cities thanking that my race is low in death,
Come, O come, with storm, come darkness! Speed my clouds on Winter's breath!"

Thus his voice keeps ringing, ringing, till appears the dreary dawn,
And the traveler, looking backward, sees the ashes on the lawn,
Sees the smoke crowd to the hilltops, torn away, and hurried south,
Hears a shrieking answer speeded from the Winter's snowy mouth.

❧ *Celia Thaxter*

THE KITTIWAKES

Like white feathers blown about the
  rocks,
Like soft snow-flakes wavering in the air,
Wheel the kittiwakes in scattered flocks,
Crying, floating, fluttering everywhere.

Shapes of snow and cloud, they soar and
  whirl:
Downy breasts that shine like lilies
  white;
Delicate, vaporous tints of grey and
  pearl,
Laid upon their arching wings so light.

Eyes of jet, and beaks and feet of gold,—
Lovelier creatures never sailed in air;
Innocent, inquisitive and bold,
Knowing not the dangers that they dare.

Stooping low above a beckoning hand,
Following gleams of waving kerchiefs
  white,
What should they of evil understand,
Though the gun awaits them full in
  sight?

Though their blood the quiet wave
  makes red,
Though their broken plumes float far
  and wide,
Still they linger, hovering overhead,
Still the gun deals death on every side.

O, begone, sweet birds, or higher soar!
See you not your comrades low are laid?
But they only flit and call the more—
Ignorant, unconscious, undismayed.

Nay, then, boatman, spare them! Must
  they bear
Pangs like these for human vanity?
That their lovely plumage we may wear,
Must these fair, pathetic creatures die?

Let the tawny squaws themselves
  admire.
Decked with feathers—we can wiser be.
Ah! beseech you, boatman, do not fire!
Stain no more with blood the tranquil
  sea!

THE GREAT BLUE HERON

The Great Blue Heron stood all alone
    By the edge of the solemn sea,
On a broken bowlder of gray trap-stone
    He was lost in a reverie.

And when I climbed over the low rough wall
    At the top of the sloping beach,
To gather the drift-wood great and small
    Left scattered to dry and to bleach,

I saw, as if carved from the broken block
    On which he was standing, the bird,
Like a part of the bowlder of blue-gray rock;
    For never a feather he stirred.

I paused to watch him. Below my breath,
    "O beautiful creature!" I cried,
"Do you know you are standing here close to your death,
    By the brink of the quiet tide?

"You can not have heard of the being called Man—
    The lord of creation is he;
And he slays earth's creatures wherever he can,
    In the air or the land or the sea.

"He's not a true friend of your race! If he sees
    Some beautiful wonderful thing
That runs in the woodland, or floats in the breeze
    On the banner-like breadth of its wing,

"Straight he goes for his gun, its sweet life to destroy,
    For mere pleasure of killing alone.
He will ruin its beauty and quench all its joy,
    Though 't is useless to him as a stone."

Then I cried aloud: "Fly! before over the sand
    This lord of creation arrives
With his powder and shot, and his gun in his hand
    For the spoiling of innocent lives!"

Oh, stately and graceful and slender and tall,
    The Heron stood silent and still,
As if careless of warning and deaf to my call,
    Unconscious of danger or ill.

"Fly! fly to some lonelier place, and fly fast!
    To the very north pole! Anywhere!"
Then he rose and soared high and swept eastward at last,
    Trailing long legs and wings in the air.

'Now perhaps you may live and be happy," I said;
    "Fly, Heron, as fast as you can!
Put the width of the earth and the breadth of the sea
    Betwixt you and the being called Man!"

❧ Lizzie M. Hadley

A SECRET

"I'll tell you something," says little Belle,
"If you're certain, sure, you'll never tell.

"Well, then," whispers the little maid,
"My papa, a great, big man, 's afraid."

"Oh, isn't that funny enough?" laughed Sue.
"Your papa's afraid, and mine is, too.

"Not of bears or tigers or bumble-bees;
  It's something a thousand times worse than these.

  It's a terrible thing, that goes up and down
  Through every city, village and town.

  And my papa says he almost knows
  That things will be ruined wherever it goes."

"Yes, isn't it dreadful?" says Belle, with a sigh
"It will swear and, papa says, steal and lie.

  I s'pect it has horns and cloven feet;
  And, Sue! what do you s'pose it will eat?"

Then closer together drew each little maid,
Looking about as if half afraid

They might see this thing with cloven feet,
And find it liked little girls to eat.

And then they fancied they heard it roar,
As it gobbled them up and cried for more.

"Oh, its name," cries Belle, "is so dreadful, too;
  Does your papa call it 'Republican,' Sue?"

Sue shakes her head. "Oh, it can't be that,
For my papa calls it a 'Democrat.'"

DEATH AND AFFLICTION

"Cora" [pseudonym] (age 13)

THE STAR

"From thy lofty home, thou star so bright,
  On what dost thou shed thy radiant light?"
I shed my light upon shadowy vales,
  Cool'd by gentle and fragrant gales;
On mountains rugged, and bare, and steep,
  And on the foaming and roaring deep;
On weeping willow and towering pine,
  On creeping moss and luxuriant vine;
On the hermit's silent and lonely cell,
  Buried deep in some shadowy dell;
On the splendid palace and fire-fly's glow;
  On glittering pomp and on humble wo;
On the monarch's throne, and the monarch's grave;
  On the triumph and fall of the noble and brave;
On the cell where the captive wretch resides;
  And my light the murderer's weapon guides.
I witness the ship on the dashing wave,
  Crashing and sinking, and naught to save;
I've witnessed fervent and ardent love,
  So pure that it might have dwelt above;
And vows of eternal friendship broke,
  And hearts that were scared by the sudden stroke.

Phoebe Cary

NEARER HOME

One sweetly-solemn thought
  Comes to me o'er and o'er;
I am nearer home to-day
  Than I ever have been before.
Nearer my Father's house,
  Where the many mansions be;
Nearer the great white throne;
  Nearer the crystal sea;
Nearer the bound of life,
  Where we lay our burdens down;

Nearer leaving the cross;
  Nearer gaining the crown.
Jesus, perfect my trust,
  Strengthen the hand of my faith;
Let me feel thee near when I stand
  On the edge of the shore of death;
Feel thee near when my feet
  Are slipping over the brink;
For, it may be, I'm nearer home—
  Nearer now than I think.

JESUS LOVES ME

[excerpts from novel co-written with Susan Warner]

I. Was it wearily that the song was given? Faith could not tell,—she could not name those different notes in the voice,—she could only feel that the octave reached from earth to heaven.

"'How kind is Jesus, Lord of all!
To hear my little feeble call.
How kind is Jesus, thus to be
Physician, Saviour, all to me!

'How much he loves me he doth shew;
How much he loves I cannot know.
I'm glad my life is his to keep,
Then he will watch and I may sleep.

'Jesus on earth, while here I lie;
Jesus in heaven, if I die:
I'm safe and happy in his care,
His love will keep me, here or there.

'An angel he may send for me,
And then an angel I shall be.
Lord Jesus, through thy love divine,
Thy little child is ever thine.'"

Faith had drawn her chair a little back and with her head leaning on the back of Mr. Linden's chair, listened—in a spirit not very different from Johnny's own. She looked up then when it was done, with almost as childlike a brow. It had quieted him, as with a charm, and the little smile he gave Faith was almost wondering why she looked grave.

II. And for a while then Faith had nothing to do but to look and listen; to listen to the soft measured steps through the room, to watch the soothing, resting effect of the motion on the sick child, as wrapped in Mr. Linden's arms he was carried to and fro. She could tell how it wrought from the quieter, unbent muscles—from the words which by degrees Johnny began to speak. But after a while, one of these words was, "Sing."—Mr. Linden did not stay his walk, but though his tone was almost as low as his footsteps, Faith heard every word.

"Jesus loves me—this I know,
For the Bible tells me so:

Little ones to him belong,—
They are weak, but he is strong.
"Jesus loves me,—he who died
Heaven's gate to open wide;
He will wash away my sin,
Let his little child come in.

"Jesus loves me—loves me still,
Though I'm very weak and ill;
From his shining throne on high
Comes to watch me where I lie.

"Jesus loves me,—he will stay
Close beside me all the way.
Then his little child will take
Up to heaven for his dear sake."

There were a few silent turns taken after that, and then Mr. Linden came back to the rocking-chair, and told Faith in a sort of bright cheerful way—meant for her as well as the child—that Johnny wanted her to brush his hair and give him something to eat. Which Johnny enforced with one of his quiet smiles. Faith sprang to do it, and both offices were performed with hands of tenderness and eyes of love, with how much inner trembling of heart neither eyes nor hands told. Then, after all that was done, Faith stood by the table and began to swallow coffee and bread on her own account, somewhat eagerly.

❧ Louisa May Alcott (about age 12)

DESPONDENCY

Silent and sad,
When all are glad,
And the earth is dressed in flowers;
When the gay birds sing
Till the forest ring,
As they rest in woodland bowers.

Oh why these tears,
And these idle fears
For what may come to-morrow?
The birds find food
From God so good,
And the flowers know no sorrow.

If he clothes these
And the leafy trees,
Will He not cherish thee?
Why doubt his care;
It is everywhere,
Though the way we may not see.

Then why be sad
When all are glad,
And the world is full of flowers?
With the gay birds sing,
Make life all Spring,
And smile through the darkest hours.

ONLY A CHILD

"The Press *of May 27 publishes an account of the suicide in the House of Refuge at Philadelphia of a boy who was only twelve years old. He was locked up in solitary confinement. They found him hanging by the neck dead and cold. Tired of waiting for the release that never came, he had at last escaped—from that House of Refuge!"*—THE WORLD.

They found him hanging dead, you know,
In the cell where he had lain
Through many a day of restless woe
And night of sleepless pain.
The heart had ceased its beating,
The little hands were numb,
And the piteous voice entreating
In death at last was dumb.

No doubt it was a painful fact
For them to contemplate;
They felt the horror of the act,
But felt it rather late.
There was none to lay the blame to—
That, each one understands;
And the jury found—he came to
His death by his own hands!

Poor little hands! that should have known
No subtler arts than these—
To seek for violets newly blown
Beneath the April breeze,
Or gaily bind unchidden
The daisies into sheaves,
Or reach the bird's nest hidden
Among the budding leaves.

Poor little hands! And little heart
That ached so long alone,
With none to ease its secret smart
And none to hear its moan;
As he lay where they had cast him
In the dark upon the floor,
And heard the feet go past him
Outside his prison door.

Think of him, you whose children lie
Soft sleeping overhead;
All day he could not see the sky,
All night he had no bed.
Your walls of brick and mortar
To shut the child's soul in,
And starving on bread and water
For—some little childish sin!

So in the darkness there he lay
While the hours crawled along,
And thought of the woodlands far away
Awake with the robin's song;
And thought of the green grass growing
And the boys at play outside,
And the breath of heaven blowing
O'er the country far and wide.

Perhaps he saw his mother's face
Bend o'er him in the gloom;
But when he leaned to catch her dress
She vanished from the room;
And though he tried to remember
The prayer he used to say,
In a pitiful, broken stammer
On his lips it died away.

His little hands had nought to do
But beat against the wall,
Until at last too tired they grew—
Poor little hands—so small!
And so he lay there voiceless,
Alone upon the ground;
If he wept, his tears were noiseless,
For he feared to hear their sound.

At last perhaps the silence grew
Too deep—it dazed his head—
And his little hands had naught to do;
And so—they found him dead!
In a Christian town it happened,
In a home for children built,
And God knows whose soul shall answer
For the burden of this guilt!

But He who bade the children come
And not be turned away,
Has surely taken the homeless home,
And we need not mourn to-day;
For our lives are all God-given,
The poorest to him is dear,
And the Father has room in heaven
For the children we don't want here!

❧ Julia C. R. Dorr

GOD KNOWS

"Perhaps your young readers will be interested in this incident with the wrecking of the emigrant ship
'Northfleet.' The baby's grave is in the church-yard of Lydd, near Dungeness, England."
—Extract from Author's note.

Oh! wild and dark was the winter night,
  When the emigrant ship went down,
But just outside of the harbor bar,
  In the sight of the startled town!
The winds howled, and the sea roared,
  And never a soul could sleep,
Save the little ones on their mothers'
    breasts,
  Too young to watch and weep.

No boat could live in the angry surf,
  No rope could reach the land;
There were bold, brave hearts upon the
    shore,
  There was many a ready hand:
Women who prayed, and men who strove
  When prayers and work were vain,—
For the sun rose over the awful void
  And the silence of the main!

All day the watchers paced the sands—
  All day they scanned the deep;
All night the booming minute-guns
  Echoed from steep to steep.

"Give up thy dead, O cruel sea!"
  They cried athwart the space;
But only a baby's fragile form
  Escaped from its stern embrace!

Only one little child of all
  Who with the ship went down,
That night, when the happy babies slept
  So warm in the sheltered town!
Wrapped in the glow of the morning
    light,
  It lay on the shifting sand,
As fair as a sculptor's marble dream,
  With a shell in its dimpled hand.

There were none to tell of its race or kin,
  "God knoweth," the Pastor said,
When the sobbing children crowded to
    ask
  The name of the baby dead.
And so when they laid it away at last
  In the church-yard's hushed repose,
They raised a stone at the baby's head
  With the carven words,—"God
    knows!"

STEPHEN TO MARY

*Found in Mary Walton's work-box, after the decease of Stephen Ricks, who died at the
Shelter for Colored Orphans*, in the 2d month, 1832.*

Mary, once I feared to go
From a world of care and woe;
But thou taught me how to die—
How to fix my hopes on high;
Bade my childish fears depart,
And revived my trembling heart;
Told me in a heavenly land,
With a chosen seraph band,
I should join in singing praise,
And my feeble anthems raise.
Yes! thou taught a little child,
With affection meek and mild,
That his home was far above,
In a land of peace and love;
Told me Jesus sweetly smiled
On a humble, sable child.
Oh then, dearest Mary, still
With thy kind, persuasive skill,
Lead a little orphan band
To this bright, celestial land,
Where the colored people share

In redeeming mercy fair.
In that holy, heavenly spot,
Jesus says, "Forbid them not;
Suffer them to come to me,
They shall of my goodness see."
And when Mary's glass is run,
When her work on earth is done,
Here a little ransomed band
Shall before her joyful stand,
Welcome to a land of love,
To a "shelter" far above,
Where no little orphan's tear
Shall distress a heart sincere;
Where no parting funeral knell
Shall a long, sad farewell tell.
Oh then, dearest Mary, stay—
Teach the orphans how to pray;
Lead them all to Jesus fair,
Make them thy peculiar care—
Bid their infant hearts arise,
Lead them to the blissful skies.

*This *Shelter for Colored Orphans* is in Philadelphia. Some account of it was given in the
Slave's Friend No. 7. It was built by the Society of Friends. [original note]

❧ Adeline Groves (age 14)

ORIGINAL COMPOSITION, LINES ON JOSEPH'S GRAVE

Joseph was the son of Mrs.—, with whom Adeline then lived as a servant, 1822.

"Dear Joseph, I've survey'd this ground,
And I have walk'd this grave around;
And now I shed the mournful tear,
To leave your relics lying here.

I'd fondly nurse thee in my arms,
And guard thee safe from every harm;
Yes, shoulds't lean upon my breast,
Or on some downy pillow rest;

But God declares, this shall not be,
Indulgent home, no more you'll see;
You now must slumber in this grave,
Nor father dear his son could save.

The God who reigns above the sky,
And bids your body here to lie,
Commands me here on earth to stay;
But soon will bear me too away.

I oft have gamboll'd at your side,
My follies you would often chide;
But now those happy days are o'er;
Your gentle smiles are seen no more.

No more you'll see your father's face,
Mamma, her son no more embrace,
On you Louisa always smil'd,
And kiss'd you as her fav'rite child."

Frances E. W. Harper

JAMIE'S PUZZLE

There was grief within our household
   Because of a vacant chair.
Our mother, so loved and precious,
   No longer was sitting there.

Our hearts grew heavy with sorrow,
   Our eyes with tears were blind,
And little Jamie was wondering,
   Why we were left behind.

We had told our little darling,
   Of the land of love and light,
Of the saints all crowned with glory,
   And enrobed in spotless white.

We said that our precious mother,
   Had gone to that land so fair,
To dwell with beautiful angels,
   And to be forever there.

But the child was sorely puzzled,
   Why dear grandmamma should go
To dwell in a stranger city,
   When her children loved her so.

But again the mystic angel
   Came with swift and silent tread,
And our sister, Jamie's mother,
   Was enrolled among the dead.

To us the mystery deepened,
   To Jamie it seemed more clear;
Grandma, he said, must be lonesome,
   And mamma has gone to her.

But the question lies unanswered
   In our little Jamie's mind,
Why she should go to our mother,
   And leave her children behind;

To dwell in that lovely city,
   From all that was dear to part,
From children who loved to nestle
   So closely around her heart.

Dear child, like you, we are puzzled,
   With problems that still remain;
But think in the great hereafter
   Their meaning will all be plain.

Charlotte F. Bates

THE WISH

A little child white-robed for sleep
   Is lying with upturned eyes;
The mother is singing; the moon looks in,
   The little one dreamily cries:

"Come nearer, nearer me, great moon,
   And make me just as bright
As the angels mother sings about
   Are, up with God to-night."

A little child white-robed for sleep
   Is lying with closed eyes;
The mother is weeping; the moon looks in
   On her who will never arise.

Nearer the great moon seems to come,
   Wrapping her in its light,—
Ay, brighter than moon or star, in heaven
   She shines with God to-night.

❦ R. S. Chilton

THE LITTLE PEASANT

Unstrung by her heart's first sorrow,
  In the dawn of her life she stands,
With listless fingers holding
  A vacant nest in her hands.

The grass at her feet no longer
  Is bright with the light of the skies,
As downward she looks through the
    tear-drops
  That stand in her heaven-blue eyes.

For the nest, so cold and forsaken,
  Has taught her the lesson to-day,
That the dearest of earthly treasures
  Have wings and can fly away.

Yet she clings to the empty casket,
  And sighs that no more is left,—
As a mother clings to the cradle
  Of its dimpled treasure bereft.

❦ Frank Printz Bixon (before age 15)

A TREASURE

Oh! there are depths in the human heart
  As there are depths in the sea,
Where the richest of treasures lie hidden apart
  From the sun's rich brilliancy.

And oft where we least would look for them,
  As the diver in the sea,
We find the richest and purest gems
  Where we thought that none would be.

But oftener far they remained unknown,
  Their lustre hid by the night,
None knowing how brightly they would have shone
  In the fulness of the light.

Or it may be that they will gleam and glow
  Like meteors in the night,
But the brightened world will never know
  The sources of its light.

THE DEAF GIRL'S THOUGHT OF MUSIC

O tell me what is music like?
　　What bright form that I see
Resembles most that wondrous thing
　　Ne'er yet revealed to me?

They say the angels long ago
　　Sang at Creation's birth,
And ever since heaven-born strains
　　Have floated o'er the earth.

And such is music's origin,
　　But its delicious spell
Has never roused my slumb'ring ear,
　　Or made my pulses thrill.

I hear no answ'ring gush of sound
　　When o'er the tuneful keys,
The skillful fingers lightly sweep,
　　Waking sweet melodies.

The mighty organ's swelling notes,
　　The anthem's peal sublime,
That bears the kindling spirit up
　　Beyond the bounds of time,—

The simple lay, the mother sings
　　Above her infant's rest,
The strains that soothe the couch of pain,
　　Or calm the suffering breast,—

The merry song that's carolled by
　　Glad lips from sorrow free,
And the low, mournful dirge,—are all
　　Mysterious to me.

They tell me Nature's realm is full
　　Of voices, grand and sweet,
That sing together evermore
　　In harmony complete;

But not for me, the music wild
　　Of bird and murm'ring bee,
Or the unending symphony
　　Of the blue, restless sea.

Yet, though my ear can never list
　　To melody of earth,
I know that it shall be unsealed
　　At my celestial birth.

And O, what rapture shall be mine
　　When that new sense is given!
How blissful, even now, to think,
　　That I shall hear in heaven!

Nathaniel Parker Willis

SATURDAY AFTERNOON

I love to look on a scene like this,
  Of wild and careless play,
And persuade myself that I am not old,
  And my locks are not yet gray;
For it stirs the blood of an old man's heart,
  And makes his pulses fly,
To catch the thrill of a happy voice,
  And the light of a pleasant eye.

I have walked the world for fourscore years;
  And they say that I am old,
And my heart is ripe for the reaper, Death,
  And my years are well nigh told.
It is very true; it is very true;
  I'm old, and I "'bide my time:"
But my heart will leap at a scene like this
  And I half renew my prime.

Play on, play on; I am with you there,
  In the midst of your merry ring;
I can feel the thrill of the daring jump,
  And rush of the breathless swing.
I hide with you in the fragrant hay,
  And I whoop the smother'd call,
And my feet slip up on the seedy floor,
  And I care not for the fall.

I am willing to die when my time shall come,
  And I shall be glad to go;
For the world is at best a weary place,
  And my pulse is getting low;
But the grave is dark, and the heart will fail
  In treading its gloomy way;
And it wiles my heart from its dreariness,
  To see the young so gay.

Louisa May Alcott

OUR LITTLE GHOST

Oft in the silence of the night,
  When the lonely moon rides high,
When wintry winds are whistling,
  And we hear the owl's shrill cry;
In the quiet, dusky chamber,
  By the flickering firelight,
Rising up between two sleepers,
  Comes a spirit all in white.

A winsome little ghost it is,
  Rosy-cheeked, and bright of eye,
With yellow curls all breaking loose
  From the small cap pushed awry;
Up it climbs among the pillows,
  For the "big dark" brings no dread,
And a baby's boundless fancy
  Makes a kingdom of a bed.

A fearless little ghost it is:
  Safe the night as is the day;
The lonely moon to it is fair,
  The sighing winds to it are gay.
The solitude is full of friends,
  And the hour brings no regrets;
For, in this happy little soul,
  Shines a sun that never sets.

A merry little ghost it is,
  Dancing gayly by itself,
On the flowery counterpane,
  Like a tricksy household elf;

Nodding to the fitful shadows,
  As they flicker on the wall,
Talking to familiar pictures,
  Mimicking the owl's shrill call.

A thoughtful little ghost it is;
  And when lonely gambols tire,
With chubby hands on chubby knees
  Sits winking at the fire;
Fancies innocent and lovely
  Shine before those baby-eyes;
Sunny fields of dandelions,
  Brooks, and birds, and butterflies.

A loving little ghost it is,
  When crept into its nest,
Its hand on father's shoulder laid,
  Its head on mother's breast,
It watches each familiar face
  With a tranquil, trusting eye,
And, like a sleepy little bird,
  Sings its own soft lullaby.

Then those who feigned to sleep before,
  Lest baby play till dawn,
Wake and watch their folded flower,
  Little rose without a thorn!
And, in the silence of the night,
  The hearts that love it most,
Pray tenderly above its sleep,
  "God bless our little ghost!"

SISSY'S RIDE IN THE MOON

What if I climbed the mountain tall,
    And could see the moon close by?
My papa says it is not so small
    As it looks, 'way off in the sky.

Maybe it comes so near, up there,
    That it touches the mountain side;
And what if it has a door somewhere?
    Then I could get in and ride.

Away I'd go,—'way up in the sky
    To the house of the angels, where
All the dear little babies that die
    With the white, white angels are.

And then I would coax our Baby May
    Into the moon with me,
And we'd sail away, and sail away,
    As happy as we could be.

We would reach our hands out either
    side,
    And gather the stars close by;
And, after a while, the moon would slide
    To the other edge of the sky.

Soon as it reached the mountain there,
    We would both get out of the moon,
And call papa, who would know just
    where
    To come, and would find us soon.

And then he would see little Baby May,
    And would take her upon his arm,
And hold my hand, and we'd walk away
    Down the hills to papa's farm.

Then mamma would see us coming, I
    know,
    And run to the gate and say,
"Why, little Sissy! where did you go?"
    And then she would see little May,—

And then she would laugh,—O, it makes
    me cry,
    To think how glad she would be!
She would say, "Who has been 'way up
    in the sky
    To get my baby for me?"

"It was little Sissy," papa would say,
    "She went in the moon to-night,
And found little May, and coaxed her away
    From the angels all so white."

Then mamma would kiss me, and call
    me good,
    And we'd all go in at the door,
And have some supper; and May never
    would
    Go up in the sky any more.

HIDING THE BABY

Hold him close, and closer hold him,
  (Ah, but this is time to cry!)
Bring his pretty cloak and fold him
  From the Old Man going by.
What Old Man ? You can not guess?
  Not the Old Man of the Sea,
Or the Mountains, I confess,
  Can be half so old as he.

Could we only catch and bind him,
  To some prison, shutting low,
Where the sun could never find him,
  This Old Man should surely go.
We would steal his scythe away,
  (Grass should grow about our feet,)
And he should not take to-day
  From us while to-day was sweet.

Gypsy-ways he has, most surely,
  (Gypsy-ways are hardly right,)
Wandering, stealing, yet securely
  Keeping, somehow, out of sight.
From our trees the fruit he shakes,
  Silver, lace, or silk, we miss
From our houses—this he takes,
  This and other things than this.

Here he comes with buds that wither,
  Here he comes with birds that fly!
Pretty playthings he brings hither,
  Just to take them bye and bye.
He could find you in the night,
  Though you should put out the moon—
He can see without a light.
  He will take the Baby soon.

Head with gold enough about it
  Just to light this whole world through,
Ah, what shall we do without it?—
  Children, say, what shall we do?
Tell me, is there any place
  We can hide the Baby? Say.
Can we cover up his face
  While the Old Man goes this way?

There is one place, one place only,
  We can hide him, if we must—
Very still and low and lonely;
  We can cover him with dust.
Shut a wild-rose in his hand,
  Set a wild-rose at his head:—
This Old Man, you understand,
  Cannot take from us the dead.

Mary E. Wilkins [Freeman]

TWO LITTLE BIRDS IN BLUE

Two little birdies all in blue
Airily flitted the garden thro'.
(Pink blows the brier in summer-weather.)

And they could whistle a rondel true
Which all of the neighbors loved and knew.
(Pink blows the brier in summer-weather.)

Now through the garden the north wind goes,
And the bush is bent to the ground with snows.
(Black turns the brier in winter-weather.)

Where are the little blue birds—who knows?
And where, oh where! is the pink brier-rose?
(Ah, sweet things come and depart together!)

Hannah Flagg Gould

THE CHILD'S ADDRESS TO THE KENTUCKY MUMMY

And now, Mistress Mummy, since thus you've been found
   By the world, who has long done without you,
In your snug little hiding-place far under ground—
Be pleased to speak out as we gather around,
   And let us hear something about you!

By the style of your dress you are not Madam Eve—
   You of course had a father and mother;
No more of your line have we power to conceive,
As you furnish us nothing by which to believe
   You had husband, child, sister, or brother.

We know you have lived, though we cannot tell when,
   And that too by eating and drinking,
To judge by your teeth, and the lips you *had then*;
And we see you are one of the children of men,
   Though long from their looks you've been shrinking.

Who was it that made you a cavern so deep,
   Refused your poor head a last pillow,
And bade you *sit still* when you'd sunken to sleep,
And they'd bound you and muffled you up in a heap
   Of clothes made of hempen and willow?

Say, whose was the ear that could hear with delight
  The musical trinket found nigh you?
And who had the eye that was pleased with the sight
Of this form (whose queer face might be brown, red, or white,)
  Trick'd out in the jewels kept by you?

We think, could we hold up a glass to that face,
  And show its odd shape and expression,
Your own native likeness you hardly would trace—
You'd perceive you'd grown old, and would ask us to place
  Your toys in another's possession!

Your hands that in bonny companionship meet,
  We wonder what hands they have shaken—
With what kind of feelings your heart used to beat—
If your eyes ever wept; and we look on your feet,
  And wonder what paths they have taken.

Come, say, if in anger, in joy, or in woe,
  In what sort of way you would shew them;
In what kind of language your thoughts used to flow—
By whom you were buried, and how long ago—
  From only yourself can we know them.

We see you were taught both to work and to play,
  By the things in the bags kept so near you;
But had you a mother who taught you to pray—
To sing a sweet hymn at the close of each day,
  And to feel that your Maker could hear you?

If so, from this clay now so shrunken and dried,
  That we know not on earth who would save it,
We trust that your spirit went up, when you died,
With its sins all forgiven, its cares laid aside,
  To live with the Being who gave it!

Lydia Sigourney

INDIAN GIRL'S BURIAL*

A wail upon the prairies,—
  A cry of woman's woes,—
That mingleth with the autumn blast,
  All fitfully and low.
It is a mother's wailing!
  Hath Earth another tone,
Like that with which a mother mourns
  Her lost, her only one?—

Pale faces gather round her,—
  They mark'd the storm swell high,
That rends and wrecks the tossing soul,
  But their cold, blue eyes were dry.
Pale faces gaze upon her,
  As the wild winds caught her moan,—
But she was an Indian mother,—
  So she wept those tears alone.

Long, o'er that wasted idol,
  She watch'd, and toil'd, and pray'd:
Tho' every dreary dawn reveal'd
  Some ravage Death had made:
Till the fleshless sinews started,
  And Hope no opiate gave,
And hoarse and hollow grew her voice,
  An echo from the grave.

She was a gentle creature,
  Of raven eye and tress;
And dovelike were the tones that breath'd
  Her bosom's tenderness;—
Save when some quick emotion,
  The warm blood strongly sent
To revel in her olive-cheek,
  So richly eloquent.

I said Consumption smote her,
  And the healer's art was vain;
But she was an Indian maiden,
  So none deplor'd her pain;—
None, save that widow'd mother,
  Who now by her open tomb,
Is writhing like the smitten wretch,
  Whom judgment marks for doom.

Alas! that lowly cabin,
  That bed beside the wall,
That seat beneath the mantling vine,
  They're lone and empty all.
What hand shall pluck the tall, green corn
  That ripeneth on the plain?
Since she for whom the board was spread,
  Must ne'er return again.

Rest, rest, thou Indian maiden!—
  Nor let thy murmuring shade
Grieve that those pale-brow'd ones with
    scorn
  Thy burial-rite survey'd;
There's many a king whose funeral
  A black-rob'd realm shall see,
For whom no tear of grief is shed,
  Like that which falls for thee.—

Yea, rest thee, forest maiden!—
  Beneath thy native tree;
The proud may boast their little day,
  Then sink to dust like thee:—
But there's many a one whose funeral
  With nodding plumes may be,
Whom Nature nor affection mourn,
  As now they mourn for thee.

*Editors' note: Much altered, the poem reappeared in Sigourney's *Select Poems* (1838) with the following headnote: "In the vicinity of Montrose, Wisconsin Territory, the only daughter of an Indian woman of the Sac tribe, died of lingering consumption, at the age of 18. A few of her own race, and a few of the pale-faces were at the grave, but none wept, save the poor mother."
—*Herald of the Upper Mississippi*

HONOR'S DREAM

In the glorious Christmas weather
All the stars came flocking together,—
Flocking into the frosty sky,
Jostling and sparkling, brightening and darkling,
Winking and blinking, far and nigh.

Proud Orion, high and large,
Looked, as he leaned on his silver targe,
At Cassiopeia's jewelled chair,
While his heart-beats played with belt and blade,
Bickering and flickering everywhere.

He heeded not the rabble of stars,
Nor the balanced and blood-red spear of Mars,
Nor the angry torch of Sirius, nay,
Nor the light like dawn, where the splendid swan
With wide-stretched wings swept the Milky Way.

And just as little they heeded him,—
The lovesick giant with glittering limb,—
For they were noting the bells in the spires.
The cheer and mirth on the dark round earth,
And the lighting of happy Christmas fires.

The wind was blowing aloft that night,—
Blowing the thin clouds high and light
To airy ribbons, till one hung down,
Gleaming and glimmering, shining and shimmering,
A gauzy veil from the Northern Crown.

And under the folds of the vaporous veil
There grew the semblance of features pale,
Of floating hair, and of shadowy eyes
Gazing and growing, glooming and glowing
In the face of the Queen of the Winter Skies,—

The darkly radiant Queen, who knew
The nook of each frozen drop of dew,
The fortunes of all beneath her reign,
The brooks that bubble in icy trouble,
The frost-flowers stealing across the pane.

And she counted the little children, too,
And sent them such dreams, the long night through,
Of cousins and chums and sleds and drums,
Of gay disguises and glad surprises,
Of stockings and tarts, and wonderful plums!

Out of the cold and tingling dark
Lit by so many a diamond spark,
Till, close on the breaking edge of day,
Through casements stooping the Dreams came trooping,
Rollicking, frolicking, ready for play.

Darling Bessie, so white and so fair,
The pillow all rich with her yellow hair,
Was clasping a doll with angel-wings,
While a queer dream rocked her, and told her the Doctor
And Santa Claus were the self-same things.

And who was so gay at the dawn of day
As Bessie and Marian, Maud and May,
When joyful Harry came bursting through,
And grinned like a gaby, and said a new baby—
A sister! he'd kissed her!—had brought the dream true?

But long ere the Christmas sunrise came,
Wrapping the white world with rosy flame,
The kind Queen questioned if all were done;
For, with so many children, 'twas fairly bewildering
To choose the fit dream for every one.

And she shivered when, searching far and wide,
She saw on the lonely common's side,
Where the winds from their four wild quarters blow,
There lay little Honor with nothing upon her
Save the careless coverlet of the snow.

For Honor no stocking hung over the hearth,
No hand prepared the morrow's mirth,
Only around her the loose drift whirled
Where the child had dropped when her tired feet stopped,—
For no one loved her in all the world.

Though the Queen of its jewels stripped her crown,
She could make no snowdrift as warm as down,
She could give the smile on no mother's face,—
The flying gleam of some happy dream
Was all she could cast across the place.

"Since to-morrow the child must beg her way,
  To-night," cried the Queen, "let her heart be gay.
  Deck her, O Dreams, a Christmas-tree
  With branches that even reach into heaven!"
"And we," sang the stars, "will the candles be!"

Straight from the pitiful Queen's far realm,
Into the boughs of a bending elm,
Darted a bevy of flashing Dreams,
While each icy spray caught an azure ray,
And tossed it back in a mist of beams.

Then from every stem a smiling sprite
Scattered glory upon the night,
And from bough to bough a rainbow flew;
The icicles tinkled, the gay stars twinkled,
And cherub faces came peering through.

And grander and greater, as Honor dreamed,
The height of the glittering elm-tree seemed,
Till over Orion its branches were creeping,
And their mystical dances of banners and lances
Beneath it the Northern Lights were keeping.

What smiles on the cherub faces bloomed!
What shining shadows around her loomed!
What pillowing arms bore her high and higher!
How this seraph's pinions cleft the blue dominions,
As the white flame fans from some sacred fire!

Forgotten the frozen sleep below,
Where the wild winds tossed the careless snow,
The constellations that over her wheeled,—
Such warmth and lustre about her cluster
In faces like flowers of some fadeless field!

For such music breathes over happy Honor,
Such beautiful angels are crowding upon her,
Such a tender hand has its blessing given!
Ah, waken who may at the dawn of day,
But Honor already has waked in Heaven!

THE RIVER

O tell me, pretty river!
    Whence do thy waters flow?
And whither art thou roaming,
    So pensive and so slow?

"My birthplace was the mountain.
    My nurse, the April showers;
My cradle was a fountain,
    O'ercurtained by wild flowers.

"One morn I ran away,
    A madcap, hoyden rill—
And many a prank that day
    I play'd adown the hill!

"And then, 'mid meadow banks,
    I flirted with the flowers
That stoop'd with glowing lips
    To woo me to their bowers.

"But these bright scenes are o'er,
    And darkly flows my wave—
I hear the ocean's roar,
    And there must be my grave!"

Sarah Piatt

THE FUNERAL OF A DOLL

They used to call her Little Nell,
    In memory of that lovely child
Whose story each had learned to tell.
    She, too, was slight and still and mild,
    Blue-eyed and sweet; she always
        smiled,
And never troubled any one
Until her pretty life was done.
And so they tolled a tiny bell,
    That made a wailing fine and faint,
As fairies ring, and all was well.
    Then she became a waxen saint.

Her funeral it was small and sad.
    Some birds sang bird-hymns in the air.
The humming-bee seemed hardly glad,
    Spite of the honey everywhere.
    The very sunshine seemed to wear
Some thought of death, caught in its gold,
That made it waver wan and cold.
Then, with what broken voice he had,
    The preacher slowly murmured on
(With many warnings to the bad)
    The virtues of the Doll now gone.

A paper coffin rosily-lined
    Had Little Nell. There, drest in white,
With buds about her, she reclined,
    A very fair and piteous sight—
    Enough to make one sorry, quite.
And, when at last the lid was shut
Under white flowers, I fancied——
No matter. When I heard the wind
    Scatter Spring-rain that night across
The Doll's wee grave, with tears half-
        blind
    One child's heart felt a grievous loss.

"It was a funeral, Mama. Oh,
    Poor Little Nell is dead, is dead.
How dark!—and do you hear it blow?
    She is afraid." And as she said
    These sobbing words, she laid her head
Between her hands, and whispered: "Here
Her bed is made, the precious dear—
She cannot sleep in it, I know.
    And there is no one left to wear
Her pretty clothes. *Where did she go?*
    ——See, this poor ribbon tied her hair!"

Eugene Field

LITTLE BOY BLUE

The little toy dog is covered with dust,
    But sturdy and stanch he stands;
And the little toy soldier is red with rust,
    And his musket moulds in his hands.
Time was when the little toy dog was new
    And the soldier was passing fair,
And that was the time when our Little Boy Blue
    Kissed them and put them there.

"Now, don't you go till I come," he said,
    "And don't you make any noise!"
So toddling off to his trundle-bed
    He dreamt of the pretty toys.
And as he was dreaming, an angel song
    Awakened our Little Boy Blue,—
Oh, the years are many, the years are long,
    But the little toy friends are true.

Ay, faithful to Little Boy Blue they stand,
    Each in the same old place,
Awaiting the touch of a little hand,
    The smile of a little face.
And they wonder, as waiting these long years through,
    In the dust of that little chair,
What has become of our Little Boy Blue
    Since he kissed them and put them there.

James Whitcomb Riley

THE HAPPY LITTLE CRIPPLE

I'm thist a little cripple boy, an' never goin' to grow
An' git a great big man at all!—'cause Aunty told me so.
When I was thist a baby onc't, I falled out of the bed
An' got "The Curv'ture of the Spine"—'at's what the Doctor said.
I never had no Mother nen—fer my Pa runned away
An' dassn't come back here no more –'cause he was drunk one day
An' stobbed a man in thish-ere town, an' couldn't pay his fine!
An' nen my Ma she died—an' I got "Curv'ture of the Spine!"

I'm nine years old! An' you can't guess how much I weigh, I bet!—
Last birthday I weighed thirty-three!—An' I weigh thirty yet!
I'm awful little fer my size—I'm purt' nigh littler 'nan
Some babies is!—an' neighbors all calls me "The Little Man!"
An' Doc one time he laughed an' said: "I 'spect, first thing you know,
You'll have a little spike-tail coat an' travel with a show!"
An' nen I laughed—till I looked round an' Aunty was a-cryin'—
Sometimes she acts like that, 'cause I got "Curv'ture of the Spine."

I set—while Aunty's washin'—on my little long-leg stool,
An' watch the little boys an' girls a-skippin' by to school;
An' I peck on the winder, an' holler out an' say:
"Who wants to fight The Little Man 'at dares you all to-day?"
An' nen the boys climbs on the fence, an' little girls peeks through,
An' they all says: "Cause you're so big, you think we're 'feard o' you!"
An' nen they yell, an' shake their fist at me, like I shake mine—
They're thist in fun, you know, 'cause I got "Curv'ture of the Spine!"

At evening, when the ironin's done, an' Aunty's fixed the fire,
An' filled an' lit the lamp, an' trimmed the wick an' turned it higher,
An' fetched the wood all in fer night, an' locked the kitchen door,
An' stuffed the ole crack where the wind blows in up through the floor—
She sets the kittle on the coals, an' biles an' makes the tea,
An' fries the liver an' the mush, an' cooks a egg fer me;
An' sometimes—when I cough so hard—her elderberry wine
Don't go so bad fer little boys with "Curv'ture of the Spine!"

But Aunty's all so childish-like on my account, you see,
I'm 'most afeard she'll be took down—an' 'at's what bothers me!—
'Cause ef my good ole aunty ever would git sick an' die,
I don't know what she'd do in heaven—till *I* come, by an' by:—
Fer she's so ust to all my ways, an' ever'thing, you know,
An' no one there like me, to nurse an' worry over so!—
'Cause all the little childerns there's so straight an' strong an' fine,
They's nary angel 'bout the place with "Curv'ture of the Spine!"

FAIRY AND FOLK

ELFIN JACK

CALLING THE FAIRY

Whistle once more, whistle once more,
  Whistle again, little Willie;
What body knows but he's under the rose
  Or fast asleep in the lily?

Dreaming his wee bit dream, my lad;
  Fighting his battles again;
Leading his men with a conqueror's pride
  On through the fiery rain.

His grape and canister, peas and beans;
  His arrows, needles and pins,—
Sharpest of steel,—and *steal* them
    he will,—
  That's how the fairy sins.

He grows his silk on the waving corn,
  His doublet is cut from its leaves;
His bonnet is hid in the kernel's heart
  He gives us the useless sheaves.

The milk-weed's pod is his fishing-boat,—
  It has weathered many a gale;
And a stolen bodkin forms the mast,
  Where floats a gossamer sail.

A butterfly's wing is his lady's fan,
  Her plume the willow-tree bears;
The spider weaves her Honiton lace,
  And gay are the gowns she wears;

All sparkling with jewels, and powdered
    with gold,
  And streaked with the rainbow's hue,
And (tell not your sister, my wise little lad)
  Her bravery always is new.

But whistle no more, whistle no more,
  My darling! be watchful and wary!
Hush! hear the birds singing, the happy
    news bringing,
  "Day breaks!"—so good-bye to the fairy.

Oliver Herford

THE FAIRIES' CONCERT

In a fairy forest known
To the fairy-folk alone,
Where the grasses meet and spread
Like a green roof overhead,
Where the dandelion tree
Towers tall as tall can be,
And the ferns lift up their high
Fairy ladders to the sky,
For the elves to climb upon—
Here are merry goings-on.

From the forest far and near
All the fairy-folk are here,
For to-day there is to be
Music 'neath the daisy-tree.
And the creatures of the wood,
One and all, have been so good
And obliging as to say,
They will gladly come and play
For the elves a serenade,
In the fairy forest glade.
All the little birds have come;
And the bumblebees that hum;
And the gnats that twang the lute;
And the frogs that play the flute;
And the kind of frog whose toots
Seem to come from out his boots;
And the great big green and yellow
Frog that plays upon the 'cello;
And the katydid, in green,
Who is oftener heard than seen;
With the little ladybird
Who is oftener seen than heard;
And the cricket, never still
With his lively legs and trill.
And, in short, each forest thing
That can hum, or buzz, or sing,
Each and all have come to play
For the little elves to-day.

Now the crawfish takes the stand
To conduct the fairy band.
First there is a moment's pause,
Then the leader lifts his claws,
Waves his wand, and—one, two, three!
All at once, from gnat and bee,
Frog, and katydid, and bird
Such a melody is heard
That the elves and fairies wee,
Clapping little hands with glee,
Make their mushroom seat to sway
In a very risky way.
And the creatures in delight
Play away with all their might,
Feeling very justly proud
That the elves applaud so loud.

Now the sun is getting low,
And the elves to bed must go
Ere the sleepy flowers close
In whose petals they repose;
For if they were late they might
Have to stay outside all night.
So the last good-byes are said;
Every one goes home to bed;
And the creatures as they fly
Play a fairy lullaby,
Growing faint and fainter still,
Fainter and more faint, until
All is silent—and the shade
Creeps upon the fairy glade.

Julia Bacon

LOOKING FOR THE FAIRIES

I've peeped in many a blue-bell,
  And crept among the flowers,
And hunted in the acorn-cups,
  And in the woodland bowers;
And shook the yellow daffodils,
  And search'd the gardens round,
A-looking for the little folk
  I never, never found.

I've linger'd till the setting sun
  Threw out a golden sheen,
In hope to see a fairy troupe
  Come dancing on the green;
And marvell'd that they did not come
  To revel in the air,
And wondered if they slept, and where
  Their hiding-places were.

I've wandered with a timid step
  Beneath the moon's pale light,
And every blazing dew-drop seemed
  To be a tiny sprite;
And listened with suspended breath,
  Among the grand old trees,
For fairy music floating soft
  Upon the evening breeze.

Ah me! those pleasant, sunny days,
  In youthful fancies wild,—
Rambling through the wooded dells,
  A careless, happy child—
And now, I sit and sigh to think
  Age from childhood varies,
And never more may we be found
  Looking for the fairies.

Harriet McEwen Kimball

THE FAIRY TAPER

Above me all the stars of night
Thick clustering make the darkness
  bright;
And in the darkling grass below
Shines out with swift, responsive glow
A tiny, steadfast, lucid ray;
Anon as swiftly dies away.
Again it comes; again it goes;
And still with equal lustre glows.
—Now I bethink me 'tis the light
Of some sweet fairy of the night;
A taper-flame of emerald hue
Put out by silver showers of dew!
But O the invisible hands that bear
The fairy candlestick in air,—

To see them strike the fairy light
And lift the flame in mortal sight,
To guide her hastening lover true
The forest of the grasses through!

Fall faster yet an[d] fall you must,
Small dew that lays the fairy dust!
Oft as you quench her lovely light
This little lady of the night
Will still renew the gem-like flame
That hour by hour will burn the same;
While lover fond and lady true
Defy the darkness and the dew!

"Who told you?" (whispered in my ear)
  A little Glow-worm told me, dear!

🍀 *Rose Terry [Cooke]*

A CHILD'S WISH

"Be my fairy, mother,
    Give me a wish a day;
Something, as well in sunshine
    As when the rain-drops play."

"And if I were a fairy,
    With but one wish to spare,
What should I give thee, darling,
    To quiet thine earnest prayer?"

"I'd like a little brook, mother,
    All for my very own,
To laugh all day among the trees
    And shine on the mossy stone;

"To run right under the window,
    And sing me fast asleep,
With soft steps and a tender sound,
    Over the grass to creep.

"Make it run down the hill, mother,
    With a leap like a tinkling bell,
So fast I can never catch the leaf
    That into its fountain fell.

"Make it as wild as a frightened bird,
    As crazy as a bee,
And a noise like the baby's funny laugh;
    That's the brook for me!"

🍀 *Esther Aswell*

NOTHING BUT TOADSTOOLS

Well, yes! Mr. Gradgrind, if so you prefer
To instruct the young Gradgrinds, I shall not demur.
And yes! Mr. Botanist, *you* shall be heard!
"Agaricus" does tell the tale in one word!
But nevertheless I affirm and maintain—
And my senses are sharp and my intellect sane—
That I *saw with these eyes,* as I climbed Annanance—
These bodily eyes, without dreamwork or trance—
The following marvels. They lay in my road
As I wandered alone through the hoary wild wood.
Did you think that the bears and the foxes, perchance,
Were the only tax-payers on old Annanance?
Then who are the citizens there, if you please,
Who own and make use of such objects as these?

A hundred umbrellas, now sober, now gay—
All textures, all fashions, each fit for a fay—
Now domed for a Turk, now flat for a Chinaman—
Big ones for deacons, and small ones for tiny men—
Black ones for showers, and tough as sole leather,
Scarlet and orange and white for fair weather—

Satin and sheen, fine enough for a trousseau—
And one that belonged, I believe, to R. Crusoe;
Rough-thatched and strong-ribbed and stout-handled I ween,
As quaint an umbrella as ever was seen.
And there they all stood unsuspicious of Vandals,
And balanced themselves on their ivory handles.

Ah! *if* I might see but just one of the throng
Of gay little folksies to whom they belong!
For there were their bonnets, besides, you must know,
More dainty and charming than those of Virôt,
More piquant and *chic* than the Gainsborough hat,
And ten times as useful—I'll guarantee that!
A caftan! a gypsy! the cap of a *bonne!*
A monk's hood! a cardinal's hat farther on!
And just a step more, on the faith of the writer,
Revealed to my gaze a remarkable mitre!
"Soho," I exclaimed—but with awe, as I should,
"There be prelates and hierarchs here in the wood!"
Then *helmets*—I vouch for it—fitted with visors
To hide the mustachios of Carls and of Kaisers—
And gear for a chieftain and gear for a khan,
And thatching of every fashion and plan,
From the fez of a Turk or the cap of a Rajah.
To the marvelous pride of a doughty drum-major—
While high on a lance of fine pearl, as befitted,
The cap of our goddess had not been omitted.
"Ods bodkins!" said I, "who'd believe it—who *could*—
That wonders like these may be found in a wood?"

But this was as nothing, for lo, by and by,
A minster, a temple, mine eyes did descry!
A marvel of skill, made of pure alabaster,
And fashioned, be sure, by the hand of a master.
How can I describe it, you've heard of the Taj?
I vow this was rarer, of course not so large—
But daintier, airier, pillared more fine,
And carven more richly, this temple of mine.
The arches how perfect! How fair every column!
The porches how friendly! The cloisters how solemn!
I gazed, and I stared, and I wondered apace,
To find such a nonpareil, there in such place—
And I lingered and loitered, and hoped I should see
Some one of the worshippers, winsome and wee—

But never a soul ventured forth to my ken,
And I took up my staff and went onward again.

Now the powers of the wood had decided—the elves—
To show quite a different phase of themselves;
And so from the Lofty and Grand and Majestic,
They dropped me at once to the purely Domestic.
For the very next thing that appeared in my path—
Tell it in Askalon, publish in Gath!—
Was a pile of good griddle cakes, velvety, tempting,
Which I barely was able to keep from pre-empting—
And a score of small pâtés—my honor I pledge!
Distractingly scalloped and worked round the edge!
Then a dozen or twenty of crisp macaroons,
Some tiny *jaune manges,* to be eaten with spoons,
And some cocoanut cakes fine enough to set frantic
The souls of all bakers this side the Atlantic;
So round, so symmetrical, luscious and plump;
Browned off in such circles, they lay on a stump.
That 'twas all I could do, in the way of just dealing,
To keep my ten fingers from picking and stealing.
Then came a fine custard, and some sort of jelly,
And something that looked like done-brown vermicelli,
A pudding, more pasties, and bannocks *galore.*
One muffin like Chater's—perhaps there were more—
Some fanciful biscuit—most like for the kinder,
And nine baked potatoes—all burnt to a cinder!
"Alas!" I exclaimed, "these adorable midgets
Are pestered like us, with perfunctory Bridgets."

One item remains in the edible line—
Some golden-brown russets—you'd say, "extra fine."
But they prove themselves nothing but apples of Sodom—
For to ashes and powder they turn if you prod 'em!
"The jokes of these practical jokers are good,"
I said to myself as I climbed through the wood.

For the tables and stools that I found in my clamber—
Their name it was Legion—their substance was amber.
Or ivory or leather, or mother-of-pearl,
Or satin embroidered, and fit for an earl,
Or velvet brocade, with a framework of agate—
Your head is quite turned now—else why do you wag it?
And if I had properly studied Mnemonics,

I'd think of the rest—but one was of onyx—
I'm certain of *that*—and it stood on a leg
As precious and rare as the famous gold peg
That belonged to the heiress of Kilmansegg.
And then there were salvers, and *tazzas* and *paterae*
That carried my heart with assault and with battery,
(And so they would *yours*, Madam, if that your mind
Is toward Keramics the leastwise inclined)
And one peerless saucer, too rare for a prince,
So bewitching in texture, devices and tints
That I've been in a glamour, I think, ever since.

That wee bittie saucer—it couldn't be matched—
No, not if an agent should straight be dispatched
To Dresden or Paris, or yet to Japan,
Or the Flowery Realm—and the mighty Chin Chan
Should issue an edict, and order his bosses
To burn krinkum-krankums, and pray to their josses,
And then—if the article wasn't forthcoming—
To set up a pounding and clattering and drumming,
And plunge the whole land in a big Saturnalia,
Their pig-tails the forfeit, in case of failure!

My memory halts—but I think of a basin
As costly, I trow, as the fleeces of Jason—
A trumpet, a funnel, some gilt-headed nails,
Some porcelain ditto—and here the list fails.
'Tis only a catalogue, now I have done;
But if I could paint, and could dip in the sun,
In the ocean and rainbow, my brush, you'd infer
How exquisite-dainty these treasure-troves were.
But still, Mr. Gradgrind—he never retracts
His remark about "Toadstools"—for "Toadstools are Facts"—
And the microscope-man smiles at fancy and fables,
And still pins his faith on his long Latin labels;
But Bessie, and Johnny, and dear little Trix,
Choose my Annannce story three nights out of six.

Emily Dickinson

THE SEA OF SUNSET

This is the land the sunset washes,
　These are the banks of the Yellow Sea;
Where it rose, or whither it rushes,
These are the western mystery!

Night after night her purple traffic
Strews the landing with opal bales;
Merchantmen poise upon horizons,
Dip, and vanish with fairy sails.

Mary E. Wilkins [Freeman]

ONCE UPON A TIME

Now, once upon a time, a nest of fairies
Was in a meadow 'neath a wild rose-tree;
And, once upon a time, the violets clustered
So thick around it one could scarcely see;
And, once upon a time, a troop of children
Came dancing by upon the flowery ground;
And, once upon a time, the nest of fairies,
With shouts of joy and wonderment they found;
And, once upon a time, the fairies fluttered
On purple winglets, shimmering in the sun;
And, once upon a time, the nest forsaking,
They flew off thro' the violets, every one;
And, once upon a time, the children followed
With loud halloos along the meadow green;
And, once upon a time, the fairies vanished,
And never more could one of them be seen;
And, once upon a time, the children sought them
For many a day, but fruitless was their quest,
For, once upon a time, amid the violets,
They only found the fairies' empty nest.

❧ *Mary E. Wilkins [Freeman]*

THE SICK FAIRY

Brew some tea o' cowslips, make some poppy-gruel,
Serve it in a buttercup—ah, 'tis very cruel,
That she is so ailing, pretty Violetta!
Locust, stop your violin, till she's feeling better.

❧ *Mary E. Wilkins [Freeman]*

A LITTLE PEACHLING

A Japanese Folk-lore Story

At the foot of the Golden Dragon Hill,
   Ages ago, in a snug little house
With a roof of dark-brown, velvety thatch,
   There lived an old woodman and his
     spouse.

One morning his bill-hook the old man
   took:
  "To the mountain, to cut me a fagot, I'll
   hie,
While you, O Koyo, the linen can wash
   In the river which rushes and gurgles
    by."

Oh! the merry old man to the mountain
   hied,
   Past young rice-fields in the morning
    sun,
Toward the dark fir-trees on the mountain
   side,
   Standing forth in its silence, every one.

From wild camellias and white plum-trees,
   In his twinkling old eyes the spider-webs
    swung;
And he merrily brushed by the green
   bamboos,
   With his bill-hook over his shoulder
    hung.

And a uguisu sang in a tall cherry-tree
   As the smiling old wife to the river-side
    went:
"Oh, red is the sun!" she cheerily sang,
   As she patiently over her washing bent.

"Oh, red is the sun! and the rice-fields
   green—
   Now what is that in the river I see?
It's the rosiest peach in the whole of Japan;
   And it's coming a-floating, a-floating to
    me.

"Now, here is a feast for my darling old
   man,
   Oh, the great Shogun not a finer can get!
Some stewed lily-bulbs, and this beautiful
   peach,
   When he comes home from work, before
    him I'll set."

Soon down from the mountain the old man
   came,
   And fast on his back his fagot was
    bound.
"Oh! hasten you, husband," his loving wife
   cried,
   "And taste this beautiful peach that I
    found."

But just as he took it the peach split in
    twain,
    And a fat little baby with raven-black
      hair
Was cradled right in the heart of the
    peach,
    And lay a-twinkling and blinking there.

"Oh! you brave little boy, you shall be our
    own son;
    And Momotaro shall have for a name,
Or Little Peachling, since out of a peach,
    You dear little fellow, this morning you
      came."

Oh! the rice-fields blossomed for twenty
    years,
    While the gurgling old river amongst
      them ran;
Oh! for twenty years grew the slim
    bamboo,
    And Little Peachling was grown to a
      man.

"Some millet-dumplings pray make
    for me,"
    To his good foster-mother he said
      one day,
"And off to the ogres' castle I'll go,
    And the whole of their treasure will
      bring away.

"As thick in the ogres' treasure-vaults
    The jewels are lying as sea-shore sands;
With blue snow-gates on the mountain-
    top,
    The ogres' castle all proudly stands—

"With blue snow-gates that are stronger
    than steel;
    But I will enter, and bring to you
The wealth from the ogres' treasure-vaults,
    Hung over with pearls, like flowers with
      dew."

"I have made you the dumplings," his good
    mother said,
    "But I fear lest the ogres should do you
      a harm."
But the little Peachling danced gayly away,
    With the millet-dumplings under his
      arm.

A dog leapt out of a cluster of pines:
    "And what have you there, Little
      Peachling, pray?"
"The best millet-dumplings in all Japan,
    And I'm to the ogres' castle away."

"For one of your dumplings with you
    I'll go,
    And the ogres' castle will help subdue."
"Well, you can bark at the castle-gate;
    So here is a dumpling, friend dog,
      for you."

An ape swung down from a roadside tree:
    "*Kia, kia*, what have you, I say?"
"The best millet-dumplings in all Japan,
    And I'm to the ogres' castle away."

"One of your dumplings pray give to me,
    And the ogres' castle I'll help subdue."
"Well, you can climb o'er the castle-gate;
    So here is a dumpling, friend ape,
      for you."

"Ken, ken," cried a pheasant, "and what
    have you there,
    Little Peachling, tucked in your girdle,
      I pray?"
"The best millet-dumplings in all Japan,
    And I'm to the ogres' castle away."

"For one of your dumplings with you
    I'll go,
    And the ogres' castle will help subdue."
"Well, you can fly o'er the castle-gate;
    So here is a dumpling, friend pheasant,
      for you."

Oh, the castle stood high on the
    mountain-top,
  And over its turrets a hurricane blew;
But up to its terrible blue snow-gates
  Little Peachling marched with his
    retinue.

Then the ogres swarmed out on the castle-
    towers,
  The drums beat loud, and the trumpets
    brayed,
And magical arrows came rustling
    around—
  But our brave little rônin was not afraid.

For his pheasant flew over the castle-wall,
  And his ape undid the castle-gate;
And brave Little Peachling, his dog at heel,
  Into the castle then marched in state.

His little dog snapped at the ogres' heels;
  His pheasant picked at their round green
    eyes;
And his ape tweaked away at the ogres'
    locks,
  As only an ape can do when he tries.

And the little rônin, around him he laid,
  With his muramasa so thick and fast,
That the king of the ogres was prisoner
    made;
  And the ogres' castle was taken at last.

Oh, measures of pearls and wedges of gold!
  Oh, the jars of musk and the coral-bars,
Amber and emeralds, tortoise-shells,
  And diamonds shining like strings of
    stars!

Gold-brocade coats, and wonderful gems
  That regulated the green sea-tide!
It's always the loveliest things in the world
  Which the treasure-castles of ogres
    hide.

With the treasures, the dog, the pheasant
    and ape,
  Little Peachling home to his parents ran;
And the old woodman and his loving wife
  Were the happiest couple in all Japan.

☘ *Mary E. Wilkins [Freeman]*

DOWN IN THE CLOVER

(a duet, with sheep obligato)

Mid feeding lambs and springing grass
There sat a little lad and lass,
A green umbrella overhead,
The flickering shade of boughs instead,
And read a book of fairy rhyme,
All in their gay vacation time.

Quoth he: "The dearest, queerest story
  Was that one of the fairy prince,
Who sailed down stream in his pearl dory,
  'Neath boughs of rose and flowering
    quince,

To save the lovely princess whom
  The wicked, white-haired, old witch-lady
Kept in a tower of awful gloom,
  Deep in a magic forest shady:
How proud he tossed his plumèd head
Before the witch's door, and said"—

Sheep: *Ba-a, ba-a! Honey-sweet the clover's
    blowing.*
Ba-a, ba-a! Juicy-green the grass is growing.

"I think," quoth she, "there's one that's
    better:
  About that little fairy girl,

Who bound the ogre with a fetter
   Of spiderwort and grass and pearl;
Then singing in the gateway sat,
   Till up the road the prince came
      prancing,
A jewelled feather in his hat,
   And set the cherry-boughs a-dancing.
How low he bent his handsome head
Before the fairy girl, and said"—

Sheep: *Ba-a, ba-a! Who the day so sweetly*
      passes
   As a lamb who never stops,
But from dawn to twilight crops
   Clover-heads and dewy grasses?

"Well, by and by I think I'll be
A fairy prince as brave as he:
I'll wind a silver bugle clear,
Low and dim you'll hear it, dear;
A sword with jewelled hilt I'll bear,
A cap and heron-plume I'll wear,
And I will rescue you," quoth he.
"Fast to the witch's tower I'll fly,
   And beat upon the gate, and cry"—

Sheep: *Ba-a, ba-a! Sweet the simple life we're*
      leading,
   In the sweet green pasture feeding!

Then quoth the little reader fair,
"I've changed my mind, for I don't dare
To stay there in the witch's tower;
I'll be the dame who found a flower
Of gold and rubies—in the tale—
And sold it for a fairy veil,
Which made her look so sweet and true
That she was dearly loved; then you"—

Sheep: *Ba-a, ba-a! Turn the juicy morsel over.*
   Who would be a lad or lass,
      If he could his summer pass
As the sheep amongst the clover?
Grasshoppers on daisies teeter,
Dew-drops clover sweeten sweeter.
Who can care for stupid tales,
Fairy horns and fairy veils,
Fairy princess, fairy prince?
Yet we must not blame them, since
(Turn the juicy morsel over)
They cannot be sheep in clover.

❦ *Sarah Piatt*

THE END OF THE RAINBOW

"May you go to find it?" You must, I fear,—
   Ah, lighted young eyes, could I show you how!
"Is it past those lilies that look so near?"
   It is past all flowers. Will you listen now?

The pretty new moons faded out of the sky,
   The bees and butterflies out of the air;
And sweet wild songs would flutter and fly
   Into wet dark leaves and the snow's white glare.

There were winds and shells full of lonesome cries;
   There were lightnings and mists along my way;
And the deserts glittered against my eyes,
   Where the beautiful phantom-fountains play.

At last, in a place very dusty and bare,
   Some little dead birds I had petted to sing,
Some little dead flowers I had gathered to wear,
   Some withered thorns, and an empty ring,

Lay scattered. My fairy story is told.
   (It does not please her,—she has not smiled.)
What is it you say?—"Did I find the gold?"
   Why, I found the End of the Rainbow, child!

❧ *Sarah Piatt*

AN EAST INDIAN FAIRY STORY

All day she was yellow and gray and thin;
   All day she was troubled with time and tears;
All day she was dressed in the withered skin
   Of a woman who lived a hundred years.

All day she begged, through the heavy heat,
   For a drop of water, a grain of rice;
But she sat, in the twilight, still and sweet,
   Close to the leaves of the blossoming spice.

At a fairy fountain dim in the air,
   In a garment white as a priestess wears,
With a lotus-bud in her lovely hair,
   And her hand in the water, she said her prayers.

"Oh, well do I hide my beauty all day
   From the sun and the cruel eyes I dread;
But the gods can see me when I pray,
   And I must look fair to the gods," she said.

Hannah Flagg Gould

THE MERMAID'S SONG

Come, mariner, down in the deep with me,
  And hide thee under the wave;
For I have a bed of coral for thee,
And quiet and sound shall thy slumber be
  In a cell in the Mermaid's cave!

On a pillow of pearls thine eye shall sleep,
  And nothing disturb thee there;
The fishes their silent vigils shall keep;
There shall be no grass thy grave to sweep,
  But the silk of the Mermaid's hair.

And she, who is waiting with cheek so pale,
  As the tempest and ocean roar,
And weeps when she hears the menacing gale,
Or sighs to behold her mariner's sail
  Come whitening up to the shore—

She has not long to linger for thee!
  Her sorrows will soon be o'er;
For the cord shall be broken, the prisoner free;
Her eye shall close, and her dreams will be
  So sweet she will wake no more!

Lucretia Davidson (age 15)

THE MERMAID

Maid of the briny wave and raven lock,
Whose bed's the sea-weed, and whose throne's the rock,
Tell me, what fate compels thee thus to ride
O'er the tempestuous ocean's foaming tide?

Art thou some naiad, who, at Neptune's nod,
Flies to obey the mandate of that god?
Art thou the syren, who, when night draws on,
Chaunt'st thy farewell to the setting sun?

Or, leaning on thy wave-encircled rock,
Twining with lily hand thy raven lock;
Dost thou, in accents wild, proclaim the storm,
Which soon shall wrap th' unwary sailor's form?

Or dost thou round the wild Charybdis play,
To warn the seaman from his dangerous way?
Or, shrieking midst the tempest, chaunt the dirge
Of shipwrecked sailors, buried in the surge?

Tell me, mysterious being, what you are ?
So wild, so strange, so lonely, yet so fair!
Tell me, O tell me, why you sit alone,
Singing so sweetly on the wave-washed stone?

And tell me, that if e'er I find my grave,
Beneath the ocean's wildly troubled wave,
That thou with weeds wilt strew my watery bed,
And hush the roaring billows o'er my head.

Laura E. Richards

THE MERMAIDENS

The little white mermaidens live in the sea,
In a palace of silver and gold;
And their neat little tails are all covered with scales,
Most beautiful for to behold.

On wild white horses they ride, they ride,
And in chairs of pink coral they sit;
They swim all the night, with a smile of delight,
And never feel tired a bit.

Laura E. Richards

THE PALACE

It's far away under the water,
And it's far away under the sea,
There's a beautiful palace a-waiting
For my little Rosy and me.

The roof is made of coral,
And the floor is made of pearl,
And over it all the great waves fall
With a terrible tumble and whirl.

The fishes swim in at the window,
And the fishes swim out at the door,
And the lobsters and eels go dancing
    quadrilles
All over the beautiful floor.

There's a silver throne at one end,
    And a golden throne at the other;
    And on them you see, as plain as can be,
"Queen Rosy" and "Queen Mother."

And I will sit on the silver throne,
    And Rosy shall sit on the gold;
    And there we will stay, and frolic and
        play,
    Until we're a thousand years old.

Oliver Wendell Holmes

THE BALLAD OF THE OYSTERMAN

It was a tall young oysterman lived by the river-side,
His shop was just upon the bank, his boat was on the tide;
The daughter of a fisherman, that was so straight and slim,
Lived over on the other bank, right opposite to him.

It was the pensive oysterman that saw a lovely maid,
Upon a moonlight evening, a-sitting in the shade;
He saw her wave her handkerchief, as much as if to say,
"I'm wide awake, young oysterman, and all the folks away."

Then up arose the oysterman, and to himself said he,
"I guess I'll leave the skiff at home, for fear that folks should see;
I read it in the story-book, that, for to kiss his dear,
Leander swam the Hellespont,—and I will swim this here."

And he has leaped into the waves, and crossed the shining stream,
And he has clambered up the bank, all in the moonlight gleam;
Oh there were kisses sweet as dew, and words as soft as rain,—
But they have heard her father's step, and in he leaps again!

Out spoke the ancient fisherman,—"Oh what was that, my daughter?"
"'Twas nothing but a pebble, sir, I threw into the water."
"And what is that, pray tell me, love, that paddles off so fast?"
"It's nothing but a porpoise, sir, that's been a-swimming past."

Out spoke the ancient fisherman,—"Now bring me my harpoon!
I'll get into my fishing-boat, and fix the fellow soon;"
Down fell that pretty innocent, as falls a snow-white lamb,
Her hair drooped round her pallid cheeks, like seaweed on a clam.

Alas for those two loving ones! she waked not from her swound,
And he was taken with the cramp, and in the waves was drowned;
But Fate has metamorphosed them, in pity of their woe,
And now they keep an oyster-shop for mermaids down below.

❧ *John Greenleaf Whittier*

RED RIDING-HOOD

On the wide lawn the snow lay deep,
Ridged o'er with many a drifted heap;
The wind that through the pine-trees sung
The naked elm boughs tossed and swung;
While, through the window, frosty-
    starred,
Against the sunset purple barred,
We saw the somber crow flap by,
The hawk's gray fleck along the sky,
The crested blue-jay flitting swift,
The squirrel poising on the drift,
Erect, alert, his thick gray tail
Set to the north wind like a sail.

It came to pass, our little lass,
With flattened face against the glass,
And eyes in which the tender dew
Of pity shone, stood gazing through
The narrow space her rosy lips
Had melted from the frost's eclipse:
"Oh, see," she cried, "the poor blue-jays!
What is it that the black crow says?
The squirrel lifts his little legs
Because he has no hands, and begs;
He's asking for my nuts, I know;
May I not feed them on the snow?"

Half lost within her boots, her head
Warm-sheltered in her hood of red,
Her plaid skirt close about her drawn,
She floundered down the wintry lawn;
Now struggling through the misty veil
Blown round her by the shrieking gale;
Now sinking in a drift so low
Her scarlet hood could scarcely show
Its dash of color on the snow.

She dropped for bird and beast forlorn
Her little store of nuts and corn,
And thus her timid guests bespoke:
"Come, squirrel, from your hollow oak,—
Come, black old crow,—come, poor
    blue-jay,
Before your supper's blown away!
Don't be afraid; we all are good;
And I'm mamma's Red Riding-Hood!"

❧

O Thou, whose care is over all,
Who heedest e'en the sparrow's fall,
Keep in the little maiden's breast
The pity which is now its guest!
Let not her cultured years make less

The childhood charm of tenderness,
But let her feel as well as know,
Nor harder with her polish grow!
Unmoved by sentimental grief
That wails along some printed leaf,
But, prompt with kindly word and deed
To own the claims of all who need,
Let the grown woman's self make good
The promise of Red Riding-Hood!

❧ *James Whitcomb Riley*

LITTLE ORPHANT ANNIE

Little Orphant Annie's come to our house to stay,
An' wash the cups an' saucers up, an' brush the crumbs away,
An' shoo the chickens off the porch, an' dust the hearth, an' sweep,
An' make the fire, an' bake the bread, an' earn her board-an'-keep ;
An' all us other childern, when the supper things is done,
We set around the kitchen fire an' has the mostest fun
A-list'nin' to the witch-tales 'at Annie tells about,
An' the Gobble-uns 'at gits you
     Ef you
          Don't
               Watch
                    Out!

Onc't they was a little boy wouldn't say his prayers,—
An' when he went to bed at night, away up stairs,
His Mammy heerd him holler, an' his Daddy heerd him bawl,
An' when they turn't the kivvers down, he wasn't there at all!
An' they seeked him in the rafter-room, an' cubby-hole, an' press,
An' seeked him up the chimbly-flue, an' ever'wheres, I guess;
But all they ever found was thist his pants an' roundabout:—
An' the Gobble-uns'll git you
     Ef you
          Don't
               Watch
                    Out!

An' one time a little girl 'ud allus laugh an' grin,
An' make fun of ever'one, an' all her blood an' kin;
An' onc't, when they was "company," an' ole folks was there,
She mocked 'em an' shocked 'em, an' said she didn't care!
An' thist as she kicked her heels, an' turn't to run an' hide,
They was two great big Black Things a-standin' by her side,
An' they snatched her through the ceilin' 'fore she knowed what she's about!
An' the Gobble-uns'll git you
      Ef you
             Don't
                    Watch
                          Out!

An' little Orphant Annie says, when the blaze is blue,
An' the lamp-wick sputters, an' the wind goes *woo-oo*!
An' you hear the crickets quit, an' the moon is gray,
An' the lightnin'-bugs in dew is all squenched away,—
You better mind yer parents, an' yer teachers fond an' dear,
An' churish them 'at loves you, an' dry the orphant's tear,
An' he'p the pore an' needy ones 'at clusters all about,
Er the Gobble-uns'll git you
      Ef you
             Don't
                    Watch
                          Out!

THE BLIND MEN AND THE ELEPHANT: A HINDOO FABLE

I.

It was six men of Indostan
 To learning much inclined,
Who went to see the Elephant
 (Though all of them were blind),
That each by observation
 Might satisfy his mind.

II.

The *First* approached the Elephant,
 And happening to fall
Against his broad and sturdy side,
 At once began to bawl:
"God bless me! but the Elephant
 Is very like a wall!"

III.

The *Second*, feeling of the tusk,
 Cried: "Ho!—what have we here
So very round and smooth and sharp?
 To me 'tis mighty clear
This wonder of an Elephant
 Is very like a spear!"

IV.

The *Third* approached the animal,
 And happening to take
The squirming trunk within his hands,
 Thus boldly up and spake:
"I see," quoth he, "the Elephant
 Is very like a snake!"

V.

The *Fourth* reached out an eager hand,
 And felt about the knee.
"What most this wondrous beast is like
 Is mighty plain," quoth he;
"'Tis clear enough the Elephant
 Is very like a tree!"

VI.

The *Fifth*, who chanced to touch the ear,
 Said: "E'en the blindest man
Can tell what this resembles most;
 Deny the fact who can,
This marvel of an Elephant
 Is very like a fan!"

VII.

The *Sixth* no sooner had begun
 About the beast to grope,
Than, seizing on the swinging tail
 That fell within his scope,
"I see," quoth he, "the Elephant
 Is very like a rope!"

VIII.

And so these men of Indostan
 Disputed loud and long,
Each in his own opinion
 Exceeding stiff and strong,
Though each was partly in the right,
 And all were in the wrong!

MORAL

So, oft in theologic wars
 The disputants, I ween,
Rail on in utter ignorance
 Of what each other mean,
And prate about an Elephant
 Not one of them has seen!

THE NINE LITTLE GOBLINS

They all climbed up on a high board-fence—
  Nine little goblins, with green-glass eyes—
Nine little goblins that had no sense,
    And couldn't tell coppers from cold mince pies;
      And they all climbed up on the fence, and sat—
      And I asked them what they were staring at.

And the first one said, as he scratched his head
  With a queer little arm that reached out of his ear
And rasped its claws in his hair so red—
  "This is what this little arm is fer!"
      And he scratched and stared, and the next one said,
      "How on earth do you scratch your head?"

And he laughed like the screech of a rusty hinge—
  Laughed and laughed till his face grew black;
And when he clicked, with a final twinge
  Of his stifling laughter, he thumped his back
      With a fist that grew on the end of his tail
      Till the breath came back to his lips so pale.

And the third little goblin leered round at me—
  And there were no lids on his eyes at all—
And he clucked one eye, and he says, says he,
  "What is the style of your socks this fall?"
      And he clapped his heels—and I sighed to see
      That he had hands where his feet should be.

Then a bald-faced goblin, gray and grim,
  Bowed his head, and I saw him slip
His eyebrows off, as I looked at him,
  And paste them over his upper lip;
      And then he moaned in remorseful pain—
      "Would—Ah, would I'd me brows again!"

And then the whole of the Goblin band
  Rocked on the fence-top to and fro,
And clung, in a long row, hand in hand,
  Singing the songs that they used to know—
      Singing the songs that their grandsires sung
      In the goo-goo days of the goblin-tongue.

And ever they kept their green-glass eyes
     Fixed on me with a stony stare—
Till my own grew glazed with a dread surmise,
     And my hat whooped up on my lifted hair,
          And I felt the heart in my breast snap to
          As you've heard the lid of a snuff-box do.

And they sang "You're asleep! There is no board-fence,
     And never a goblin with green-glass eyes!—
'Tis only a vision the mind invents
     After a supper of cold mince-pies,—
          And you're doomed to dream this way," they said,—
          "And you shan't wake up till you're clean plum dead!"

✤ *Margaret Sangster*

WHERE THE TROLLS ARE BUSY

Where the trolls are busy,
     Underneath the snow,
There is stirring, there is whirring,
     Of flowers that yet will blow.

The little trolls are spinning
     The crocus garments gay,
Cups of honey, colors sunny,
     To see the light one day.

Beneath the great oak's foot, dears,
     And by the frozen stream,
On her pillow Pussywillow
     Is waking from a dream.

For, oh! the trolls are busy,
     When wintry breezes blow,
Weaving flowers for summer hours,
     Deep down beneath the snow.

✤ *Palmer Cox*

THE BROWNIES ON BICYCLES

One evening Brownies, peeping down
From bluffs that overlooked the town,
Saw wheelmen passing to and fro
Upon the boulevard below.
"It seems," said one, "an easy trick.
The wheel goes 'round so smooth and
     quick;
You simply sit and work your feet
And glide with grace along the street.
The pleasure would be fine indeed

If we could thus in line proceed."
"Last night," another answer made,
"As by the river's bank I strayed,
Where here and there a building
     stands.
And town and country-side join hands,
Before me stood a massive wall
With engine-rooms and chimneys tall
To scale the place a way I found,
And, creeping in, looked all around;

There bicycles of every grade
Are manufactured for the trade;
Some made for baby hands to guide,
And some for older folk to ride.
Though built to keep intruders out,
With shutters thick and casings stout,
I noticed twenty ways or more,
By roof, by window, wall and door,
Where we, by exercising skill,
May travel in and out at will."
Another spoke, in nowise slow
To catch at pleasures as they go,
And said, "Why let another day
Come creeping in to drag away?
Let's active measures now employ
To seize at once the promised joy.
On bicycles quick let us ride.
While yet our wants may be supplied."
So when the town grew hushed and still,
The Brownies ventured down the hill.
And soon the band was drawing nigh
The building with the chimneys high.
When people lock their doors at night,
And double-bolt them left and right.
And think through patents, new and old,
To leave the burglars in the cold,
The cunning Brownies smile to see
The springing bolt and turning key;
For well they know if fancy leads
Their band to venture daring-deeds,
The miser's gold, the merchant's ware
To them is open as the air.
Not long could door or windows stand
Fast locked before the Brownie band;
And soon the bicycles they sought
From every room and bench were
    brought.
The rogues ere long began to show
As many colors as the bow;
For paint and varnish lately spread
Besmeared them all from foot to head.
Some turned to jay-birds in a minute,

And some as quick might shame the
    linnet
While more with crimson-tinted breast
Seemed fitted for the robin's nest.
But whether red or green or blue,
The work on hand was hurried through;
They took the wheels from blacksmith
    fires.
Though wanting bolts and even tires,
And rigged the parts with skill and speed
To answer well their pressing need.
And soon, enough were made complete
To give the greater part a seat,
And let the rest through cunning find
Some way of hanging on behind.
And then no spurt along the road,
Or 'round the yard their carnage showed,
But twenty times a measured mile
They wheeled away in single file,
Or bunched together in a crowd
If width of road or skill allowed.

NE evening Brownies, peeping down
    From bluffs that overlooked the town,
    Saw wheelmen passing to and fro
    Upon the boulevard below.
"It seems," said one,
    "an easy trick,
The wheel goes 'round so
    smooth and quick;
You simply sit and work
    your feet
And glide with grace along
    the street.

PALMER COX

At tunes, while rolling down the grade,
Collisions some confusion made,
For every member of the band,
At steering wished to try his hand;
Though some, perhaps, were not designed
For labor of that special kind.
But Brownies are the folk to bear
Misfortunes with unruffled air;
So on through rough and smooth they
    spun
Until the turning-point was won.
Then back they wheeled with every
    spoke,
An hour before the thrush awoke.

🍀 *Palmer Cox*

THE BROWNIES IN CHINA

Through many trials hard to face
The Brownies moved from place to place.
Now camping on some dreary wild,
Now in some village domiciled,
In waiting till a better chance
Was offered for a safe advance,
Until before their wondering eyes
They saw the strange pagodas rise,
And saw the wall built long ago
To keep aloof a plundering foe,
And then they knew not far away
The "Flowery Kingdom" smiling lay.
Without a ladder, rope, or line,
Or aught except a clinging vine,
To aid them in their steep ascent,
Upon the wall the Brownies went.
Said one: "'T is here this very hour
We show indeed superior power.
This wall that kept the Tatars out
Two thousand years, or thereabout,
Has failed to keep the Brownie hand
For fifteen minutes from the land."
The Brownies many wonders found
While through that empire roaming
    round.
'T was large enough to let them range
Through fertile plains and cities strange
For weeks and months, and still pursue
Their way through scenes and wonders
    new.

Said one: "The oldest country spread
Upon the world we Brownies tread;
Great nations rose and swept away
Their neighbors' lines, and had their day,
Then crumbled to a final fall.
But this old empire lived through all.
Three thousand years have left no trace
Upon the customs of the race;
Still eating rice and drinking tea,
Behind their wall from trouble free,
They live content to be alone
Among their shrines of wood and stone."
Another said "'T is well that they
Are inclined from home to stray,
For if the sea they venture o'er
They'll find small welcome at the shore."
The Brownies climbed the towers grand
That are so common in the land,
And freely did their views exchange
About the architecture strange.
Said one: "Not often do we find
A place where builders are so kind.
Here shelves abound where one can stop
And rest while climbing to the top:
By easy stages we can rise
And view the land that round us lies,
And what seemed like a trying task
Is sport as good as one could ask.
No slippery spire of tin or slate,
To which we have to trust our weight

We here encounter as we go
But wood that suits both hand and toe,
And they must be but common people
To lose their hold on such a steeple."
At times too many rushed to view
An object that attention drew,
And then the odd-shaped roof would bend
Or yield, and with its load descend,
And only mystic powers could save
The Brownies from an early grave.
It has to be a fearful squall,
It has to be a stunning fall.
It needs must be a wild affair
In shape of beast, or bird of air
That can subdue the lively band,
Or bring their actions to a stand.

Oh, could we mortals, toiling here
Upon this fast-revolving sphere
Like them surmount the greatest ill
And bravely face the music still,
We might do many things I trow
We'll leave unfinished when we go!
Not often strangers penetrate
Into that country old and great,
And when they do some years go by
While they one half its wonders spy.
So do not marvel that the band
Were some weeks passing through
  the land,
And oft were prompted to declare
It paid them well to journey there.

❧ *Palmer Cox*

THE BROWNIES IN RUSSIA

Russian ground no lengthy stay
The Brownies made to work or play.
Said one: "If we had not to go
Across this country, as you know,
While circling the terrestrial ball
We'd hardly give the place a call.
From poorest peasant up to peer
There's too much secret plotting here,
Too many mines and bombs concealed
In city, village, road, and field.
'T is hardly safe to touch a briar
Or twig, lest it should wake a fire
That would not leave a foot or hand
Or head intact of all the band.
However dark may be the night
A sentinel will pop in sight
So we're compelled to hide away
Through hours of night as well as day.
They stand on guard o'er mill and mine
O'er bridges, boats, and pipes of wine.
Some stand to guard the ruler's bed,

More watch his baker bake the bread,
For fear some poison he might throw
With vengeful hand amid the dough;
More watch the chemist while he tries
The coffee that the cook supplies;
The horse is guarded on all sides
On which the Czar at morning rides.
For fear they'd deck it well at night
With cartridges of dynamite
To scatter him around the street
The moment that he takes his seat.
At times up to the ears in snow
They struggled through a valley low,
And only that the band possessed
Endurance equal to the best,
Some place like that to-day would hold
The bones of every Brownie bold.
Of Moscow, as they hurried through
The land, the Brownies gained a view.
There on a bridge the wondering band
Before the Kremlin paused to stand

And mark the many-towered pile
That glowed in Oriental style.
Once while they crossed a lonely waste
A pack of wolves the Brownies chased,
For miles and miles, well was their need.
They scampered at their highest speed
Through broken ground of every kind
And still could hear the howls behind,
Now sinking to a muffled wail,
Now rising louder on the gale,
Until the frosty hills around
Gave answer to the awful sound.
But as the pack with bristling hair
And open mouths and fiery glare,
Above a snowy ridge appeared,
A friendly tree the Brownies neared.
For this they ran, and well they might
With half a hundred wolves in sight.
Each brute prepared to stow away
A breakfast with but small delay.
But ere they reached the tree in view
The howling terrors closer drew
With bristling backs and clashing jaws,
Bright flashing eyes and nimble paws.
But, though they skirmished left and right
At closest range they failed to bite
As if the cunning rogues surmised
A mystic prey they had surprised
Of quite a different form and caste
From those they had devoured last.
Meanwhile the Brownies ne'er forgot
The tree that graced that lonely spot,
And kept alive and in the race
Until they reached its rugged base.
The hugging, climbing, scratching now,
As each one sought to gain a bough
Might bring a smile to every face
Had this not been a serious case
That did in greatest manner plead

For mystic exercise indeed.
If that old tree, that long had grown
Upon the frozen plain alone,
Had been designed with special care
To meet the need of Brownies there,
It hardly could be better planned
In fitness for the lively band.
Through all that night with hungry eyes
The wolves sat glaring at the prize,
In hopes some branch would snap at last
With overweight, or else a blast
Might shake a shower from the tree
That patience might rewarded be.
At length, as night her mantle rent,
The wolves appeared to catch the scent
Of something on a distant hill
That seemed to promise better still;
So in a trice the siege was raised,
And all the Brownies, much amazed,
Descended from the tree in haste
And made their way across the waste.

HOLIDAYS

Clement Clarke Moore

ACCOUNT OF A VISIT FROM ST. NICHOLAS

'Twas the night before Christmas, when all through the house
Not a creature was stirring, not even a mouse;
The stockings were hung by the chimney with care,
In hopes that ST. NICHOLAS soon would be there;
The children were nestled all snug in their beds,
While visions of sugar-plums danced in their heads;
And mamma in her 'kerchief, and I in my cap,
Had just settled our brains for a long winter's nap,
When out on the lawn there arose such a clatter,
I sprang from the bed to see what was the matter.
Away to the window I flew like a flash,
Tore open the shutters and threw up the sash.
The moon on the breast of the new-fallen snow
Gave the lustre of mid-day to objects below,
When, what to my wondering eyes should appear,
But a miniature sleigh, and eight tiny reindeer,
With a little old driver, so lively and quick,
I knew in a moment it must be St. Nick.
More rapid than eagles his coursers they came,
And he whistled, and shouted, and called them by name;
"Now, Dasher! now, Dancer! now, Prancer and Vixen!
On, Comet! on, Cupid! on, Donder and Blitzen!
To the top of the porch! to the top of the wall!
Now dash away! dash away! dash away all!"
As dry leaves that before the wild hurricane fly,
When they meet with an obstacle, mount to the sky;
So up to the house-top the coursers they flew,
With the sleigh full of Toys, and St. Nicholas too.
And then, in a twinkling, I heard on the roof
The prancing and pawing of each little hoof.
As I drew in my head, and was turning around,
Down the chimney St. Nicholas came with a bound.
He was dressed all in fur, from his head to his foot,
And his clothes were all tarnished with ashes and soot;
A bundle of Toys he had flung on his back,
And he looked like a pedlar just opening his pack.
His eyes—how they twinkled! his dimples how merry!
His cheeks were like roses, his nose like a cherry!
His droll little mouth was drawn up like a bow
And the beard of his chin was as white as the snow;

The stump of a pipe he held tight in his teeth,
And the smoke it encircled his head like a wreath;
He had a broad face and a little round belly,
That shook when he laughed, like a bowlful of jelly.
He was chubby and plump, a right jolly old elf,
And I laughed when I saw him, in spite of myself;
A wink of his eye and a twist of his head,
Soon gave me to know I had nothing to dread;
He spoke not a word, but went straight to his work,
And filled all the stockings; then turned with a jerk,
And laying his finger aside of his nose,
And giving a nod, up the chimney he rose;
He sprang to his sleigh, to his team gave a whistle,
And away they all flew like the down of a thistle,
But I heard him exclaim, ere he drove out of sight,
"Happy Christmas to all, and to all a good-night."

Author Unknown

SANTA CLAUS

He comes in the night! He comes in the night!
    He softly, silently comes;
When the little brown heads on the pillows so white
    Are dreaming of bugles and drums.
He cuts through the snow like a ship through the foam,
    While the white flakes around him whirl;
Who tells him I know not, but he soon finds the home
    Of each good little boy and girl.

His sleigh it is long, and deep, and wide;
    It will carry a host of things,
While dozens of drums hang over the side,
    With the sticks sticking under the strings.
And yet not the sound of a drum is heard,
    Not a bugle blast is blown,
As he mounts to the chimney-top like a bird,
    And drops to the hearth like a stone.

The little red stockings he silently fills,
    Till the stockings will hold no more;
The bright little sleds for the great snow hills
    Are quickly set down on the floor.

Then Santa Claus mounts to the roof like a bird,
  And springs to his seat in the sleigh;
Not the sound of a bugle or drum is heard
  As he noiselessly gallops away.

He rides to the East, he rides to the West,
  Of his goodies he touches not one;
He waits for the crumbs of the Christmas feast
  When the dear little folks are done.
Old Santa Claus doeth all that he can;
  This beautiful mission is his;
Then, children, be kind to the little old man,
  When you find who the little man is.

❧ *Mary Mapes Dodge*

STOCKING SONG ON CHRISTMAS EVE

Welcome, Christmas! heel and toe,
Here we wait thee in a row.
Come, good Santa Claus, we beg,—
Fill us tightly, foot and leg.

Fill us quickly ere you go,—
Fill us till we overflow.
That's the way! and leave us more
Heaped in piles upon the floor.

Little feet that ran all day
Twitch in dreams of merry play;
Little feet that jumped at will
Lie all pink, and warm, and still.

See us, how we lightly swing;
Hear us, how we try to sing.
Welcome, Christmas! heel and toe,
Come and fill us ere you go.

Here we hang till some one nimbly
Jumps with treasure down the chimney.
Bless us! how he'll tickle us!
Funny old St. Nicholas!

A Song of St. Nicholas

COME, ho! sing, ho! ye chimney sprit
  Come and a riddle unravel:
  Tell us true, by the dancing lights,
    Where does Saint Nicholas travel?

❧ Thomas Bailey Aldrich

KRISS KRINGLE
(Written in a child's album)

Just as the moon was fading amid her misty rings,
And every stocking was stuffed with childhood's precious things,
Old Kriss Kringle looked round, and saw on the elm-tree bough,
High-hung, an oriole's nest, silent and empty now.
"Quite like a stocking," he laughed, "pinned up there on the tree!
Little I thought the birds expected a present from me!"
Then old Kriss Kringle, who loves a joke as well as the best,
Dropped a handful of flakes in the oriole's empty nest.

❧ James Russell Lowell

HOB GOBBLING'S SONG

Not from Titania's Court do I
Hither upon a night-moth fly;
I am not of those Fairies seen
Tripping by moonlight on the green,
Whose dewdrop bumpers, nightly
    poured,
Befleck the mushroom's virgin board,
And whose faint cymbals tinkling clear
Sometimes on frosty nights you hear.

No, I was born of lustier stock,
And all their puling night-sports mock:
My father was the Good Old Time,
Famous in many a noble rhyme,
Who reigned with such a royal cheer
He made one Christmas of the year,
And but a single edict passed,
Dooming it instant death to fast.

I am that earthlier, fatter elf
That haunts the wood of pantry-shelf,
When minced-pies, ranged from end
    to end,
Up to the gladdened roof ascend;
On a fat goose I hither rode,
Using a skewer for a goad,

From the rich region of Cockayne,
And must ere morn be back again.

I am the plump sprite that presides
O'er Thanksgiving and Christmas tides;
I jig it not in woods profound;
The barn-yard is my dancing-ground,
Making me music as I can
By drumming on a pattypan;
Or if with songs your sleep I mar,
A gridiron serves me for guitar.

When without touch the glasses clink,
And dishes on the dresser wink
Back at the fire, whose jovial glance
Sets the grave pot-lids all adance;
When tails of little pigs hang straight,
Unnerved by dreams of coming fate;
When from the poultry-house you hear
Midnight alarums,—I am near.

While the pleased housewife shuts
    her eyes,
I lift the crust of temperance pies,
And slip in slyly two or three
Spoonfuls of saving *eau de vie*;

And, while the cookmaid rests her
   thumbs,
I stone a score of choicer plums,
And hide them in the pudding's corner,
In memory of the brave Jack Horner.

I put the currants in the buns,
A task the frugal baker shuns;
I for the youthful miner make
Nuggets of citron in the cake;
'T is I that down the chimney whip,
And presents in the stockings slip,

Which Superstition's mumbling jaws
Ascribe to loutish Santa Claus.

'T is I that hang, as you may see,
With presents gay the Christmas-tree;
But, if some foolish girl or boy
Should chance to mar the common joy
With any sulky look or word,
By them my anger is incurred,
And to all such I give fair warning
Of nightmares ere tomorrow morning.

Elizabeth Stuart Phelps

THE LITTLE MUD SPARROWS

I like that old sweet legend
   Not found in Holy Writ
And wish that John or Matthew
   Had made Bible out of it.

But though it is not Gospel
   There is not law to hold
The heart from growing better
   That hears the story told:—

How the little Jewish children
   Upon a summer day
Went down across the meadows
   With the Child Christ to play,

And in the gold-green valley
   Where low the reed-grass lay,
They made them mock mud-sparrows
   Out of the meadow-clay.

So, when these all were fashioned
   And ranged in flocks about,
"Now," said the little Jesus,
   "We'll let the birds fly out."

Then all the happy children
   Did call, and coax, and cry—
Each to his own mud-sparrow:
   "Fly, as I bid you—fly!"

But earthen were the sparrows
   And earth they did remain,
Though loud the Jewish children
   Cried out and cried again—

Except the one bird only
   The little Lord Christ made.
The earth that owned Him Master,
   —His earth heard and obeyed.

Softly He leaned and whispered:
   "Fly up to Heaven! fly!"
And swift his little sparrow
   When soaring to the sky.

And silent all the children
   Stood awe-struck looking on,
Till deep into the heavens
   The bird of earth had gone.

I like to think for playmate
   We have the Lord Christ still,
And that still above our weakness,
   He works his mighty will,

That all our little playthings
   Of earthen hopes and joys
Shall be by his commandment
   Changed into heavenly toys.

Our souls are like the sparrows
   Imprisoned in the clay—
Bless Him who came to give them wings,
   Upon a Christmas Day!

Harriet E. Prescott [Spofford]

CHRISTMAS

Over the hills of Palestine
The silver stars began to shine;
Night drew her shadows softly round
The slumbering earth, without a sound.

Among the fields and dewy rocks
The shepherds kept their quiet flocks,
And looked along the darkening land
That waited the Divine command.

When lo! through all the opening blue
Far up the deep, dark heavens withdrew,
And angels in a solemn light
Praised God to all the listening night.

Ah! said the lowly shepherds then,
The Seraph sang good-will to men:
O hasten, earth, to meet the morn,
The Prince, the Prince of Peace is born!

Again the sky was deep and dark,
Each star relumed his silver spark,
The dreaming land in silence lay,
And waited for the dawning day.

But in a stable low and rude,
Where white-horned, mild-eyed oxen
    stood,
The gates of heaven were still displayed,
For Christ was in the manger laid.

Henry Wadsworth Longfellow

CHRISTMAS BELLS

I heard the bells on Christmas Day
Their old, familiar carols play,
    And wild and sweet
    The words repeat
Of peace on earth, good-will to men!

And thought how, as the day had come,
The belfries of all Christendom
    Had rolled along
    The unbroken song
Of peace on earth, good-will to men!

Till, ringing, singing on its way,
The world revolved from night to day
    A voice, a chime,
    A chant sublime
Of peace on earth, good-will to men!

Then from each black, accursed mouth,
The cannon thundered in the South,
    And with the sound
    The carols drowned
Of peace on earth, good-will to men!

It was as if an earthquake rent
The hearth-stones of a continent,
    And made forlorn
    The households born
Of peace on earth, good-will to men!

And in despair I bowed my head;
"There is no peace on earth," I said;
    "For hate is strong
    And mocks the song
Of peace on earth, good-will to men!"

Then pealed the bells more loud and
        deep:
"God is not dead; nor doth he sleep!
    The Wrong shall fail,
    The Right prevail,
With peace on earth, good-will to men!"

A CHRISTMAS MEMORY

Ma she's home.—An' I'm 'way here
  At my A'nty's, visitun'!
A'nty allus calls me "Dear,"
  An' is lets me romp an' run
  An' don't never scold me none
Like sometimes she ust to do
When my Ma she be here, too.

Pa he bringed me here to stay
  'Til my Ma she's well.—An' nen
He's go' hitch up, Chris'mus-day,
  An' come take me back again
Wher' my Ma's at! Won't I be
Tickled when he comes fer me!

My Ma an' my A'nty they
  'Uz each-uvvers sisters. Pa—
A'nty telled me, th' other day;—
  He comed here an' married Ma . . .
A'nty said nen, "Go run play,
  I must work now!" . . . An' I saw,
When she turn' her face away,
  She 'uz-cryin'.—An' nen I
  'Tend-like I "run play"—an' cry.

This-here house o' A'nty's wher'
They 'uz borned—my Ma an' her!—
An' her Ma 'uz my Ma's Ma,
An' her Pa 'uz my Ma's Pa—
Ain't that funny?—An' they're dead:
An' this-here's "th' ole Homestead."—
An' my A'nty said, an' cried,
It's mine, too, ef my Ma died—
Don't know what she mean—'cause my
Ma she's nuver go' to die!

When Pa bringed me here t'uz night—
  'Way dark night! An' A'nty spread
Me a piece—an' light the light
  An' say I must go to bed.—
  I cry not to—but Pa said,
  "Be good boy now, like you telled
  Mommy 'at you're go' to be!"
  An', when he 'uz kissin' me
    My good-night, his cheek's all wet
An' taste salty.—An' he held
  Wite close to me an' rocked some
  An' laughed-like—'tel A'nty come
    Git me while he's rockin' yet.

A'nty he'p me, 'til I be
Purt'-nigh strip-pud—nen hug me
In bofe arms an' lif' me 'way
Up in her high bed—an' pray
  Wiv me,—'Bout my Ma—an' Pa—
An' ole Santy Claus—an' Sleigh—
  An' Reindeers an' little Drum—
  Yes, an' Picture-books, "Tom
    Thumb,"
An' "Three Bears," an' ole "Fee-Faw"—
  Yes, an' "Tweedle-Dee" an' "Dum,"
  An' "White Knight" an'
    "Squidjicum,"
An' most things you ever saw!—
  An' when A'nty kissed me, she
  'Uz all cryin' over me!

Don't want Santy Claus—ner things
Any kind he ever brings!—
Don't want A'nty !—Don't want Pa!—
I ist only want my Ma!

Eugene Field

JEST 'FORE CHRISTMAS

Father calls me William, sister calls me Will,
Mother calls me Willie, but the fellers call me Bill!
Mighty glad I ain't a girl—ruther be a boy,
Without them sashes, curls, an' things that's worn by Fauntleroy!
Love to chawnk green apples an' go swimmin' in the lake—
Hate to take the castor-ile they give for belly-ache!
'Most all the time, the whole year round, there ain't no flies on me,
But jest 'fore Christmas I'm as good as I kin be!

Got a yeller dog named Sport, sick him on the cat;
First thing she knows she doesn't know where she is at!
Got a clipper sled, an' when us kids goes out to slide,
'Long comes the grocery cart, an' we all hook a ride!
But sometimes when the grocery man is worrited an' cross,
He reaches at us with his whip, an' larrups up his hoss,
An' then I laf an' holler, "Oh, ye never teched *me!*"
But jest 'fore Christmas I'm as good as I kin be!

Gran'ma says she hopes that when I git to be a man,
I'll be a missionarer like her oldest brother, Dan,
As was et up by the cannibuls that lives in Ceylon's Isle,
Where every prospeck pleases, an' only man is vile!
But gran'ma she has never been to see a Wild West show,
Nor read the life of Daniel Boone, or else I guess she'd know
That Buff'lo Bill an' cow-boys is good enough for me!
Excep' jest 'fore Christmas, when I'm good as I kin be!

And then old Sport he hangs around, so solemn-like an' still,
His eyes they keep a-sayin': "What's the matter, little Bill?"
The old cat sneaks down off her perch an' wonders what's become
Of them two enemies of hern that used to make things hum!
But I am so perlite an' 'tend so earnestly to biz,
That mother says to father: "How improved our Willie is!"
But father, havin' been a boy hisself, suspicions me
When, jest 'fore Christmas, I'm as good as I kin be!

For Christmas, with its lots an' lots of candies, cakes, an' toys,
Was made, they say, for proper kids an' not for naughty boys;
So wash yer face an' bresh yer hair, an' mind yer p's an' q's,
An' don't bust out yer pantaloons, an' don't wear out yer shoes;
Say "Yessum" to the ladies, an' "Yessur" to the men,
An' when they's company, don't pass yer plate for pie again;
But, thinkin' of the things yer'd like to see upon that tree,
Jest 'fore Christmas be as good as yer kin be!

Stephen Crane (about age 9)

I'D RATHER HAVE—

Last Christmas they gave me a sweater,
  And a nice warm suit of wool,
But I'd rather be cold and have a dog,
  To watch when I come from school.

Father gave me a bicycle,
  But that isn't much of a treat,
Unless you have a dog at your heels
  Racing away down the street.

They bought me a camping outfit,
  But a bonfire by a log
Is all the outfit I would ask,
  If I only had a dog.

They seem to think a little dog
  Is a killer of all earth's joys;
But oh, that "pesky little dog"
  Means hours of joy to the boys.

Mary E. Wilkins [Freeman]

THE SPOILED DARLING

Oh the ruffles there were on that little dress, Fanny!
  Her mamma does dress her so sweetly, you know;
And the prettiest sash of pale rose-colored satin
  Tied at her waist in a butterfly-bow.

And her soft, flossy hair, almost a rose-yellow,
  Like the roses we had in our garden last year,
Cut short round the fairest blue-veined little forehead—
  Oh, if Miss Marion wasn't a dear!

Just perfect she was, the mite of a darling,
  From her flower of a head to her pink slipper-toes!
You will laugh, but she seemed as I looked at her, Fanny,
  A little girl copied right after a rose!

Well, you know how it is: they have petted the darling,
  Her papa and mamma, her uncles and aunts—
Till, saving the moon, which they can't get for princes,
  There isn't a thing but she has if she wants.

So, last night at the Christmas-tree, Fanny,
  —It was so funny I laugh at it now—
There was Miss Marion sweeter than honey,
  All in her ruffles and butterfly-bow;

She had presents, I thought, enough for a dozen,
  But she seemed heavy-hearted in spite of it all;

Her sweet little mouth was all of a quiver,
    And there was a teardrop just ready to fall.

The aunts and the cousins all round her came crowding;
  "And what is the matter, my darling, my dear?"
She didn't look sulky, but grieved; and I saw it
    Roll down her pink cheek, that trembling tear;

And she lisped out so honest, "Mamie and Bessie,
    And the rest, have pwesents—and 'twas my Tristmas-tree;
And when I tame in, I fought that the pwesents—
    The whole of them on it—of tourse were for me!"

I scarcely could blame her—she didn't seem angry,
    But grieved to the heart, the queer little mite!
And 'twasn't her fault—she'd been fed so much honey,
    All the sweet in the world she took as her right.

❧ Katharine Lee Bates

THE KINGS OF THE EAST

The Kings of the East are riding
  To-night to Bethlehem.
The sunset glows dividing,
The Kings of the East are riding;
A star their journey guiding;
  Gleaming with gold and gem,
The Kings of the East are riding
  To-night to Bethlehem.

To a strange sweet harp of Zion
  The starry host troops forth;
The golden-glaived Orion
To a strange, sweet harp of Zion;

The Archer and the Lion,
  The Watcher of the North;
To a strange sweet harp of Zion
  The starry host troops forth.

There beams above a manger
  The child-face of a star;
Amid the stars a stranger,
It beams above a manger;
What means this ether-ranger
  To pause where poor folk are?
There beams above a manger
  The child-face of a star.

❧ Katharine Lee Bates

CHRISTMAS ISLAND

Fringed with coral, floored with lava,
Threescore leagues to south of Java,
So is Christmas Island charted
By geographers blind-hearted,—

Just a dot, by their dull notion,
On the burning Indian Ocean;
Merely a refreshment station
For the birds in long migration;

Its pomegranates, custard-apples
That the dancing sunshine dapples,
Cocoanuts with milky hollows,
Only feast wing-weary swallows,
Or the tropic fowl there dwelling.
Don't believe a word they're telling!
Christmas Island, though it seem land,
Is a floating bit of dreamland
'Gone adrift from childhood, planted
By the winds with seeds enchanted,
Seeds of candied plum and cherry;
Here the Christmas Saints make merry.

Even saints must have vacation;
So they chose from all creation,
As a change from iceberg castles
Hung with snow in loops and tassels,
Christmas Island for a summer
Residence. The earliest comer
Is our own saint, none diviner,
Santa Claus. His ocean-liner
Is a sleigh that's scudding fast.
Mistletoe climbs up the mast,
And the sail, so full of caper,
Is of tissue wrapping-paper.
As he steers he hums a carol;
But instead of fur apparel
Smudged with soot, he's spick and
    spandy
In white linen, dear old dandy,
With a Borealis sash on
And a palm-leaf hat in fashion
Wreathed about with holly-berry.
Welcome, Santa! Rest you merry!

Next, his chubby legs bestriding
Such a Yule-log, who comes riding
Overseas, the feast to dish up,
But—aha!—the boys' own bishop,

Good St. Nicholas! And listen!
Out of Denmark old Jule-nissen,
Kindly goblin, bent, rheumatic,
In the milk-bowl set up attic
For his Christmas cheer, comes bobbing
Through the waves. He'll be hobnobbing
With Knecht Clobes, Dutchman true,
Sailing in a wooden shoe.
When the sunset gold enamels
All the sea, three cloudy camels
Bear the Kings with stately paces,
Taking island for oases,
While a star-boar brings Kriss Kringle.
Singing "Noel" as they mingle,
Drinking toasts in sunshine sherry,
How the Christmas Saints make merry!

While a gray contralto pigeon
Coos that loving is religion.
How they laugh and how they rollick,
How they fill the isle with frolic!
Up the Christmas trees they clamber,
Lighting candles rose and amber,
Till the sudden moonbeams glisten.
Then all kneel but old Jule-nissen,
Who, a heathen elf, stiff-jointed,
Doffs his nightcap red and pointed;
For within the moon's pure luster
They behold bright figures cluster;
Their adoring eyes look on a
Silver-throned serene Madonna,
With the Christ-Child, rosy sweeting,
Smiling to their loyal greeting.
Would that on this Holy Night
We might share such blissful sight,—
We might find a fairy ferry
To that isle where saints make merry!

Lydia Maria Child

A NEW ENGLAND BOY'S SONG ABOUT THANKSGIVING DAY

Over the river, and through the wood,
To grandfather's house we go;
    The horse knows the way,
    To carry the sleigh,
Through the white and drifted snow.

Over the river, and through the wood,
To grandfather's house away!
    We would not stop
    For doll or top,
For 't is Thanksgiving Day.

Over the river, and through the wood,
Oh, how the wind does blow!
    It stings the toes,
    And bites the nose,
As over the ground we go.

Over the river, and through the wood,
With a clear blue winter sky,
    The dogs do bark,
    And children hark,
As we go jingling by.

Over the river, and through the wood,
To have a first-rate play—
    Hear the bells ring
    Ting a ling ding,
Hurra for Thanksgiving Day!

Over the river, and through the wood—
No matter for winds that blow;
    Or if we get
    The sleigh upset,
Into a bank of snow.

Over the river, and through the wood,
To see little John and Ann;
    We will kiss them all,
    And play snow-ball,
And stay as long as we can.

Over the river, and through the wood,
Trot fast, my dapple grey!
    Spring over the ground,
    Like a hunting hound,
For 't is Thanksgiving Day!

Over the river, and through the wood,
And straight through the barn-yard gate;
    We seem to go
    Extremely slow,
It is so hard to wait.

Over the river, and through the wood—
Old Jowler hears our bells;
    He shakes his pow,
    With a loud bow wow,
And thus the news he tells.

Over the river, and through the wood—
When grandmother sees us come,
    She will say, Oh dear,
    The children are here,
Bring a pie for every one.

Over the river, and through the wood—
Now grandmother's cap I spy!
    Hurra for the fun!
    Is the pudding done?
Hurra for the pumpkin pie!

THE VOLUNTEER'S THANKSGIVING

The last days of November, and everything so green!
A finer bit of country my eyes have never seen.
'T will be a thing to tell of, ten years or twenty hence,
How I came down to Georgia at Uncle Sam's expense.

Four years ago this winter, up at the district school,
I wrote all day, and ciphered, perched on a white-pine stool;
And studied in my atlas the boundaries of the States,
And learnt the wars with England, the history and the dates.

Then little I expected to travel in such haste
Along the lines my fingers and fancy often traced,
To bear a soldier's knapsack, and face the cannon's mouth,
And help to save for Freedom the lovely, perjured South.

That red, old-fashioned school-house! what winds came sweeping through
Its doors from bald Monadnock, and from the mountains blue
That slope off south and eastward beyond the Merrimack!
O pleasant Northern river, your music calls me back

To where the pines are humming the slow notes of their psalm
Around a shady farm-house, half hid within their calm,
Reflecting in the river a picture not so bright
As these verandahed mansions,—but yet my heart's delight.

They're sitting at the table this clear Thanksgiving noon;
I smell the crispy turkey, the pies will come in soon,—
The golden squares of pumpkin, the flaky rounds of mince,
Behind the barberry syrups, the cranberry and the quince.

Be sure my mouth does water,—but then I am content
To stay and do the errand on which I have been sent.
A soldier mustn't grumble at salt beef and hard-tack:
We'll have a grand Thanksgiving if ever we get back!

I'm very sure they'll miss me at dinner-time to-day,
For I was good at stowing their provender away.
When mother clears the table, and wipes the platters bright,
She'll say, "I hope my baby don't lose his appetite!"

But oh! the after-dinner! I miss that most of all,—
The shooting at the targets, the jolly game of ball,
And then the long wood-ramble! We climbed, and slid, and ran,—
We and the neighbor-children,—and one was Mary Ann,

Who (as I didn't mention) sat next to me at school:
Sometimes I had to show her the way to work the rule
Of Ratio and Proportion, and do upon her slate
Those long, hard sums that puzzle a merry maiden's pate.

I wonder if they're going across the hills to-day;
And up the cliffs I wonder what boy will lead the way;
And if they'll gather fern-leaves and checkerberries red,
And who will put a garland of ground-pine on her head.

O dear! the air grows sultry: I'd wish myself at home
Were it a whit less noble, the cause for which I've come.
Four years ago a school-boy; as foolish now as then!
But greatly they don't differ, I fancy,—boys and men.

I'm just nineteen to-morrow, and I shall surely stay
For Freedom's final battle, be it until I'm gray,
Unless a Southern bullet should take me off my feet.—
There's nothing left to live for, if Rebeldom should beat;

For home and love and honor and freedom are at stake,
And life may well be given for our dear Union's sake;
So reads the Proclamation, and so the sermon ran;
Do ministers and people feel it as soldiers can?

When will it all be ended? 'T is not in youth to hold
In quietness and patience, like people grave and old:
A year? three? four? or seven?—O then, when I return,
Put on a big log, mother, and let it blaze and burn,

And roast your fattest turkey, bake all the pies you can,
And, if she isn't married, invite in Mary Ann!
Hang flags from every window! we'll all be glad and gay,
For Peace will light the country on that Thanksgiving Day.

Rose Terry Cooke

TURKEY: A THANKSGIVING ODE

When is the turkey handsomest?
With sunshine on his brazen breast,
When every feather is like a scale
On a glittering suit of knightly mail;
When his tail is spread, a splendid fan,
As he struts before his faithful clan
With blue, bald head and threatening
    eye,
And wattles red as a stormy sky?
With lofty step and war-cry loud
He marshals forth the quittering crowd,
Or leads their dance across the plain,
Or heads their march through waving
    grain,
Intent on plunder, red with pride,
Like warrior not to be defied,
In all the pomp of battle drest,—
Then is the turkey handsomest?

When is the turkey handsomest?
When he is killed and plucked and
    dressed;
His spurs hacked off and thrown aside
With all the trappings of his pride,
He lies, a goodly shape of snow,
On stall or dresser, making show
Of swelling breast and rampant legs;
Or, dangling from the larder's pegs,
Tells to the cook-maid's practised eye
How fast the days are flitting by,

How soon appears the day of days,
The hour of Turkey's reign and praise;—
There, hanging in his smooth white vest,
Is not the turkey handsomest?

When is the turkey handsomest?
Ah! when again he shows his breast,
Brown with the sunshine of the fire,
Crisp as a lady's silk attire,
With unctuous juices dripping down
In pools of gravy rich and brown;
Odorous as any spicy air
That blows across an orchard.
His bosom swelled with savory meat
Of sausages and bread-crumbs sweet,
His pinions neatly skewered and tied
With giblets tucked in either side;
His legs resigned to any fate,
Rampant no more, but meekly straight;
Beside him cranberry, ruby clear,
With groves of brittle celery near:
As stately as a king he lies,
The centre of admiring eyes.
Now is the turkey handsomest,
Arrayed before the hungry guest,
Of all the viands first and best!
His life well lived, his woes at rest,
And the platter he lies on gayly dressed,
Now is the turkey handsomest!

❧ Anna M. Pratt

THE TURKEY'S OPINION

"What dost thou think of drumsticks?"
    I asked a barn-yard bird.
He grinned a turkey grin, and then
    He answered me this word:

"They're good to eat, they're good to beat,
    But sure as I am living,
They're best to run away with
    The week before Thanksgiving."

❧ M.A., Sisters of Mercy

SAINT PATRICK'S DAY

Holy Patrick, patron blest
Of the land I love the best,
Once thy day brought joy and gladness,
Chasing far each thought of sadness,
When we sped at early morning,
Ditch, and hedge, and damp feet scorning,
To seek out some sheltered nook
Where the shamrocks greenest look,
Then sped home prepared for Mass,
Fixing high the triple grass
In boy's cap or young girl's bonnet
Where all eyes must rest upon it.
Sad the day I left my childhood,
As the time when some fair wild-wood
Where a myriad flowers bloom brightly,
And young fawns are bounding lightly,
Where rich berries hang in clusters,
And wild birds hold merry musters,
Is *cut down* and cleaned for tilling,
At some stern, old owner's willing.
Home is but a memory
Now, alas, to mine and me—
But from thee we've learned to know
That our home is not below:
Thou wert exiled, why not we?
Oh were we but like thee!
Dear St. Patrick, won't you pray
For those scattered far away,—
From the Isle whose very air
Breathes of God, of faith, of prayer,
Where, as in a record vast
We may ready the hallowed past?
Wreck and ruin and decay
Cannot blot that scroll away.

🍀 *M.A., Sisters of Mercy*

ST. PATRICK'S DAY WITHOUT SHAMROCKS

We sought them 'neath the snow-flakes
  And o'er the frosty ground,
But no leaflet like the Shamrock
  On St. Patrick's day we found.
And our hearts went back to Erin,
  To her dewy vales and hills,
Where the Shamrock twines and
    clusters
  O'er the fields and by the rills.

Oh, no more, no more, my Country!
  Shall thy loving daughter lay
Down her head upon thy bosom
  While she weeps her tears away.
There the primrose and the daisy
  Bloom as in the days of old,
And the violet comes up purple
  And the buttercup in gold.

But thy child, thine exiled daughter,
  She is far from thee to-day,
Dreary walls of brick surround her,
  Dreary miles of foreign clay.
For no home is hers, no country,
  Willville now is with the past,
On the chapel, on the graveyard
  She hath sadly looked her last.

Kildare's broad fields are fragrant
  With the Shamrock's breath to-day,
Shamrocks bloom from Clare to Antrim,
  From Killarney to Lough Neagh;
And they speak of Patrick's preaching
  With a quiet, voiceless lore,
And they breathe of Faith and Heaven
  All the trefoiled island o'er.

Wandering listless by the Liffey,
  Stoop and pluck the shamrock green;
What an emblem plain and simple
  Of the one true faith is seen!

Of the Father and the Spirit
  Speaks the mystic triune leaf,
Of the Son in anguish dying
  On the cross, in love and grief.

Well humility may choose it
  For an emblem fair and sweet,
Close beside the poorest cabin
  Is its pouring fragrance sweet.
Modest is our darling Shamrock,
  Useful, charitable, kind,
Clothing mean, deserted places
  With its green leaves intertwined.

With the dew drops shining pearly
  As bright gems within its heart,
Pure as purity it seemeth,
  True as nature, fair as art.
Fortitude and perseverance
  Hath the leaf we love so well,
For 'tis green through all the winter
  In some shady nook or dell.

Many a lesson it teaches,
  Many a wholesome thought recalls,
Many a tear-drop all unbidden
  To its cherished memory falls.
For the green of Erin's banner
  Still must stir the Irish heart,
Which in Erin's many sorrows
  Ever, ever must have part.

Oh be true, be true to Erin,
  True to Faith and true to God,
To St. Patrick, his Apostle,
  Who redeemed your native sod!
Never more her mystic emblem
  In green Erin may you see,
Let the faith it symbolizes
  Be the dearer unto thee.

THE MAGICAL DOOR

There's a door in the wall of the ages—
    A door that no man sees;
For the angel who writes in the Book of
      Time
    Is the keeper of the keys.
Once in the year it opens,
    At the solemn midnight hour,
When the children sleep, and the old
      clocks keep
    Awake in the tall church tower.

And then, as it swings on its hinges,
    Whoever might peer inside
Would catch a glimpse of the centuries
    That behind in the silence hide.
Egypt and Rome and Tyre,
    All in that mythical place
Where the old years rest that were once
      possessed
    By the wonderful human race.

The shadowy door swings open,
    And a pilgrim enters in,
Bowed with a twelve-months' struggle
    In this world of strife and sin.

Waft him a farewell greeting!
    He will pass no more this way—
This weary year who must disappear
    In the haven of yesterday.

The door still swingeth open,
    And outward another comes,
With a stir of banners and bugles
    And the beat of friendly drums;
His hands are full of beauty—
    The cluster, the song, the sheaf,
The snow-flake's wing, and the budding
      spring,
    And the foam on the crested reef.

This is the New Year, darlings,
    Oh! haste to give him cheer.
Only the Father knoweth
    The whole of his errand here.
This is the New Year, darlings;
    A year for work and play,
For doing our best, and for trusting
      the rest
    To the Maker of night and day.

Lucy Larcom

IN TIME'S SWING

Father Time, your footsteps go
Lightly as the falling snow.
In your swing I'm sitting, see!
Push me softly; one, two, three,
Twelve times only. Like a sheet
Spreads the snow beneath my feet.
Singing merrily, let me swing
Out of winter into spring.

Swing me out, and swing me in!
Trees are bare, but birds begin
Twittering to the peeping leaves
On the bough beneath the eaves.
Wait,—one lilac-bud I saw.
Icy hillsides feel the thaw.
April chased off March to-day;
Now I catch a glimpse of May.

O the smell of sprouting grass!
In a blur the violets pass.
Whispering from the wild-wood come
Mayflowers' breath, and insects' hum.
Roses carpeting the ground;
Thrushes, orioles, warbling sound:—
Swing me low, and swing me high,
To the warm clouds of July.

Slower now, for at my side
White pond-lilies open wide.
Underneath the pine's tall spire
Cardinal-blossoms burn like fire.
They are gone; the golden-rod
Flashes from the dark green sod.
Crickets in the grass I hear;
Asters light the fading year.

Slower still! October weaves
Rainbows of the forest-leaves.
Gentians fringed, like eyes of blue,
Glimmer out of sleety dew.
Meadow-green I sadly miss:
Winds through withered sedges hiss.
O, 't is snowing; swing me fast,
While December shivers past!

Frosty-bearded Father Time,
Stop your footfall on the rime!
Hard your push, your hand is rough;
You have swung me long enough.
"Nay, no stopping," say you? Well,
Some of your best stories tell,
While you swing me—gently, do!—
From the Old Year to the New.

"Kruna" [Julia Pratt Ballard]

THE BOYS' "FOURTH OF JULY"

There, can't you see the line, my boys,
    And toe the mark precisely?
Dick, just step back a foot or two—
    You three have hit it nicely.

I want you all to make me proud—
    Show your very neatest drilling,
Or else your captain's honor, boys,
    Will not be worth a shilling.

Now! forward, march! quick even step,
    Eye raised a trifle higher,
And throw into your souls, my boys,
    A little extra fire!

Forget that Grant has conquered Lee;
    Forget that Richmond's taken;
Forget that ditch—the *very* last,
    Jeff Davis has forsaken.

The glorious Fourth is just ahead,
    We'll save for that our thunder,
And *then* declare Secession dead,
    And buried ten feet under!

By the beating of the drums,
Something of an army comes!
Victory lighting every eye,
See them proudly marching by!
    With the beat, beat,
    And the tramping feet,
"Yankee Doodle" chimes complete!

And now a halt! and "three times three"—
Nine cheers for Grant—three groans
      for Lee;
    Rebels shaken,
    Richmond taken,
And an apple-bough for Jefferson D.!

Hurrah, hurrah, boys! be alive
To the glorious Fourth of *'sixty-five;*
'Twas a wonderful day in 'seventy-six,
But the British were never in such a fix
As the grand Confederate host to-day
With their leader in *dress-goods led away!*
Hurrah, hurrah, boys! be alive
To the glorious Fourth of *'sixty five!*

Nora Perry

BOSTON BOYS (GRANDFATHER'S STORY)

What! you want to hear a story all about that old-time glory,
When your grandsires fought for freedom against the British crown;
When King George's red-coats mustered all their forces, to be flustered
By our Yankee raw recruits, from each village and each town;

And the very best boys protested, when they thought their rights molested?
My father used to tell us how the British General stared
With a curious, dazed expression when the youngsters in procession
Filed before him in a column, not a whit put out or scared.

Then the leader told his story,—told the haughty, handsome Tory
How his troops there, on the mall there (what you call "the common," dears),
All the winter through had vexed them, meddled with them and perplexed them,
Flinging back to their remonstrance only laughter, threats, and sneers.

"What!" the General cried in wonder,—and his tones were tones of thunder,—
"Are these the rebel lessons that your fathers taught you, pray?
Did they send such lads as you up here, to make such bold ado here,
And flout King George's officers upon the King's highway?"

Up the little leader started, while heat lightning flashed and darted
From his blue eyes, as he answered, stout of voice, with all his might:
"No one taught us, let me say, sir,—no one sent us here to-day, sir;
But we're Yankees, Yankees, Yankees, and the Yankees know their rights!

"And your soldiers at the first, sir, on the mall there, did their worst, sir;
Pulled our snow-hills down we'd built there, broke the ice upon our pond.
'Help it, help it if you can, then!' back they answered every man then,
When we asked them, sir, to quit it; and we said, 'This goes beyond

Soldiers' rights or soldiers' orders, for we've kept within our borders
To the south'ard of the mall there, where we've always had our play!'"
"Where you always shall hereafter, undisturbed by threat or laughter
From my officers or soldiers. Go, my brave boys, from this day

"Troops of mine shall never harm you, never trouble or alarm you,"
Suddenly the British Gen'ral, moved with admiration, cried.
In a minute caps were swinging, five and twenty voices ringing
In a shout and cheer that summoned every neighbor far and wide.

And these neighbors told the story how the haughty, handsome Tory,
Bowing, smiling, hat in hand there, faced the little rebel band;
How he said, just then and after, half in earnest, half in laughter:
"So it seems the very children strike for freedom in this land!"

So I tell you now the story all about that old-time glory,
As my father's father told it long ago to me;
How they met and had it out there, what he called their bloodless bout there;
How he felt—"What! was he there, then?" Why, the *leader*, that was he!

HISTORIES

Joaquin Miller

COLUMBUS

Behind him lay the gray Azores,
Behind, the Gates of Hercules;
Before him not the ghost of shores,
Before him only shoreless seas.
The good mate said, "Now must we pray,
For lo! the very stars are gone;
Brave Adm'r'l, speak, what shall I say?"
"Why, say, 'Sail on! sail on! and on!'"

"My men grow mutinous day by day,
My men grow ghastly wan and weak."
The stout mate thought of home; a spray
Of salt wave washed his swarthy cheek.
"What shall I say, brave Adm'r'l, say,
If we sight naught but seas at dawn?"
"Why, you may say, at break of day,
'Sail on! sail on! sail on! and on!'"

They sailed and sailed, as winds might
    blow,
Until at last the blanched mate said:
"Why, now not even God would know
Should I and all my men fall dead.

These very winds forget their way,
For God from these dread seas is gone.
Now speak, brave Adm'r'l; speak and
    say—"
He said, "Sail on! sail on! and on!"

They sailed. They sailed. Then spake
    the mate:
"This mad sea shows his teeth to-night;
He curls his lip, he lies in wait
With lifted teeth as if to bite!
Brave Adm'r'l, say but one good word:
What shall we do when hope is gone?"
The words leaped like a leaping sword:
"Sail on! sail on! sail on! and on!"

Then, pale and worn, he kept his deck,
And peered through darkness. Ah, that
    night
Of all dark nights! and then a speck—
A light! A light! A light! A light!
It grew, a starlit flag unfurled!
It grew to be Time's burst of dawn.
He gained a world; he gave that world
Its grandest lesson: "On! sail on!"

❧ James Russell Lowell

THE FATHERLAND

Where is the true man's fatherland?
    Is it where he by chance is born?
    Doth not the yearning spirit scorn
In such scant borders to be spanned?
Oh yes! his fatherland must be
As the blue heaven wide and free!

Is it alone where freedom is,
    Where God is God and man is man?
    Doth he not claim a broader span
For the soul's love of home than this?
Oh yes! his fatherland must be
As the blue heaven wide and free!

Where'er a human heart doth wear
    Joy's myrtle-wreath or sorrow's gyves,
    Where'er a human spirit strives
After a life more true and fair,
There is the true man's birth-place
        grand,
His is a world-wide fatherland!

Where'er a single slave doth pine,
    Where'er one man may help another,—
    Thank God for such a birthright,
        brother,—
That spot of earth is thine and mine!
There is the true man's birthplace grand,
His is a world-wide fatherland!

❧ Celia Thaxter

THE PRETTY PURITAN

Light she trips across the snow—
Downcast eyes and cheeks that glow,
While her golden hair escapes
O'er the daintiest of capes.

Berries of the holly bright,
Which she holds with clasp so light!
Her red lips have stolen from you
Tint as fresh as morning dew.

Fairer picture ne'er was seen
The bare wintry boughs between!
Like some rich and lovely flower
Blooming in a frosty hour.

All alight with color sweet.
Beautiful from head to feet.
'Neath her quiet lids demure
Hide her glances shy and pure.

Thoughts like lilies, snow-drops, daisies.
Look forth when those lids she raises.
Happy little maiden she,
Gentle rose of modesty!

ଛ *Seba Smith*

REVOLUTIONARY TEA

There was an old lady lived over the sea,
    And she was an Island Queen;
Her daughter lived off in a new countrie,
    With an ocean of water between.

The old lady's pockets were full of gold,
    But never contented was she;
So she called to her daughter to pay her a tax
    Of "thrippence" a pound on her tea.

"Now, mother, dear mother," the daughter replied,
    "I shan't do the thing that you ax;
I'm willing to pay a fair price for the tea,
    But never the thrippenny tax.

"You shall," quoth the mother, and reddened with rage,
    "For you're my own daughter, ye see;
And sure 'tis quite proper the daughter should pay
    Her mother a tax on her tea."

And so the old lady her servants called up,
    And pack'd off a budget of tea,
And, eager for thrippence a pound, she put in
    Enough for a large familie.

She ordered her servants to bring home the tax,
    Declaring her child should obey,
Or, old as she was, and almost woman-grown,
    She'd half whip her life away.

The tea was conveyed to the daughter's door,
    All down by the ocean side,
And the bouncing girl poured out every pound
    In the dark and boiling tide.

And then she called out to the Island Queen,
    "Oh, mother, dear mother," quoth she,
"Your tea you may have, when 'tis steeped enough,
    But never a tax from me—
    No, never a tax from me."

PAUL REVERE'S RIDE

Listen, my children, and you shall hear
Of the midnight ride of Paul Revere,
On the eighteenth of April, in Seventy-Five;
Hardly a man is now alive
Who remembers that famous day and year.

He said to his friend,—"If the British march
By land or sea from the town to-night,
Hang a lantern aloft in the belfry arch
Of the North-Church-tower, as a signal light,—
One if by land, and two if by sea;
And I on the opposite shore will be,
Ready to ride and spread the alarm
Through every Middlesex village and farm,
For the country folk to be up and to arm."

Then he said "Good-night!" and with muffled oar
Silently rowed to the Charlestown shore,
Just as the moon rose over the bay,
Where swinging wide at her moorings lay
The Somerset, British man-of-war:
A phantom ship, with each mast and spar
Across the moon like a prison bar,
And a huge black hulk, that was magnified
By its own reflection in the tide.

Meanwhile, his friend, through alley and street
Wanders and watches, with eager ears,
Till in the silence around him he hears
The muster of men at the barrack-door,
The sound of arms, and the tramp of feet,
And the measured tread of the grenadiers,
Marching down to their boats on the shore.

Then he climbed to the tower of the church,
Up the wooden stairs, with stealthy tread,
To the belfry-chamber overhead,
And startled the pigeons from their perch
On the sombre rafters, that round him made
Masses and moving shapes of shade,—
Up the light ladder, slender and tall,

To the highest window in the wall,
Where he paused to listen and look down
A moment on the roofs of the town,
And the moonlight flowing over all.

Beneath, in the churchyard, lay the dead,
In their night encampment on the hill,
Wrapped in silence so deep and still,
That he could hear, like a sentinel's tread,
The watchful night-wind, as it went
Creeping along from tent to tent,
And seeming to whisper, "All is well!"
A moment only he feels the spell
Of the place and the hour, and the secret dread
Of the lonely belfry and the dead;
For suddenly all his thoughts are bent
On a shadowy something far away,
Where the river widens to meet the bay,—
A line of black that bends and floats
On the rising tide, like a bridge of boats.

Meanwhile, impatient to mount and ride,
Booted and spurred, with a heavy stride,
On the opposite shore walked Paul Revere.
Now he patted his horse's side,
Now gazed at the landscape far and near,
Then impetuous stamped the earth,
And turned and tightened his saddle-girth;
But mostly he watched with eager search
The belfry tower of the old North Church,
As it rose above the graves on the hill,
Lonely and spectral and sombre and still.

And lo! as he looks, on the belfry's height,
A glimmer, and then a gleam of light!
He springs to the saddle, the bridle he turns,
But lingers and gazes, till full on his sight
A second lamp in the belfry burns!

A hurry of hoofs in a village street,
A shape in the moonlight, a bulk in the dark,
And beneath, from the pebbles, in passing, a spark
Struck out by a steed that flies fearless and fleet:
That was all! And yet, through the gloom and the light,
The fate of a nation was riding that night;

And the spark struck out by that steed, in his flight,
Kindled the land into flame with its heat.

It was twelve by the village-clock
When he crossed the bridge into Medford town.
He heard the crowing of the cock,
And the barking of the farmer's dog,
And felt the damp of the river-fog,
That rises after the sun goes down.

It was one by the village clock,
When he rode into Lexington.
He saw the gilded weathercock
Swim in the moonlight as he passed,
And the meeting-house windows, blank and bare,
Gaze at him with a spectral glare,
As if they already stood aghast
At the bloody work they would look upon.

It was two by the village-clock,
When he came to the bridge in Concord town.
He heard the bleating of the flock,
And the twitter of birds among the trees,
And felt the breath of the morning-breeze
Blowing over the meadow brown.
And one was safe and asleep in his bed
Who at the bridge would be first to fall,
Who that day would be lying dead,
Pierced by a British musket-ball.

You know the rest. In the books you have read
How the British Regulars fired and fled,—
How the farmers gave them ball for ball,
From behind each fence and farmyard-wall,
Chasing the red-coats down the lane,
Then crossing the fields to emerge again
Under the trees at the turn of the road,
And only pausing to fire and load.

So through the night rode Paul Revere;
And so through the night went his cry of alarm
To every Middlesex village and farm,—
A cry of defiance, and not of fear,
A voice in the darkness, a knock at the door,
And a word that shall echo for evermore!

For, borne on the night-wind of the Past,
Through all our history, to the last,
In the hour of darkness and peril and need,
The people will waken and listen to hear
The hurrying hoof-beat of that steed,
And the midnight message of Paul Revere.

❧ *Oliver Wendell Holmes*

GRANDMOTHER'S STORY OF BUNKER-HILL BATTLE: AS SHE SAW IT FROM THE BELFRY

'Tis like stirring living embers when, at eighty, one remembers
All the achings and the quakings of "the times that tried men's souls;"
When I talk of *Whig* and *Tory*, when I tell the *Rebel* story,
To you the words are ashes, but to me they're burning coals.

I had heard the muskets' rattle of the April running battle;
Lord Percy's hunted soldiers, I can see their red coats still;
But a deadly chill comes o'er me, as the day looms up before me,
When a thousand men lay bleeding on the slopes of Bunker's Hill.

'Twas a peaceful summer's morning, when the first thing gave us warning
Was the booming of the cannon from the river and the shore:
"Child," says grandma, "what's the matter, what is all this noise and clatter?
Have those scalping Indian devils come to murder us once more?"

Poor old soul! my sides were shaking in the midst of all my quaking
To hear her talk of Indians when the guns began to roar:
She had seen the burning village, and the slaughter and the pillage,
When the Mohawks killed her father, with their bullets through his door.

Then I said, "Now, dear old granny, don't you fret and worry any,
For I'll soon come back and tell you whether this is work or play;
There can't be mischief in it, so I won't be gone a minute"—
For a minute then I started. I was gone the live-long day.

No time for bodice-lacing or for looking-glass grimacing;
Down my hair went as I hurried, tumbling half-way to my heels;
God forbid your ever knowing, when there's blood around her flowing,
How the lonely, helpless daughter of a quiet household feels!

In the street I heard a thumping; and I knew it was the stumping
Of the Corporal, our old neighbor, on that wooden leg he wore,
With a knot of women round him,—it was lucky I had found him,
So I followed with the others, and the Corporal marched before.

They were making for the steeple,—the old soldier and his people;
The pigeons circled round us as we climbed the creaking stair,
Just across the narrow river—oh, so close it made me shiver!
Stood a fortress on the hill-top that but yesterday was bare.

Not slow our eyes to find it; well we knew who stood behind it,
Though the earthwork hid them from us, and the stubborn walls were dumb:
Here were sister, wife, and mother, looking wild upon each other,
And their lips were white with terror as they said, "THE HOUR HAS COME!"

The morning slowly wasted, not a morsel had we tasted,
And our heads were almost splitting with the cannons' deafening thrill,
When a figure tall and stately round the rampart strode sedately;
It was PRESCOTT, one since told me; he commanded on the hill.

Every woman's heart grew bigger when we saw his manly figure,
With the banyan buckled round it, standing up so straight and tall;
Like a gentleman of leisure who is strolling out for pleasure,
Through the storm of shells and cannon-shot he walked around the wall.

At eleven the streets were swarming, for the red-coats' ranks were forming;
At noon in marching order they were moving to the piers;
How the bayonets gleamed and glistened, as we looked far down and listened
To the trampling and the drum-beat of the belted grenadiers!

At length the men have started, with a cheer (it seemed faint-hearted),
In their scarlet regimentals, with their knapsacks on their backs,
And the reddening, rippling water, as after a sea-fight's slaughter,
Round the barges gliding onward blushed like blood along their tracks.

So they crossed to the other border, and again they formed in order;
And the boats came back for soldiers, came for soldiers, soldiers still:
The time seemed everlasting to us women faint and fasting,—
At last they're moving, marching, marching proudly up the hill.

We can see the bright steel glancing all along the lines advancing—
Now the front rank fires a volley—they have thrown away their shot;
Far behind the earthwork lying, all the balls above them flying,
Our people need not hurry; so they wait and answer not.

Then the Corporal, our old cripple (he would swear sometimes and tipple),—
He had heard the bullets whistle (in the old French war) before,—
Calls out in words of jeering, just as if they all were hearing,—
And his wooden leg thumps fiercely on the dusty belfry floor:—

"Oh! fire away, ye villains, and earn King George's shillin's,
But ye'll waste a ton of powder afore a 'rebel' falls;
You may bang the dirt and welcome, they're as safe as Dan'l Malcolm
Ten foot beneath the gravestone that you've splintered with your balls!"

In the hush of expectation, in the awe and trepidation
Of the dread approaching moment, we are well-nigh breathless all;
Though the rotten bars are failing on the rickety belfry railing,
We are crowding up against them like the waves against a wall.

Just a glimpse (the air is clearer), they are nearer,—nearer,—nearer,
When a flash—a curling smoke-wreath—then a crash—the steeple shakes—
The deadly truce is ended; the tempest's shroud is rended;
Like a morning mist it gathered, like a thunder-cloud it breaks!

Oh the sight our eyes discover as the blue-black smoke blows over!
The red-coats stretched in windrows as a mower rakes his hay;
Here a scarlet heap is lying, there a headlong crowd is flying
Like a billow that has broken and is shivered into spray.

Then we cried, "The troops are routed! they are beat—it can't be doubted!
God be thanked, the fight is over!"—Ah! the grim old soldier's smile!
"Tell us, tell us why you look so?" (we could hardly speak, we shook so)
"Are they beaten? *Are* they beaten? A R E they beaten?"—"Wait a while."

Oh the trembling and the terror! for too soon we saw our error:
They are baffled, not defeated; we have driven them back in vain;
And the columns that were scattered, round the colors that were tattered,
Toward the sullen silent fortress turn their belted breasts again.

All at once, as we are gazing, lo the roofs of Charlestown blazing!
They have fired the harmless village; in an hour it will be down!
The Lord in heaven confound them, rain his fire and brimstone round them,—
The robbing, murdering red-coats, that would burn a peaceful town!

They are marching, stern and solemn; we can see each massive column
As they near the naked earth-mound with the slanting walls so steep.
Have our soldiers got faint-hearted, and in noiseless haste departed?
Are they panic-struck and helpless? Are they palsied or asleep?

Now! the walls they're almost under! scarce a rod the foes asunder!
Not a firelock flashed against them! up the earthwork they will swarm!
But the words have scarce been spoken, when the ominous calm is broken,
And a bellowing crash has emptied all the vengeance of the storm!

So again, with murderous slaughter, pelted backward to the water,
Fly Pigot's running heroes and the frightened braves of Howe;
And we shout, "At last they're done for, it's their barges they have run for:
They are beaten, beaten, beaten; and the battle's over now!"

And we looked, poor timid creatures, on the rough old soldier's features,
Our lips afraid to question, but he knew what we would ask:
"Not sure," he said; "keep quiet,—once more, I guess, they'll try it—
Here's damnation to the cut-throats!"—then he handed me his flask,

Saying, "Gal, you're looking shaky; have a drop of old Jamaiky;
I'm afraid there'll be more trouble afore this job is done;"
So I took one scorching swallow; dreadful faint I felt and hollow,
Standing there from early morning when the firing was begun.

All through those hours of trial I had watched a calm clock dial,
As the hands kept creeping, creeping,—they were creeping round to four,
When the old man said, "They're forming with their bayonets fixed for storming:
It's the death grip that's a coming,—they will try the works once more."

With brazen trumpets blaring, the flames behind them glaring,
The deadly wall before them, in close array they come;
Still onward, upward toiling, like a dragon's fold uncoiling—
Like the rattlesnake's shrill warning the reverberating drum!

Over heaps all torn and gory—shall I tell the fearful story,
How they surged above the breastwork, as a sea breaks over a deck;
How, driven, yet scarce defeated, our worn-out men retreated,
With their powder-horns all emptied, like the swimmers from a wreck?

It has all been told and painted; as for me, they say I fainted,
And the wooden-legged old Corporal stumped with me down the stair:
When I woke from dreams affrighted the evening lamps were lighted,—
On the floor a youth was lying; his bleeding breast was bare.

And I heard through all the flurry, "Send for WARREN! hurry! hurry!
Tell him here's a soldier bleeding, and he'll come and dress his wound!"
Ah, we knew not till the morrow told its tale of death and sorrow,
How the starlight found him stiffened on the dark and bloody ground.

Who the youth was, what his name was, where the place from which he came was,
Who had brought him from the battle, and had left him at our door,
He could not speak to tell us; but 'twas one of our brave fellows,
As the homespun plainly showed us which the dying soldier wore.

For they all thought he was dying, as they gathered 'round him crying,—
And they said, "O, how they'll miss him!" and, "What *will* his mother do?"
Then, his eyelids just unclosing like a child's that has been dozing,
He faintly murmured, "Mother!"—and—I saw his eyes were blue.

—"Why, grandma, how you're winking!"—Ah, my child, it sets me thinking
Of a story not like this one. Well, he somehow lived along;
So we came to know each other, and I nursed him like a—mother,
Till at last he stood before me, tall, and rosy-cheeked, and strong.

And we sometimes walked together in the pleasant summer weather;
—"Please to tell us what his name was?"—Just your own, my little dear,—
There's his picture Copley painted: we became so well acquainted,
That—in short, that's why I'm grandma, and you children all are here!

Publisher's note: "As this Poem is written expressly for this Memorial, and not intended for
publication elsewhere, the Publishers request that it not be copied or reprinted."

SHERIDAN'S RIDE

Up from the South at break of day,
Bringing to Winchester fresh dismay,
  The affrighted air with a shudder bore,
  Like a herald in haste, to the chieftain's door,
  The terrible grumble, and rumble, and roar,
  Telling the battle was on once more,
And Sheridan twenty miles away.

And wider still those billows of war,
Thundered along the horizon's bar;
And louder yet into Winchester rolled
The roar of that red sea uncontrolled,
Making the blood of the listener cold,
As he thought of the stake in that fiery fray,
And Sheridan twenty miles away.

But there is a road from Winchester town,
A good, broad highway leading down;
And there, through the flush of the morning light,
A steed as black as the steeds of night,
Was seen to pass, as with eagle flight,
As if he knew the terrible need;
He stretched away with his utmost speed;
Hills rose and fell; but his heart was gay,
With Sheridan fifteen miles away.

Still sprung from those swift hoofs, thundering South,
The dust, like smoke from the cannon's mouth;
Or the trail of a comet, sweeping faster and faster,
Foreboding to traitors the doom of disaster.
The heart of the steed, and the heart of the master
Were beating like prisoners assaulting their walls,
Impatient to be where the battle-field calls;
Every nerve of the charger was strained to full play,
With Sheridan only ten miles away.

Under his spurning feet the road
Like an arrowy Alpine river flowed,
And the landscape sped away behind
Like an ocean flying before the wind,
And the steed, like a bark fed with furnace ire,
Swept on, with his wild eye full of fire.

But lo! he is nearing his heart's desire;
He is snuffing the smoke of the roaring fray,
With Sheridan only five miles away.

The first that the general saw were the groups
Of stragglers, and then the retreating troops,
What was done? what to do? a glance told him both,
Then striking his spurs, with a terrible oath,
He dashed down the line 'mid a storm of huzzas,
And the wave of retreat checked its course there, because
The sight of the master compelled it to pause.
With foam and with dust the black charger was gray;
By the flash of his eye, and the red nostril's play,
He seemed to the whole great army to say,
"I have brought you Sheridan all the way
From Winchester, down to save the day!"

Hurrah! hurrah for Sheridan!
Hurrah! hurrah for horse and man!
And when their statues are placed on high,
Under the dome of the Union sky,
The American soldier's Temple of Fame;
There with the glorious general's name,
Be it said, in letters both bold and bright,
    "Here is the steed that saved the day,
By carrying Sheridan into the fight,
    From Winchester, twenty miles away!"

John Greenleaf Whittier

BARBARA FRIETCHIE

Up from the meadows rich with corn,
Clear in the cool September morn,

The clustered spires of Frederick stand
Green-walled by the hills of Maryland.

Round about them orchards sweep,
Apple- and peach-tree fruited deep,

Fair as the garden of the Lord
To the eyes of the famished rebel horde,

On that pleasant morn of the early fall
When Lee marched over the mountain-
    wall,—

Over the mountains winding down,
Horse and foot, into Frederick town.

Forty flags with their silver stars,
Forty flags with their crimson bars,

Flapped in the morning wind: the sun
Of noon looked down, and saw not one.

Up rose old Barbara Frietchie then,
Bowed with her fourscore years and ten;

Bravest of all in Frederick town,
She took up the flag the men hauled
    down;

In her attic window the staff she set,
To show that one heart was loyal yet.

Up the street came the rebel tread,
Stonewall Jackson riding ahead.

Under his slouched hat left and right
He glanced: the old flag met his sight.

"Halt!"—the dust-brown ranks stood fast.
"Fire!"—out blazed the rifle-blast.

It shivered the window, pane and sash;
It rent the banner with seam and gash.

Quick, as it fell, from the broken staff
Dame Barbara snatched the silken scarf;

She leaned far out on the window-sill,
And shook it forth with a royal will.

"Shoot, if you must, this old gray head,
But spare your country's flag," she said.

A shade of sadness, a blush of shame,
Over the face of the leader came;

The nobler nature within him stirred
To life at that woman's deed and word;

"Who touches a hair of yon gray head
Dies like a dog! March on!" he said.

All day long through Frederick street
Sounded the tread of marching feet:

All day long that free flag tossed
Over the heads of the rebel host.

Ever its torn folds rose and fell
On the loyal winds that loved it well;

And through the hill-gaps sunset light
Shone over it with a warm good-night.

Barbara Frietchie's work is o'er,
And the Rebel rides on his raids no more.

Honor to her! and let a tear
Fall, for her sake, on Stonewall's bier.

Over Barbara Frietchie's grave,
Flag of Freedom and Union, wave!

Peace and order and beauty draw
Round thy symbol of light and law;

And ever the stars above look down
On thy stars below in Frederick town!

J. T. Trowbridge

THE COLOR-BEARER

'T was a fortress to be stormed:
    Boldly right in view they formed,
All as quiet as a regiment parading:
    Then in front a line of flame!
    Then at left and right the same!
Two platoons received a furious
        enfilading,
    To their places still they filed,
    And they smiled at the wild
        Cannonading.

"'T will be over in an hour!
    'T will not be much of a shower!
Never mind, my boys," said he, "a little
        drizzling!"
    Then to cross that fatal plain,
    Through the whirring, hurtling rain
Of the grape-shot, and the minie-bullets'
        whistling!
    But he nothing heeds nor shuns,
    As he runs with the guns
        Brightly bristling!

Leaving trails of dead and dying
In their track, yet forward flying
Like a breaker where the gale of conflict
        rolled them,
With a foam of flashing light
Borne before them on their bright
Burnished barrels,—O, 't was fearful to
        behold them
While from ramparts roaring loud
Swept a cloud like a shroud
To enfold them!

O, his color was the first!
Through the burying cloud he burst,
With the standard to the battle forward
        slanted!
Through the belching, blinding
        breath
Of the flaming jaws of Death,
Till his banner on the bastion to be
        planted!
By the screaming shot that fell,
And the yell of the shell,
Nothing daunted.

Right against the bulwark dashing,
Over tangled branches crashing,
'Mid the plunging volleys thundering
        ever louder,
There he clambers, there he stands,
With the ensign in his hands,—
O, was ever hero handsomer or prouder?
Streaked with battle-sweat and
        slime,
And sublime in the grime
Of the powder!

'T was six minutes, at the least,
Ere the closing combat ceased,—
Near as we the mighty moments then
        could measure,—
And we held our souls with awe,
Till his haughty flag we saw
On the lifting vapors drifting o'er the
        embrasure!
Saw it glimmer in our tears,
While our ears heard the cheers
Rend the azure!

Through the abatis they broke,
Through the surging cannon-
        smoke,
And they drove the foe before like
        frightened cattle.
O, but never wound was his,
For in other wars than this,
Where the volleys of Life's conflict roar
        and rattle,
He must still, as he was wont,
In the front bear the brunt
Of the battle.

He shall guide the van of Truth,
And in manhood, as in youth,
Be her fearless, be her peerless
        Color-Bearer!
With his high and bright example,
Like a banner brave and ample,
Ever leading through receding clouds
        of Error,
To the empire of the Strong,
And to Wrong he shall long
        Be a terror!

Margaret Sangster

A DRUMMER

I'm only a drummer; I've nothing to do
But to beat my brave drum and make music for you.

I'm only a drummer, not quite twelve years old,
But I hope that my heart is full twenty years bold.

I do not give orders, I've just to obey,
As quick as a flash, what my officers say.

There are fellows who think that my task must be light,
Just beating a drum with a merry boy's might.

Yet drummers no taller than I am are found
In low little beds in the land's holy ground.

They followed the flag, in the days long ago,
When it waved its defiance, whoe'er was the foe.

They timed to the bugles, so shrill and so sweet,
And they faltered alone when the call was retreat.

Oh, brave drummer boys! though you lived or you died,
I look at your record and stand by your side,

And beat my brave drum with the gladness of love—
'Tis the flag of our Union that's flying above!

Walt Whitman

O CAPTAIN! MY CAPTAIN!

I.

O Captain! my captain! our fearful trip is done;
The ship has weathered every rack, the prize we sought is won;
The port is near, the bells I hear, the people are exulting,
While follow eyes the steady keel, the vessel grim and daring:
   But O heart! heart! heart!
     Leave you not the little spot,
       Where on the deck my captain lies,
         Fallen cold and dead.

II.

O captain! my captain! rise up and hear the bells;
Rise up—for you the flag is flung—for you the bugle trills;
For you bouquets and ribbon'd wreaths—for you the shores a-crowding,
For you they call, the swaying mass, their eager faces turning;
   O captain! dear father!
     This arm I push beneath you;
       It is some dream that on the deck,
         You've fallen cold and dead.

III.

My captain does not answer, his lips are pale and still;
My father does not feel my arm, he has no pulse nor will:
But the ship, the ship is anchor'd safe, its voyage closed and done;
From fearful trip the victor ship, comes in with object won:
   Exult, O shores, and ring, O bells!
     But I, with silent tread,
       Walk the spot my captain lies,
         Fallen cold and dead.

❧ *"Kruna" [Julia Pratt Ballard]*

THE TWO BURIALS

In reading the *Life of Abraham Lincoln,* one is forcibly struck by the contrast in the burial of his mother—alone, in an unbroken forest, in a rude, homemade box, with no funeral service, and scarcely a witness outside of the family—and the unparalleled magnificence of the national funeral of her noble son a few years later.

In the cool, unbroken shadow,
  Where the fragile wild-flowers nod,
Dreamily above the sleeper
  Laid beneath the forest sod,

Lonely in their grief they bore her,
  With no sound of tolling bell;
Ah! the sob of crushed affection
  Was the mother's funeral-knell.

Never had that grand old forest
  Echoed to the sexton's spade;
First, within its sheltering bosom,
  Was that noble mother laid.

Lonely sleeper! he whose footsteps
    Wore a path to that lone mound—
Who with tears so oft bedewed it—
    That same sleep too quickly found.

Borne along, in bitter anguish,
    List the solemn-toiling bell;
Northern lakes to Southern waters
    Echoed back his funeral-knell.

Tolling! in the quiet village,
    Tolling! in the myriad throng,
Tolling! through the mountain gorges,
    As his form was borne along;

Tolling for the sorrow welling
    From a sudden, awful blow;
Tolling for the anguish swelling
    From a nation's bitter woe!

Lonely dust within the forest,
    Sleeper, where above the sod
Millions raised the speaking marble,
    Rest alike, beloved of God.

❧ *Hezekiah Butterworth*

WHITMAN'S RIDE FOR OREGON

I.

"An empire to be lost or won!"
    And who four thousand miles will ride
    And climb to heaven the Great Divide,
And find the way to Washington,
    Through mountain cañons, winter
        snows,
    O'er streams where free the north
        wind blows?
Who, who will ride from Walla-Walla,
    Four thousand miles, for Oregon!

II.

"An empire to be lost or won?
    In youth to man I gave my all,
    And naught is yonder mountain wall;
If but the will of Heaven be done,
    It is not mine to live or die,
    Or count the mountains low or high,
Or count the miles from Walla-Walla.
    I, I will ride for Oregon!

III.

"An empire to be lost or won?
    Bring me my Cayuse pony then,
    And I will thread old ways again,
Beneath the gray skies' crystal sun.
'Twas on those altars of the air
    I raised the flag, and saw below
    The measureless Columbia flow;
The Bible oped, and bowed in prayer,
    And gave myself to God anew,
And felt my spirit newly born;
    And to my mission I'll be true,
And from the vale of Walla-Walla
    I'll ride again for Oregon.

IV.

"I'm not my own; myself I've given,
    To bear to savage hordes the word;
If on the altars of the heaven
    I'm called to die, it is the Lord.
The herald may not wait or choose,
    'Tis his the summons to obey;
To do his best, or gain or lose,
    To seek the Guide and not the way.
He must not miss the cross, and I
    Have ceased to think of life or death;
My ark I've builded—Heaven is nigh,
    And earth is but a morning's breath!
Go, then, my Cayuse pony, bring;
    The hopes that seek myself are gone,
And from the vale of Walla-Walla
    I'll ride again for Oregon."

V.

He disappeared, as not his own,
    He heard the warning ice winds sigh;
The smoky sun flames o'er him shone,
    On whitened altars of the sky,
As up the mountain sides he rose;
    The wandering eagle round him
        wheeled,
The partridge fled, the gentle roes,

And oft his Cayuse pony reeled
Upon some dizzy crag and gazed
    Down cloudy chasms, falling storms,
While higher yet the peaks upraised
    Against the winds their giant forms.
On, on and on, past Idaho,
    On past the mighty Saline sea,
His covering at night the snow,
    His only sentinel a tree.
On, past Portneuf's basaltic heights,
    On where the San Juan Mountains lay,
Through sunless days and starless nights,
    Toward Toas [Taos] and far Sante Fé.
O'er table-lands of sleet and hail,
    Through pine-roofed gorges, cañons
        cold,
Now fording streams incased in mail
    Of ice, like Alpine knights of old,
Still on, and on, forgetful on,
    Till far behind lay Walla-Walla,
And far the fields of Oregon.

VI.

The winter deepened, sharper grew
    The hail and sleet, the frost and snow;
Not e'en the eagle o'er him flew,
    And scarce the partridge's wing below.
The land became a long white sea,
    And then a deep with scarce a coast;
The stars refused their light, till he
    Was in the wildering mazes lost.
He dropped rein, his stiffened hand
    Was like a statue's hand of clay,
"My trusty beast, 'tis the command;
    Go on, I leave to thee the way.
I must go on, I must go on,
    Whatever lot may fall to me,
On, 'tis for others' sake I ride,
    For others I may never see,
And dare thy clouds, O Great Divide,
    Not for myself, O Walla-Walla,
Not for myself, O Washington,
But for thy future, Oregon."

VII.

And on and on the dumb beast pressed
    Uncertain, and without a guide,
And found the mountain's curves of rest
    And sheltered ways of the Divide.
His feet grew firm, he found the way
    With storm-beat limbs and frozen
        breath,
As keen his instincts to obey
    As was his master's eye of faith,
Still on and on, still on and on,
    And far and far grew Walla-Walla,
And far the fields of Oregon.

VIII.

That spring, a man with frozen feet
    Came to the marble halls of state,
And told his mission but to meet
    The chill of scorn, the scoff of hate.
"Is Oregon worth saving?" asked
    The treaty-makers from the coast,
And him, the church with questions
        tasked,
    And said, "Why did you leave your
        post?"
Was it for this that he had braved
    The warring storms of mount and sky?
Yes!—yet that empire he had saved,
    And to his post went back to die,
Went back to die for others' sake,
    Went back to die from Washington,
Went back to die for Walla-Walla,
    For Idaho and Oregon.

IX.

At fair Walla-Walla one may see
    The city of the Western North,
And near it graves unmarked there be
    That cover souls of royal worth;
The flag waves o'er them in the sky
    Beneath whose stars are cities born,
And round them mountain-castled lie
    The hundred states of Oregon.

Augusta [Joyce] Crocheron

A SCENE OF THE EARLY DAYS

Out of their peaceful slumbers
    The little children woke,
When the tramp of armed and angry men
    The night's deep silence broke.
And, shuddering, they listened to
    The threatened doom they swore,
And their father's step as he rose to meet
    The mobbers at the door.

'Twas cold, and dark the night looked,
    But colder, darker yet
The hearts and faces of the men
    The Mormon father met.
Many a month of hardship,
    Many a sleepless night,
While the hungry cried, and his dear
      ones clung
    Around him in their fright,

Had worn his strength to weakness,
    And now he stood at bay,
A hunted soul—and in despair
    Heard what they had to say:
"Bring out your Mormon children!
    Nor dare our word defy,
For we are firm, and the oath is sworn
    That you and they must die."

No anger kindled in his eye;
    His cheek was wan and thin;
But pity melted not their hearts,
    As he went slowly in.
The feeble candle threw its light
    Upon the door-yard bare—
Shone on their rifles, steely cold—
    The stern eyes' evil glare.

He spread a quilt before them,
    Then, from the lowly bed,
Without a kiss, without a word,
    Lifted each little head.
In his true arms he bore them,
    And 'neath the midnight sky,
Place one by one his children dear
    Before their God to die!

And standing 'mid them, faithful,
    With bared and reverent head,
"Now, shoot them if God will let you,"
    Were all the words he said.
The mobbers looked in each other's eyes;
    Not one had voice to say
The answer word, but each one turned
    And silent rode away.

From hate and power of mobbers
    Their guiltless lives were spared;
Their steps were led through desert
      paths
    And perils wild they dared.
Then followed years of peace and joy,
    Of plenty and sweet rest—
His children's children throng his home,
    His name is honored, blest.

But hark! his soul so long on watch,
    Hath caught a far-off sound—
The foeman's step; oppressions might
    Approach our rightful ground.
O Father, reach out thine arm again,
    Thy children still to save;
Make strong thy hosts, thy banners bid
    O'er all thy temples wave.

THE FLAG GOES BY

Hats off!
Along the street there comes
A blare of bugles, a ruffle of drums,
A flash of color beneath the sky:
Hats off!
The flag is passing by!

Blue and crimson and white it shines,
Over the steel-tipped, ordered lines.
Hats off!
The colors before us fly;
But more than the flag is passing by.

Sea-fights and land-fights, grim and
      great,
Fought to make and to save the State;
Weary marches and sinking ships;
Cheers of victory on dying lips;

Days of plenty and years of peace;
March of a strong land's swift increase;
Equal justice, right and law,
Stately honor and revered awe;

Sign of a nation, great and strong
To ward her people from foreign wrong:
Pride and glory and honor, all
Live in the colors to stand or fall.

Hats off!
Along the street there comes
A blare of bugles, a ruffle of drums;
And loyal hearts are beating high:
Hats off!
The flag is passing by!

GRANNY'S STORY

Yes, lads, I'm a poor old body;
    My wits are not over clear;
I can't remember the day o' the week,
    And scarcely the time o' year.
But one thing is down in my mem'ry
    So deep, it is sure to stay;
It was long ago, but it all comes back
    As if it had happened to-day.

Here, stand by the window, laddies.
    Do you see, away to the right,
A long black line on the water,
    Topped with a crest of white?
That is the reef Defiance,
    Where the good ship Gaspereau
Beat out her life in the breakers,
    Just fifty-six years ago.

I mind 't was a raw Thanksgiving,
    The sleet drove sharp as knives,
And most of us here at the harbor
    Were sailors' sweethearts and wives.
But I had my goodman beside me,
    And everything tidy and bright,
When, all of a sudden, a signal
    Shot up through the murky night,

And a single gun in the darkness
    Boomed over and over again,
As if it bore in its awful tone
    The shrieks of women and men.
And down to the rocks we crowded,
    Facing the icy rain,
Praying the Lord to be their aid,
    Since human help was vain.

Then my goodman stooped and kissed me,
    And said, "It is but to die:
Who goes with me to the rescue?"
    And six noble lads cried "I!"
And crouching there in the tempest,
    Hiding our faces away,
We heard them row into the blackness,
    And what could we do but pray?

So long, when at last we heard them
    Cheering faint, off the shore,
I thought I had died and gone to heaven,
    And all my trouble was o'er.
And the white-faced women and children
    Seemed like ghosts in my sight,
As the boats, weighed down to the water,
    Came tossing into the light.

Eh, that was a heartsome Thanksgiving,
    With sobbing and laughter and prayers:
Our lads with their brown, dripping faces,
    And not a face missing from theirs.
For you never can know how much dearer
    The one you love dearest can be,
Till you've had him come back to you
        safely
    From out of the jaws of the sea.

And little we cared that the breakers
    Were tearing the ship in their hold.
There are things, if you weigh them fairly,
    Will balance a mint of gold.
And even the bearded captain
    Said, "Now let the good ship go,
Since never a soul that sailed with me
    Goes down in the Gaspereau."

THE COAST GUARD

Do you wonder what I am seeing,
  In the heart of the fire, aglow
Like cliffs in a golden sunset,
  With a summer sea below?
I see, away to the eastward,
  The line of a storm-beat coast,
And I hear the tread of the hurrying
    waves
  Like the tramp of a mailèd host.

And up and down in the darkness,
  And over the frozen sand,
I hear the men of the coast-guard
  Pacing along the strand.
Beaten by storm and tempest,
  And drenched by the pelting rain,
From the shores of Carolina,
  To the wind-swept bays of Maine.

No matter what storms are raging,
  No matter how wild the night,
The gleam of their swinging lanterns
  Shines out with a friendly light.
And many a shipwrecked sailor
  Thanks God, with his gasping breath,
For the sturdy arms of the surfmen
  That drew him away from death.

And so, when the wind is wailing,
  And the air grows dim with sleet,
I think of the fearless watchers
  Pacing along their beat.
I think of a wreck, fast breaking
  In the surf of a rocky shore,
And the life-boat leaping onward
  To the stroke of the bending oar.

I hear the shouts of the sailors,
  The boom of the frozen sail,
And the creak of the icy halyards
  Straining against the gale.
"Courage!" the captain trumpets,
  "They are sending help from land!"
God bless the men of the coast-guard,
  And hold their lives in His hand!

ROBINSON CRUSOE

"The night was thick and hazy,
  When the Piccadilly Daisy
Carried down the crew and captain in
    the sea;
  And I think the water drowned 'em,
  For they never, never found 'em,
And I know they didn't come ashore
    with me.

"Oh! 'twas very sad and lonely
  When I found myself the only
Population on this cultivated shore;
  But I've made a little tavern
  In a rocky little cavern,
And I sit and watch for people at the door.

"I spent no time in looking
  For a girl to do my cooking,
As I'm quite a clever hand at making
    stews;
  But I had that fellow Friday
  Just to keep the tavern tidy,
And to put a Sunday polish on my shoes.

"I have a little garden
  That I'm cultivating lard in,
As the things I eat are rather tough and
    dry;
  For I live on toasted lizards,
  Prickly pears, and parrot gizzards,
And I'm really very fond of beetle-pie.

"The clothes I had were furry,
  And it made me fret and worry
When I found the moths were eating off
    the hair;
  And I had to scrape and sand 'em,
  And I boiled 'em and I tanned 'em,
'Till I got the fine morocco suit I wear.

"I sometimes seek diversion
  In a family excursion
With the few domestic animals you see;
  And we take along a carrot
  As refreshment for the parrot,
And a little can of jungleberry tea.

"Then we gather as we travel
  Bits of moss and dirty gravel,
And we chip off little specimens of stone;
  And we carry home as prizes
  Funny bugs of handy sizes,
Just to give the day a scientific tone.

"If the roads are wet and muddy,
  We remain at home and study,—
For the Goat is very clever at a sum,—
  And the Dog, instead of fighting,
  Studies ornamental writing,
While the Cat is taking lessons on the
    drum.

"We retire at eleven,
  And we rise again at seven,
And I wish to call attention as I close,
  To the fact that all the scholars
  Are correct about their collars,
And particular in turning out their toes."

A PRESIDENT AT HOME*

I passed a President's House to-day—
  "A President, mamma, and what is
    that?"
O, it is a man who has to stay
  Where bowing beggars hold out the hat
For something,—a man who has to be
The Captain of every ship that we
Send with our darling flag to the sea,—
The Colonel at home who has to
    command
Each marching regiment in the land.

This President now has a single room,
  That is low and not much lighted,
    I fear;
Yet the butterflies play in the sun and
    gloom
  Of his evergreen avenue, year by year;
And the childlike violets up the hill

Climb, sweetly wayward, about him still;
And the bees blow by at the winds' wide
    will;
And the cruel river, that drowns men so,
Looks pretty enough in the shadows
    below.

Just one little fellow (named Robin) was
    there,
  In a red spring vest, and he let me pass
With that charming, careless, high-bred
    air
  Which comes of serving the great! In
    the grass
He sat half-singing, with nothing to do—
No, I did not see the President too:
His door was locked (what I say is true),
And he was asleep, and has been, it
    appears,
  Like Rip Van Winkle, asleep for years!

*At North Bend, Ohio River,—the tomb of General Harrison. [Piatt's note]

ONLY A SOLDIER
Harlem, New York

Only a soldier, gallant and true:
Fearlessly sparkles his eye of blue
Under the lashes, golden brown,
Over his red cheek sweeping down,—
Cheek and chin and lip in mould
Like the Iron Duke's of old.

Only a sabre-stroke, cruel and keen.
Two little uniform buttons between.
Just as the battle was lost and won,

Just as the day's fell work was done,
What seemed our soldier, turned pale
    and cold,—
But *he* was walking in streets of gold.

Only a quiet grass-grown grave;
Around it willows weeping wave;
Over his breast wild roses twine
With sprays of graceful eglantine,
And on the air no sound doth float
But the song of the bee and the wild
    bird's note.

BESS AND BEN

Sunny days, and sunny days,
  And all day long,
Here they go, and there they go,
  In and out the throng.

Here they go, and there they go,
  Up and down the street;
Benjie grinding out the tune,
  Bessie singing sweet.

Singing loud, and singing low,
  Trilling out the tune,
Not as Benjie grinds it out,
  But as birds in June

Lift and lift their voices up
  Out of pure delight;
Singing loud and singing low,
  Morning, noon, and night.

What! you never heard our Bess?
  Never heard her sing
"John Brown's soul is marching on,"
  And "The Lord is King"?

Why, where've you lived, I wonder,
  Never to have heard
Bessie with her tambourine,
  Singing like a bird?

Singing up and down the street,
  Singing high and low,
Since a little child of three,
  Twice three years ago.

It is twice three years, and more,
  Since that summer day
When the news from Gettysburg
  Told how Sergeant May,

Through the thickest of the fight,
  Through the rush and roar
Of the shout and shot and shell,
  Held the flag he bore,

Firmly, till the very last,
  When they found him lying
By the famous old stone-wall,
  In the twilight,—dying.

Dying, faltering at the last,
  "Little Bess and Ben!
They'll miss their father sorely—
  Who'll look out for them when—"

And that was all,—the words broke off
  In this world, for the other,
And little Bess and Ben were left
  With neither father, mother.

And this is why that through the street,
  In and out the throng,
Sunny days and sunny days,
  And all day long,

Here they go, and there they go,—
  Up and down the street;
Benjie grinding out the tune,
  Bessie singing sweet.

SONG
Air—"All the Blue Bonnets Are over the Border"

I.

March, march, mothers and grand-
    mammas!
Come from each home that stands in
    our border!
March, march, fathers and grand-papas!
Now young America waits in good order!
    Here is a flower show,
    Grown under winter snow,
Ready for spring with her sunshine
    and showers;
    Here every blossom grows
    Shamrock, thistle and rose,
And fresh from our hillside the Pilgrim's
    May flowers.

II.

Here is the New World that yet shall
    be founded;
Here are our Websters, our Sumners
    and Hales,
And here, with ambition by boat-racing
    bounded,
Perhaps there may be a new Splitter of
    rails.
    Here our are future men,
    Here are John Browns again;
Here are young Phillipses eyeing our
    blunders;
    Yet may the river see
    Hunt, Hosmer, Flint and Lee
Stand to make Concord hills echo their
    thunders.

III.

Here are the women who make no
    complaining,
Dumb-bells and clubs chasing vapors away,
Queens of good health and good humor
    all reigning,
Fairer and freer than we of to-day;
    Fullers with gifted eyes,
    Friendly Eliza Frys,
Nightingales born to give war a new
    glory;
    Britomarts brave to ride
    Thro' the world far and wide,
Righting all wrongs, as in Spenser's sweet
    story.

IV.

Come now from Barrett's mill, Bateman's
    blue water,
Nine Acre Corner, the Centre and all;
Come from the Factory, the North and
    East Quarter,
For here is a Union that never need fall;
    Lads in your blithest moods,
    Maids in your pretty snoods,
Come from all homes that stand in our
    border;
    Concord shall many a day
    Tell of the fair array
When young America met in good order.

Charlotte Perkins Gilman

LITTLE CELL

Little Cell! Little Cell! with a heart as
    big as heaven—
Remember that you are but a part!
This great longing in your soul
Is the longing of the whole—
And your work is not done with your
    heart!

Don't imagine, Little Cell,
That the work you do so well
Is the only work the world needs to do!
You are wanted in your place

For the growing of the race,
But the growing does not all depend on
    you!

Little Cell! Little Cell! with a race's
    whole ambition—
Remember there are others growing,
    too!
You've been noble—you've been
    strong—
Rest a while and come along—
Let the world take a turn and carry you!

Author Unknown

DISTANT WORLDS

About this earth, above the sky,
Worlds on worlds unnumbered lie;
And each around its own bright sun
Year after year its course doth run;
True as the dial to the day,
Each moves in its allotted way.
Uranus hangs so far from earth,
That, on the morn of Moses' birth,
Had a race-horse from it started,
And through the cloud and sunshine
    darted,
And never halted in its flight,
But ever galloped day and night,
Without pausing, without sleeping,
Ever onward, downward sweeping,
Not half its journey would be done,
Not half the distance now be run,
Had it set out for this earth,
On the morn of Moses' birth.
Oft glittering like the light of noon,
Are seen the mountains in the moon,
On whose high tops the sunbeams glow,
While gloomy shadows sleep below;

We see Mount Tycho's towering height
Throw back the sun's reflected light;
Through Ross's telescope while gazing,
Some have seen vast volcanoes blazing,
And reddening wide the valleys deep,
Which round the moon's piled
    mountains sleep.
Comets that travel wide and far,
Perchance have passed by every star;
By every world beyond our sight,
They move with half the speed of light;
Yet oft some planet's mighty force
Will twist them from their onward
    course,
Or hurl them, quick as lightning's pace,
'Mid the immensity of space.
The sun in Mercury doth appear
Six times larger than seen here,
And it shineth six times brighter,
And makes that planet six times lighter
Than the earth on which we dwell;
Such brilliancy no tongue can tell.
The stars there hang in Syrian skies,

Glitter like gems of richest dyes,
Blazing on high they there are seen
In robes of purple, gold and green.
Those bright and shooting stars we see,
Are still to us a mystery,
Rushing by each golden star

Which on us shineth from afar;
Whence they come, or whither go,
Mortal man may never know;
Angels may all God's wonders tell,
When in eternity we dwell.

M. B. Whiting

THE SEVEN AGES

It was an age of Fire,
    Long, long years ago,
When great melted rocks,
With earthquake shocks,
    In torrents of flame did flow.

It was an age of Mollusks,
    Long, long years ago,
When the clam and the oyster,
With the mussel much moister,
    By the sad sea waves sang low.

It was an age of Fishes,
    Long, long years ago,
When the shark and the gar-fish,
With the dear little star-fish,
    Swam about stately and slow.

It was an age of Carbons,
    Long, long years ago,
When the fern and the pine,
And other plants fine,
    Were made into coal, you know.

It was an age of Reptiles,
    Long, long years ago,
When the ichthyosaurus,
By the banks of the Taurus,

And the pterodactyl,
By the gurgling rill,
    Danced in the moonbeam's glow.

It was an age of Mammals,
    Long, long years ago,
When the wild mastodon,
With his war-paint on,
The behemoth wooed,
And the mammoth sued,
    Where glaciers once did go.

It is the age of Man!
Now tell me, if you can,
Why no more on the hills
March the pterodactyls?
Why the ancient tapirs,
Through the morning vapors,
Chase not the whale,
Or the sportive snail?

And when men have gone,
What next will come on
This peculiar earth,
Which had its birth,
As you surely know,
In an age of fire,
Long years ago—
Yes, long ago?

Emily Dickinson

SIMPLICITY

How happy is the little stone
That rambles in the road alone,
And does n't care about careers,
And exigencies never fears;
Whose coat of elemental brown
A passing universe put on;
And independent as the sun,
Associates or glows alone,
Fulfilling absolute decree
In casual simplicity.

Mary Mapes Dodge

[OH, NO!]

Oh, no!
'Tisn't so!
Papa's watch
Won't go?

It *must* go—
Guess I know!
Last night
I wound it tight,
And greased it nice
With camphor-ice.

Mary Mapes Dodge

GOOD MISTRESS SUNDIAL

"Good Mistress Sundial, what is the hour?"
    "Alack! to tell you I've not the power.
It rains; and I only can work, you see,
When the sun is casting his light on me.
I'm nothing at all but a senseless block
    Whenever his beautiful rays depart;
But ask my neighbor, the Four-o'clock;
    She carries the time o' day in her heart."

[IF THIS LITTLE WORLD TONIGHT]

If this little world tonight
  Suddenly should fall thro' space
In a hissing, headlong flight,
  Shrivelling from off its face,
As it falls into the sun,
  In an instant every trace
Of the little crawling things—
  Ants, philosophers, and lice,
Cattle, cockroaches, and kinds,
  Beggars, millionaires, and mice,
Men and maggots all as one
  As it falls into the sun—
Who can say but at the same
  Instant from some planet far
A child may watch us and exclaim,
  "See the pretty shooting star!"

C. P. Cranch

THE EARTH, THE MOON AND THE COMET

The old Earth was sleepy, and rolled into bed,
And the clouds were the pillows under his head;
While the Moon, his old wife, stood by with her light,
And tucked him up snugly and bade him "good-night."

But neither the Earth nor the Moon was aware
There was coming a star with a singular glare,
And a terrible tail, across their track,
That wasn't set down in their almanac.

But the Moon soon awoke and discovered this Star
Plunging along through the night from afar;
And she nudged her husband, and bade him look
    out,
For a fiery monster was roaming about!

And nearer and nearer the Comet came,
With his blazing head and his tail of flame
Some millions of miles in length, they say:
And the poor Earth trembled with sore dismay.

For the Comet was robed in fire and mist,
And frowned and glared and doubled his fist,
Till the Earth's round face grew long with
   affright,
And the Moon, in her terror, let fall her light.

But all on a sudden their terror was gone,
For the Comet wheeled by on his way to the Sun;
And they laughed as they saw him go tearing his
   hair,
Far away in the distance, in rage and despair.

"Ha, ha!" laughed the Earth, and "Ho, ho!" cried the Moon;
"I don't think you'll scare us again very soon.
 You make a great show in the sky as you pass;
 But astronomers say you are nothing but gas!"

 *Ella Wheeler Wilcox*

A NAUGHTY LITTLE COMET

There was a little comet who lived near the Milky Way!
She loved to wander out at night and jump about and play.

The mother of the comet was a very good old star;
She used to scold her reckless child for venturing out too far.

She told her of the ogre, Sun, who loved on stars to sup,
And who asked no better pastime than in gobbling comets up.

But instead of growing cautious and of showing proper fear,
The foolish little comet edged up nearer, and more near.

She switched her saucy tail along right where the Sun could see,
And flirted with old Mars, and was as bold as bold could be.

She laughed to scorn the quiet stars who never frisked about;
She said there was no fun in life unless you ventured out.

She liked to make the planets stare, and wished no better mirth
Than just to see the telescopes aimed at her from the Earth.

She wondered how so many stars could mope through nights and days,
And let the sickly faced old Moon get all the love and praise.

And as she talked and tossed her head and switched her shining trail
The staid old mother star grew sad, her cheek grew wan and pale.

For she had lived there in the skies a million years or more,
And she had heard gay comets talk in just this way before.

And by and by there came an end to this gay comet's fun.
She went a tiny bit too far—and vanished in the Sun!

No more she swings her shining trail before the whole world's sight,
But quiet stars she laughed to scorn are twinkling every night.

Celia Thaxter

DUST

Here is a problem, a wonder for all to see,
    Look at this marvelous thing I hold in my hand!
This is a magic surprising, a mystery
    Strange as a miracle, harder to understand.

What is it? Only a handful of earth: to your touch
    A dry rough powder you trample beneath your feet,
Dark and lifeless; but think for a moment, how much
    It hides and holds that is beautiful, bitter, or sweet.

Think of the glory of color! The red of the rose,
    Green of the myriad leaves and the fields of grass,
Yellow as bright as the sun where the daffodil blows,
    Purple where violets nod as the breezes pass.

Think of the manifold form, of the oak and the vine.
    Nut and fruit, and cluster, and ears of corn;
Of the anchored water-lily, a thing divine,
    Unfolding its dazzling snow to the kiss of morn.

Think of the delicate perfumes borne on the gale,
    Of the golden willow catkin's odor of spring,
Of the breath of the rich narcissus waxen-pale,
    Of the sweet pea's flight of flowers, of the nettle's sting.

Strange that this lifeless thing gives vine, flower, tree
    Color and shape and character, fragrance too;
That the timber that builds the house, the ship for the sea,
    Out of this powder its strength and its toughness drew!

That the cocoa among the palms should suck its milk
    From this dry dust, while dates from the self-same soil
Summon their sweet rich fruit: that our shining silk
    The mulberry leaves should yield to the worm's slow toil.

How should the poppy steal sleep from the very source
    That grants to the grape-vine juice that can madden or cheer ?
How does the weed find food for its fabric coarse
    Where the lilies proud their blossoms pure uprear?

Who shall compass or fathom God's thought profound?
    We can but praise, for we may not understand;
But there's no more beautiful riddle the whole world round
    Than is hid in this heap of dust I hold in my hand.

❧ *Nancy Minerva Haynes Miller*

THE WIND

"What is the wind, mamma?"
    "'Tis air in motion, child."
"Why can I never see the wind
    That blows so fierce and wild?"

"Because the gases, dear,
    Of which the air is made,
Are quite transparent; that is, we
    See through, but see no shade."

"And what are gases, ma?"
    "Fluids, which, if we squeeze
In space too small, will burst with force."
    "And what are fluids, please?"

"Fluids are what will flow,
    And gases are so light
That, when we give them room enough,
    They rush with eager flight."

"What gases, dear mamma,
    Make up the air or wind?"
"'Tis oxygen and nitrogen
    That chiefly there we find;

"And when the air is full
    Of oxygen, we're gay,
But when there's not quite enough,
    We're dull or faint away."

❧ Leila Lee

CONVERSATION UPON ICE

MOTHER AND DAUGHTER

"Come, dear," said Mrs. Jones one day,
    To Jane, her little daughter,
"Come, look at this large block of ice,
    Now floating in the water!

"You could not lift it from the ground,
    If you should try all day,
And yet, like a mere feather, now,
    You see it float away."

"Oh, yes, mamma, it does seem strange,
    That it should never sink,
Why that large block of ice should float,
    I'm sure I cannot think.

"How very kind it is in God
    To freeze the waters so,
That on the top the ice remains
    And cannot sink below!

"For, while our winters are so cold,
    How short a time 'twould take
To form one solid mass of ice,
    In river, pond, or lake!

"And thus, from year to year, mamma,
    Winter would ever reign,
For such a mass could never melt
    When summer came again.

"But tell me how the ice is formed,
    And what can make it float
Upon the surface of the lake,
    Just like a little boat?"

"Our Heavenly Father, Jane, has filled
    With bubbles full of air,
Each lump of ice—and we may see
    His goodness everywhere.

"The air expands within the ice,
    Just as its Maker pleases,

And rarifies to make it light,
    Whene'er the water freezes.

"Thin cakes thus form in layers, Jane,
    As you may often see
One ring within another, round
    The body of a tree,

"And thus 't is piled from week to week,
    While Jack Frost is about,
Until the men with horses come,
    To float the treasure out."

"And what a luxury, mamma,
    These large ice blocks will be
When summer comes, and we again
    Such sultry weather see!

"Last August, I remember well,
    When I came home from school,
How good the water used to taste,
    With ice to make it cool.

"And then, you know, we used to have
    Our butter hard and nice,
Our cake kept cool, and fish, and meat,
    Preserved with lumps of ice."

"Yes, dearest, God is ever kind—
    How constant is his care!
He gives not only food and drink,
    And clothes for us to wear,—

"But happy homes with luxuries filled,
    And this bright world of ours
Is stored with precious gifts of love,
    Abundant fruits and flowers,

"To gratify the taste of man,
    And fill his heart with joy;
Then, should not grateful thoughts of God
    Each passing hour employ?"

"Yes, dear mamma, for warbling birds
    Send up their sweetest lays,
To thank Him for his gifts of love,
    And we should offer praise

"To the great God, our dearest friend,
    Who lives and reigns above;
Will you not pray to Him, mamma,
    To fill my heart with love?"

John Townsend Trowbridge

DARIUS GREEN AND HIS FLYING-MACHINE

If ever there lived a Yankee lad,
Wise or otherwise, good or bad,
Who, seeing the birds fly, didn't jump
With flapping arms from stake or stump,
    Or, spreading the tail
    Of his coat for a sail,
Take a soaring leap from post or rail,
    And wonder why
    He couldn't fly,
And flap and flutter and wish and try,—
If ever you knew a country dunce
Who didn't try that as often as once,
All I can say is, that's a sign
He never would do for a hero of mine.

An aspiring genius was D. Green:
The son of a farmer,—age fourteen;
His body was long and lank and lean,—
Just right for flying, as will be seen;
He had two eyes as bright as a bean,
And a freckled nose that grew between,
A little awry;—for I must mention
That he had riveted his attention
Upon his wonderful invention,
Twisting his tongue as he twisted the
        strings,
And working his face as he worked the
        wings,
And with every turn of gimlet and screw
Turning and screwing his mouth round
        too,
    Till his nose seemed bent
    to catch the scent,
Around some corner, of new-baked pies,

And his wrinkled cheeks and his
        squinting eyes
Grew puckered into a queer grimace,
That made him look very droll in
        the face,
    And also very wise.

And wise he must have been, to do more
Than ever a genius did before,
Excepting Daedalus of yore
And his son Icarus, who wore
    Upon their backs
    Those wings of wax
He had read of in the old almanacs.
Darius was clearly of the opinion,
That the air was also man's dominion,
And that, with paddle or fin or pinion,
    We soon or late
    Should navigate
The azure as now we sail the sea.
The thing looks simple enough to me;
    And, if you doubt it,
Hear how Darius reasoned about it:

  "The birds can fly,
    an' why can't I?
    Must we give in,"
    says he with a grin,
  "'T the bluebird an' phoebe
    Are smarter'n we be?
Jest fold our hands, an' see the swaller
An' blackbird an' catbird beat us holler?
Does the leetle, chatterin', sassy wren,
No bigger'n my thumb, know more
        than men?

Jest show me that!
   Er prove 't the bat
Hez got more brains than's in my hat,
An' I'll back down, an' not till then!"

He argued further: "Ner I can't see
What's th' use o' wings to a bumble-bee,
Fer to git a livin' with, more'n to me;—
   Ain't my business
   Importanter'n his'n is?
   That Icarus
   Was a silly cuss,—
Him an' his daddy Daedalus;
They might 'a' knowed wings made o' wax
Wouldn't stan' sun-heat an' hard whacks:
   I'll make mine o' luther,
   Er suthin' er other."

And he said to himself, as he tinkered
      and planned:
"But I ain't goin' to show my hand
To nummies that never can understand
The fust idee that's big an' grand.
   They'd 'a' laft an' made fun
O' Creation itself afore 'twas done!"
So he kept his secret from all the rest,
Safely buttoned within his vest;
And in the loft above the shed
Himself he locks, with thimble and thread
And wax and hammer and buckles and
      screws,
And all such things as geniuses use;—
Two bats for patterns, curious fellows!
A charcoal-pot and a pair of bellows;
An old hoop-skirt or two, as well as
Some wire, and several old umbrellas;
A carriage-cover, for tail and wings;
A piece of harness; and straps and strings;
   And a big strong box,
   In which he locks
These and a hundred other things.

His grinning brothers, Reuben and Burke
And Nathan and Jotham and Solomon,
      lurk
Around the corner to see him work,—
Sitting cross-leggéd, like a Turk,
Drawing the waxed-end through with a
      jerk,
And boring the holes with a comical quirk
Of his wise old head, and a knowing
      smirk.
But vainly they mounted each other's
      backs,
And poked through knot-holes and pried
      through cracks;
With wood from the pile and straw from
      the stacks
He plugged the knot-holes and calked the
      cracks;
And a bucket of water, which one would
      think
He had brought up into the loft to drink
   When he chanced to be dry,
   Stood always nigh,
   For Darius was sly!
And, whenever at work he happened to
      spy

At chink or crevice a blinking eye,
He let a dipper of water fly:
Take that! an', ef ever ye git a peep,
Guess ye'll ketch a weasel asleep!"
   And he sings as he locks
   His big strong box:

"The weasel's head is small an' trim,
An' he is leetle an' long an' slim,
An' quick of motion an' nimble of limb,
   An', if yeou'll be
   Advised by me,
Keep wide awake when ye're ketchin'
      him!"

So day after day
He stitched and tinkered and hammered
    away,
  Till at last 'twas done,—
The greatest invention under the sun!
"An' now," says Darius, "hooray fer some
    fun!"

  'Twas the Fourth of July,
   and the weather was dry,
And not a cloud was on all the sky,
Save a few light fleeces, which here and
    there,
  Half mist, half air,
Like foam on the ocean went floating by,—
Just as lovely a morning as ever was seen
For a nice little trip in a flying-machine.

Thought cunning Darius, "Now I shan't
    go
Along 'ith the fellers to see the show:
I'll say I've got sich a terrible cough!
An' then, when the folks 'ave all gone off,
  I'll hev full swing
   fer to try the thing,
An' practyse a little on the wing."

"'Ain't goin' to see the celebration?"
Says brother Nate. "No; botheration!
I've got sich a cold—a toothache—I—
My gracious!—feel's though I should fly!"
  Said Jotham, "Sho!
  guess ye better go."
  But Darius said, "No!
Shouldn't wonder 'f yeou might see me,
    though,
'Long 'bout noon, ef I git red
O' this jumpin', thumpin' pain 'n my
    head."
For all the while to himself he said,
  "I tell ye what!
I'll fly a few times around the lot,
To see how 't seems, then soon's I've got
The hang o' the thing, ez likely's not,

I'll astonish the nation,
  an' all creation,
By flyin' over the celebration!
Over their heads I'll sail like an eagle;
I'll balance myself on my wings like a
    sea-gull;
I'll dance on the chimbleys; I'll stan' on
    the steeple;
I'll flop up to winders, an' scare the
    people!
I'll light on the libbe'ty-pole, an' crow;
An' I'll say to the gawpin' fools below,
  'What world's this 'ere
   that I've come near?'
Fer I'll make 'em b'lieve I'm a chap f'm
    the moon;
An' I'll try a race 'ith their ol' balloon!"

  He crept from his bed;
And, seeing the others were gone, he said,
"I'm a-gittin' over the cold 'n my head."
  And away he sped,
To open the wonderful box in the shed.

His brothers had walked but a little way,
When Jotham to Nathan chanced to say,
"What on airth is he up to, hey?"
"Don'o',—the' 's suthin' er other to pay,
Er he wouldn't 'a' stayed to hum to-day."
Says Burke, "His toothache's all 'n his eye!
He never'd miss a Fo'th-o'-July,
Ef he hedn't got some machine to try."
Then Sol, the little one, spoke: "By darn!
Le's hurry back, an' hide 'n the barn,
An' pay him fer tellin' us that yarn!"
"Agreed!" Through the orchard they
    creep back,
Along by the fences, behind the stack,
And one by one, through a hole in the
    wall,
In under the dusty barn they crawl,
Dressed in their Sunday garments all;
And a very astonishing sight was that,
When each in his cobwebbed coat and hat

Came up through the floor like an
     ancient rat.
   And there they hid;
   and Reuben slid
The fastenings back, and the door undid.
"Keep dark!" said he,
"While I squint an' see what the' is to
     see."

As knights of old put on their mail,—
   From head to foot
   an iron suit,
Iron jacket and iron boot,
Iron breeches, and on the head
No hat, but an iron pot instead,
   And under the chin the bail,—
(I believe they called the thing a helm)—
And, thus accoutred, they took the field,
Sallying forth to overwhelm
The dragons and pagans that plagued the
     realm;
   So this modern knight
   prepared for flight,
Put on his wings and strapped them
     tight,—
Jointed and jaunty, strong and light,—
Buckled them fast to shoulder and hip,—
Ten feet they measured from tip to tip!
And a helm had he, but that he wore,
Not on his head, like those of yore,
   But more like the helm of a ship.

   Hush!" Reuben said,
   "he's up in the shed!
He's opened the winder,—I see his head!
   He stretches it out, an' pokes it about,
Lookin' to see 'f the coast is clear,
   An' nobody near;—
Guess he don'o' who's hid in here!
He's riggin' a spring-board over the sill!
Stop laffin', Solomon!   Burke, keep still!
He's a climbin' out now—Of all the
     things!

What's he got on? I van, it's wings!
An' that 'other thing? I vum, it's a tail!
An' there he sets like a hawk on a rail!
Steppin' careful, he travels the length
Of his spring-board, and teeters to try its
     strength.
Now he stretches his wings, like a
     monstrous bat;
Peeks over his shoulder, this way an' that,
Fer to see 'f the' 's any one passin' by;
But the' 's on'y a ca'f an' a goslin' nigh."
They turn up at him a wonderin' eye,
To see—The dragon! he's goin' to fly!
Away he goes!   Jimminy! what a jump!
   Flop—flop—an' plump
   to the ground with a thump!
Flutt'rin' an' flound'rin', all 'n a lump!"

As a demon is hurled by an angel's spear,
Heels over head, to his proper sphere,—
Heels over head, and head over heels,
Dizzily down the abyss he wheels,—
So fell Darius. Upon his crown,
In the midst of the barn-yard, he came
     down,
In a wonderful whirl of tangled strings,
Broken braces and broken springs,
Broken tail and broken wings,
Shooting-stars, and various things,—
Barn-yard litter of straw and chaff,
And much that wasn't so sweet by half.
Away with a bellow fled the calf,
And what was that? Did the gosling laugh?
   'Tis a merry roar
From the old barn-door,
And he hears the voice of Jotham crying;
"Say, D'rius! how de yeou like flyin'?"

Slowly, ruefully, where he lay,
Darius just turned and looked that way,
As he stanched his sorrowful nose with
     his cuff,
"Wal, I like flyin' well enough,"

He said; "but the' ain't sich a thunderin'
     sight
O' fun in 't when ye come to light."
I just have room for the MORAL here:
And this is the moral,—Stick to your
     sphere;

Or, if you insist, as you have the right,
On spreading your wings for a loftier
     flight,
The moral is—Take care how you light.

&❧ *M. E. B.*

TEDDY THE TEAZER: A MORAL STORY
WITH A VELOCIPEDE ATTACHMENT

He wanted a velocipede,
     And shook his saucy head;
He thought of it in day time,
     He dreamed of it in bed,
He begged for it at morning,
     He cried for it at noon,
And even in the evening
     He sang the same old tune.

He wanted a velocipede!
     It was no use to say
He was too small to manage it,
     Or it might run away,
Or crack his little occiput,
     Or break his little leg—
It made no bit of difference,
     He'd beg, and beg, and beg.

He wanted a velocipede,
     A big one with a gong
To startle all the people,
     As they saw him speed along;
A big one, with a cushion,
     And painted red and black,
To make the others jealous
     And clear them off the track.

He wanted a velocipede,
     The largest ever built,
Though he was only five years old
     And wore a little kilt,

And hair in curls a-waving,
     And sashes by his side,
And collars wide as cart-wheels,
     Which hurt his manly pride!

He wanted a velocipede
     With springs of burnished steel;
He knew the way to work it—
     The treadle for the wheel,
The brake to turn and twist it,
     The crank to make it stop,
My! hadn't he been riding
     For days, with Jimmy Top?

He wanted a velocipede!
     Why, he was just as tall
As six-year-old Tom Tucker,
     Who wasn't very small!
And feel his muscle, will you?
     And tell him, if you dare,
That he's the sort of fellow
     To get a fall, or scare?

They got him a velocipede;
     I really do not know
How they could ever do it,
     But then, he teased them so,
And so abused their patience,
     And dulled their nerves of right,
That they just lost their senses
     And brought it home one night.

They bought him a velocipede—
　　O woe the day and hour!
When proudly seated on it,
　　In pomp of pride and power,
His foot upon the treadle,
　　With motion staid and slow
He turned upon his axle,
　　And made the big thing go.

Alas, for the velocipede!
　　The way ran down a hill—
The whirling wheels went faster,
　　And fast, and faster still,
Until, like flash of rocket,
　　Or shooting star at night,
They crossed the dim horizon
　　And rattled out of sight.

So vanished the velocipede,
　　With him who rode thereon;
And no one, since that dreadful day,
　　Has found out where 'tis gone!
Except a floating rumor
　　Which some stray wind doth blow.
When the long nights of winter
　　Are white with frost and snow,
Of a small fleeting shadow,
　　That seems to run astray
Upon a pair of flying wheels,
　　Along the Milky Way.

And this they think is Teddy!
　　Doomed for all time to speed—
A wretched little phantom boy,
　　On a velocipede!

❧ *Amos Russel Wells*

THE SONG OF THE LAWN-MOWER

'Twas the gayest lawn-mower that ever was seen,
Its body was red and its handle was green.
It ran on the lawn for most of the day,
And oh! how it rattled and clattered away!
It had a wide mouth and a long, twisted tongue,
And this is the song that the lawn-mower sung:

"Ke-clickety, clickety, clickety, klot!
The work, it is hard, and the day, it is hot.
But Susie will like it, the dear little lass;
How happy she is in the newly cut grass!
It's good for her tennis and good for croquet,
And gladly for Susie I'll labor away
　　With my clickety, clickety, klot!

"Ke-clickety, clickety, clickety, klot!
The work, it is hard, and the day, it is hot,
And Charley, the lad who is pushing me now,
He carries a terrible frown on his brow.
For Charley is lazy and Charley's a shirk,
But spite of it all I must stick to my work
　　With my clickety, clickety, klot!

"Ke-clickety, clickety, clickety, klot!
The work, it is hard, and the day, it is hot,
But all of the sparrows are grateful to me,
And all of the robins are coming, you see.
The crickets and worms they can easily spy,
So they pounce on their dinner when I have gone by
    With my clickety, clickety, klot!

"Ke-clickety, clickety, clickety, klot!
The work, it is hard, and the day, it is hot,
And down in the grass, when I listen, I hear
The grasshoppers squeaking, half crazy with fear.
The ants and the worms and the katydids dread
To hear me come clattering on overhead
    With my clickety, clickety, klot!

"Ke-clickety, clickety, clickety, klot!
The work, it is hard, and the day, it is hot.
O Charley, and crickets, and ants, and the rest,
I'd like to please all, but I'm doing my best.
As long as I work I am happy and gay,
And so keep pegging and pegging away
    With my clickety, clickety, klot!"

&* *John Godfrey Saxe*

HOW CYRUS LAID THE CABLE
A Ballad

Come, listen all unto my song;
    It is no silly fable;
'T is all about the mighty cord
    They call the Atlantic Cable.

Bold Cyrus Field he said, says he,
    I have a pretty notion
That I can run a telegraph
    Across the Atlantic Ocean.

Then all the people laughed, and said,
    They'd like to see him do it;
He might get half-seas-over, but
    He never could go through it;

To carry out his foolish plan
    He never would be able;
He might as well go hang himself
    With his Atlantic Cable!

But Cyrus was a valiant man,
    A fellow of decision;
And heeded not their mocking words,
    Their laughter and derision.

Twice did his bravest efforts fail,
    And yet his mind was stable;
He wa'n't the man to break his heart
    Because he broke his cable.

"Once more, my gallant boys!" he cried;
  "*Three times*!—you know the fable,—
  (I'll make it *thirty*," muttered he,
    "But I will lay the cable!")

Once more they tried,—hurrah! hurrah!
  What means this great commotion?
The Lord be praised! the cable's laid
  Across the Atlantic Ocean!

Loud ring the bells,—for, flashing
    through
  Six hundred leagues of water,
Old Mother England's benison
  Salutes her eldest daughter!

O'er all the land the tidings speed,
And soon, in every nation,
They'll hear about the cable with
Profoundest admiration!

Now long live James, and long live Vic,
And long live gallant Cyrus;
And may his courage, faith, and zeal
With emulation fire us;

And may we honor evermore
The manly, bold, and stable;
And tell our sons, to make them brave,
How Cyrus laid the cable!

  Gertrude Heath

THE BIRD AND THE WIRES

'Twas a cold, little sparrow came my way,
  Sing hey! sing ho! little bird.
And what goes on the world, I pray?
  "Speak low, O low," said the bird.
"O I sit on the wires, and under my feet
 Go words of sorrow, O sad! O sweet!"
  Speak soft, speak low, little bird.

 Now tell me the words that the strange wires say,
 O sweet, O cold little stray:
"Says one: 'Our mother is lying dead.'
 Another: 'Our Julia to-day is wed.'
 And again: 'Rejoice, for a son is born.'
 And another: 'I only am left forlorn.'
 And the wires they tremble beneath my feet
 And over and over the words repeat.
 For now 'tis a smile, and now 'tis a sigh
 That under my feet goes hurrying by,
 'Tis a queer old world I have often heard.
 Sing hey! sing ho!" said the wise little bird.

Josephine Preston Peabody

THE JOURNEY

I never saw the hills so far,
And blue, the way the pictures are;

And flowers, flowers, growing thick,
But not a one for me to pick!

The land was running from the train,
All blurry through the window-pane;

And then it all looked flat and still,
When up there jumped a little hill!

I saw the windows, and the spires,
And sparrows sitting on the wires;

And fences running up and down;
And then we cut straight through a town.

I saw a valley like a cup;
And ponds that twinkled, and dried up;

I counted meadows that were burnt;
And there were trees, and then there
      weren't!

We crossed the bridges with a roar,
Then hummed the way we went before.

And tunnels made it dark and light
Like open-work of day and night;

Until I saw the chimneys rise,
And lights, and lights, and lights, like
      eyes;

And when they took me through the
      door,
I heard it all begin to roar.

I thought—as far as I could see—
That everybody wanted me!

Anne L. Huber

THE LOCOMOTIVE

There goes the train for Harlem,
    It is moving very slow;
The locomotive puffs and blows,
    Just so, just so, just so.

Now they are going faster,
    Don't you see, don't you see, don't
      you see;
I think the people in the cars
    Will soon at Harlem be.

The bell rings, the whistle screams,
    What an awful noise they make;
And now they're near the depot,
    And down goes every brake.

Oh! what a cloud of smoke;
    Now the train is coming back,
Almost like a streak of lightning;
    Look out there, clear the track!

WHAT THE TRAIN RAN OVER

When the train came shrieking down,
  Did you see what it ran over?
I saw heads of golden brown,
  Little plump hands filled with clover.
Yes, I saw them, boys and girls,
  With no look or thought of flitting,
Not a tremble in their curls;—
  Where the track runs they were
    sitting.

From the windows of the train
  I could see what they were doing:
I could see their faces, plain;
  Some with dreamy eyes pursuing
Flight of passing cloud or bird;
  Others childish ditties flinging
On the air,—I almost heard
  What the song was they were singing.

They were well-known faces, too;
  Do you marvel that I shiver
As I picture them to you
  Playing there beside the river?
With them I myself have played
  On that very spot. I wonder
Why I never was afraid
  Of the coming railway-thunder.

Little sunburnt, barefoot boys
  In the shallow water wading,
Sea-birds scattering with your noise,
  Ragged hats your rogue-looks shading,
Will your sparkling eyes upon
  Yonder waves again flash never?
Is your heartsome laughter gone
  From this tired old world forever?

Dimpled Ruth, with brow of snow,—
  Never thought I to outlive her,
While we watched the white boats go
  Up and down the small-tide river,
Past dark steeps of juniper,
  Ever widening, ever flowing
To the sea; I mourn for her,
  Gone so far beyond my knowing!

Well, the cruel train rolls on.
  What! your eyes with tears are filling
For my pretty playmates gone?
  Child, I am to blame for chilling
All your warm young fancies so:
  There are real troubles, plenty.
They lived—forty years ago;
  And the road has run here twenty.

And those children,—I was one,—
  Busy men and women, wander
Under life's midsummer sun.
  One or two have gone home yonder
Out of sight. But still I see
  Golden heads amid the clover
On the railway-track; to me
  This is what the train runs over.

Malcolm Douglas

BABY ON THE RAILROAD

Baby's on the railroad—click-click-click-click-click—
Those are flat cars going by with Philadelphia brick—
Click-click-click-click-click-click-click—there, the last one's past!
Bumpety-bumpety—that's a switch—and now we're off at last,
With a-chick-a-choo-a-chick-a-choo-a-chick-a-chick-a-choo,
And the tootle on the choo-choo screaming zip-a-zip-a-hoo!
See the horsey-worseys scatter, kicking up their heels;
There's a piggy-wiggy running—goodness, how he squeals!
Rumble-umble—that's a bridge—and glug-a-glug-a-glug—
That's a tunnel in which one'll have a chance to hug!
Creepy-weepy—Sleepy-weepy—this train goes right through,
With a-chick-a-choo-a-chick-a-choo-a-chick-a-chick-a-choo,
And lots of more a-chick-a-choos, until the brakemen shout:
"Laststationdreamyweamypassengersallout!"

Mrs. S. C. Stone

THE PUNJAUBS OF SIAM

"Toot, toot!" puffed Mrs. Punjaub,
   Loud trumpeting with fear,
"I do believe what they call '*men*'
   Have been invading here!
And that they've spun their railroad,—
   There's so much talk about,—
Right through our quiet jungle
   I haven't, now, a doubt!"

Thus spake a lady elephant
   In her own far Siam;
But Mr. Punjaub bore the news
   Just like a ponderous lamb.

He laid his ears back lightly
   As though he barely heard,
And took a second bite of tree
   Before he spoke a word.

"These so-called men are pigmies!
   Pray, what can creatures do

Who have no tusks, nor even trunks,
   Who're so inferior, too?
Once let them show their faces here—
   I'll scatter them like chaff!"
And then he smiled a lordly smile;
   She laughed a wifely laugh.

They really quite enjoyed their fun,
   So pleasant 'tis to feel
Superior to some weaker sort,
   And turn upon one's heel!

Till, one day, through their solitudes
   There pierced a dreadful screech!
When, Mrs. Punjaub, fainting, caught
   The nearest branch in reach!

Right down upon their silent haunts
   There tore a shrieking train;
At which it seemed Punjaub, himself,
   Would never breathe again!

One moment thus he quailed, and then
  On that fast-flying train
He strove to turn; but it had passed,
  And all was still again.

The Punjaubs caught each other's eyes;
  They winked, but did not speak;
Since Punjaub hardly would have told
  His knees felt rather weak.
Though what to say they did not know,
  Just what to do they did:
With one accord they galloped off
  And straightway went and hid.

But Punjaub soon began to scold
  And tear around and fret,
Declare he'd never been afraid
  Of any humbug, yet!
So, when that same invading train
  Came slowly shrieking back,
Old Punjaub thundered boldly down
  To storm along the track.

Nor would he leave the gleaming lines,—
  He roared: "This wild is mine!
And I shall go, or I shall stay,
  Whichever I incline!"

So pigmy man turned on his steam
  And laughed with sly aside:
"If that's your tune, old Juggernaut,
  We'll treat you to a ride!"

And, as the train rolled pointing on
  Straight towards big Punjaub's legs,
The cow-catcher soon tossed his weight
  Quite off those useful pegs.

Perhaps things wore an aspect new
  As, crouching like a dog,
The startled beast was whirled away
  At quite a lightning jog.

Unwilling though he were to ride,
  He dared not drop his feet,
And so he did the next best thing,—
  He humbly kept his seat.
But when the playful man was tired,
  And gave him half a chance,
Bewildered Punjaub found his feet
  And fled with frantic prance.

And, as he went, with baffled rage
  He pulled up mighty trees,
That so he might somehow secure
  His injured spirit's ease.
Great Punjaub never rode again;—
  The sun had scarcely set
Ere he had nailed a ticket up:—
"This Jungle is TO LET."

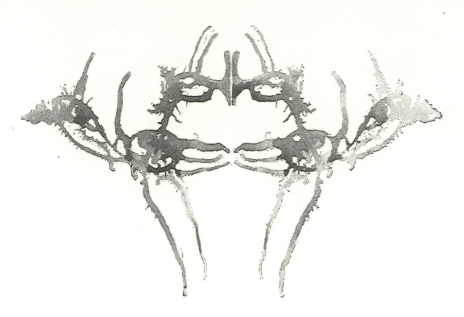

IN THE X-RAY

Cathode fairy,
Light and airy,
Sunny weather,
Two together,
Caring nothing why or whether
Flesh or blood or bone or feather
Shows on such a summer day
'Neath the Cathode's magic ray.

A GAS-LOG REVERIE

As I sit, inanely staring
   In the Gas-log's lambent flame,
Far away my fancy's faring
   To a land without a name,—
To the country of Invention,
   Where I roam in ecstasy,
Where all things are mere pretension,
   Nothing what is seems to be.

Folded in a calm serenic,
   On a jute-bank I recline,
Where mid moss of hue arsenic,
   Millinery flowers entwine.
Cambric blooms—glass-dew beshowered,
   Gay with colors aniline,
Ever eagerly devoured
   By the mild, condensed milch kine.

Now the scene idyllic changes
   From the meadows aniline,
And my faltering fancy ranges
   Down a dismal, deep decline,

Scene of some age past upheaval,
   Where no foot of man has fared,
To a Gas-log grove primeval,
   Where I find me, mute, and scared
Of—I know not—Goblins, Banshees,
   And the ancient Gas-trees toss
Gnarled and flickering giant branches,
   Hoary with asbestos moss.

Now I come to where are waving
   Painted palms, precisely planned,
Rearing trunks of cocoa shaving,
   By electric zephyrs fanned,
Soothing me with sound seraphic
   Till I sink into a swoon,
Dreaming cinematographic
   Dreams beneath an arc-light moon.

HOMEWORK AND HANDWORK

HER SAMPLER

By Anna B. Patten

To think Great-Grandmother could be
   A little girl of eight,
In pinafore of dimity,
   Or sunbonnet, sedate.
This Sampler, faded now and worn,
   Her childish fingers made;
Each stitch, of patient labor born,
   With careful touch was laid.

"Wrought in the eighth year of her age
   By Polly Simms," I read.
Ah, what a sober, little sage
   Our ancestor, indeed!
"In 1700—March—5th day—"
   These words she doth indite:—
"Children, your parents should obey,
   'T is seemly in God's sight!"

The Alphabet runs, row on row,
   In letters large and small;
The numbers—"1-2-3-"—below,
   "Etc.", ending all.
And then, the border-stitch around,
   So neat and so precise,
In faded crewels, on a ground
   Of cunning, quaint device.

Sometimes, I seem to see her there,
   With little, busy hands;
Her pretty, smoothly-parted hair
   Plaited in silky bands.
Sitting sedately on a stool,
   Close to her mother's side,
Sewing her "stent," by given rule,
   With watchful eye to guide.

Oh, did she ever romp and play,
   And get in mischief, too;
Or did she walk in formal way,
   As she was taught to do!
This little, Puritanic maid,
   Whom I can seem to see,
Sorting her silks, of somber shade,
   Her Sampler on her knee!

Anna B. Patten

HER SAMPLER

To think Great-Grandmother could be
    A little girl of eight,
In pinafore of dimity,
    Or sunbonnet, sedate.
This sampler, faded now and worn,
    Her childish fingers made;
Each stitch, of patient labor born,
    With careful touch was laid.

"Wrought in the eighth year of her age
    By Polly Simms," I read.
Ah, what a sober, little sage
    Our ancestor, indeed!
"In 1700—March—5th day—"
    These words she doth indite:—
"Children, your parents should obey,
    'Tis seemly in God's sight!"

The Alphabet runs, row on row,
    In letters large and small;
The numbers—"1-2-3"—below,
    "Etc.", ending all.

And then, the border-stitch around,
    So neat and so precise,
In faded crewels, on a ground
    Of cunning, quaint device.

Sometimes, I seem to see her there,
    With little, busy hands;
Her pretty, smoothly-parted hair
    Plaited in silky bands.
Sitting sedately on a stool,
    Close to her mother's side,
Sewing her "stent," by given rule,
    With watchful eye to guide.

Oh, did she ever romp and play,
    And get in mischief, too;
Or did she walk in formal way,
    As she was taught to do!
This little, Puritanic maid,
    Whom I can seem to see,
Sorting her silks, of somber shade,
    Her Sampler on her knee!

A GATHERING OF SAMPLER VERSES, C. 1790–1840

[Superscript letters indicate where the sampler writer could not fit all the words in the given space.—Karen Kilcup and Angela Sorby.]

❧ *Wrought by Betsy Gail, Marblehead, Massachusetts, c.1790 (9 years old)*

Plain as This Canvas was as Plain we Find
Unletterd Unadornd The Female Mind
No Nice Ideas Fill The Vacant Soul
No Graceful Colouring Animate The Wh^{ole}
With Close Attention Carefully Inwrought
Fair Education Paints The Pleasing Thought
Inserts The Curious Lines On Proper Gro^{und}
Completes The Work And Scatters Rose^{s}
$_{round}$

❧ *Wrought by Lucretia McClure, 1800 (age unknown)*

The little ant for one poor grain
Labours & tugs & strives
But we who have a Heaven to obtain
[unfinished]

❧ *Maker Unknown, 1801*

I cannot perceive This business design'd
For anything more Than to pleas a raw mind

❧ *Wrought by Elizabeth Lord, Dover, New Hampshire, 1801 (10 years old)*

Friendship's a name to few confined
The offspring of a noble Mind:
A generous warmth which fills the breast
And better felt than eer exprest.

❧ *Wrought by Mary Sluman, probably New Hampshire, 1802 (13 years old)*

I Sigh Not for Beauty Nor Languish for Wealth
But Grant Me Kind Providence Vertue and Health
Then Rich as a King and happy as they
My Days Shall Pass Sweetly and Swiftly awa^{y}

THE RURAL SCEN[E]

Sweet contemplation to pursue
Behold a rural scene in view
The bleating herds the lowing kine
The spreading oak the tow'ring pine
The air from noxious vapours free
Whilst squirrels trip from tree to tree
And the sweet songsters hover round
Fruit herbs and flowers enrich the ground
And each their various fruit produce
Some for delight and some for use
Behold in youth this scene and see
What nature's god hath given to the[e]
With wonder view his great designs
In which superior wisdom shines
Revere his name admire his love
And raise thy thoughts to worlds above

❧ *Wrought by Rachel Anderson, 1803 (10 years old)*

When I am dead   When this you see
And laid in Grave   Pray think on me
And all my flesh decayd   A poor young harmless maid

❧ *Wrought by Lydia Cogswell, Dover, New Hampshire,1804 (11 years old)*
   and Elizabeth Wentworth, Dover, New Hampshire, 1804 (13 years old)

When my short glass its latest sand shall run
And death approach to fright the lookers on
Softly may I sigh out my soul in air
Stand thou my pitying guardian angel there
Guide and conduct me through the Milky Way
To the bright region of eternal day
Then shall I Joy to leave this clay behind
And peace in better happier mansion find

❧ Wrought by Harriot Roach, Charleston, South Carolina, 1805 (age unknown)

1. Plain as this canvas was, as plain we find,
   Unlettered unadorned the female mind.
   No fine ideas fill the vacant soul,
   No graceful coloring animates the whole.

2. With close attention carefully inwrought,
   Fair education paints the pleasing thought,
   Inserts the curious line on proper ground,
   Completes the whole, and scatters flowers around.

3. My heart exults, while to the attentive eyes
   The curious needle spreads the enamell'd dyes,
   While varying shades the pleasing task beguile,
   My friends approve me, and my parents smile.

❧ Wrought by Mary Lithgow, Augusta, Maine, 1807 (9 years old)

A generous friendship no cold medium knows,
Warms with one love—with one resentment shows,
One should our interests, one our passions be,
My friend must slight the one that injures me.

❧ Wrought by Susan Prandall, 1808 (9 years old)

In fair proportion see the letters stand
A beauteous equal and impressive band
With eye of care we must their structure raise
A point too much the hand unskilled betrays
A thread misplaced their symmetry despoils
And the fond hope of excellence beguiles
So my sweet girl the path of life survey
And tread with caution o'er devious way
An erring step would blast thy budding fame
And with dishonor stamp my Mary's name
From rules of virtue shouldst thou careless stray
Nor sighs nor tears can e'er the forfeit pay
For female reputation wounded dies
No blest Panaceas this wide world supplies.

Wrought by Abigail Ayer, Essex, Massachusetts, 1808 (14 years old)

Of female arts in usefulness The needle far excels
the rest in ornament there is no device Affords adorn
ment half so nice While thus we practice every art
To adorn and grade our mortal part Let us with no
Less care devise To improve the mind that never dies

Wrought by Fanny Rand Hammatt, Boston, 1809 (age unknown)

If e'er you are by Grief oppressed
Repose it in a mother's breast
Unfold each secret of your heart
Use no disbuse[?] detest all art

Be candid open and sincere
A mother's love you cannot fear
She'll be a kind and faithful
Friend tell you your faults
And how to mend

Wrought by Sophia Catherine Bier, 1810 (age unknown)

Virtue and wit, with science join'd
Refine the manners, form the mind

And when with industry they meet
The female character's complete.

Maker Unknown, 1811

I live in a cottage & yonder it stands
And while I can work with these two honest hands
I'm as happy as those that have houses and lands.

Maker Unknown, 1813

The traveler if he chances to stray
May turn uncensored to his way
Polluted streams again are pure

The deepest wounds admit a cure,
But woman no redemption knows,
The wounds of honor never close.

Wrought by Eliza Catherine Gale, Charlestown, Massachusetts, 1813 (12 years old)

When Nature sheds her beauties rare
Oer tree and shrub, plant and gay parterre
Mark how the bee employs each hour
Extracting sweets from every flower
So gentle maid while youth shall last
Eer the gay morn of life is past
Select each sweet with care and art

To store the head and mend the heart
Happy the woman who can find
Constant amusement in her mind
Thrice happy is she whose chief enjoyment
Is placed in regular employment
In works of genius, use or taste
Nor lets one moment run to waste.

❧ *Wrought by Polly Warner, 1817 (11 years old)*

1. Ye sprightly are whose gentle mind incline
   To all that's joyous innocent and fine
   With admiration in your works are read
   The various texture of the twining thread.

2. Then let the needle whose unrivalled skill
   Exalts the needle above the noble quill.

❧ *Wrought by Ruth Davis, 1817 (11 years old)*

This work I did to let you see
What care my Papy took of me

❧ *Wrought by Ariadne Hackney, Mercer, Pennsylvania, 1817 (age unknown)*

Believe not each aspersing tongue
As most week persons do

But still believe the story wrong
Which ought not to be true.

❧ *Wrought by Ann Barriere, Baltimore, 1820 (8 years old; African American)*

May Heaven protect may God defend and
   fortune smile until time shall end
That every one prove Just and true shall ever be my prayer adieu

Count that day lost whose low [?] des‸ending sun views
from thy hand no virtuous actions done

❧ *Maker Unknown, 1821*

Convince the world that you are just and true
   Be just in all you say and all you do
What soever be your birth your sure to be
   A man of the first Magnitude to me.

❧ *Wrought by Louisa Gaffreau, New York City, 1821 (8 years old)*

A MA MÈRE

La rose mort en un instant
En un moment est flétrie
Mais ce que pour vous mon coeur sent
Ne finira qu'avec ma vie.

[TO MY MOTHER]

[The rose dies in an instant
In a moment it will fly
But all that my heart feels for you
Ends only when I die.]

[Editors' translation.]

❧ Wrought by Mary O. Randall, 1822 (age unknown)

Science adorns and virtue beams divine
How bright their radience when they both combine.

❧ Wrought by Emma Anna Gailliard, Charleston. South Carolina, 1823 (9 years old)

May virtue in your heart preside
May prudence all your actions guide

May peace attend your future hours
May love your pathway strew with
    flowers.

❧ Maker Unknown, 1824

No other care than this I knew
But perseverance brought me through.

❧ Wrought by Mary Wing Dodge, Ohio, 1826 (12 years old)

Swift to award a parent's cares,
    A parent's hopes to crown,
Roll on in peace ye blooming years
    With virtue and renown.

❧ Wrought by Mary B. Gove, Deering, New Hampshire, 1827 (13 years old)

As thus my hand with artful aim
Confirms the useful needle's fame
So may my actions every part
Be aimed alone to mend my heart.

❧ Wrought by Sarah Ann Engle, Pennsylvania, 1827 (age unknown) (partial)

By holiness and watchful care
    Be vain desire confined,
Guard O my soul against this snare,
    A carnal earthly mind.
Peace constant then serene and full,
    Would like a river flow.
Courage divine would arm my soul,
    And bear down every foe.

❧ Wrought by Eliza Longfellow, Machias, Maine, 1828 (9 years old)

Whence did the wondrous mystic
   Art arise
Of painting speech and speaking
   to the eyes

That we by tracing magic lines are
   taught
How both to colour and embody
   thought.

❧ Maker Unknown, before 1830

Let no one in tears pass my cot
To whom I can render relief

But may I make happy their lot
And dry up the source of their grief.

❧ Wrought by Sarah Ballinger, Ohio, 1830 (11 years old)

O what great need there is indeed
   To make good use of time
That thou mayst find true peace of mind
   Now in thy youthful prime

❧ Wrought by Mary Pets (or Marie Petz), Baltimore, 1831
   (about 10 years old; African American)

VIRTUE

Virtue is the chiefest beauty of
   the mind
The noblest ornament of human kind

Virtue's our safeguard and our
   guiding star
That stirs up reason when our senses [err]

❧ Wrought by Maria Wise, Ohio, 1837 (16 years old)

When this you see
Remember me
So many miles
We distent be

Remember me
As you pass by
As you are now
So wonce was I
As I am now
So you must be
Prepare for death
And follow me

❧ Wrought by Martha Jane Reynolds, Ohio, 1839 (8 years old)

With my needle and my thread
Which now appear so neat
Before I was quite nine years old
I did this work complete.
It will still show when I am old
Or laid into the tomb
How I employed my little hands
While I was in my bloom.

❧ Wrought by S. E. Wheeler, Ohio, 1840 (age unknown)

The Friend on whose bosom
We in sorrow repose
That Friend is the winters
Lone beautiful rose.

❧ Wrought by Eliza R. Johnson, Ohio, 1840 (age unknown)

Oh lonely is our old green fort, Perrysburg.
Where oft in days of old,
Our soldiers bravely fought
Gainst savage allies bold.

SARAH ORNE'S SAMPLER

Wrought ye year 1763.

A hundred years ago, and down to within a much later period, a young lady's education was not thought to be finished until she had wrought a sampler, that is, had made in cross-stitch, on canvas, with silk, the letters of the alphabet and her own name, and had added to this work a knowledge of hem-stitch, chain-stitch, feather-stitch, and sundry other stitches, all which were to be turned to practical use in making, ornamenting, and marking the piles of linen, often homespun, which were so toilfully and so exquisitely fashioned by hand before the days of sewing-machines and stencil-plates. In the search for centennial relics, one of these ancient samplers was found at North Andover. The name on it was unrecognized by anyone living in the neighborhood. Subsequently it was ascertained to have been that of the maternal great-grandmother of the Hon. George B. Loring. While the name was still a mystery, the following lines were written (1875), a tribute to the unknown embroiderer.
—Abbot Courant.

Of thee, O Sarah Orne,
That on bright summer morn
A hundred years agone,
Or dreary winter night,
The long hours' tedious flight
Didst mark in colors bright,

Token hath earth nor air,
Nor marble anywhere
Doth name or lineage bear,
Or memory record
When thou thy life's reward
Didst welcome from thy Lord.

Was thine sweet childish face
That bowed these lines to trace,
Ye year of heavenly grace,
Or matron's brow of care,
Or age's silver hair
And placid forehead fair?

Or wast thou maid forlorn,
The butt of jest and scorn,
O unknown Sarah Orne,
Thy figure straight and slim,
Thy faded eyes and dim
Straining to cross-stitch prim?

Whate'er thou wast or art,
Thou speakest to my heart,
To work some humble part
Upon time's canvas vast,
In colors that shall last
When centuries are past.

JANE AND HER NEEDLE

My shining needle! much I prize
Thy tender form and slender size,
   And well I love thee now;
Though when I first began to sew,
Before thy proper use I knew,
And often pricked my fingers too,
   A trial sore wert thou.
Then speed thee on my needle bright,
The love of thee makes labor light.

Oh, soon thy motions to control,
In collar, wristband, button-hole,
   My ready hand attains;
And with thee I can help to form,
Full many a garment stout and warm,
To shield from winter's wind and storm,
   The aged and the blind.
Then speed thee on my needle bright,
The love of thee makes labor light.

L. J. K.

FINGER LESSON

Now, fingers, stand up for your lessons;
The short one, the thick one, the tall,
The long one must put on the thimble;
The others should wear none at all.

But don't think you may ever be idle,
Or guess you'll have nothing to do;
You each must learn to be nimble
And do the work fitted for you.

Now, thumb and forefinger, attention!
The needle I put in your care.
Short finger, both you and your neighbor
To manage the thread you're the pair.

Left fingers, pay all close attention:
No needle or thread I've for you,
But what's just as needful in sewing
Is what you must every one do.

It is very, yes, very important
To hold the work even and true,
And so you must try to be careful,
For this work depends upon you.

Ten fingers, you've all had your lessons,
I pray you, remember them well;
Let none of you e'er be found napping—
How naughty that would be to tell.

🍀 *G. B. D.*

THE IDLE GIRL'S SERENADE

There is an idle girl, her name is Lazy
    Jane,
She's a dunce long ago, long ago,
At books, at work, and play all the same,
She is lazy and idle and slow.

Chorus—
Put away the needle and thread,
Go without supper to bed.
Oh, lazy Jane, how can you ever learn,
While you idle and trifle so?

Her clothes are all hanging in tatters and
    rags,
Her dress, oh, it is not very clean;
The buttons are all off her coat and her
    shoes;
Her sacque isn't fit to be seen.

Chorus—
Put away the needle and thread,
Go without supper to bed.
Oh, lazy Jane, how can you ever learn,
While you idle and trifle so?

Her hair is uncombed from morning till
    night;
Her apron is hanging in rags;
Her face and her hands for dirt are a
    sight.
Her hood all in tatters and tags.

Chorus—
Put away the needle and thread,
Go without supper to bed.
Oh, lazy Jane, how can you ever learn,
While you idle and trifle so?

🍀 *L .J. K.*

TRY, O TRY

O stitching is witching,
And hemming as well,
But what is distressing
Is turning a fell.
I'm sick of such seaming,
And ready to cry,
But I hear the word ringing,
"Try, little one, try;
Try, try; try, try."
I hear the word ringing,
"Try, little one, try."

And so I am striving,
As hard as can be.
To keep back my crying,
Just so I can see.
And may be with helping,
At last I shall learn
The worst fringy edges
Most neatly to turn.
"Try, try; try, try;"
I hear the word ringing,
"Try, little one, try."

ᐯᔑ Islay Walden

DEDICATED TO M.W.W., ON MAKING, FOR THE FIRST TIME, A SHIRT

Mary, my shirt is neatly made,
   Each stitch is in its proper place;
There's not a wrinkle to be seen.
   Nor basting thread that will deface.

I've criticised with all my might;
   I thought the button holes were
     shirked,
But I was struck with much surprise
   To find they all were neatly worked.

I turned it in and turned it out,
   I sought to find some fault with it;
I tried it on, and tried it off,
   I never had so neat a fit.

I think I see within it stitched,
   A figure of your daily life;
It surely tells that you will make,
   Some happy man a thrifty wife.

And now I speak unto the hand
   That never made a shirt before:—
Work hard to cultivate the mind,
   Then arduous task's will soon be o'er.

ᐯᔑ Rosa Graham

SOW, SEW, AND SO

Sow, sow, sow,
So the farmers sow!
Busy, busy, all the day,
While the children are at play,
Stowing, stowing close away
Baby wheat and rye in bed,
So the children may be fed,
   So, so, so.

Sew, sew, sew,
So the mothers sew!
Busy, busy, all the day,
While the children are at play,
Sewing, sewing fast away,
So the children may have frocks,
Trowsers, coats, and pretty socks,
   So, so, so,

Sew, sew, so,
So they sow and sew;
s, and o, and w,
This is what the farmers do;
Put an E, in place of o,
This is how the mothers sew,—
So they sow and sew for you,
So without the w,
   So, so, so.

Laura E. Richards

SEWING SONG
Air, "A Hundred Pipers and A' "

Oh, it's thread and needle and thimble, too.
  It's wax and scissors and emery, too.
O, wonderful, wonderful things I'll do,
  With my thread and needle and thimble, too.

I'll make a bag for my own Mamma.
  I'll hem a kerchief for dear Pappa;
And a doll I'll dress for our little wee Bess,
  With a frock and mantle and petticoat, too.

Oh, it's cutting and basting and hemming, too,
  It's stitching and felling and gathering, too;
There's really no end to the things I can do
  With my cutting and basting and gathering, too.

And oh, what pleasure to sing and sew.
  And feel I am helping Mamma, you know;
And still more pleasure beyond all measure,
  When work is finished and off I go!

Margaret Vandegrift

A SAD CASE

Miss Dorothea Dimpleton, whenever she went out,
Held in her neatly mittened hand a silken reticule;
When she went to shop, to market, or to visit all about,
She carried it, as if upon her way to sewing-school.
'Twas always full, and yet her dearest friends had never heard
What 'twas full of, so they all agreed her conduct was absurd.

Miss Dorothea Dimpleton had early learned to sew;
She could hem, and fell, and overseam, could gather and could gore;
And she said, "This is an art that every woman ought to know,
But, alas! my sex disdains to learn the useful any more!
Yet I will not be discouraged; I will do my small endeavor,
And perchance I may prevent the art from being lost forever!"

So she filled with pretty "hussifs" her ample reticule,
Each stocked with thimble, needlecase, and scissors all complete,
And she stopped the little maidens on their way from morning school,

And to each of them she kindly gave a "hussif" fresh and neat.
And the little maids said, "Thank you, Ma'am!" and curtseyed to the ground.
And then went and hid the "hussifs" where they seldom could be found.

Miss Dorothea Dimpleton felt very sure, at last,
That every little girl in town was sewing with a will;
And it was not till at least a year of feeling sure was past,
That she heard a truth so dreadful that it really made her ill:
Of all those lovely "hussifs" she had given in the place,
There had not been a needle in one single needle-case!

But that, you know, was years ago, before it had been said,
"Be sure you're right and" (please observe the "then") "*then* go ahead!"

&ℛ *William Oland Bourne*

THE BUSY KNITTER

Little Helen on her chair—
   Patiently at work was she,
And in ringlets fell her hair—
   Lovely did she seem to me.
     She was sitting,
     Knitting, knitting.

Busy little girl! thought I,
   How I love to see your skill!
I am half inclined to try,
   And I almost think I will!
     See her sitting,
     Knitting, knitting.

In a whirl the fingers fly
   First one needle, then the next!
She might with her mother vie;
   But for me, I am perplexed.
     She was sitting,
     Knitting, knitting.

Then a zig-zag cross this way,
   Then a curious whirl again—
How she makes the fingers play;
   It's no business for the men,
     To be sitting,
     Knitting, knitting.

Now the curious seam is made;
   How to do it I can't tell,
But the skill she has displayed
   Makes me think she does it well.
     She was sitting,
     Knitting, knitting.

Now the toe is closed and done—
   What a pretty sock is this!
It is knitting number one!
   Go and get your mother's kiss!
     She was sitting,
     Knitting, knitting.

Busy little girl! thought I,
   How I love to see your skill!
And the pleasure in her eye
   Made my heart with pleasure fill—
     Helen sitting,
     At her knitting.

THE KNITTING LESSON

Grandmother knows how a stocking grows,
Ribbing and purling and heels and toes;
Now she is teaching our little Rose.
  "Put in the needle,
    Throw over the thread,
Out with the needle, and off it goes!"

Grandmother's mouth gives a little twitch,
Watching so slyly the eager witch,
Ready to help at the smallest hitch.
  "Put in the needle,
    Throw over the thread,
Out with the needle, and there's the stitch!"

Grandmother sees in a misty dream,
Her eyes still fixed on the needles' gleam,
Pastured flocks and a gurgling stream—
  "Grandma! oh, we forgot the seam!"
  "Bring the thread forward,
The needle this side,
Then over—off—and we've made the seam."

Grandmother knows how a stocking grows,
Ribbing and purling and heels and toes;
Now she is teaching our little Rose.

Lucy Larcom

A LITTLE OLD GIRL

What is this round world to Prudence,
  With her round, black, restless eyes,
But a world for knitting stockings,
  Sweeping floors, and baking pies?

'T is a world that women work in,
  Sewing long seams, stitch by stitch;
Barns for hay, and chests for linen;
  'T is a world where men grow rich.

Ten years old is little Prudence;
  Ten years older still she seems,
With her busy eyes and fingers,
  With her grown-up thoughts and
    schemes.

Sunset is the time for candles;
  Cows are milked at fall of dew,
Beans will grow, and melons ripen,
  When the summer skies are blue.

Is there more than work in living?
　　Yes; a child must go to school.
And to meeting every Sunday;
　　Not a heathen be, or fool.

Something more has haunted Prudence
　　In the song of bird and bee,
In the low wind's dreamy whisper
　　Through the light-leaved poplar-tree.

Something lingers, bends above her,
　　Leaning at the mossy well;
Some sweet murmur from the meadows,
　　On the air some gentle spell.

But she will not stop to listen:——
　　May be there are witches yet!
So she runs away from beauty,
　　Tries its presence to forget.

'Tis the way her mother taught her;
　　Prudence is not much to blame.
Work is good for child or woman;
　　Childhood's jailer—'t is a shame!

Meanwhile at the romping children
　　Their grave heads the gossips shake;
Saying, with a smile for Prudence,
　　"What a good wife she will make!"

Louisa May Alcott

A SONG FROM THE SUDS

Queen of my tub, I merrily sing,
　　While the white foam rises high,
And sturdily wash, and rinse, and wring,
　　And fasten the clothes to dry;
Then out in the free fresh air they swing,
　　Under the sunny sky.

I wish we could wash from our hearts and
　　　　our souls
　　The stains of the week away,
And let water and air by their magic make
　　Ourselves as pure as they;
Then on the earth there would be indeed
　　A glorious washing day!

Along the path of a useful life
　　Will heart's-ease ever bloom;
The busy mind has no time to think
　　Of sorrow, or care, or gloom;
And anxious thoughts may be swept away
　　As we busily wield a broom.

I am glad a task to me is given
　　To labor at day by day;
For it brings me health, and strength, and
　　hope,
　　And I cheerfully learn to say,—
"Head, you may think; Heart, you may
　　feel;
　　But Hand, you shall work alway!"

BALLAD OF THE PLYMOUTH WASHING

When Captain Standish of Plymouth town
(Able and strong while the weak went down),
With the six good men left sound and well,
Labored for all, strange things befell!
Half o' the folk were under the snow;
Famine and fever had laid them low;
And the sick, too feeble for work or care,
Were a burden the seven men must bear:

Guardians, nurses, and serving-men,
They showed the stuff they were made of then!
Nothing too lowly they found to do,
Nor shirked to try when little they knew.
They cooked, they cleaned, and their rough hands tried
The tasks the women's had thrown aside.
They soothed and tended as best they might;
They mothered the orphaned babes at night.
They gathered the garments foul, forgot,
And linen stripped from the fever-cot,
And sturdily faced, as a foe at bay,
The toilsome terrors of washing-day!
Brows bent sternly and anxious eye,
Weapon unslung and sleeves rolled high,
Brawny back bent over the tub,
Great hands awkward to wring and rub,
And lean, strong arms in the sudsy snow
Tossing the linen to and fro—

Strange to the peering sick folks' eyes
Captain Standish in such a guise!
His sword-hand, used to grip o' the hilt,
Dealt but ill with a cradle-quilt.
Alack for the Dutch-wove white and blue,
Frayed where a hero's thumb went through!
Alack for the stitches, tiny as pearls,
Sewn in the shifts of the Deacon's girls!
The tender mother who set them there,
So fine for her dear little maids to wear,
Little might guess a soldier's hand
Should scrub the gathers from wrist and band,

Nor ever her housewife's soul could dream
That cruel rending of cloth and seam,
While, strong and steady, he hummed a strain
Of a marching air with a deep refrain.

Strong and steady, and yet, good lack!
He learned the ache of a wearied back.
He had rubbed right often his brightening blade,
Yet, work of a man 'gainst work of a maid,
Harder he found, by the strained arms' feel,
Clothes to cleanse than the fleckéd steel:
A maiden's lawns, fair, fine, and frail,
Than the warrior's helmet, sword and mail!

Bold Miles Standish, grim at your tub,
Down through the years we see you rub,
And the water that whitens the web you hold
Brightens your name till it shines like gold
Clear and clean o' the pride of war!
Was fame ever won at the wash before?

Never a care for praise or blame,
Never a thought of mock or shame,
Soldier and captain, brave o' the brave,
Drudging, ungrudging, to serve and save!

❧ *Amos Russel Wells*

PATENT APPLIED FOR

MY DEAR MR. CARPENTER:
    Please call at eight,
All prepared with your tools to mend my front gate.
The latch has been broken. And pray bring with you
Not one latch, but though it seem strange, sir, bring two.
For I have a notion. It's awkward, you know,
Half the time, when you pass a gateway, to throw
Your arm over the pickets, and fumble around
For a latch, out of sight. And now, sir, I've found
A remedy for this: *one latch on each side!*
There's a notion worth having! In fact, I've applied
For a patent upon it. Remember,—at eight,
With your tools, and *two latches.*
                        Yours,
                        J. ADDLE PATE.

✿ Amos Russell Wells

WHAT HE PROFESSES

I know a professor of Greek and of Latin;
His nouns and his verbs he is not at all pat in,
But he knows how to wield the plane, hammer, and saw,
He knows how to paint, how to etch and to draw,
  How to decorate dishes and satin.

He can play on the flute and the violin-cello,
He raises fine fruit, large and juicy and mellow,
He will write you a sonnet, an ode, or a play,
He will sing you a song in an elegant way;
  He's a very versatile fellow.

But I know a shrewd student whose impudent guess is,—
(To account for the way the professor digresses
From his Latin and Greek, art and farming unto),—
That these are the things the professor can *do*,
  While the classics he merely—*professes*!

✿ I. R.

GERMS OF GENIUS

My son is a genius. 'Tis easy to see,
By the drawings he makes on his slate
And all the fly-leaves of available books,
That his name in the land will be great.
His beasts have such horn, and his birds have such claw,

      Such carnivorous jaw,
      So capacious of maw,
Such archings of back, and such ponderous paw,
Such freedom from all anatomical law,
As the eye of a genius alone ever saw.
      And Gustave Doré
      In his night-marish way
Never pictured such terrible creatures as they;
For ichthyosauri or pliocene snakes
Would look gentle as doves by the drawings he makes.

Now some of the pictures of Rosa Bonheur
Are rather good animal drawings—for her;
              But *she* copies Nature's
              Mere external features,
And has no conception of these sorts of creatures;
And as for the paintings of Edwin Landseer,
With the endless and wearisome horses and deer,
              His feelings I spare;
              I forbear
              To compare
His pitiful portraits of badger and hare
With these masterly sketches, dashed off as they are,—
For no finish of antler or gloss upon hair
Can atone for the loss of their wildness of air,
From his smallest bull-pup with the impudent stare
To his biggest brass lion on Trafalgar Square.

Now here on the page of my latest review,
That I happened to leave but a moment or two,
What is it I find? A man full of dread,
              With a circular head
On a triangle body, with legs at the base,
              And arms with no joint in
              Horizontally pointing
Trifurcated ends out in opposite ways,
              Is receiving a blow
              From the blade of a foe
That cuts through the skull like a keel through the water;
              While a rectangle grin
              Shows the grim teeth within,
And the terrible slayer's delight in the slaughter.

The grouping is natural, the drawing correct;
That foreshortened arm has a striking effect;
But the malice and wrath on the face of the victor
Are what give the wonderful charm to the picture.
I will tear out this drawing and fold it away;
He shall have it again on that glorious day
When high on the walls of the Temple of Art
   The mighty cartoon is unfurled;
For if he goes on with his pencil in hand
   He will make a great mark in the world.

Author's note—not marked in poem, but referencing illustration 1: "Particular attention
is called to the masterly introduction of the other eye in the profile view."

THE ALPHABET

Little boys with pockets,
    Little boys with none,
Little bright-eyed lassies
    Gather, every one!
Crowd around me closely.
    Would you master books?
You must first discover
    How each letter looks.

A has a bar
    Where a fairy might ride;

B is a post
    With two loops at the side.

C might be round
    If a piece you would lend;

D is a buck-saw
    Standing on end.

E has a peg
    In the middle, they say;

F is an E
    With the bottom away.

G is like C,
    With a block on one end;

H has a seat
    That would hold you, depend.

I is so straight
    It would do for a prop;

J is a crook
    With a bar at the top.

K is a stick
    With a crotch fastened to it;

L is a roost,
    If the chickens but knew it.

M has four parts,
    As you quickly may see;

N the poor fellow!
    Is made out of three.

O is so round
    It would do for a hoop;

P is a stick
    With a top like a loop.

Q to be curly
    Is constantly trying;

R is like B,
    With the bottom loop flying.

S is a snake,
    All crooked and dread;

T is a pole
    With a bar for a head.

U it is plain,
    Would make a good swing;

V is as sharp
    As a bumble-bee's sting.

W ought
    To be called double-V;

X is a cross,
    As you plainly can see;

Y is just formed
    Like a V on a stand;

Z is the crookedest
    Thing in the land!

FAMILY TIES

&% Margaret Sangster

SOMETHING NEW

There's something new at our house—I'm s'prised you didn't know it;
It makes papa feel awful proud, although he hates to show it.
The thing is not so very big, but money couldn't buy it;
If any fellow thinks it could, I'd like to see him try it.

It's half a dozen things at once—a dove, a love, a flower;
Mamma calls it a hundred names, and new ones every hour;
It is a little music-box, with tunes for every minute;
You haven't got one at your house, and so you are not in it.

It puckers up its wee, wee mouth, as if it meant to whistle;
A gold mine weighed against it then were lighter than a thistle;
Papa said so the other night—I thought it sounded splendid,
And said it to myself until I fell asleep, and ended.

Of course you guessed it by this time—our gift that came from heaven;
Mamma declares the darling thing was by the angels given.
But then some folks are very slow, and some are stupid; maybe
I ought to say, right straight and plain, come home and see our baby!

&% Laura E. Richards

LITTLE OLD BABY

Little old baby, pretty old baby,
   Screams and cries at his little old bath,
Pours on the head of his little old mother
   All the full vials of baby wrath.

Little old baby, pretty old baby,
   If you could see just how queer you look,—
Arms and legs in a knot together,
   Face twisted up in a terrible crook,—

How you would straighten out every feature,
   Masculine vanity all aflame!
Fie! what a noise from a little wee creature!
   Did they abuse him! and *was* it a shame!

Little old baby, pretty old baby,
   Curls himself over and goes to sleep.
Ah! such is life, my little old baby,
   Sleep and forget it, or wake and weep!

LITTLE BROWN BABY

Little brown baby wif spa'klin' eyes,
   Come to yo' pappy an' set on his knee.
What you been doin', suh—makin' san' pies?
   Look at dat bib—you's ez du'ty ez me.
Look at dat mouf—dat's merlasses, I bet;
   Come hyeah, Maria, an' wipe off his han's.
Bees gwine to ketch you an' eat you up yit,
   Bein' so sticky an sweet—goodness lan's!

Little brown baby wif spa'klin' eyes,
   Who's pappy's darlin' an' who's pappy's chile?
Who is it all de day nevah once tries
   Fu' to be cross, er once loses dat smile?
Whah did you git dem teef? My, you's a scamp!
   Whah did dat dimple come f'om in yo' chin?
Pappy do' know you—I b'lieves you's a tramp;
   Mammy, dis hyeah's some ol' straggler got in!

Let's th'ow him outen de do' in de san',
   We do' want stragglers a-layin' 'roun' hyeah;
Let's gin him 'way to de big buggah-man;
   I know he's hidin' erroun' hyeah right heah.
Buggah-man, buggah-man, come in de do',
   Hyeah's a bad boy you kin have fu' to eat.
Mammy an' pappy do' want him no mo',
   Swaller him down f'om his haid to his feet!

Dah, now, I t'ought dat you'd hug me up close.
   Go back, ol' buggah, you sha'n't have dis boy.
He ain't no tramp, ner no straggler, of co'se;
   He's pappy's pa'dner an playmate an' joy.
Come to you' pallet now—go to yo' res';
   Wisht you could allus know ease an' cleah skies;
Wisht you could stay jes' a chile on my breas'—
   Little brown baby wif spa'klin' eyes!

Anna M. Pratt

A PROMISE

We won't forget the birthday
   Of a noble little boy
Till hatchets climb the cherry-trees
   And clap their hands for joy.
And we truly will remember
   That he didn't tell a lie,
Till cherry-stones
With moats and groans
   Devour a hatchet pie.

A. R. Wells

GOING! GOING!

Attention, good people! A baby I'm selling.
His folks are all tired of his crowing and yelling.
If a price that's at all within reason you'll pay,
You may have the young rascal, and take him away.
The Mountains have bid every gem in their store;
The Ocean has bid every pearl on its floor;
By the Land we are offered ten million of sheep,—
But we have no intention of selling so cheap!
Compared with his value our price is not high—
How much for a baby? what offer? who'll buy?

Katharine Forrest Hamill

THE NEW BROTHER

I.

Got a new kid in our house;
   'Bout gives me a fit,
The fuss that ev'rybody is
   A-making over it.
All 'long I've been the pet, you see,
   'Twas *me* they tried to please,
But now, this other fellow has
   Them all upon their knees!

II.

He's just about the ugliest!
   And really doesn't seem
Able to do another thing
   But double up and scream.
He's got no teeth, he's got no hair,—
   Worst curiosity!
I'd like some one to tell me *why*
   He counts for more than me!

THE WORLD-WIDE CONSOLATION

From north to south, from east to west,
    All over Christendom,
One consolation sure and blest
Is by each baby heart confessed,
    Though baby lips are dumb.

'Tis neither twang of harp or lute,
    Nor beat of noisy drum,
Nor squeak of fife, nor thrill of flute,
Nor silver rattle played to suit
    Nor ivory keys to thrum,

Nor barking dog, nor wailing cat,
    Nor cake of softest crumb,
New shoes, new toys, blue-ribboned hat,
These all fail Baby and fall flat
    But never—Baby's thumb!

When slumber shuns his willful eyes
    And nurse is cross and grum,
And things go wrong, and mother sighs,
For a brief moment Baby cries,
    Then hies him to his thumb!

Once in his red mouth safely set,
    Embraced by each small gum,
Though storms may rage and rulers fret,
Baby has consolation yet,
    That dear and faithful thumb!

Oh me! how would poor mothers fare,
    And how they would succumb,
Had not kind Nature, everywhere,
All the world over, taken care
    To give each babe a thumb!

LITTLE DORA'S SOLILOQUY

I tan't see what our baby boy is dood for, anyway:
He don' know how to walk or talk, he don' know how to play;
He tears up ev'ry single zing he posser-bil-ly tan,
An' even tried to break, one day, my mamma's bestest fan.
He's al'ays tumblin' 'bout ze floor, an' give us awful scares,
An' when he goes to bed at night, he never says his prayers.
On Sunday, too, he musses up my go-to-meetin' clothes,
An' once I foun' him hard at work a-pinc'in' Dolly's nose;
An' ze uzzer day zat naughty boy (now what you s'pose you zink?)
Upset a dreat big bottle of my papa's writin' ink;
An', 'stead of kyin' dood an' hard, as course he ought to done,
He laughed, and kicked his head 'most off, as zough he zough't was fun.
He even tries to reach up high, an' pull zings off ze shelf,
An' he's al'ays wantin' *you*, of course, jus' when you wants you'self.
I rather dess, I really do, from how he pulls my turls,
Zey all was made a-purpose for to 'noy us little dirls;
An' I wish zere wasn't no such zing as naughty baby boys—
Why—why, zat's him a-kyin' now; he makes a drefful noise.
I dess I better run and see, for if he has—boo-hoo!—
Felled down ze stairs and killed his-self, *whatever s-s-s'all I do!*

🍀 Anna C. Vincent

JAPANESE BABIES

A little bird sings from over the sea:
"I've been to a land that pleases me.
'Tis a fabulous land where babies don't cry
From the time they are born till the time they die.

You queer little baby, way over the sea,
Tell us, oh, tell us, how can it be,
Aren't Japanese baby clothes ever too tight?
Don't Japanese babies wake up in the night?

Do Japanese teeth come through without pain?
Or Japanese children tease babies in vain?
Don't Japanese pins have points that prick?
Won't Japanese colic make little folk sick?

You queer little baby, if secret there be
Send it, oh, send it way over the sea!
There is no such secret. Far off in Japan
Some babies *can* cry, and they'll prove that they can!

❧ Samuel W. Duffield

LITTLE BEAR

There lives with us an Indian—
    A Paw-knee, I declare—
And he utters dreadful war-whoops,
    And his name is Little Bear.

A braver foe in a battle,
    When his hands are in your hair,
There is none in all my knowledge
    Than this same Little Bear.

But when the firelight shining
    Lights the room up with its glare,
I often camp on the hearth-rug,
    Good friends with Little Bear.

And I'm very sure I should miss him
    If ever he wasn't there—
This irrepressible Indian,
    By the name of Little Bear!

❧ Ella Wheeler Wilcox

THE AH-GOO TONGUE

The queerest languages known to man,
Sanskrit, Hebrew, Hindoostan,
Are all translated and made as free
And comprehensive as A B C.

Yet the oldest language talked or sung,
The strange mysterious Ah Goo tongue,
The royal language of Babyland
No man living can understand.

Every soul in the world to-day
Was one time anchored in Babyland Bay,
And quarantined there for a year or more
Before he even could step on shore.

And everybody in Babyland Bay
Talks the Ah Goo tongue, so people say,
But once on land—why not a word
Do they understand of it when 'tis heard.

For the fairy rulers of Babyland
Who guard the kingdom on every hand,
Have willed that no one shall keep the
    key
Who crosses into the Grownup Sea.

So the sweet court language has never
    been made
A common parlance of strife or trade,
But is kept in the kingdom where natives
    come
Versed in the language of Babydom.

They are all of them royal and that is how
The Grown-up people all kneel and bow,
When they hear that language talked or
    sung—
The strange mysterious Ah Goo tongue.

"A Lady of Boston" [Nancy Sproat]

PUDDING AND MILK

The sun is set, the schools are done,
The boys and girls are all come home;
And now they want their supper quick,
Come, Betty, get the pudding-stick—
And see! the cows have left the dale,
Come, Peggy, run and catch your pail,
And milk as fast as e'er you can,
And strain it in the largest pan:
Now get some bowls and dip it out,
And drop the pudding all about.
Come now, dear children, come and eat,
Your pudding's hot, your milk is sweet.
Then quietly retire up stairs,
With grateful hearts, and fervent prayers;
Undress, and go to bed and sleep,
Till morning light begins to peep.

Allen G. Bigelow

MY SWEETHEART

I'm in love with a fair little maiden—
   With her eyes, with her lips, with her hands,
With her dozens of dear little dimples;—
      And although she's petite
      On her sweet little feet,
   'T is a wonder to me how she stands.

And she loves me, this dear little maiden;
   And her hands, and her eyes, and her lips,
And her dimples, all giving me welcome—
      In a sweet, artless way
      Have their say, every day,
   As to meet me she lovingly trips.

Will she wed me, this sweet little maiden?
   —Bless you, no! That she never will do.
But, when I have told you the reason,
      I haven't a fear
      'T will appear to you queer;
   For I'm thirty—while she's only two!

THE CHILDREN'S HOUR

Between the dark and the daylight,
    When the night is beginning to lower,
Comes a pause in the day's occupation,
    That is known as the children's hour.

I hear in the chamber above me
    The patter of little feet,
The sound of a door that is opened,
    And voices soft and sweet.

From my study I see in the lamplight,
    Descending the broad hall stair,
Grave Alice, and laughing Allegra,
    And Edith with golden hair.

A whisper and then a silence:
    Yet I know by their merry eyes,
They are plotting and planning together,
    To take me by surprise.

A sudden rush from the stairway,
    A sudden raid from the hall!
By three doors left unguarded
    They enter my castle wall!

They climb up into my turret
    O'er the arms and back of my chair;
If I try to escape, they surround me,
    They seem to be everywhere.

They almost devour me with kisses,
    Their arms about me entwine,
Till I think of the Bishop of Bingen
    In his Mouse-Tower on the Rhine!

Do you think, O blue-eyed banditti,
    Because you have scaled the wall,
Such an old mustache as I am
    Is not a match for you all?

I have you fast in my fortress
    And will not let you depart,
But put you down in the dungeon
    In the round-tower of my heart.

And there will I keep you forever,
    Yes, forever and a day,
Till the walls shall crumble to ruin,
    And moulder in dust away!

THE CHILDREN

Come to me, O ye children!
    For I hear you at your play,
And the questions that perplexed me
    Have vanished quite away.

Ye open the eastern windows,
    That look towards the sun,
Where thoughts are singing swallows
    And the brooks of morning run.

In your hearts are the birds and the
        sunshine,
    In your thoughts the brooklet's flow;
But in mine is the wind of Autumn
    And the first fall of the snow.

Ah! what would the world be to us
    If the children were no more?
We should dread the desert behind us
    Worse than the dark before.

What the leaves are to the forest,
    With light and air for food,
Ere their sweet and tender juices
    Have been hardened into wood,—

That to the world are children;
    Through them it feels the glow
Of a brighter and sunnier climate
    Than reaches the trunks below.

Come to me, O ye children!
    And whisper in my ear
What the birds and the winds are singing
    In your sunny atmosphere.

For what are all our contrivings,
    And the wisdom of our books,
When compared with your caresses,
    And the gladness of your looks?

Ye are better than all the ballads
    That ever were sung or said;
For ye are living poems,
    And all the rest are dead.

Louisa May Alcott (age 15)

TO MOTHER

I hope that soon, dear mother,
    You and I may be
In the quiet room my fancy
    Has so often made for thee,—

The pleasant, sunny chamber,
    The cushioned easy-chair,
The book laid for your reading,
    The vase of flowers fair;

The desk beside the window
    Where the sun shines warm and bright:
And there in ease and quiet
    The promised book you write;

While I sit close beside you,
    Content at last to see
That you can rest, dear mother,
    And I can cherish thee.

THE LAY OF A GOLDEN GOOSE

Long ago in a poultry yard
   One dull November morn,
Beneath a motherly soft wing
   A little goose was born.

Who straightway peeped out of the shell
   To view the world beyond,
Longing at once to sally forth
   And paddle in the pond.

"Oh! be not rash," her father said,
   A mild Socratic bird;
Her mother begged her not to stray
   With many a warning word.

But little goosey was perverse,
   And eagerly did cry,
"I've got a pair of lovely wings,
   Of course I ought to fly."

In vain parental cacklings,
   In vain the cold sky's frown,
Ambitious goosey tried to soar,
   But always tumbled down.

The farm-yard jeered at her attempts,
   The peacocks screamed, "Oh fie!
You're only a domestic goose,
   So don't pretend to fly."

Great cock-a-doodle from his perch
   Crowed daily loud and clear,
"Stay in the puddle, foolish bird,
   That is your proper sphere."

The ducks and hens said, one and all,
   In gossip by the pool,
"Our children never play such pranks;
   My dear, that fowl's a fool."

The owls came out and flew about,
   Hooting above the rest,
"No useful egg was ever hatched
   From transcendental nest."

Good little goslings at their play
   And well-conducted chicks
Were taught to think poor goosey's flights
   Were naughty, ill-bred tricks.

They were content to swim and scratch,
   And not at all inclined
For any wild-goose chase in search
   Of something undefined.

Hard times she has as one may guess,
   That young aspiring bird,
Who still from every fall arose
   Saddened but undeterred.

She knew she was no nightingale,
   Yet spite of much abuse,
She longed to help and cheer the world,
   Although a plain gray goose.

She could not sing, she could not fly,
   Nor even walk with grace,
And all the farm-yard had declared
   A puddle was her place.

But something stronger than herself
   Would cry, "Go on, go on!
Remember, though an humble fowl,
   You're cousin to a swan."

So up and down poor goosey went,
   A busy, hopeful bird.
Searched many wide unfruitful fields,
   And many waters stirred.

At length she came unto a stream
   Most fertile of all *Niles*,
Where tuneful birds might soar and sing
   Among the leafy isles.

How did she build a little nest
   Beside the waters still,
Where the parental goose could rest
   Unvexed by any *bill*.

And here she paused to smooth her
    plumes,
    Ruffled by many plagues;
When suddenly arose the cry,
    "This goose lays golden eggs."

At once the farm-yard was agog;
    The ducks began to quack;
Prim Guinea fowls relenting called,
    "Come back, come back, come back."

Great chanticleer was pleased to give
    A patronizing crow,
And the contemptuous biddies clucked,
    "I wish my chicks did so."

The peacocks spread their shining tails,
    And cried in accents soft,
"We want to know you, gifted one,
    Come up and sit aloft."

Wise owls awoke and gravely said,
    With proudly swelling breasts,
"Rare birds have always been evoked
    From transcendental nests!"

News-hunting turkeys from afar
    Now ran with all thin legs
To gobble facts and fictions of
    The goose with golden eggs.

But best of all the little fowls
    Still playing on the shore,
Soft downy chicks and goslings gay,
    Chirped out, "Dear Goose, lay more."

But goosey all these weary years
    Had toiled like any ant,
And wearied out she now replied,
    "My little dears, I can't.

"When I was starving, half this corn
    Had been of vital use,
Now I am surfeited with food
    Like any Strasbourg goose."

So to escape too many friends,
    Without uncivil strive,
She ran to the Atlantic pond
    And paddled for her life.

Soon up among the grand old Alps
    She found two blessed things,
The health she had so nearly lost,
    And rest for weary limbs.

But still across the briny deep
    Couched in most friendly words,
Came prayers for letters, tales, or verse,
    From literary birds.

Whereat the renovated fowl
    With grateful thanks profuse,
Took from her wing a quill and wrote
    This lay of a Golden Goose.

BEX, SWITZERLAND, AUGUST, 1870

THE RAGGEDY MAN

O the Raggedy Man! He works fer Pa;
An' he's the goodest man ever you saw!
He comes to our house every day,
An' waters the horses, an' feeds 'em hay;
An' he opens the shed—an' we all ist laugh
When he drives out our little old wobble-ly calf;
An' nen—ef our hired girl says he can—
He milks the cow fer 'Lizabuth Ann.—
     Ain't he a' awful good Raggedy Man?
        Raggedy! Raggedy! Raggedy Man!

W'y, The Raggedy Man—he's ist so good,
He splits the kindlin' an' chops the wood;
An' nen he spades in our garden, too,
An' does most things 'at boys can't do.—
He clumbed clean up in our big tree
An' shooked a' apple down fer me—
An' 'nother 'n', too, fer 'Lizabuth Ann—
An' 'nother 'n', too, fer The Raggedy Man.—
     Ain't he a' awful kind Raggedy Man?
        Raggedy! Raggedy! Raggedy Man!

An' The Raggedy Man, he knows most rhymes,
An' tells 'em, ef I be good, sometimes:
Knows 'bout Giunts, an' Griffuns, an' Elves,
An' the Squidgicum-Squees 'at swallers the'rselves:
An', wite by the pump in our pasture-lot,
He showed me the hole 'at the Wunks is got,
'At lives 'way deep in the ground, an' can
Turn into me, er 'Lizabuth Ann!
     Ain't he a funny old Raggedy Man?
        Raggedy! Raggedy! Raggedy Man!

The Raggedy Man—one time, when he
Wuz makin' a little bow-'n'-orry fer me,
Says "When *you're* big like your Pa is,
Air you go' to keep a fine store like his—
An' be a rich merchunt—an' wear fine clothes?—
Er what *air* you go' to be, goodness knows!"
An' nen he laughed at 'Lizabuth Ann,
An' I says "'M go' to be a Raggedy Man!—
     I'm ist go' to be a nice Raggedy Man!"
Raggedy! Raggedy! Raggedy Man!

🍀 *D. G.*

DID YOU EVER?

Did you ever see a puppy with legs behind his tail?
Did you ever see an elephant talking to a snail?
Did you ever see a crocodile walking up the street?
Did you ever see a mackerel with boots upon its feet?
Did you ever see a billy-goat draw water from a well?
Did you ever see a pussy-cat learning how to spell?
A stranger sight than any of these things I can tell,
To see men take to drinking because they don't feel well!

Did you ever see a pony playing with a kite?
Did you ever see a peacock learning how to write?
Did you ever see a spider in a fashionable hat?
Did you ever see a flagstaff looking plump and fat?
Did you ever see an oyster climbing up a tree?
Did you ever see a mushroom growing in the sea?
Well, none of these queer sights would seem so strange to me,
As to see a man go drinking from troubles to get free.

🍀 *Thad Oliver*

A NICE LITTLE TIME

I saw a little doggery upon a little hill;
I saw a little ugly man a-coming from the mill.
And in the little doggery the little man did go,
To take a little merry grog with his little neighbor Joe.
And when they took a little grog they felt a little big;
They laughed a little hearty laugh and danced a little jig.
They took a little more, and then they got a little tight;
They disagreed on politics, and had a little fight.
And when they had a little fight they felt as large as life;
Each staggered to his little home and whipped his little wife.

SINCE PAPA DOESN'T DRINK

FOR A GIRL.

My papa's awful happy now, and mamma's happy too,
'Cause papa drinks no more the way he used to do.
And everything's so jolly now—'tain't like it used to be
When papa never stayed at home with poor mamma and me.
It made me feel so very bad to see my mamma cry.
And though she'd smile I'd spy the tears a-hiding in her eye.
But now she laughs just like we girls—it sounds so 'cute, I think
And sings such pretty little songs—since papa doesn't drink.

You ought to see my Sunday dress—it's every bit all new;
It ain't made out of mamma's dress the way she used to do,
And mamma's got a pretty cloak all trimmed with funny fur.
And papa's got some nice new clothes and goes to church with her.
My papa says that Christmas-time will soon be here,
And maybe good old Santa Claus will find our house this year.
I hope he'll bring some candy, and a dolly that can wink,
He'll know where our home is, I'm sure—since papa doesn't drink.

A LAMENT

My brother Will he used to be
The nicest kind of girl;
He wore a little dress like me,
And had his hair in curl.
We played with dolls and tea sets then,
And every kind of toy;
But all those good old times are gone—
Will's turned into a boy.

Mamma has made him little suits,
With pockets in the pants,
And cut off all his yellow curls
And sent them to my aunts;
And Will he was so pleased, I b'lieve
He almost jumped for joy;
But I declared I didn't like
Will turned into a boy.

And now he plays with horrid tops
I don't know how to spin,
And marbles that I try to shoot,
But never hit or win;
And leap-frog—I can't give a "back"
Like Charley, Frank, or Roy.
Oh! no one knows how bad I feel
Since Will has turned a boy!

I have to wear the frocks he left,
And, oh! they're awful tight;
I have to sit and just be good,
While he can climb and fight;
I have to keep my dresses nice,
And wear my hair in curl,
And worst—oh, *worstest* thing of all!—
I have to *stay* a girl.

And maybe he'll be President
Or Emperor or King;
For boys can be just what they please,
But girls can't be a thing.
It's awful dull to sit and play
With Nelly, Lill, aud Floy;
Why was I choosed to be a girl,
And Will to be a boy?

LIZA ANN'S LAMENT [WUSH'T I WUZ A BOY]

Wush't I wuz a boy!
  So I could jump an' run
An' yell real loud, an' whistle,
  An' fight an' have the mostest fun,
    Like boys duz.
Wush't I wuz a boy!

Wush't I wuz a boy!
  So's maw won't allus say:
"Don't straddle the fence, now, Liza Ann;
  Nice girls don't do that way."
    But boys duz.
Wush't I wuz a boy!

Wush't I wuz a boy!
  'N when they call me names:
"Tomboy," "Tag-tail," an' "Whistlin' Ann,"
  'N I could fight same's
    Billy duz.
Wush't I wuz a boy!

Wush't I wuz a boy!
  'N me an' John could play
At "skin-the-cat" an' "leap-frog," too;
  My dress is in the way—
    Boys' pants ain't.
Wush't I wuz a boy!

Wush't I wuz a boy!
  All gurl's good fur—jist
To dust an' sweep, an' scold,
  An' sew on buttons what yo mus't
    Sewin' on last week.
Wush't I wuz a boy!

Wush't I wuz a boy!
  Wush't God'd make gurls boys,
An' made boys gurls—'t 'd bin the same;
  'N I'd bin "John," an' John
Bin "Liza Ann," by name.
    Wush't He had!
Wush't I wuz a boy!

"WISH'T I WUZ A GURL"

Wish't I wuz a gurl,
  'Stid uv bein' a boy,
An' bang my hair, an' eat ice-cream,
An' ride ahind my feller's team,
  Like gurls duz—
    Wish't I wuz a gurl!

Wish't I wuz a gurl,
  An' when 't come Sunday night
I'd whack the old pianner,
  Just clean up outen site,
An' I'd marry some rich feller
  Like gurls duz—
    Wish't I wuz a gurl!

 Wish't I wuz a gurl!
  I'd just chaw gum an' talk,
An' when out ter promenade,
I'd take up all the walk,
  Like some gurls does—
    Wish't I wuz a gurl!

Wish't I wuz a gurl!
  All boy's good fer is't
Ter carry coal an' run odd jobs,
An' git off the walk fer dudy snobs,
  Like I did t'other night—
    Wish't I wuz a gurl!

Wish't I wuz a gurl!
  Wish't the Lord made all boys gurls,
An' made gurls boys, 'tud been the same
  An' I'd been Lizy Ann by name,
An' she'd been John or Joe 'stid of Jane.
    Wish't He had—
    Wish't I wuz a gurl!

ROSEBUD

O little maid in your rosebud-bower,
  Dreaming of growing old,
Wishing youth always would linger, a flower
  Never in haste to unfold;
Lift from the shadow your sunshiny head,
Growing old is nothing to dread.

O little maid in the rose-tree shade,
  See how its dry boughs shoot!
The green leaves fall and the blossoms fade;
  But youth is a living root.
There are always buds in the old tree's heart,
Ready at beckon of Spring to start.

O little maid, there is joy to seek,—
  Glory of earth and sky,
When the rosebud-streak fades out of your cheek,
  And the dewy gleam from your eye;
Deeper and wider must life take root;
Redder and higher must glow its fruit.

O little maid, be never afraid
  That youth from your heart will go:—
Reach forth unto heaven, through shower and shade!
  We are always young, while we grow.
Breathe out in a blessing your happy breath!
For love keeps the spirit from age and death.

Anna Maria Wells

THE LITTLE MAID

When I was a little maid,
    I waited on myself;
I washed my mother's teacups,
    And set them on the shelf.

I had a little garden
    Most beautiful to see;
I wished that I had somebody
    To play in it with me.

Nurse was in mamma's room;
    I knew her by the cap;

She held a lovely baby boy
    Asleep upon her lap.

As soon as he could learn to walk,
    I led him by my side,—
My brother and my playfellow,—
    Until the day he died!

Now I am an old maid,
    I wait upon myself;
I only wipe one teacup,
    And set it on the shelf.

Priscilla Jane Thompson

TO A LITTLE COLORED BOY

Oh, pure and sportive little child,
    Be happy while you may:
Ring out your laughter loud and clear;
    Be blithe, enjoy your day.

Your eyes of sloe, they sparkle bright;
    Your rounded, dusky cheeks,
Are ever dimpled in a smile,
    From each week into weeks.

Build high your castles in the air;
    Dream on of manhood's fame;
What matter, if your pure, young, heart,
    Deems each man's chance the same.

I hold your little hand in mine;
    Fast wags your childish tongue;
Your prospects doth look bright to you,
    Because you are so young.

Thou knoweth not, poor little boy,
    What Future holds for thee,
Thy dreams are not extravagant,
    And yet, they canst not be.

This mass of midnight curly hair,
    This soft and dusky skin,
Will bring not fortune's smile to you,
    When childhood's day will end.

Thou art a child, of promise rare;
    God, for some cause, profound,
Hath cast thee in a finer mold,
    Than most about you found.

E'en now your little high-aimed heart,
    A pris'ner seems to be,
And with impatience beats the bars,
    Of helpless infancy.

You'll bloom a rare high-minded man;
    Surpassing fair-faced men;
Would God, the Future, held for you,
    The hope it holds for them.

Would that your path of life could be,
    Like theirs, with roses strewn;
Would that your thorns, be brushed aside,
    As often as their own.

Would that the world, which you must face,
　　Were free from this low sin,
To meanly wrong a fellow-man,
　　For darkness of his skin.

I look me deep into thine eyes;
　　My love is mixed with grief;
To think that naught, within my power,
　　Can later, bring relief.

But pure and sportive little boy,
　　When time his trials lend,
Think not that you are destitute;
　　In me you have a friend.

☙ *Authors Unknown*

LINES SPOKEN AT A PUBLIC EXAMINATION 1821, BY TWO FEMALE PUPILS (TWINS) WRITTEN FOR THE OCCASION

　　Ladies and gentl'men, here you see
As pretty a sight as well can be:
We look alike, eyes, nose, and chins;
No wonder this, for we are twins.
We live as sisters ought to do,
We feel as one, though we are two:
We seldom grieve our parent's heart,
And seldom from each other part.
'Tis said of twins in days of old,
　　From thirst of fame, or love of gold;
They form'd two bands, resolv'd to see
Which should obtain the victory.
So furious grew the wicked strife,
That Remus yielded up his life;
Rome's famous name to t'other owes,
For he was named Romulus.
Here friends, in sable skin you find
Two children who possess one mind;
So form'd by nature to agree,
That none more happy are than we.

A KANSAS NURSERY

"The baby?" we asked, as with mop and
    broom
    Its mother came to the ranch one day.
"Oh, she's *picketed out* across the way!
    I dare not leave her alone in the room."

And the busy mother looked for a tub,
While we saddled our horses and rode to
    see
How the lonely baby fared, while we
Had stolen its mother to sweep and to
    scrub.

For the babies we were accustomed to
Could never have kept their silk and lace
And little be-ribboned hats in place,
With only a tree for their nurse, we knew.

But this Kansas baby had no hat;
And it laughed as if it thought silk and
    lace
Would have been entirely out of place
On a prairie,—or, for matter of that,

Anywhere else. It could only go
The length of the rope; but its little feet
Pattered about where the grass was sweet,
Just as it pleased; and that, you know,

Is more than city babies do:
For, trundled under the city trees,
They are carried just where the nurses
    please,
Which I shouldn't like at all; should you?

As I thought it over, it seemed to me
That a city darling has less to hope,
"Picketed out" with invisible rope
To a somewhat less reliable tree!

Charlotte Perkins Gilman

IF MOTHER KNEW

If mother knew the way I felt,—
    And I'm sure a mother should,—
She wouldn't make it quite so hard
    For a person to be good!

I want to do the way she says;
    I try to all day long;
And then she just strips all the right,
    And pounces on the wrong!

A dozen times I do a thing,
    And one time I forget;
And then she looks at me and asks
    If I can't remember yet?

She'll tell me to do something,
    And I'll really start to go;
But she'll keep right on telling it
    As if I didn't know.

Till it seems as if I couldn't—
    It makes me kind of wild;
And then she says she never saw
    Such a disobliging child.

I go to bed all sorry,
    And say my prayers, and cry,
And mean next day to be so good
    I just can't wait to try.

And I get up next morning,
    And mean to do just right;
But mother's sure to scold me
    About something, before night.

I wonder if she really thinks
    A child could go so far,
As to be perfect all the time
    As the grown up people are!

If she only knew I tried to,—
    And I'm sure a mother should,—
She wouldn't make it quite so hard
    For a person to be good!

Mary Mapes Dodge

THE NAUGHTY BOY

"Och, save us!" cried Betty, "I'm 'most driven wild;
    Would you shtep here a moment, ma'am, please?
For the sowl of me, ma'am, I can't ready the child
    While he keeps up such doin's as these.

"I might better be curlin' a porkerpine quill,
    Or washin' the face of a eel,
Than be dressin' of him—for he never bees still
    'Less I howld him by neck an' by heel.

"It's three blissed times since I put on his clothes
    That he's wriggled stret off o' the chair;
Not a moment ago he attack-ted me nose,
    And it's twice he's been into me hair.

"If ye'll credit me, ma'am, wid his cryin' an' kickin',
    He's brought tears to me eyelids, like rain—
If he wasn't so bad, ma'am, I wouldn't be speaking',
    For I niver was one to complain."

Thus summoned, I went to the nursery-door,
    There sat master Johnny, a-pout.
And I said, as I lifted him up from the floor,
    "Why, Johnny, what's all this about?'

A scream was his answer. His flushed little face
    Looked angrily up into mine;
"Oo hurt!" "Do I, Johnny? Where?—show me the place!"
    But his cry only changed to a whine.

In a moment, I found out the cause of the trouble—
    'Twas a pin, pricking deep in his side;
And she, in her roughness, had bent the thing double—
    No wonder my darling had cried!

Poor Johnny! He sobbed on my shoulder awhile,
    Then held up his face to be kissed;
(If Betty went back to the Emerald Isle,
    I know where she wouldn't be missed.)

Soon, meek as a lamb when the tempest is whirling,
    And the shepherd is deaf to his bleat,
Our Johnny submitted to washing and curling,
    Till Betty proclaimed him "complete."

            In "righting" each other,
                (As Betty would say),
            If we find there's a bother
                That stands in the way—

            Perhaps 'twould be well,
                Before crying, "Sin,"
            And running to tell,
                To look for the pin!

Anna Maria Wells

NO, YOU CAN'T

Let me into the breakfast-room, Bridget,—
  I'll be a good girl if you will;
And see if I can't be a lady,
  And see if I don't sit still.

You wash me and curl me and dress me,
  Yet say that I do not look fit.
You think that I'll tease for the sugar;
  I won't do it—hardly a bit.

I won't put my foot on the table,
  Nor make the least atom of fuss;
I won't drum at all with my teaspoon,
  I won't pull the cloth in a muss.

Papa, if he only had seen me,
  I know would have said, "Let her stay."
But just as I pushed the door open,
  You came there and snatched me away.

Don't say, "No, you can't," and then kiss me,—
  You're not half so kind as you seem.
I don't wan't to stay with you, Bridget:
  O dear! I'm afraid I shall scream!

I wonder if folks that are grown up,
  And thinking to have what they want,
Are patient when doors are shut on them,
  And good when *they*'re told, "No, YOU CAN'T!"

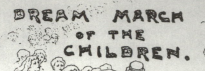

DREAM MARCH
OF THE
CHILDREN.

By James Whitcomb Riley.

WAS N'T it a funny dream? — perfectly bewild'rin'! —
Last night, and night *before*, and night before *that*, —
Seemed like I saw the march o' regiments o' children,
 Marching to the robin's fife and cricket's rat-ta-tat!
Lily-banners overhead, with the dew upon 'em,
 On flashed the little army, as with sword and flame;
Like the buzz o' bumble-wings with the honey on 'em,
 Came an eerie, cheery chant, chiming as it came:

Where go the children? Traveling! Traveling!
 Where go the children, traveling ahead?
Some go to kindergarten; some go to day-school;
 Some go to night-school; and some go to bed!

Smooth roads or rough roads, warm or winter weather
 On go the children, tow-head and brown,
Brave boys and brave girls, rank and file together,
 Marching out of Babyland, over dale and down:
Some go a-gipsying out in country places —
 Out through the orchards, with blossoms on the boughs
Wild, sweet, and pink and white as their own glad faces;
 And some go, at evening, calling home the cows.

Where go the children? Traveling! Traveling!
 Where go the children, traveling ahead?
Some go to foreign wars and camps by the firelight —
 Some go to glory so; and some go to bed!

Some go through grassy lanes leading to the city —
 Thinner grow the green trees and thicker grows the dust;
Ever, though, to little people any path is pretty
 So it leads to newer lands, as they know it must.
Some go to singing less; some go to list'ning;
 Some go to thinking over ever nobler themes;
Some go anhungered, but ever bravely whistling,
 Turning never home again only in their dreams.

Where go the children? Traveling! Traveling!
 Where go the children, traveling ahead?
Some go to conquer things; some go to try them;
 Some go to dream them; and some go to bed!

DREAM-MARCH OF THE CHILDREN

Wasn't it a funny dream?—perfectly bewild'rin!—
  Last night, and night *before*, and night before *that,*
Seemed like I saw the march o' regiments o' children,
  Marching to the robin's fife and cricket's rat-ta-tat!
Lily-banners overhead, with the dew upon 'em,
  On flashed the little army, as with sword and flame;
Like the buzz o' bumble-wings with the honey on 'em,
  Came an eerie, cheery chant, chiming as it came:

> *Where go the children? Traveling! Traveling!*
>   *Where go the children, traveling ahead?*
> *Some go to kindergarten; some go to day-school;*
>   *Some go to night-school; and some go to bed!*

Smooth roads or rough roads, warm or winter weather
  On go the children, tow-head and brown,
Brave boys and brave girls, rank and file together,
  Marching out of Babyland, over dale and down:
Some go a-gipsying out in country places—
  Out through the orchards, with blossoms on the boughs
Wild, sweet, and pink and white as their own glad faces;
  And some go, at evening, calling home the cows.

> *Where go the children? Traveling! Traveling!*
>   *Where go the children, traveling ahead?*
> *Some go to foreign wars and camps by the firelight—*
>   *Some go to glory so; and some go to bed!*

Some go through grassy lanes leading to the city—
  Thinner grow the green trees and thicker grows the dust;
Ever, though, to little people any path is pretty
  So it leads to newer lands, as they know it must.
Some go to singing less; some go to listn'ning;
  Some go to thinking over ever nobler themes;
Some go anhungered, but ever bravely whistling,
  Turning never home again only in their dreams.

> *Where go the children? Traveling! Traveling!*
>   *Where go the children, traveling ahead?*
> *Some go to conquer things; some go to try them;*
>   *Some go to dream them; and some go to bed!*

❧ Gertrude Heath

WHAT RODDY SAW

Roddy stood at the window
  Watching the western sky;
The sun had sunk behind the hills,
  And clouds went sailing by.

The moon rose o'er the garden trees,
  A crescent clear and pale:
And Roddy cried, "O Mamma, come!
  I see God's finger-nail!"

❧ Mary Mapes Dodge

AT THE WINDOW

In and out, in and out,
  Through the clouds heaped about,
Wanders the bright moon.

What she seeks, I do not know;
Where it is, I cannot show.

I am but a little child,
And the night is strange and wild.

In and out, in and out,
  Wanders the bright moon;

In and out, in and out,
  She will find it soon.

There she comes! as clear as day,
  Now the clouds are going away.
She is smiling, I can see,
  And she's looking straight at me.

Pretty moon, so bright and round,
Won't you tell me what you found?

❧ Agnes Lee

RACING WITH THE MOON

When by the river run I will,
The moon peeps up behind the mill,
And with a laugh and merrily
It starts to run a race with me.

The moon it starts to run a race,
And nothing seems to keep its place:
The trees advance with rapid stride
To meet me, and the houses glide.

They glide and pass me silently,
And every window winks its eye.
All glide to greet, at evening gray,
Except the moon, that runs my way.

It runs with me the river past,
And when I hurry, hurries fast;
Or slackens, if I slacken do.
And when I stop, the moon stops, too.

☙ *Agnes Lee*

O ROUNDY MOON

O Roundy moon above the dune!
This little kindness show me:
To let me rise and through thine eyes
Behold the world below me;

To let me look on woody nook,
And river smooth and even,
And wander down the silver town,
From hazy heights of heaven!

☙ *Sarah Piatt*

MY BABES IN THE WOOD

I know a story, fairer, dimmer, sadder,
   Than any story painted in your books.
You are so glad? It will not make you gladder;
   Yet listen, with your pretty restless looks.

"Is it a Fairy Story?" Well, half fairy—
   At least it dates far back as fairies do;
And seems to me as beautiful and airy;
   Yet half, perhaps the fairy half, is true.

You had a baby sister and a brother,
   The very dainty people, rosy white,
Sweeter than all things except each other!
   Older yet younger—gone from human sight!

And I, who loved them, and shall love them ever,
   And think with yearning tears how each light hand
Crept toward bright bloom or berries—I shall never
   Know how I lost them. Do you understand?

Poor slightly golden heads! I think I missed them,
   First in some dreamy, piteous, doubtful way;
But when and where with lingering lips I kissed them,
   My gradual parting, I can never say.

Sometimes I fancy that they may have perished
   In shadowy quiet of wet rocks and moss,
Near paths whose very pebbles I have cherished,
   For their small sakes, since my most bitter loss.

I fancy, too, that they were softly covered
   By robins, out of apple-flowers they knew,
Whose nursing wings in far home sunshine hovered,
   Before the timid world had dropped the dew.

Their names were—what yours are! At this you wonder.
   Their pictures are,—your own, as you have seen;
And my bird-buried darlings, hidden under
   Lost leaves—why, it is your dead Selves I mean!

Grace Denio Litchfield

MY OTHER ME

Children, do you ever,
   In walks by land or sea,
Meet a little maiden
   Long time lost to me?

She is gay and gladsome,
   Has a laughing face,
And a heart as sunny;
   And her name is Grace.

Naught she knows of sorrow,
   Naught of doubt or blight;
Heaven is just above her—
   All her thoughts are white.

Longtime since I lost her,
   That other Me of mine;
She crossed into Time's shadow
   Out of Youth's sunshine.

Now the darkness keeps her;
   And call her as I will,
The years that lie between us
   Hide her from me still.

I am dull and pain-worn,
   And lonely as can be—
Oh, children, if you meet her,
   Send back my other Me!

THE ORCHARD ON THE HILL

Grandfather's home!—that dear old place,
  A house with gables wide
Embowered in trees, a great red barn
  With haystacks at its side,
A brook spanned by a rustic bridge,
  A gloomy, rumbling mill,
And set against a dreamy sky
  An orchard on a hill!

Oh, every summer I go there,
  When school is out, to stay;
I look for hens' nests, drink new milk,
  And tumble on the hay.
Grandfather is the best of men,—
  He lets me start the mill,—
And oh, the pippins growing in
  The orchard on the hill!

Grandmother's old, too, but so sweet!
  She's sprightly, though she's gray;
She feeds the chickens, milks the cows,
  And churns, 'most every day,
Such yellow butter! And her pies
  The pastry-cupboard fill;
They're made of yellow harvests from
  The orchard on the hill.

Across the farm I love to run,
  Through fields of grass and grain,
And fight the thistles by the brook,
  The mulleins in the lane.
I love the dear old garden set
  With rosemary, rue, and dill;
But best of all, and most of all,
  The orchard on the hill!

Oh, the berries from the briers!
  Oh, the melons green and gold!
We put them in the spring-house
  To make them good and cold;
And from the beehives, now and then,
  A honey-bowl we fill,
To sweeten our baked quinces from
  The orchard on the hill.

At night Grandfather tells me tales
  Of long and long ago,
Grandmother knits and knits and smiles
  To see her stocking grow,
While all outdoors it is so calm,
  So dusky and so still,
And then the moon rolls up behind
  The orchard on the hill.

At nine o'clock we have our prayer,
  And then I go to bed,
Away off in the darkest room,
  And cover up my head,
'Most scared to death, and listen to
  The lonesome whippoorwill
Calling to its mate across
  The orchard on the hill.

Josephine Preston Peabody

WINDOWS

Once, and in the daytime too, I made myself afraid:
Playing Eyelids Up and Down, with the window-shade.
Till the Houses seemed to watch the People going by;
And they kept me looking too,—wondering Where, and Why.

(If I were that other Boy,—if I were those Men
Going by with things to sell,—Oh, who would I be then?)

Windows with their eyebrows high; windows like a frown,—
Ones that think it over so,—with the curtains down;
Tall ones, that are somehow sad; shallow ones that blink,
All the Windows you can see, make you think and think.

(If I were that Old Man,—and I looked up at Me,
Watching from the window here, Oh then, how would it be?)

Sometimes they are golden, with shining in their Eyes;
Every time the sun sets, it happens like surprise,
And so bright,—I almost forget the dream I made.
But I keep it for the days I want to make myself Afraid,—

(If I were that Boy who Limps,—now it's dark, and snowing,
And if I were going Home,—oh, where would I be going?)

Eugene Field

SEEIN' THINGS

I ain't afeard uv snakes, or toads, or bugs, or worms, or mice,
An' things 'at girls are skeered uv I think are awful nice!
I'm pretty brave, I guess; an' yet I hate to go to bed,
For, when I'm tucked up warm an' snug an' when my prayers are said,
Mother tells me, "Happy Dreams!" an' takes away the light,
An' leaves me lyin' all alone an' seein' things at night!

Sometimes they're in the corner, sometimes they're by the door,
Sometimes they're all a-standin' in the middle uv the floor;
Sometimes they are a-sittin' down, sometimes they're walkin' round
So softly and so creepylike they never make a sound!
Sometimes they are as black as ink, an' other times they're white—
But the color ain't no difference when you see things at night!

Once, when I licked a feller 'at had just moved on our street,
An' father sent me up to bed without a bite to eat,
I woke up in the dark an' saw things standin' in a row,
A-lookin' at me cross-eyed an' p'intin' at me—so!
Oh, my! I wuz so skeered that time I never slep' a mite—
It's almost alluz when I'm bad I see things at night!

Lucky thing I ain't a girl, or I'd be skeered to death!
Bein' I'm a boy, I duck my head an' hold my breath;
An' I am, oh, *so* sorry I'm a naughty boy, an' then
I promise to be better an' I say my prayers again!
Gran'ma tells me that's the only way to make it right ,
When a feller has been wicked an' sees things at night!

An' so, when other naughty boys would coax me into sin,
I try to skwush the Tempter's voice 'at urges me within;
An' when they's pie for supper, or cakes 'at's 's big an' nice,
I want to—but I do not pass my plate f'r them things twice!
No, ruther let Starvation wipe me slowly out o' sight
Than I should keep a-livin' on an' seein' things at night!

e❧ *Lucy Larcom*

MY CHILDHOOD'S ENCHANTRESS

When purple dusk fell on the sea,
And the white moon looked in at me,
Where, wakeful and alone, I lay,
Watching unshapen shadows play
In huddling groups beneath the eaves;
And fears, that childish fancy weaves
Of airy nothing, banished sleep,
A step upon the stairway steep
Made gladness blossom out of fear;—
The step of my enchantress dear!

She came and sat upon my bed;
An aureole-ring was round her head,
Of golden light—her own bright hair,
Falling in wavy crinkles fair
Upon her shoulders—while she told
Tale after tale, that seemed to fold
My life in wonder-robes complete,
Wrapped in romance from head to feet.

She waved her wand; rare folks she knew
One after one came gliding through
The raftered attic's vista dim:—
What pencil would their portraits limn,
Their motley grouping?—Knights in mail,
And rescued ladies, lily-pale,
Fairy and giant, dwarf and sprite,
Walked in procession down the night.

Little Bo-Peep; Red Riding Hood;
The Babes that wandered in the wood;
Bold Humpty-Dumpty, hobbling after
Hop o' my Thumb, with elfin laughter;
And Mother Hubbard—dog and dame
With slippered Cinderella came;
Jack trailed along his beanstalk vine;
Aladdin and his lamp were mine;

Briar-Rose, half-waked, smiled on her
   Prince—
How tame are story people since!

The patchwork quilt that covered me
Was like the enchanted tapestry
Of Eastern tales; for in my dreams
I walked by unknown shores and
   streams,
Where trees could talk, and magic lights
Dropped splendor from the Arabian
   Nights.—
She made the far-off seem so near!
My golden-haired enchantress dear!

And more she stirred my fledgling
   wings,
And led my flight to loftier things
Than fairy-fancies ever shaped:
From earth together we escaped,
And caught the glance, and heard the
   song
Of seraph and archangel strong,

And knew there was no near nor far:—
The world we lived on was a Star!

Her elf-land mists melt not away:
Their lambent tints around me play,
Now I am old. Her clear blue eye,
That seemed an opening to the sky—
The heaven that makes of earth a place
Worth living in, unfolding space
Of spirit-realms—it haunts me still,
Wakening the old ecstatic thrill.

She gave me what no queen could give;
Keys to the secret, How to Live,
Fancy is good, but faith is better:
I am to my enchantress debtor,
Whose doors swung wide to both. And
   she—
How did she find her way to me?—
God sent her hither, long before
I came: he taught sweet mother-lore
To sister-lips. Oh, dear and fair,
My sister with the shining hair!

Lucy Larcom

A CHILD'S NIGHT-THOUGHTS

They put her to bed in the darkness,
  And bade her be quiet and good;
But she sobbed in the silence, and
    trembled,
    Though she tried to be brave as
    she could.

For the Night was so real, so awful!
  A mystery closing around,
Like the walls of a deep, deep dungeon,
  That hid her from sight and sound.

So stifling, so empty, so dreary—
  That horror of loneliness black!
She fell asleep, moaning and fearing
  That morning would never come back.

A baby must bear its own sorrow,
  Since none understands it aright;
But at last, from her bosom was lifted
  That terrible fear of the night.

One evening, the hands that undressed
    her
    Led her out of the floor close by,
And bade her look up for a moment
  Up into the wonderful sky,

Where the planets and constellations,
  Deep-rooted in darkness, grew
Like blossoms from black earth
    blooming,
    All sparkling with silvery dew.

It seemed to bend down to meet her—
  That luminous purple dome;
She was caught up into a glory,
  Where her baby-heart was at home,

Like a child in its father's garden.
  As glad as a child could be,
In the feeling of perfect protection
  And limitless liberty.

And this had been all around her,
  While she shuddered alone in bed!
The beautiful, grand revelation,
  With ecstasy sweet she read.

And she sank into sound child-slumber,
  All folded in splendors high,
All happy and soothed with blessings
  Breathed out of the heart of the sky.

And in dreams her light, swift footsteps
  Those infinite spaces trod;
A fearless little explorer
  Of the paths that lead up to God.

The darkness now was no dungeon,
  But a key unto wide release;
And the Night was a vision of freedom—
  A Presence of heavenly peace.

And I doubt not that in like manner
  Might vanish, as with a breath,
The gloom and the lonely terror
  Of the mystery we call Death.

TALK ABOUT GHOSTS [AT BED-TIME]
"Each of us carries within him a future ghost."

What *is* a ghost? "It is something white,
  (And I guess it goes barefooted, too,)
That comes from the graveyard in the night,
  When the doors are lock'd, and breaks right through."
    What does it do?

"Oh, it frightens people ever so much,
  And goes away when the chickens crow;
And—doesn't steal any spoons, or touch
  One thing that is n't its own, you know."
    Who told you so?

"Somebody—every body, almost;
  Or I knew, myself, when this world begun.
Not even a General could kill a ghost—
  I wish the Lord had never made one.
    They hate the sun!"

No, sweetest of all wee brown-eyed girls,
  They love the light—'t is the dark they fear;
Love riches and power, love laces and pearls;
  Love—all the preacher calls vanity here.
    This much is clear.

"Do they love to be dead?" I can but tell
  That few of them greatly love to die:
Perhaps they doubt whether all is well
  In the place where ghosts—yes, "up in the sky."
    You wonder why?

They love their clothes (and want to keep dress'd:)
  Whether new and prettily white and red,
Or gray and ragged, 't is hard, at best,
  To take them off—though the prayers are said—
    And go to bed.

Elizabeth Lincoln Shackford

A LITTLE MAID'S WISH

I'd like to have a perfect face,
I'd like a body full of grace.
Brain packed with thoughts as comb
    with honey,
And then I'd like a little money,
And still I want a few things more—

Please give me true friends by the score,
A little voice to sing and trill,
Two clever hands to do my will,
Then grant, besides these blessings
    seven,
For future use, a little Heaven.

Eugene Field

LADY BUTTON-EYES

When the busy day is done,
And my weary little one
Rocketh gently to and fro;
When the night winds softly blow,
And the crickets in the glen
Chirp and chirp and chirp again;
When upon the haunted green
Fairies dance around their queen—
Then from yonder misty skies
Cometh Lady Button-Eyes.

Through the murk and mist and gloam
To our quiet, cozy home,
Where to singing, sweet and low,
Rocks a cradle to and fro;
Where the clock's dull monotone
Telleth of the day that's done;
Where the moonbeams hover o'er
Playthings sleeping on the floor—
Where my weary wee one lies
Cometh Lady Button-Eyes.

Cometh like a fleeting ghost
From some distant eerie coast;
Never footfall can you hear
As that spirit fareth near—
Never whisper, never word

From that shadow-queen is heard.
In ethereal raiment dight,
From the realm of fay and sprite
In the depth of yonder skies
Cometh Lady Button-Eyes.

Layeth she her hands upon
My dear weary little one,
And those white hands overspread
Like a veil the curly head,
Seem to fondle and caress
Every little silken tress;
Then she smooths the eyelids down
Over those two eyes of brown—
In such soothing, tender wise
Cometh Lady Button-Eyes.

Dearest, feel upon your brow
That caressing magic now;
For the crickets in the glen
Chirp and chirp and chirp again,
While upon the haunted green
Fairies dance around their queen,
And the moonbeams hover o'er
Playthings sleeping on the floor—
Hush, my sweet! from yonder skies
Cometh Lady Button-Eyes!

GOOD NIGHT!

What do I see in Baby's eyes

So bright?

I see the blue, I see a spark,
I see a twinkle in the dark

Of light.

What do I see in Baby's eyes

Shut tight?

The blue is gone, the light is hid—
I'll lay a soft kiss on each lid.

Good night!

THE SAND MAN

☙ Paul Laurence Dunbar

THE SAND-MAN

I know a man
  With face of tan,
But who is ever kind;
  Whom girls and boys
  Leaves games and toys
Each eventide to find.

When day grows dim,
  They watch for him,
He comes to place his claim;
  He wears the crown
  Of Dreaming-town;
The sand-man is his name.

When sparkling eyes
  Droop sleepywise
And busy lips grow dumb;
  When little heads
  Nod towards the beds,
We know the sand-man's come.

☙ Mary Mapes Dodge

THE SAND MAN

Oho! but he travels the country over,
The queer little, kind little, elfish rover!
Lightly he bears in his tricksome hand
A silvery horn full of sleepy sand,
Shaking it here, and shaking it there,
Till the blossoms nod in the drowsy air;
Till the sunlight creeps down hill to bed,
Or slips through the sky where clouds are red;
Till the lambkins bleat a soft "good-night!"
And birds grow still in the tree-tops bright,
While sweet little eyelids, all over the land,
Droop with the weight of the silvery sand.
Oho! Oho! where the Sand Man goes
Every one wonders and nobody knows;
For just when the right time comes to peep,
Little and big are falling asleep.
He steals to the cradles, the cribs, the bed,
And sprinkles his sand over children's heads,
Till bright little faces lie warm and still,
Smiling or grave, at the Sand Man's will.
He catches them often at full mid-day,
And bids them stop at their merry play—

With a "Ho! my darling," "Hi! my dear,"
"I'll sing a dream-song into your ear."

Some on the carpet, some on the chairs,
Some curled up on the nursery stairs;
Some in the grass where the shadows play,
Some hidden deep in the fragrant hay,
And some who, folded in mother's embrace,
Float in a lullaby, pressing her face.
Oho! but he travels the country over,
The queer little, kind little, elfish rover!
And whence he comes, and whither he goes,
Every one wonders, and nobody knows;
For just when the right time comes to peep,
All the children are falling asleep.

❧ *Louisa May Alcott*

LULLABY

"Now the day is done
  Now the shepherd sun
Drives his white flocks from the sky;
  Now the flowers rest
  On their mother's breast,
Hushed by her low lullaby.

"Now the glowworms glance,
  Now the fireflies dance,
Under fern-boughs green and high;
  And the western breeze
  To the forest trees
Chants a tuneful lullaby.

"Now 'mid shadows deep
  Falls blesséd sleep,
Like dew from the summer sky;
  And the whole earth dreams,
  In the moon's soft beams,
While night breathes a lullaby.

"Now, birdlings, rest,
  In your wind-rocked nest,
Unscared by the owl's shrill cry;
  For with folded wings
  Little Brier swings,
And singeth your lullaby."

DUTCH LULLABY [WYNKEN, BLYNKEN, AND NOD]

Wynken, Blynken, and Nod one night
    Sailed off in a wooden shoe,—
Sailed on a river of misty light
    Into a sea of dew.
"Where are you going, and what do you wish?"
    The old moon asked the three.
"We have come to fish for the herring fish
    That live in this beautiful sea;
    Nets of silver and gold have we!"
            Said Wynken,
            Blynken,
            And Nod.

The old moon laughed and sang a song,
    As they rocked in the wooden shoe,
And the wind that sped them all night long
    Ruffled the waves of dew;
The little stars were the herring fish
That lived in that beautiful sea.
"Now cast your nets wherever you wish
    But never afeard are we!"
    So cried the stars to the fishermen three,
            Wynken,
            Blynken,
            And Nod.

All night long their nets they threw
    For the fish in the twinkling foam,
Then down from the skies came the wooden shoe,
    Bringing the fishermen home;
'T was all so pretty a sail, it seemed
    As if it could not be,
And some folks thought 't was a dream they'd dreamed
    Of sailing that beautiful sea;
    But I shall name you the fishermen three:
            Wynken,
            Blynken,
            And Nod.

Wynken and Blynken are two little eyes,
    And Nod is a little head,
And the wooden shoe that sailed the skies
    Is a wee one's trundle-bed;
So shut your eyes while Mother sings
    Of wonderful sights that be,
And you shall see the beautiful things
    As you rock in the misty sea,
    Where the old shoe rocked the fishermen three:
        Wynken,
        Blynken,
        And Nod.

Eugene Field

THE ROCK-A-BY LADY

The Rock-a-By Lady from Hushaby street
    Comes stealing; comes creeping;
The poppies they hang from her head to her feet,
And each hath a dream that is tiny and fleet—
She bringeth her poppies to you, my sweet,
    When she findeth you sleeping!

There is one little dream of a beautiful drum—
  "Rub-a-dub!" it goeth;
There is one little dream of a big sugar-plum,
And lo! thick and fast the other dreams come
Of popguns that bang, and tin tops that hum,
    And a trumpet that bloweth!

And dollies peep out of those wee little dreams
    With laughter and singing;
And boats go a-floating on silvery streams,
And the stars peek-a-boo with their own misty gleams,
And up, up, and up, where the Mother Moon beams,
    The Fairies go winging!

Would you dream all these dreams that are tiny and fleet?
    They'll come to you sleeping;
So shut the two eyes that are weary, my sweet,
For the Rock-a-By Lady from Hushaby Street,
With poppies that hang from her head to her feet,
    Comes stealing; comes creeping.

J. G. Holland

A LULLABY

Rockaby, lullaby, bees in the clover!—
Crooning so drowsily, crying so low—
Rockaby, lullaby, dear little rover!
    Down into wonderland—
    Down to the underland—
      Go, oh go!
Down into wonderland go!

Rockaby, lullaby, rain on the clover!
Tears on the eyelids that waver and
      weep;
Rockaby, lullaby—bending it over
    Down on the mother-world,
    Down on the other world!
      Sleep, oh sleep!
Down on the mother-world sleep!

Rockaby, lullaby, dew on the clover!
Dew on the eyes that will sparkle at
      dawn!
Rockaby, lullaby, dear little rover!
    Into the stilly world—
    Into the lily-world
      Gone, oh gone!
Into the lily-world, gone!

Thomas Bailey Aldrich

"CRADLE SONG"

Who is it opens her blue bright eye,
Bright as the sea, and blue as the sky?—
    Chiquita!
Who has the smile that comes and goes
Like sunshine over her mouth's red
      rose?—
    Muchachita!

What is the softest laughter heard,
Gurgle of brook or trill of bird,
    Chiquita?
Nay, 't is thy laughter makes the rill
Hush its voice and the bird be still,
    Muchachita!

Ah, little flower-hand on my breast,
How it soothes me and gives me rest.
    Chiquita!
What is the sweetest sight I know?
Three little white teeth in a row,
Three little white teeth in a row,
    Muchachita!

❧ E. Pauline Johnson [Tekahionwake; Mohawk]

THE BIRDS' LULLABY

I

Sing to us, cedars; the twilight is creeping
    With shadowy garments, the wilderness through;
All day we have carolled, and now would be sleeping,
    So echo the anthems we warbled to you;
        While we swing, swing,
        And your branches sing,
    And we drowse to your dreamy whispering.

II

Sing to us, cedars; the night-wind is sighing,
    Is wooing, is pleading, to hear you reply;
And here in your arms we are restfully lying,
    And longing to dream to your soft lullaby;
        While we swing, swing,
        And your branches sing.
    And we drowse to your dreamy whispering.

III

Sing to us, cedars; your voice is so lowly,
    Your breathing so fragrant, your branches so strong;
Our little nest-cradles are swaying so slowly,
    While zephyrs are breathing their slumberous song.
        And we swing, swing,
        While your branches sing,
    And we drowse to your dreamy whispering.

❧ E. Pauline Johnson [Tekahionwake; Mohawk]

LULLABY OF THE IROQUOIS

Little brown baby-bird, lapped in your nest,
    Wrapped in your nest,
    Strapped in your nest,
Your straight little cradle-board rocks you to rest;
    Its hands are your nest,
    Its bands are your nest;
It swings from the down-bending branch of the oak;

You watch the camp flame, and the curling gray smoke;
But, oh, for your pretty black eyes; sleep is best,—
Little brown baby of mine, go to rest.

Little brown baby-bird swinging to sleep,
        Winging to sleep,
        Singing to sleep,
Your wonder-black eyes that so wide open keep,
        Shielding their sleep,
        Unyielding to sleep.
The heron is homing, the plover is still,
The night-owl calls from his haunt on the hill,
Afar the fox barks, afar the stars peep,—
Little brown baby of mine, go to sleep.

&⅜ *Sarah Piatt*

IF I HAD MADE THE WORLD

If I had made the world—ah me!
    I might have left some things undone!
But as to *him*—my boy, you see,
A pretty world this world would be,
    I'd say, without George Washington!

Would I have made the Baby? Oh,
    There were no need of anything
Without the Baby, you must know!
——I'm a Republican, and so
    I never would have made "the King."

I might have made the President—
    Had I known how to make him right!
——Columbus? Yes, if I had meant
To find a flowering continent
    Already made for me, I might.

I would have made one poet too—
    Has God made more?—Yes, I forgot,
There is no need of asking you;
You know as little as I do.
    A poet is—well, who knows who?

And yet a poet is, my dear,
    A man who writes a book like this,
(There never *was* but one, I hear;)
    ——Yes, it is hard to spell S-h-a-k-e-s-p-e-a-r-e.
    So, now, Good-night.—and here's a kiss.

You are not tired?—you want to know
    What else I would have made? Not much.
A few white lambs that would not grow;
Some violets that would stay; some snow
    Not quite too cold for you to touch.

I'd not have taught my birds to fly;
    My deepest seas would not be deep!—
My highest mountains hardly high;
My deserts full of dates should lie—
    But why will you not go to sleep?

I'd *not* have made the wind, because
    It's made of—nothing. Never mind.
Nor any white bears—they have claws;
(Nor "Science," no, nor "Nature's laws!")
    Nor made the North Pole hard to find!

I'd *not* have made the monkeys—(then
    No one could ever prove to me
There ever was a season when
All these fine creatures we call men
    Hung chattering in some tropic tree!)

Once more, Good-night. This time you hear?
    Please hear as well my morning call.
    ——Yes, first I'll tell you something queer:
If *I* had made the world, I fear—
    I'd not have made the world at all!

❧ Sarah Piatt

KEEPING THE FAITH

How long must you believe in Fairy-land?
   Forever, child. You must not bear to doubt
That one true country sweeter than this honey,
   Where little people surely go about
And buy and sell with grains of golden sand,
Which they, indeed, the foolish things, call money!

Believe, while out of broken bits of dew,
   For window-panes, something you cannot see—
Something that never *was* a bird—is peeping,
   And whispering what you cannot hear to you,
Shy as a shadow, where some good old tree,
Close by, its friendly watch and ward is keeping.

Who have believed in it? Why, all the men
   In all the world—and all the women, too.
Because it is so pleasant to believe in:
   There are so many pretty things to do,
Such light to laugh and dance in; yes, and then
Such lonesome, rainy woods for one to grieve in.

Believe in it. Until he sailed from Spain
   Columbus did. (But keep it out of sight.)
Yes, he found Fairy-land, and found it surely,
   (And landed there as one who had a right;)
But reached his hand for it, and caught a chain,
   Which in his coffin he can keep securely.

Then captains have believed in it and gone
   With swords and soldiers there to fight for it,
And torn their plumes and spoiled their scarlet sashes,
   But mended matters for us scarce a whit.
Why, Cinderella, her glass slippers on,
   Goes there—yes, now—from kitchen-smoke and ashes!

Did I believe in Fairy-land? I do.
   The young believe in it less than the old.
As eyes grow blind and heads grow white and whiter
   (The heads that dreamed about it in their gold)
We change its name to Heaven. That makes it true,
And all the light of all the stars grows lighter.

OFFERS FOR THE CHILD

In the dim spaces of a dream, you see—
    Somewhere, perhaps, or else not anywhere,
(Remember in a dream what things may be)—
    I met a stranger with the whitest hair.

From his wide, wandering beard the snow-flakes whirled—
    (His face when young, no doubt, was much admired:)
His name was Atlas, and he held the world;
    I held a child—and both of us were tired.

"A handsome boy," he courteously said;
    "He pleases my old fancy. What fine eyes!"
"Yes, father, but he wearies me. My head
    Is aching, too, and—listen how he cries!"

"If you would let me take him"—and he spread
    All his fair laces and deep velvets wide;
Then hid them from my smile, and in their stead,
    Sweet jewels and vague sums of gold he tried.

Then ships, all heavy with the scents and sounds
    Of many a sea, the stains of many a sun;
Then palaces, with empires for their grounds,
    Were slowly offered to me, one by one.

"Then take the world! It will amuse you. So,
    Watch while I move its wires." An instant, then,
He laughed. "Look, child, at this quick puppet-show:"
    I saw a rich land dusk with marching men.

"This puppet with the smile inscrutable,
    You call The Emperor; these, Statesmen; these—
No matter; this, who just now plays the fool,
    Is"—"Not our"—"It is, madam, if you please!"*

"Hush!—" "Take the world and move them as you will!—
    Give me the boy."
                            —Then, shivering with affright,
I held the close cheek's dimples closer still,
    And bade the old Peddler—for I woke—good-night!

*186–.

Fr. John Banister Tabb

SLEEP

When he is a little chap,
    We call him *Nap.*
When he somewhat older grows,
    We call him *Doze.*
When his age by hours we number,
    We call him *Slumber.*

Mary E. Wilkins [Freeman]

AT THE DREAMLAND GATE

The winds go down in peace, dear child,
The birds are circling o'er the sea;
The Dreamland gate before thee swings
With murmur soft as drowsy bee;
Now enter in, dear child, nor fear, nor fear lest harm should come to thee.

Beyond the gate I cannot go,
But here I'll stand, nor stir away,
While, with the Dreamland children, thou
Shalt frolic till the break of day;
Fear not to enter in, dear child; for close beside the gate I'll stay.

And if in Dreamland's lovely woods
Some harmless giant lay in wait,
Some straggler from thy fairy tales,
He'll take to flight disconsolate—
Just say, "Away! or I will tell my mother at the Dreamland gate!"

ᏻᎦ Mary McNeil Fenollosa

GOOD-LUCK DREAMS

Last night I dreamed of Fuji-San,
　I saw its snowy crest.
Of all the dreams in all Japan
　This dream is quite the best.

Some splendid luck it always brings.
　I wonder what I'll choose
There are so very many things
　A boy like me can use.

My little brother wants a kite.
　I'm far too old for that.

I heard my sister pray last night
　To find a lonesome cat.

Poor babies! Well, it isn't right
　To keep my luck alone.
Perhaps I'll dream again to-night
　And see a bigger cone.

I'll dream of egg-plants in a row;
　Of falcons flying free.
Of all the dreams a boy may know
　These are the lucky three.

ᏻᎦ Sarah Piatt

LAST WORDS
Over a little bed at night

Good-night, pretty sleepers of mine—
　I shall never see you again:
Ah, never in shadow or shine;
　Ah, never in dew or in rain!

In your small dreaming-dresses of white,
　With the wild-bloom you gathered to-day
In your quiet shut hands, from the light
　And the dark you will wander away.

Though no graves in the bee-haunted grass,
　And no love in the beautiful sky,
Shall take you as yet, you will pass,
　With this kiss, through these tear-drops. Good-by!

With less gold and more gloom in their hair,
　When the buds near have faded to flowers,
Three faces may wake here as fair—
　But older than yours are, by hours!

Good-night, then, lost darlings of mine—
　I never shall see you again:
Ah, never in shadow or shine;
　Ah, never in dew or in rain!

GOOD NIGHT

1. The sun has sunk behind the hills,
      The shadows o'er the landscape creep;
   A drowsy sound the woodland fills,
      As nature folds her arms to sleep:
            Good night—good night.

2. The chattering jay has ceased his din,
      The noisy robin sings no more;
   The crow, his mountain haunt within,
      Dreams 'mid the forest's surly roar:
            Good night—good night.

3. The sunlit cloud floats dim and pale;
      The dew is falling soft and still,
   The mist hangs trembling o'er the vale,
      And silence broods o'er yonder mill:
            Good night—good night.

4. The rose, so ruddy in the light,
      Bends on its stem all rayless now;
   And by its side a lily white,
      A sister shadow, seems to bow:
            Good night—good night.

5. The bat may wheel on silent wing,
      The fox his guilty vigils keep,
   The boding owl his dirges sing;
      But love and innocence will sleep:
            Good night—good night.

THE SHADOWS

All up and down in shadow-town
   The shadow children go;
In every street you're sure to meet
   Them running to and fro.

They move around without a sound,
   They play at hide-and-seek,
But no one yet that I have met
   Has ever heard them speak.

Beneath the tree you often see
   Them dancing in and out,
And in the sun there's always one
   To follow you about.

Go where you will, he follows still,
   Or sometimes runs before,
And, home at last, you'll find him fast
   Beside you at the door.

A faithful friend he is to lend
   His presence everywhere;
Blow out the light—to bed at night—
   Your shadow-mate is there!

Then he will call the shadows all
   Into your room to leap,
And such a pack! they make it black,
   And fill your eyes with sleep!

TABLE OF CONTENTS BY DATE

Within each date range, entries appear first by date, then alphabetically by author's last name (or, in the case of pseudonyms composed of only initials, by first initial), then alphabetically by title of poem. Works by "Author Unknown" are alphabetized under A. The sampler verses have two designations, "Wrought by" (where the maker signed her work) and "Maker Unknown" (where the sampler was un-signed). These designations are used because the embroiderers often used verses coming from parents, schoolteachers, friends, prayer books, literary texts, or other sources; thus, it is often impossible to at-tribute "authorship" to these individuals. Works by "Maker Unknown" are alphabetized under M.

Wrought by Mary O. Randall, [Science adorns and virtue beams divine], 1822

Wrought by Emma Anna Gailliard, [May virtue in your heart preside], 1823

Clement Clarke Moore, "A Visit from St. Nicholas," *The Troy* [NY] *Sentinel*, 1823

Maker Unknown, [No other care than this I knew], 1824

Author Unknown, "BEANS, PEAS &c. &c.," in Day, *New-York Cries, in Rhyme*, 1828

Author Unknown, "HOT CORN!" in Day, *New-York Cries, in Rhyme*, 1828

Author Unknown, "MATCHES!" in Day, *New-York Cries, in Rhyme*, 1828

Author Unknown, "NEW MILK," in Day, *New-York Cries, in Rhyme*, 1828

Author Unknown, "SAND O!" in Day, *New-York Cries, in Rhyme*, 1828

Wrought by Mary Wing Dodge, [Swift to award a parent's cares], 1826

Wrought by Sarah Ann Engle, "Extract" [By holiness and watchful care], 1827

Wrought by Mary B. Gove, [As thus my hand with artful aim], 1827

Author Unknown, "Pork and Beef," *Juvenile Poems; or the Alphabet in Verse: Designed for the Entertainment of All Good Boys and Girls, and No Others*, 1828

Author Unknown, "What Is Mutton," *Juvenile Poems; or the Alphabet in Verse: Designed for the Entertainment of All Good Boys and Girls, and No Others*, 1828

Author Unknown, "What Is Veal," *Juvenile Poems; or the Alphabet in Verse: Designed for the Entertainment of All Good Boys and Girls, and No Others*, 1828

Wrought by Eliza Longfellow, [Whence did the wondrous mystic Art arise], 1828

A—e, "The Idiot Boy," *The Juvenile Miscellany*, 1829

Author Unknown, "The Reindeer and the Rabbit," *The Juvenile Miscellany*, 1829

Author Unknown, "Winter," *The Juvenile Miscellany*, 1829

Lydia Maria Child, "Little Bird! Little Bird!" *The Juvenile Miscellany*, 1829

"Cora" [pseudonym] (age 13), "The Star," *The Juvenile Miscellany*, 1829

Anna Maria Wells, "Compassion," *The Juvenile Miscellany*, 1829

Maker Unknown, [Let no one in tears pass my cot], before 1830

1830s

George R. Allen (age 12), "On Slavery," in Andrews, *History of the New-York African Free-Schools*, 1830 (written in 1828)

Authors Unknown, "Lines Spoken at a Public Examination 1821, by Two Female Pupils (Twins) Written for the Occasion," in Andrews, *The History of the New-York African Free-Schools*, 1830

Author Unknown, "For there is yet a liberty unsung," *The History of the New-York African Free-Schools*, 1830 (adapted from William Cowper's "The Task," 1822)

Author Unknown, "On the Sun," in Andrews, *The History of the New-York African Free-Schools*, 1830

Wrought by Sarah Ballinger, [O what great need there is indeed], 1830

Adeline Groves (age 14), "Original Composition, Lines on Joseph's Grave," in Andrews, *The History of the New-York African Free-Schools*, 1830

Sarah Josepha Hale, "Birds," *Poems for Our Children*, 1830

Sarah Josepha Hale, "Mary's Lamb," *The Juvenile Miscellany*, 1830

Sarah Josepha Hale, "My Country," *Poems for Our Children*, 1830

Thomas S. Sidney (age 12), "On Freedom," *The History of the New-York African Free-Schools*, 1830 (written in 1828)

Andrew R. Smith, "Lines on the School Fair," *The History of the New-York African Free-Schools*, 1830

James Smith (age 14), "Night," in Charles, *The History of the New-York African Free-Schools*, 1830

"Cora" [pseudonym], "The Little Boy's Lament" and "The Little Girl's Reply," *The Juvenile Miscellany*, 1831

Hannah Flagg Gould, "The Broken Pipe," *The Juvenile Miscellany*, 1831

Hannah Flagg Gould, "The Child's Address to the Kentucky Mummy," *The Juvenile Miscellany*, 1831

Hannah Flagg Gould, "The Peach Blossoms," *The Juvenile Miscellany*, 1831

Wrought by Mary Pets (or Marie Petz), "Virtue," 1831

1850S

"Peter Parley" [Samuel Goodrich], "Butterfly and Bee," *Parley's Poetical Present*, 1850

William Oland Bourne, "The Busy Knitter," *Woodworth's Youth's Cabinet*, 1851

Hannah Flagg Gould, "The Dissatisfied Angler Boy," *The Youth's Coronal*, 1851

Hannah Flagg Gould, "The Indian Boy with His Father's Bow," *The Youth's Coronal*, 1851

Author Unknown, "Distant Worlds," *Robert Merry's Museum*, 1852

Oliver Wendell Holmes, "The Ballad of the Oysterman," *Poems*, 1852

Eliza Lee Cabot Follen, "Butterflies Are Pretty Things," *New Nursery Songs for All Good Children*, 1853

Eliza Lee Cabot Follen, "The Dog and the Cat, the Duck and the Rat," *New Nursery Songs for All Good Children*, 1853

Eliza Lee Cabot Follen, "The Farm Yard," *New Nursery Songs for All Good Children*, 1853

Eliza Lee Cabot Follen, "The Three Little Kittens," *New Nursery Songs for All Good Children*, 1853 [adapted from English traditional verse; this version from the 1856 edition of *Little Songs*]

Author Unknown, "Curious Rhymes," *Robert Merry's Museum*, 1854

William Cullen Bryant, "Robert of Lincoln," *Poems*, 1854

"Corinne," "Our Wreath of Rose Buds," *Cherokee Rose Buds*, 1854

Ralph Waldo Emerson, "So Nigh Is Grandeur," *Poems*, 1854

"Peter Parley" [Samuel G. Goodrich], "The River," in Buckley, *The Girl's First Help to Reading; or, Selections from the Best Authors*, 1854

Lily Lee (Cherokee), "Literary Day among the Birds," *Wreath of Cherokee Rose Buds*, 1855

Seba Smith, "Revolutionary Tea," *The Wide-Awake: A Know-Nothing Token for 1855*, 1855

John Greenleaf Whittier, "The Barefoot Boy," *The Little Pilgrim*, 1855

Frances E. W. Harper, "The Little Builders," *Poems*, 1857

Phoebe Cary, "Nearer Home," *The Ladies' Repository*, 1858

Leila Lee, "Conversation upon Ice," *Wee Wee Songs for Our Little Pets*, 1858

Leila Lee, "Little Lydia and the Razor," *Wee Wee Songs for Our Little Pets*, 1858

Henry Wadsworth Longfellow, "The Children," *The Courtship of Miles Standish, and Other Poems*, 1858

1860S

Henry Wadsworth Longfellow, "The Children's Hour," *Atlantic Monthly*, 1860

Anna Bartlett Warner, "Jesus Loves Me," from novel co-written with Susan Warner, *Say and Seal*, vol. 2, 1860

Louisa May Alcott, "Song," *Reports of the Selectmen and Other Officers of the Town of Concord*, 1861

"A Lady of Savannah" [pseudonym], "Willie's Political Alphabet," *For the Little Ones*, 1861

Henry Wadsworth Longfellow, "Paul Revere's Ride," *Atlantic Monthly*, 1861

Rose Terry [Cooke], "A Child's Wish," *Poems*, 1861

Anna Bartlett Warner, "Jesus Bids Us Shine," *The Children of Blackberry Hollow*, 1863

John Greenleaf Whittier, "Barbara Frietchie," *Atlantic Monthly*, 1863

Louisa May Alcott, "Lullaby," *The Rose Family: A Fairy Tale*, 1864

Author Unknown, "Sanitary Fair Limericks," Ladies of the Sanitary Commission, *The New Book of Nonsense: A Contribution to the Great Central Fair*, 1864

"Kruna" [Julia Pratt Ballard], "The Boys' 'Fourth of July,'" *Robert Merry's Museum*, 1865

Lucy Larcom, "The Volunteer's Thanksgiving," *Our Young Folks*, 1865

Henry Wadsworth Longfellow, "Christmas Bells," *Our Young Folks*, 1865

Harriet E. Prescott [Spofford], "Christmas," *Our Young Folks*, 1865

Thomas Buchanan Read, "Sheridan's Ride," *A Summer Story, Sheridan's Ride, and Other Poems*, 1865

Tacie Townsend, "The Night-Moth," *Our Young Folks*, 1865

Anna Maria Wells, "Disappointment," *Our Young Folks*, 1865

Louisa May Alcott, "Our Little Ghost," *Flag of Our Union*, 1866

J. Warren Newcomb, Jr., "Work and Play," *Our Young Folks*, 1866

Anna Maria Wells, "The Cow-Boy's Song," *Our Young Folks*, 1866

Caroline Howard Gilman, and Caroline Howard Gilman Jervey, "The Boy Is Cold," from "The Schoolboy and His Eight Troubles," *Stories and Poems by Mother and Daughter*, 1872

Caroline Howard Gilman, and Caroline Howard Gilman Jervey, "Cannot Write Poetry," from "The Schoolboy and His Eight Troubles," *Stories and Poems by Mother and Daughter*, 1872

Caroline Howard Gilman, and Caroline Howard Gilman Jervey, "Not Ready for School," from "The Schoolboy and His Eight Troubles," *Stories and Poems by Mother and Daughter*, 1872

Nora Perry, "Bess and Ben," *Our Young Folks*, 1872

Author Unknown, "The Johnny Cake," *The Nursery: A Monthly Magazine for the Youngest Readers*, 1873

Author Unknown, "To the Children of the Rich for the Children of the Poor," in M.A., Sisters of Mercy, *Poems for Catholics and Convents and Plays for Catholic Schools*, 1873

Alice Cary, "Barbara Blue," *Ballads for Little Folk*, 1873

Alice Cary, "Spider and Fly," *Ballads for Little Folk*, 1873

Alice Cary, "Telling Fortunes," *Ballads for Little Folk*, 1873

Alice Cary, "Three Bugs," *Ballads for Little Folk*, 1873

Phoebe Cary, "The Crow's Children," *Ballads for Little Folk*, 1873

Phoebe Cary, "Feathers," *Ballads for Little Folk*, 1873

Phoebe Cary, "Griselda Goose," *Ballads for Little Folk*, 1873

Phoebe Cary, "The Happy Little Wife," *Ballads for Little Folk*, 1873

Rose Terry Cooke, "Turkey: A Thanksgiving Ode," *Our Young Folks*, 1873

Anne L. Huber, "Daddy Longlegs," *The Nursery Rattle. For Little Folks*, 1873

Anne L. Huber, "How Much, and How Many," *The Nursery Rattle. For Little Folks*, 1873

Anne L. Huber, "The Kilkenny Cats," *The Nursery Rattle. For Little Folks*, 1873

Anne L. Huber, "The Little Boy's Pocket," *The Nursery Rattle. For Little Folks*, 1873

Anne L. Huber, "The Locomotive," *The Nursery Rattle. For Little Folks*, 1873

Anne L. Huber, "The Man in the Moon," *The Nursery Rattle. For Little Folks*, 1873

Anne L. Huber, "The Monkey and the Pussy Cat," *The Nursery Rattle. For Little Folks*, 1873

Anne L. Huber, "My Wife Peggy," *The Nursery Rattle. For Little Folks*, 1873

Anne L. Huber, "The Old Maid and the Bachelor," *The Nursery Rattle. For Little Folks*, 1873

Anne L. Huber, "Widow McCree," *The Nursery Rattle. For Little Folks*, 1873

Anne L. Huber, "Won't I, and I Won't," *The Nursery Rattle. For Little Folks*, 1873

M.A., Sisters of Mercy, "The Geography of Ireland," *Poems for Catholics and Convents and Plays for Catholic Schools*, 1873

John Godfrey Saxe, "The Blind Men and the Elephant: A Hindoo Fable," *The Poems of John Godfrey Saxe*, 1873

John Godfrey Saxe, "How Cyrus Laid the Cable," *The Poems of John Godfrey Saxe*, 1873

Eudora May Stone (age 12), "The Chickadee," *Our Young Folks*, 1873

M.A., Sisters of Mercy, "St. Patrick's Day," *Poems for Catholics and Convents and Plays for Catholic Schools*, 1873

M.A., Sisters of Mercy, "St. Patrick's Day without Shamrocks," *Poems for Catholics and Convents and Plays for Catholic Schools*, 1873

Islay Walden, "Dedicated to M. W. W., on Making, for the First Time, a Shirt," *Walden's Miscellaneous Poems*. Second edition, 1873

Clara Doty Bates, "The Cheated Mosquitoes," *St. Nicholas*, 1874

Rose Terry Cooke, "Peter Parrot," *St. Nicholas*, 1874

C. P. Cranch, "The Earth, the Moon and the Comet," *St. Nicholas*, 1874

Mary Mapes Dodge, "The Alphabet," *Rhymes and Jingles*, 1874

Mary Mapes Dodge, "Among the Animals," *Rhymes and Jingles*, 1874

Mary Mapes Dodge, "The Ants," *Rhymes and Jingles*, 1874

Mary Mapes Dodge, "At the Window," *Rhymes and Jingles*, 1874

Mary Mapes Dodge, "Burs," *Rhymes and Jingles*, 1874

Mary Mapes Dodge, "Farm Lessons," *Rhymes and Jingles*, 1874

Mary Mapes Dodge, "Good Mistress Sundial," *Rhymes and Jingles*, 1874

Mary Mapes Dodge, "Good-Night!" *Rhymes and Jingles*, 1874

Joel Stacy, "The Naughty Little Egyptian," *St. Nicholas*, 1877

Various, Authors Unknown, "Mary's Lamb" parodies: *Godey's Lady's Book*, 1872; *The Virginia Spectator*, 1872; Morgan, *Macaronic Poetry*, 1872; *Indiana School Journal*, 1877

M. B. Whiting, "The Seven Ages," *St. Nicholas*, 1877

John Greenleaf Whittier, "Red Riding-Hood," *St. Nicholas*, 1877

Thomas Bailey Aldrich, "Cradle Song," from *Mercedes* in *Harper's New Monthly*, 1878

Bessie Hill, "Some children roam the fields and hills," *St. Nicholas*, 1878

Samuel W. Duffield, "Little Bear," *St. Nicholas*, 1878

Howell Foster, "What Happened," *St. Nicholas*, 1878

S. Conant Foster, "The Crow That the Crow Crowed," *St. Nicholas*, 1878

Elaine Goodale [Eastman] (age 15), "Ashes of Roses," *Apple-Blossoms: Verses of Two Children*, 1878

Sarah Orne Jewett, "Only a Doll!" *St. Nicholas*, 1878

Laura E. Richards, "Belinda Blonde," *St. Nicholas*, 1878

Laura E. Richards, "Tommy's Dream, or the Geography Demon," *St. Nicholas*, 1878

Author Unknown, "Santa Claus," *St. Nicholas*, 1879

Palmer Cox, "The Funny Mandarin," *St. Nicholas*, 1879

Mary Mapes Dodge, "Snow-Flakes," *Along the Way*, 1879

"Eadgyth" [Edith Wharton] (age 15), "Only a Child," *The World* [New York], 1879

H. H. [Helen Hunt Jackson], "The Shining Little House," *St. Nicholas*, 1879

Lucy Larcom, "Rosebud," *St. Nicholas*, 1879

"M.M." [pseudonym], "The Sleeping Beauty," *Youth's Companion*, 1879

Nancy Minerva Haynes Miller, "The Wind," *Mother Truth's Melodies. Common Sense for Children. A Kindergarten*, 1879

Frederick Palmer, "There was an old man of the Nile," *St. Nicholas*, 1879

"Peter Parley" [Samuel Goodrich], "Good Night," in McGuffey, *McGuffey's Fifth Eclectic Reader*, 1879

C. Perry, "A Boy's Remonstrance," *St. Nicholas*, 1879

Laura E. Richards, "The Sad Story of the Dandy Cat," *St. Nicholas*, 1879

Margaret Vandegrift, "Catching the Cat," *St. Nicholas*, 1879

Stephen Crane (about age 9), "I'd Rather Have—," manuscript, c. 1879–1880

1880s

Mary L. Bolles Branch, "The Petrified Fern," in Bryant, *The Family Library of Poetry and Song*, 1880

R. S. Chilton, "The Little Peasant," *St. Nicholas*, 1880

Charles de Kay, "Boozy Little Bat," *Hesperus, and Other Poems*, 1880

Rosa Graham, "Sow, Sew, and So," *St. Nicholas*, 1880

Paul H. Hayne, "The Three Copecks," *St. Nicholas*, 1880

James Whitcomb Riley, "A Nonsense Rhyme," *St. Nicholas*, 1880

"Bonnie Doon" [pseudonym], "Little Dora's Soliloquy," *St. Nicholas*, 1881

Mary E. Wilkins [Freeman], "The Beggar King," *Wide Awake*, 1881

Rosa Graham, "Babel," *St. Nicholas*, 1881

T[acie] T[ownsend] Purvis, "Ruth, A Ballad of '36," *Hagar: The Singing Maiden, with Other Stories and Rhymes*, 1881

T[acie] T[ownsend] Purvis, "What the Lichens Sang," *Hagar: The Singing Maiden, with Other Stories and Rhymes*, 1881

Thomas Hall Shastid (est. age 14), "Cleopatra's Needles," *Poems*, 1881

Author Unknown, "Love in a Noah's Ark," *St. Nicholas*, 1882

H.H. [Helen Hunt Jackson], "Grab-Bag," *St. Nicholas*, 1882

Kate Lawrence, "Questions," *Wide Awake*, 1882

Mrs. S. C. Stone, "The Punjaubs of Siam," *St. Nicholas*, 1882

Celia Thaxter, "The Pretty Puritan," *St. Nicholas*, 1882

Nellie L. Tinkham, "A Question of Color," *St. Nicholas*, 1882

Esther Aswell, "Nothing But Toadstools," *Wide Awake*, 1883

Clara Doty Bates, "Naming the Kitten," *Wide Awake*, 1883

Lilian Dynevor Rice, "A Fourth of July Record," *St. Nicholas*, 1887

A. R. Wells, "Going! Going!" *St. Nicholas*, 1887

M.E.B., "Teddy the Teazer: A Moral Story with a Velocipede Attachment," in Harland, *Young People's New Pictorial Library of Poetry and Prose*, 1888

Elizabeth Lincoln Shackford, "A Little Maid's Wish," in Harland, *Young People's New Pictorial Library of Poetry and Prose*, 1888

Louisa May Alcott (about age 12), "Despondency," *Louisa May Alcott: Her Life, Letters, and Journals*, 1889

Louisa May Alcott, "The Lay of a Golden Goose," *Louisa May Alcott: Her Life, Letters, and Journals*, 1889

Louisa May Alcott (age 15), "To Mother," *Louisa May Alcott: Her Life, Letters, and Journals*, 1889

Eugene Field, "Dutch Lullaby" ["Wynken, Blynken, and Nod"], *A Little Book of Western Verse*, 1889

Eugene Field, "Little Boy Blue," *A Little Book of Western Verse*, 1889

Lucy Larcom, "My Childhood's Enchantress," *St. Nicholas*, 1889

Edward Rowland Sill, "A Baker's Duzzen Uv Wize Sawz," *The Century*, 1889

1890s

Augusta [Joyce] Crocheron, "A Scene of the Early Days," *The Children's Book: A Collection of Short Stories and Poems, a Mormon Book for Mormon Children*, 1890

Emily Dickinson, "As children bid the guest good-night," *Poems by Emily Dickinson*. First Series, 1890

Emily Dickinson, "Autumn," *Poems by Emily Dickinson*. First Series, 1890

Emily Dickinson, "A Day," *Poems by Emily Dickinson*. First Series, 1890

Emily Dickinson, "The Mountain," *Poems by Emily Dickinson*. First Series, 1890

Emily Dickinson, "The Sea of Sunset," *Poems by Emily Dickinson*. First Series, 1890

Mary Mapes Dodge, "Looking Back," *St. Nicholas*, 1890

Robert Frost (age 16), "Tenochtitlan," from "La Noche Triste," *Lawrence High School Bulletin*, 1890

Laura E. Richards, "A Howl about an Owl," *In My Nursery*, 1890

Laura E. Richards, "A Legend of Lake Okeefinokee," *In My Nursery*, 1890

Laura E. Richards, "Little Old Baby," *In My Nursery*, 1890

Laura E. Richards, "The Mermaidens," *In My Nursery*, 1890

Laura E. Richards, "An Old Rat's Tale," *In My Nursery*, 1890

Laura E. Richards, "The Owl and the Eel and the Warming-Pan," *In My Nursery*, 1890

Laura E. Richards, "The Palace," *In My Nursery*, 1890

Laura E. Richards, "Wiggle and Waggle and Bubble and Squeak," *In My Nursery*, 1890

James Whitcomb Riley, "The Happy Little Cripple," *Rhymes of Childhood*, 1890

James Whitcomb Riley, "Little Orphant Annie," *Rhymes of Childhood*, 1890

James Whitcomb Riley, "The Nine Little Goblins," *Rhymes of Childhood*, 1890

James Whitcomb Riley, "The Raggedy Man," *Rhymes of Childhood*, 1890

Lilian Taylor (age 9), "The Crimson Tree," *May Blossoms*, 1890

Ina Coolbrith, "December," *St. Nicholas*, 1891

Emily Dickinson, "In the Garden," *Poems by Emily Dickinson*. Second Series, 1891

Emily Dickinson, "Simplicity," *Poems by Emily Dickinson*. Second Series, 1891

Emily Dickinson, "The Storm," *Poems by Emily Dickinson*. Second Series, 1891

Robert Frost (age 17), "The Sachem of the Clouds," *Lawrence Daily American*, 1891

Lizzie M. Hadley, "A Secret," in Owen, *Readings, Recitations, and Impersonations*, 1891

Walt Whitman, "The Commonplace," *Leaves of Grass, 2D Annex. Good-Bye My Fancy*, 1891

Lydia Brawner, "A Lament," *Harper's Young People*, 1892

Charles E. Carryl, "Memorandrums," in *The Admiral's Caravan*, *St. Nicholas*, 1892

Charles Edward Carryl, "The Plaint of the Camel," from "The Admiral's Caravan," *St. Nicholas*, 1892

Susan Coolidge, "How the Snow-man Felt," *Rhymes and Ballads for Girls and Boys*, 1892

Susan Coolidge, "The World-Wide Consolation," *Rhymes and Ballads for Girls and Boys*, 1892

Ruth McEnery Stuart and Albert Bigelow Paine, "The Somethings," *Gobolinks, or Shadow-Pictures for Young and Old*, 1896

Ruth McEnery Stuart and Albert Bigelow Paine, "A What-Is-It," *Gobolinks, or Shadow-Pictures for Young and Old*, 1896

Sarah Loring Bailey, "Sarah Orne's Sampler," *Poems*, 1897

Gelett Burgess, "The Lazy Roof," *The Lark*, 1897

Gelett Burgess, "My Feet," *The Lark*, 1897

Gelett Burgess, "The Purple Cow" and "Envoi," *The Lark*, 1897

Mary E. Wilkins [Freeman], "At the Dreamland Gate," *Once upon a Time and Other Child-Verses*, 1897

Mary E. Wilkins [Freeman], "Caraway," *Once upon a Time and Other Child-Verses*, 1897

Mary E. Wilkins [Freeman], "Down in the Clover," *Once upon a Time and Other Child-Verses*, 1897

Mary E. Wilkins [Freeman], "The Enlightenment of Mamma," *Once upon a Time and Other Child-Verses*, 1897

Mary E. Wilkins [Freeman], "Katy-Did—Katy-Didn't," *Once upon a Time and Other Child-Verses*, 1897

Mary E. Wilkins [Freeman], "A Little Peachling," *Once upon a Time and Other Child-Verses*, 1897

Mary E. Wilkins [Freeman], "Once upon a Time," *Once upon a Time and Other Child-Verses*, 1897

Mary E. Wilkins [Freeman], "A Pretty Ambition," *Once upon a Time and Other Child-Verses*, 1897

Mary E. Wilkins [Freeman], "The Prize," *Once upon a Time and Other Child-Verses*, 1897

Mary E. Wilkins [Freeman], "Pussy-Willow," *Once upon a Time and Other Child-Verses*, 1897

Mary E. Wilkins [Freeman], "The Sick Fairy," *Once upon a Time and Other Child-Verses*, 1897

Mary E. Wilkins [Freeman], "A Silly Boy," *Once upon a Time and Other Child-Verses*, 1897

Mary E. Wilkins [Freeman], "Sliding Down Hill," *Once upon a Time and Other Child-Verses*, 1897

Mary E. Wilkins [Freeman], "A Song," *Once upon a Time and Other Child-Verses*, 1897

Mary E. Wilkins [Freeman], "The Spoiled Darling," *Once upon a Time and Other Child-Verses*, 1897

Mary E. Wilkins [Freeman], "The Three Margery Daws," *Once upon a Time and Other Child-Verses*, 1897

Mary E. Wilkins [Freeman], "Tiger Lilies," *Once upon a Time and Other Child-Verses*, 1897

Mary E. Wilkins [Freeman], "Two Little Birds in Blue," *Once upon a Time and Other Child-Verses*, 1897

Gertrude Heath, "The Bird and the Wires," *Rhymes and Jingles for a Good Child*, 1897

Gertrude Heath, "A Funny Party," *Rhymes and Jingles for a Good Child*, 1897

Gertrude Heath, "In Frogland," *Rhymes and Jingles for a Good Child*, 1897

Gertrude Heath, "A Jingle," *Rhymes and Jingles for a Good Child*, 1897

Gertrude Heath, "July," *Rhymes and Jingles for a Good Child*, 1897

Gertrude Heath, "The Reason Why," *Rhymes and Jingles for a Good Child*, 1897

Gertrude Heath, "Wake," *Rhymes and Jingles for a Good Child*, 1897

Gertrude Heath, "What Roddy Saw," *Rhymes and Jingles for a Good Child*, 1897

Gertrude Heath, "What the Fly Thinks," *Rhymes and Jingles for a Good Child*, 1897

Joaquin Miller, "Columbus," *The Complete Poetical Works of Joaquin Miller*, 1897

Frank Dempster Sherman, "Humming-Bird Song," *Little-Folk Lyrics*, 1897

Frank Dempster Sherman, "The Shadows," *Little-Folk Lyrics*, 1897

Carolyn Wells, "There once was a happy Hyena," *St. Nicholas*, 1897

Author Unknown, "Since Papa Doesn't Drink," *The Juvenile Temperance Reciter*, 1898

H[enry] H[olcomb] Bennett, "The Flag Goes By," *Youth's Companion*, 1898

Mary Norton Bradford, "Her Papa," in Witherbee, *Spanish-American War Songs*, 1898

Arthur James Burdick, "The Runaway Boy," *Just Jingles*, 1898

Mary E[lizabeth] Burt, "The Flying Squirrel," *The Kindergarten Magazine for Teachers and Parents*, 1898

D. G., "Did You Ever?" in Penny, *The Juvenile Temperance Reciter*, 1898

Charlotte Perkins Gilman, "If Mother Knew," *In This Our World*, 1898

Charlotte Perkins Gilman, "Tree Feelings," *In This Our World*, 1898

Mary Mapes Dodge, "Sunlight or Starlight," *Rhymes and Jingles,* 1904

Paul Laurence Dunbar, "The Sand-Man," *Lyrics of Sunshine and Shadow,* 1905

Paul Laurence Dunbar, "When a Feller's Itchin' to Be Spanked," *Lyrics of Sunshine and Shadow,* 1905

Mary E. Wilkins Freeman, "The Ostrich," *Harper's Monthly,* 1905

Josephine Preston Peabody, "Secrets," in "The Dreamer," *Harper's Monthly,* 1905

Adella Washee, "A Summer Day," *Sturm's Oklahoma Magazine,* 1905

Katharine Lee Bates, "The Kings of the East," *McBride's Magazine,* 1906

Katharine Forrest Hamill, "Mrs. Spider," *The Golden Age of Childhood,* 1906

Katharine Forrest Hamill, "The New Brother," *The Golden Age of Childhood,* 1906

Marie Bruckman MacDonald, "The 'Skeeter and Peter," *St. Nicholas,* 1906

Edna St. Vincent Millay (age 14), "Forest Trees," *St. Nicholas,* 1906

Anna B. Patten, "Her Sampler," *St. Nicholas,* 1907

Josephine Preston Peabody, "Windows," *Harper's Monthly,* 1908

Benjamin Franklin King, "The Cat o' Nine Tails," *Jane Jones and Some Others,* 1909

1910S

Christina Moody (age 13–16), "Advice from Uncle Enoux," *A Tiny Spark,* 1910

Christina Moody (age 13–16), "Chillun and Men," *A Tiny Spark,* 1910

Christina Moody (age 13–16), "The Depth From Whence We Came," *A Tiny Spark,* 1910

Christina Moody (age 13–16), "The Little Seed," *A Tiny Spark,* 1910

Christina Moody, (age 13–16), "Mary's Little Goat," *A Tiny Spark,* 1910

Christina Moody (age 13–16), "The Negro's Flag and Country," *A Tiny Spark,* 1910

Christina Moody (age 13–16), "Ol' Man Rain, P'ease Go Away," *A Tiny Spark,* 1910

Christina Moody (age 13–16), "The Pie That Sister Made," *A Tiny Spark,* 1910

Christina Moody (age 13–16), "Sam Found Something New and Mammy Did Too," *A Tiny Spark,* 1910

Christina Moody (age 13–16), "A Tale Told by Grandma," *A Tiny Spark,* 1910

Christina Moody (age 13–16), "To My Dear Reader," *A Tiny Spark,* 1910

Katharine Lee Bates, "Christmas Island," *The Outlook,* 1911

Edna F. Wood (age 15), "The Fairy Messenger," *St. Nicholas,* 1912

Mary McNeil Fenollosa, "Good-Luck Dreams," *Blossoms from a Japanese Garden: A Book of Child-Verses,* 1913

Mary McNeil Fenollosa, "Iris Flowers," *Blossoms from a Japanese Garden: A Book of Child-Verses,* 1913

Mary McNeil Fenollosa, "The Jishin (The Earthquake)," *Blossoms from a Japanese Garden: A Book of Child-Verses,* 1913

Mary McNeil Fenollosa, "A Typhoon," *Blossoms from a Japanese Garden: A Book of Child-Verses,* 1913

Fenton Johnson, "The Plaint of the Factory Child," *Little Dreaming,* 1913

E. Pauline Johnson [Tekahionwake; Mohawk], "The Train Dogs," *Flint and Feather: The Complete Poems of E. Pauline Johnson (Tekahionwake),* 1917

Authors Unknown, "Left Overs from Good English Week: Slogans and Rhymes by Vocational IV, Girls," *The Indian Leader,* 1919

UNKNOWN DATE OF COMPOSITION
(Compiled from Older Sources)

Author Unknown, "Bedbug," in Talley, *Negro Folk-Rhymes, Wise and Otherwise,* 1922

Author Unknown, "Bridle Up er Rat," in Talley, *Negro Folk-Rhymes, Wise and Otherwise,* 1922

Author Unknown, "Fishing Simon," in Talley, *Negro Folk-Rhymes, Wise and Otherwise,* 1922

Author Unknown, "Little Dogs," in Talley, *Negro Folk-Rhymes, Wise and Otherwise,* 1922

INDIVIDUAL-AUTHOR POETRY COLLECTIONS AND NOVELS

Alcott, Louisa May. *Aunt Jo's Scrap-Bag II*. Boston: Roberts Brothers, 1872.

Alcott, Louisa May. *Comic Tragedies*. Boston: Little, Brown, and Company, 1893.

Alcott, Louisa May. *Little Women: or, Meg, Jo, Beth, and Amy. Part First*. Boston: Roberts Brothers, 1868.

Alcott, Louisa May. *Louisa May Alcott: Her Life, Letters, and Journals*. Ed. Ednah D. Cheney. Boston: Roberts Brothers, 1889.

Alcott, Louisa May. *Morning-Glories, and Other Stories*. Boston: Horace B. Fuller, 1867.

Alcott, Louisa May. *The Rose Family: A Fairy Tale*. Boston: James Redpath, 1864.

Aldrich, Thomas Bailey. *The Poems of Thomas Bailey Aldrich*. Boston: Houghton Mifflin, 1885.

Bailey, Sarah Loring. *Poems*. Chicago: Dial Press, 1897.

Bixon, Frank Printz. *Newly Gathered Flowers: A Collection of Original Poems*. New York: Burr Printing House, 1884.

Bryant, William Cullen. *Poems*. New York: D. Appleton, 1854.

Burdick, Arthur James. *Just Jingles*. Buffalo, NY: The Peter Paul Book Co., 1898.

Burgess, Gelett. *Goops and How to Be Them*. New York: Frederick A. Stokes, 1900.

Burgess, Gelett. *More Goops and How Not to Be Them*. New York: Frederick A. Stokes, 1903.

Butterworth, Hezekiah. *Songs of History: Poems and Ballads upon Important Events in American History*. Boston: New England Publishing Co., 1887.

Carryl, Charles Edward. *The Admiral's Caravan*. Boston: Houghton Mifflin, 1892.

Cary, Alice, and Phoebe Cary. *Ballads for Little Folk*. Boston: Houghton Mifflin, 1873.

Chandler, Elizabeth Margaret. *The Poetical Works of Elizabeth Margaret Chandler*. Philadelphia: Lemuel Howell, 1836.

Child, Lydia Maria. *Flowers for Children II. For Children from Four to Six Years Old*. New York: C. S. Francis / Boston: J. H. Francis, 1844.

Clarkson [Whitelock], L[ouise]. *The Gathering of the Lilies*. Philadelphia: J. L. Sibole & Co., 1877.

[Cooke], Rose Terry. *Poems*. Boston: Ticknor and Fields, 1861.

Coolbrith, Ina. *Songs from the Golden Gate*. Boston: Houghton Mifflin, 1895.

Coolidge, Susan. *Rhymes and Ballads for Girls and Boys*. Boston: Roberts Brothers, 1892.

Cox, Palmer. *The Brownies: Their Book*. New York: The Century Co., 1887.

Cox, Palmer. *The Brownies around the World*. New York: The Century Co., 1894.

Crane, Stephen, "I'd Rather Have—," manuscript, c. 1879–1880. Stephen Crane Collection, Special Collections Research Center, Syracuse University Library, Syracuse, New York.

Crocheron, Augusta (Joyce). *The Children's Book: A Collection of Short Stories and Poems, a Mormon Book for Mormon Children*. Bountiful, UT: Augusta Crocheron, 1890.

Davidson, Lucretia. *Poetical Remains of the Late Lucretia Maria Davidson*. Philadelphia: Lea and Blanchard, 1841.

DeKay, Charles. *Hesperus, and Other Poems*. New York: Scribner's, 1880.

Dickinson, Emily. *Poems by Emily Dickinson*. First Series. Edited by Thomas Wentworth Higginson and Mabel Loomis Todd. Boston: Roberts Brothers, 1890.

Dickinson, Emily. *Poems by Emily Dickinson*. Second Series. Edited by Thomas Wentworth Higginson and Mabel Loomis Todd. Boston: Roberts Brothers, 1891.

Dickinson, Emily. *Poems by Emily Dickinson*. Third Series. Edited by Mabel Loomis Todd. Boston: Roberts Brothers, 1896.

Dodge, Mary Mapes. *Along the Way*. New York: Scribner, 1879.

Dodge, Mary Mapes. *Rhymes and Jingles*. New York: Scribner, 1874.

Dodge, Mary Mapes. *Rhymes and Jingles*. 2nd edition. New York: Scribner, 1904.

Douglas, Malcom. *My Odd Little Folk: Rhymes and Verses About Them*. Philadelphia: Henry Altemus, 1893.

Dunbar, Paul Laurence. *Lyrics of Lowly Life*. New York: Dodd, Mead, 1896

Dunbar, Paul Laurence. *Lyrics of Sunshine and Shadow*. New York: Dodd, Mead, 1905.

Dunbar, Paul Laurence. *Poems of Cabin and Field*. New York: Dodd, Mead, 1894.

Emerson, Ralph Waldo. *Poems*. Boston: James Munroe & Co., 1845.

Emerson, Ralph Waldo. *Poems*. Boston: Houghton Mifflin, 1854.

Fenollosa, Mary McNeil. *Blossoms from a Japanese Garden: A Book of Child-Verses*. New York: Frederick A. Stokes, 1913.

Field, Eugene. *A Little Book of Western Verse*. New York: Scribner, 1889.

Field, Eugene. *Love-Songs of Childhood*. New York: Scribner, 1894.

Field, Eugene. *The Writings in Prose and Verse of Eugene Field*. Vol. 4. New York: Scribner, 1894.

Follen, Eliza Lee Cabot. *Hymns, Songs, and Fables, for Young People*. Revised edition. Boston: Wm. Crosby and H. P. Nichols, 1846.

Follen, Eliza Lee Cabot. *Little Songs*. Boston: Leonard C. Bowles, 1833. Reprinted 1856.

Follen, Eliza Lee Cabot. *New Nursery Songs for All Good Children*. London: Addey & Company, 1853; London: James Blackwood, 1860.

[Freeman], Mary E. Wilkins. *Once Upon a Time and Other Child-Verses*. Boston: Lothrop, 1897.

Gilman, Caroline Howard, and Caroline Howard Gilman Jervey. *Stories and Poems by Mother and Daughter*. Boston: Lee & Shepard, 1872.

Gilman, Charlotte Perkins. *In This Our World*. Boston: Small, Maynard & Co., 1898 [c. 1893].

Gilman, Charlotte Perkins. *In This Our World, and Other Poems*. San Francisco: James H. Barry and John H. Marble, 1895 [c. 1893].

Goodrich, Samuel ["Peter Parley"]. *Parley's Poetical Present*. Worcester, MA: J. Grout, Jr., 1850.

Gould, Hannah Flagg. *Poems*. Boston: Hilliard & Gray, 1832.

Gould, Hannah Flagg. *Poems*. Vol. II. Boston: Hilliard & Gray, 1836.

Gould, Hannah Flagg. *Poems*, Vol. III. Boston: Hilliard & Gray, 1841.

Gould, Hannah Flagg. *The Youth's Coronal*. New York: D. Appleton, 1851.

Hale, Sarah Josepha. *Poems for Our Children*. Boston: Wait & Dow's, 1830.

Hamill, Katharine Forrest. *The Golden Age of Childhood*. New York: Platt & Peck, 1906.

Harper, Frances E. W. *Poems*. Philadelphia: Merrihew & Thompson, 1857.

Harper, Frances E. W. *Poems*. Philadelphia: George S. Furguson, 1895.

Heath, Gertrude. *Rhymes and Jingles for a Good Child*. Cincinnati: Editor Publishing Company, 1897.

Herford, Oliver. *Artful Anticks*. New York: The Century Co., 1894.

Herford, Oliver. *The Bashful Earthquake and Other Fables and Verses*. New York: Scribner, 1898.

Herford, Oliver. *A Child's Primer of Natural History*. New York: Scribner, 1899.

Holmes, Oliver Wendell. *Poems*. Boston: Ticknor, Reed & Fields, 1852.

Huber, Anne. *The Nursery Rattle. For Little Folks*. Philadelphia: Lippincott, 1873.

Jackson, Helen Hunt. *Bits of Talk in Verse and Prose for Young Folks*. Boston: Roberts Brothers, 1876.

Johnson, E. Pauline (Tekahionwake; Mohawk). *Canadian Born*. Toronto: Morang, 1903.

Johnson, E. Pauline (Tekahionwake; Mohawk). *Flint and Feather: The Complete Poems of E. Pauline Johnson (Tekahionwake)*. Toronto: Musson Book Co., 1917.

Johnson, E. Pauline (Tekahionwake; Mohawk). *The White Wampum*. Toronto: Copp Clark, 1895.

Johnson, Fenton. *Little Dreaming*. Chicago: Peterson Linotyping Company, 1913.

Juvenile Poems. Wendell, MA: J. Metcalf, 1828.

Juvenile Poems; or the Alphabet in Verse: Designed for the Entertainment of All Good Boys and Girls, and No Others. Philadelphia: John Adams, 1804.

Kimball, Harriet McEwen. *Swallow-Flights*. New York: Dutton, 1874.

King, Benjamin Franklin. *Ben King's Verse*. Chicago: Press Club of Chicago, 1894.

King, Benjamin Franklin. *Jane Jones and Some Others*. Chicago: Forbes & Company, 1909.

"A Lady of Savannah." *For the Little Ones*. Savannah, GA: John M. Cooper, 1861.

Larcom, Lucy. *Childhood Songs*. Boston: Houghton, Mifflin, 1874.

Larcom, Lucy. *The Poetical Works of Lucy Larcom*. Boston/New York: Houghton Mifflin, 1884.

Lee, Agnes. *The Round Rabbit*. Boston: Copeland & Day, 1898.

Lee, Leila. *Wee Wee Songs for Our Little Pets*. Boston: HV Degen, 1858.

Longfellow, Henry Wadsworth. *The Courtship of Miles Standish, and Other Poems*. Boston: Ticknor and Fields, 1858.

Longfellow, Henry Wadsworth. *Poems*. New York: Harper & Brothers, 1846.

Longfellow, Henry Wadsworth. *Poems on Slavery*. Cambridge, MA: J. Owen, 1842.

M.A., Sisters of Mercy. *Poems for Catholics and Convents and Plays for Catholic Schools*. West Chester, NY: New York Catholic Protectory, 1873.

Miller, Joaquin. *The Complete Poetical Works of Joaquin Miller*. San Francisco: Whitaker & Ray, 1897.

Miller, Joaquin. *Memorie and Rime*. New York: Funk & Wagnalls, 1884.

Miller, Nancy Minerva Haynes. *Mother Truth's Melodies. Common Sense for Children. A Kindergarten*. New York: G. W. Carleton, 1879.

Moody, Christina. *A Tiny Spark*. Washington DC: Murray Brothers, 1910.

Newell, Peter. *Peter Newell's Pictures and Rhymes*. New York: Harper & Brothers, 1899.

Peabody, Josephine Preston. *The Singing Leaves: A Book of Songs and Spells*, 1903.

Piatt, Sarah. *Poems in Company with Children*. Boston: D. Lothrop, 1877.

Piatt, Sarah. *A Voyage to the Fortunate Isles and Other Poems*. Boston: Houghton Mifflin, 1885.

Piatt, Sarah. *A Woman's Poems*. Boston: James R. Osgood and Co., 1871.

Preston, Ann. *Cousin Ann's Stories for Children*. Philadelphia: Merrihew & Thompson, 1849.

Purvis, T[acie] T[ownsend]. *Hagar: The Singing Maiden, with Other Stories and Rhymes*, 1881.

Read, Thomas Buchanan. *A Summer Story, Sheridan's Ride, and Other Poems*. Philadelphia: Lippincott, 1865.

Reese, Lizette Woodworth. *A Branch of May: Poems*. Baltimore: Cushings and Bailey, 1887.

Reese, Lizette Woodworth. *A Quiet Road*. Boston: Houghton Mifflin, 1896.

Richards, Laura E. *In My Nursery*. Boston: Little, Brown, 1890.

Riley, James Whitcomb. *The Book of Joyous Children*. New York: Scribner, 1902.

Riley, James Whitcomb. *Rhymes of Childhood*. Indianapolis: Bowen-Merrill, 1890.

Sangster, Margaret. *Little Knights and Ladies: Verses for Young People*. New York: Harper & Brothers, 1895.

Saxe, John Godfrey. *The Poems of John Godfrey Saxe*. Boston: James R. Osgood, 1873.

Scollard, Clinton. *A Boy's Book of Rhyme*. Boston: Copeland & Day, 1896.

Shastid, Thomas Hall. *Poems*. Pittsfield, IL: Thomas H. Shastid, 1881.

Sherman, Frank Dempster. *Little-Folk Lyrics*. Boston: Houghton Mifflin, 1892; 2nd edition 1897.

Sigourney, Lydia. *Poems for Children*. Hartford, CT: Canfield and Robins, 1835.

Sproat, Nancy ["A Lady of Boston"]. *Ditties for Children*. New York: Samuel Wood and Sons, 1813.

Staver, Mary Wiley. *New and True*. Boston: Lee and Shephard, 1892.

Stuart, Ruth McEnery, and Albert Bigelow Paine. *Gobolinks, or Shadow-Pictures for Young and Old*. New York: The Century Co., 1896.

Studebaker, Sue. *Ohio Is My Dwelling Place: Schoolgirl Embroideries, 1803-1850*. Athens: Ohio University Press, 2002.

Tabb, Fr. John Banister. *Child Verse: Poems Grave and Gay*. Boston: Small, Maynard, 1899.

Taylor, Lilian. *May Blossoms*. New York: G. P. Putnam's Sons, 1890.

Thaxter, Celia. *Poems for Children*. Boston: Houghton Mifflin, 1884.

Thompson, Priscilla Jane. *Ethiope Lays*. Rossmoyne, OH: Author, 1900.

Tilton, Theodore. *The Sexton's Tale, and Other Poems*. New York: Sheldon and Company, 1867.

Townsend, Hannah, and Mary Townsend, "The Anti-Slavery Alphabet." Printed for the Anti-Slavery Fair. Philadelphia: Merrihew & Thompson, 1847.

Trowbridge, J. T. *Vagabonds: and Other Poems*. Boston: Fields, Osgood, 1869.

Walden, Islay. *Walden's Miscellaneous Poems*. Second edition. Washington, DC: Author, 1873.

Warner, Anna Bartlett. *The Children of Blackberry Hollow*. London: James Nisbet and Co., 1863.

Warner, Anna Bartlett, and Susan Warner. *Say and Seal*. Philadelphia: Lippincott, 1860.

Wells, Amos Russel. *Rollicking Rhymes for Youngsters*. New York: Fleming H. Revell, 1902.

Wells, Carolyn. *The Jingle Book*. London: MacMillan, 1899.

Whitman, Walt. *Leaves of Grass*. New York: William E. Chapin, 1867.

Whitman, Walt. *Leaves of Grass, 2nd Annex, Good-Bye My Fancy*. Philadelphia: David McKay, 1891.

Wilcox, Ella Wheeler. *The Beautiful Land of Nod*. Chicago: Morrill, Higgins, 1892.

Willis, Nathaniel Parker. *Melanie and Other Poems*. New York: Saunders and Otley, 1837.

MULTI-AUTHOR COLLECTIONS AND ANTHOLOGIES

Andrews, Charles. *The History of the New-York African Free-Schools*. New York: Mahlon Day, 1830.

Barnes, Charles, ed. *New National Second Reader*. New York: A. S. Barnes, 1883.

Bolton, Ethel Stanwood, and Eva Johnston Coe. *American Samplers*. Boston: Massachusetts Society of the Colonial Dames of America, 1921.

Bryant, William Cullen, ed. *The Family Library of Poetry and Song*. New York: Fords, Howard, and Hurlbert, 1880.

Buckley, Theodore. *The Girl's First Help to Reading; or, Selections from the Best Authors*. London: G. Routledge, 1854.

Chapin, Bela. *The Poets of New Hampshire, Being Specimen Poems of Three Hundred Poets of the Granite State, with Biographical Notes*. Claremont, NH: C. H. Adams, 1883 [c. 1882].

Child, Lydia Maria, ed. *The Oasis*. Boston: Benjamin C. Bacon, 1834.

Davidson, James Wood. *Living Writers of the South*. New York: Carleton, 1869.

Day, Mahlon, ed. *New-York Cries, in Rhyme*. New York: Mahlon Day, 1828.

Harland, Marion, et al. *Young People's New Pictorial Library of Poetry and Prose*. Boston: Adams, Putnam & Co. / New York: N. D. Thompson Pub. Co., 1888.

Home Songs for Little People. New York: American Tract Society, 1872.

Jordan, Charlotte Brewster. *Mother-Song and Child-Song*. New York: Frederick A. Stokes, 1898.

Kirkwood, Louise J. *Illustrated Sewing Primer, with Songs and Music. For Schools and Families*. New York: American Book Company, 1886.

Ladies of the Sanitary Commission. *The New Book of Nonsense: A Contribution to the Great Central Fair*. Philadelphia: Ashmead & Evans, 1864.

Mackintosh, Newton, ed. *Precious Nonsense*. New York: Simpson & Lyall, 1895.

McGuffey, William Holmes, ed. *McGuffey's Fifth Eclectic Reader*. New York: American Book Company, 1879.

McKim, J. M., ed. *Voices of the True-Hearted*. Philadelphia: Merrihew & Thompson, 1846.

Memorial, Bunker Hill, 1775, June 17, 1875. Boston: J. R. Osgood & Co., 1875.

Morgan, James Appleton, ed. *Macaronic Poetry*. New York: Hurd and Houghton, 1872.

Newell, William Wells, ed. *Games and Songs of American Children*. New York: Harper & Brothers, 1883.

Owen, Ermine. *Readings, Recitations, and Impersonations*. Kirksville, MO: Journal Printing Company, 1891.

Penny, Lizzie, ed. *The Juvenile Temperance Reciter*. New York: National Temperance Society and Publishing House, 1898.

Percy's Year of Rhymes. New York: Hurd and Houghton, 1867.

Reports of the Selectmen and Other Officers of the Town of Concord. Concord, MA: Benjamin Tolman, 1861.

Spring Blossoms. New York: Turner & Fisher, 1835.

Taken from Life: Verses. New York: Doubleday & McClure, 1898.

Talley, Thomas Washington. *Negro Folk-Rhymes, Wise and Otherwise*. New York: Macmillan, 1922.

Tappan, Eva March, ed. *Old Fashioned Stories & Poems*. Boston: Houghton Mifflin, 1907.

Whittier, John Greenleaf, and Lucy Larcom, eds. *Child-Life: A Collection of Poems*. Boston: James R. Osgood & Co., 1872 [c. 1871].

The Wide-Awake: A Know-Nothing Token for 1855. New York: J. C. Derby, 1855.

Wilbor, Elsie, ed. *Werner's Readings and Recitations*. Vol. 7. Bellmar, NJ: Edgar S. Werner, 1892.

Witherbee, Sidney A., ed. *Spanish-American War Songs: A Complete Collection of Newspaper Verse during the Recent War with Spain*. Detroit: Sidney A. Witherbee, 1898.

PERIODICALS, WITH PLACE AND INCLUSIVE DATES OF PUBLICATION

Atlantic Monthly. Boston: 1857–present.
The Century. New York: 1881–1930.
Cherokee Rose Buds (after 1855: *Wreath of Cherokee Rose Buds*). Park Hill, OK: 1854–1857.
The Dial. Boston: 1840–1844.
Flag of Our Union. Boston: 1846–1870.
Godey's Lady's Book. Philadelphia: 1830–1878.
Gospel Teacher (later *Myrtle*). Boston[?]: 1840s–1849
Harper's New Monthly (after 1900: *Harper's Monthly*). New York: 1850–present.
Harper's Young People. New York: 1879–1895.
Health: A Monthly Devoted to the Cause and Cure of Disease. Altruria, CA: 1896–1907.
Indiana School Journal. Indianapolis, IN: 1856–1900.
The Indian Leader. Lawrence, KS: 1897–present.
The Juvenile Miscellany. Boston: 1826–1836; Philadelphia: January and March, 1829.
The Kindergarten Magazine for Teachers and Parents. Chicago: 1888–1912.
Ladies' Repository. Cincinnati: 1841–1876.
The Lark. San Francisco: 1895–1897.
Lawrence Daily American. Lawrence, MA: 1888–1914.
Lawrence High School Bulletin. Lawrence, MA: 1890.
The Little Pilgrim. Philadelphia: 1853–1865.
The Magazine Antiques. 152.2 (August 1997): 198-203; 165.4 (April 2004): 134-43.
McBride's Magazine (originally *Lippincott's Monthly Magazine*). Philadelphia and New York: 1868–1916.
New-York Saturday Press. New York: 1858–1866.
The Nursery: A Monthly Magazine for the Youngest Readers. Boston: 1867–1881.
Our Young Folks. Boston: 1865–1873. Select issues also published in New York (1865–1866), Philadelphia (1865–1866), and Chicago (1865–1866).
The Outlook. New York: 1893–1928.
Parley's Magazine. Boston: 1833–1844.
Primary Education. Boston: 1892–1926.
Riverside Magazine for Young People. New York: 1867–1870.
Robert Merry's Museum. Boston and New York: 1841–1872.
Scribner's Monthly. 1870–1881.
The Slave's Friend. New York: 1835–1839.
Southern Literary Messenger. Richmond: 1834–1864.
St. Nicholas. New York: 1873–1940.
Sturm's Oklahoma Magazine. Tulsa, Indian Territory [OK]: 1905–1911.
The Troy Sentinel. Troy, NY: 1823–1832.
Twin Territories. Muskogee, Indian Territory [OK]: 1898–1904.
Virginia Spectator (also called *University of Virginia Magazine*). Charlottesville, VA: 1838–1954.
The Western Adventurer. Montrose, Wisconsin Territory [IA]: 1837–1838.
Wide Awake. Boston: 1875–1893.
Woodworth's Youth's Cabinet. Boston and New York: 1837–1857.
The World. New York: 1863–1881.
Youth's Companion. Boston: 1827–1929.

AUTHOR INDEX

TITLE INDEX

ILLUSTRATION CREDITS